And They Were Not Ashamed

Strengthening Marriage through Sexual Fulfillment

LAURA M. BROTHERSON, CFLE

INSPIRE BOOK

Cover design by Douglas Dearden of A N D Works. Interior design and composition by Jenny Wilkson

Published by Inspire Book
Boise, Idaho
In collaboration with Sea Script Company
Seattle, Washington

ISBN: 1-58783-034-5

Library of Congress Catalogue Number: 2004102289

First Printing March 2004
Thirteenth Printing November 2018

DISCLAIMER

This work is not an official publication of The Church of Jesus Christ of Latter-day Saints. The views expressed herein are the responsibility of the author and do not necessarily represent the position of The Church of Jesus Christ of Latter-day Saints.

AUTHOR'S NOTE

Because everyone's situation is unique, the ideas and suggestions contained herein should not be considered a substitute for consultation with a trained counselor or therapist.

PERMISSIONS

Excerpts from *365 Questions for Couples* by Michael J. Beck, Stanis Marusak Beck, and Seanna Beck, used by permission of Adams Media © 1999. All rights reserved. Excerpts from *The Act of Marriage* (updated and expanded) by Tim and Beverly LaHaye, used by permission of The Zondervan Corporation © 1998. All rights reserved. Excerpts from *And They Shall Be One Flesh* by Lindsay R. Curtis, used by permission © 1968. All rights reserved. Personal interview with Savior excerpt, used by permission of Fred A. Baker © 2004. All rights reserved. Excerpts from *Becoming One* by Joe Beam, used by permission of Howard Publishing Co., West Monroe, LA © 1999. All rights reserved. Excerpts from *Children Are from Heaven* by John Gray, Ph.D., used by permission of HarperCollins Publishers © 1999. All rights reserved. Excerpts from Michael Farnworth's class material, used by permission of Michael Farnworth © 2004. All rights reserved. Excerpts from *The Five Love Languages* by Gary Chapman, Ph.D., used by permission of Northfield Publishing, a division of Moody Publishers © 1992. All rights reserved. Excerpt from *Freeway to Perfection* by Calvin Grondahl, used by permission of The Sunstone Education Foundation © 1978. All rights reserved. Excerpts from *A Guide for Couples Home Video Workshop Manual* and *Getting the Love You Want Couples Workshop Manual* by Harville Hendrix, used by permission of Harville Hendrix, Ph.D. Imago Relationships International © 1993 and 1997. All rights reserved. Excerpts from *How to Make Love All the Time* by Barbara DeAngelis, Ph. D., used by permission of Rawson Associates/Scribner, an imprint of Simon & Schuster Adult Publishing Group © 1986. All rights reserved. Excerpts from *Intended for Pleasure* by Ed Wheat, M.D., and Gaye Wheat, used by permission of Fleming H. Revell, a division of Baker Book House Company © 1997. All rights reserved. Excerpts from *Just for Newlyweds* by Brent A. Barlow, used by permission of Deseret Book Company © 1997. All rights reserved. Excerpts from *Keeping the Love You Find* by Harville Hendrix, Ph.D., used by permission of Atria Books, an imprint of Simon & Schuster Adult Publishing Group © 1992. All rights reserved. Excerpts from *Living, Loving and Marrying* by Lindsay R. Curtis and Wayne J. Anderson, used by permission of Deseret Book Company © 1968. All rights reserved. Excerpts from *Marriage and Divorce* by Spencer W. Kimball, used by permission of Deseret Book Company © 1976. All rights reserved. "Marriage Takes Three," poem by Perry Tanksley used by permission of Perry Tanksley of Dear Cards Co. ©. All rights reserved. Excerpts from *Mars and Venus in the Bedroom* by John Gray, Ph.D., used by permission of HarperCollins Publishers © 1995. All rights reserved. Excerpts from *Multiply and Replenish* by Romel W. Mackelprang used by permission of Signature Books, Inc. © 1994. All rights reserved. Excerpts from *One Flesh One Heart* by Carlfred Broderick, used by permission of Deseret Book Company © 1986. All rights reserved. Excerpts from *The Power of Sexual Surrender* by Marie N. Robinson, used by permission of Doubleday, a division of Random House, Inc. © 1959. All rights reserved. Excerpts from *The Power of Touch* by Phyllis K. Davis, Ph.D., used by permission of Hay House, Inc. Carlsbad, CA © 1999. All rights reserved. Excerpts from *The Power of Your Other Hand* by Lucia Capacchione and Mona Brookes, used by permission of Career Press © 2001. All rights reserved. Excerpts from *Purity and Passion* by Wendy L. Watson used by permission of Deseret Book Company © 2001. All rights reserved. Letter used by permission of Dr. Laura Schlessinger, internationally syndicated talk show host © 2001. All rights reserved. Excerpts from *Sex-Starved Marriage* by Michelle Weiner-Davis, used by permission of Simon and Schuster Adult Publishing Group © 2003. All rights reserved. Excerpts from *Sexual Happiness in Marriage* by Herbert J. Miles, used by permission of The Zondervan Corporation © 1967. All rights reserved. Excerpts from *The Teachings of Ezra Taft Benson* by Ezra Taft Benson, used by permission of Deseret Book Company © 1988. All rights reserved. Excerpts from *The Teachings of Spencer W. Kimball* by Edward L. Kimball, ed., used by permission of Deseret Book Company © 1982. All rights reserved. Excerpts from *Toward a Celestial Marriage* by Douglas E. Brinley, used by permission of Deseret Book Company © 1986. All rights reserved. Excerpt from *The Washington Post* by Kevin Klose, used by permission of The Washington Post © 1985. All rights reserved. Excerpts from *What Wives Wish Their Husbands Knew about Women* by James Dobson, Ph.D., used by permission of Tyndale House Publishers © 1975. All rights reserved. Excerpts from *You and Your Marriage* by Hugh B. Brown, used by permission of Deseret Book Company © 1960. All rights reserved.

www.InspireBook.com

My gift, from the heart, to all who seek.

EDITIONS

Hardcover

Softcover

Audio Book on CD

Other products by Laura M. Brotherson

Love 101—Learning to Love More Meaningfully
(Talk on CD)

Teaching Intimacy 101—How to Teach Your Children abour Sex and Intimacy in Marriage
(CD Audio Book)

CONTENTS

FOREWORD

When we speak to parents about how to talk to their kids about sex we tell them first to do it early, and second to build up to it by saying things like, "On your eighth birthday, we are going to tell you about the most awesome, wonderful, and beautiful thing in the world!" If parents make this "big talk" (and subsequent follow-up talks about sex) open, positive, and spiritual, they increase the chances that their kids will: (1) avoid promiscuous and experimental sexual activity, not out of fear, but because it is too special, and too beautiful for anything less than a committed marriage; and (2) have richer, more loving, and committed physical intimacy within their marriages.

We see this book as that same kind of "big talk" for adults!

Laura Brotherson may look young, but she is wise far beyond her years. Part of her wisdom is a gift from God, and part comes from her meticulous attention to *her* homework on this very important subject of marital intimacy. She has collected an enormous amount of supporting information from scripture, and from writings of latter-day prophets, as well as a vast number of insights from trusted doctors, counselors, and therapists.

With the escalating and disturbing number of divorces occurring not only nationwide, but in latter-day-saint homes, often due to the lack of education in emotional, spiritual, and physical intimacy, this book is an invaluable resource. It can help enlighten a new marriage, enrich a stable marriage, and mend a flailing one.

We are not therapists or experts in human sexuality, but we meet with and speak to thousands of parents and marriage partners every year, and we constantly wish for a way to bring about more communication, more intimacy, and more oneness. The book you are holding can be part of that way.

Speaking from our own field of expertise, let us put it this way: This book would be well worth the read even if all it did for you was to help you talk to your children about sex…and by the way, that is *not* all this book will do for you!

Richard and Linda Eyre
New York Times #1 Bestselling Authors of
How to Talk to Your Child About Sex and
Founders of www.ValuesParenting.com

ACKNOWLEDGMENTS

Thank you to the following people who played an important role in the conception and creation of this book. It has been a tremendous collaborative effort of many reviewers, editors, designers, enthusiastic supporters and those who helped light the way for me to find the answers.

Michael Farnworth

Shirley Henderson

Ron Dent

Melinda Jensen

Hart and Jory Beal

My first CES class members

Jared and Denise Mason

Morris and Elaine Bastian

Elizabeth Richards

Caralee Frederic

Ryan Orrock

Andrea Kaufman

Diane Frisbie

Carol Tuttle

Beth Farrell

Lynette Simpson

Doug Dearden

Stephanie Bird

Valerie Holladay

Melisa Brotherson

Sean Brotherson

Jenny Wilkson

Barry Reeder

Ronald S. Higginbotham

To my children Tanner, Alyssa and Tyler—thank you for enduring. I hope the blessings will outweigh the costs.

To Kevin, my eternal companion—without you this book could not have been written. Thank you for your endless sustaining efforts to provide the way for this book to be written . . . like taking three kids grocery shopping each week! You have been a true saint throughout our life's journey. I hope my love is evident in my continuing desire to learn and grow and become whole, which enables me to love you better.

To my Heavenly Father—thank you for the light and truth you've taught me and for providing the inspiration and guidance to share this with others.

PREFACE

Why I Have Written this Book

Every book has a story behind it. The story of this book's development is rooted in my own experiences and in a sense of personal obligation to the many couples who struggle with marital intimacy. Additionally, it is centered in a vision taught by God and others of the loving, fulfilling relationship and the oneness available between husband and wife.

In a frank, honest, yet sensitive manner *And They Were Not Ashamed—Strengthening Marriage through Sexual Fulfillment* shares some specific and effective solutions to the many problems that couples encounter. This book definitively declares there *are* answers to the sexual problems that plague many marriages. With my husband's blessing I share some of our learning experiences to provide hope and help to others who struggle with intimacy in marriage.

My husband and I have always tried to create a loving marriage, but for many years our sexual relationship was mediocre at best. Over time and through study, discussion and application of the suggestions in this book, we have been able to significantly improve our sexual relationship. In writing this book, I hope others will be able to find answers more quickly than we did.

The ideas in this book are not a quick fix. However, hope and help are available. Having personally overcome the sexual barriers I faced, my experience and growth have made the motivation to write this book too hard to ignore, especially as I considered the lack of resources, from a woman's perspective, currently available to address intimacy in marriage.

My own personal journey toward a more complete and fulfilling marital relationship was not an easy one. Though I had tried many times in the past to remedy our sexual dissatisfaction, some difficult life experiences made me get very serious about succeeding this time. After the birth of my third child, I realized I was struggling with depression. In my search for answers to overcome depression, I came across a book by a well-known Christian author and the founder of Focus on the Family, Dr. James Dobson. In his book, *What Wives Wish Their Husbands Knew About Women*, Dr.

Dobson identified sexual problems as one of the sources of depression among women. I knew he was right.

Strengthening Family Relationships

Wanting to do everything I could to fully overcome the depression propelled me on a quest to create a sexually fulfilling marriage. As I overcame the depression, I was able to invest myself in the discovery and application of the suggestions for sexual improvement that I share in this book. The pursuit of knowledge regarding sexual fulfillment has taught me much about God's purposes for marriage and provided the foundation for this book.

I have always had an avid interest in strengthening marriages and families and have come to know that this is one of God's purposes for me. To that end I obtained my bachelor's degree in Family Science, with an emphasis in marriage and family therapy, from Brigham Young University and plan to become a marriage and family therapist and a much-needed LDS sex therapist after my children are grown.

A few years ago my desire to bless lives, strengthen marriages and build strong families led me to teach a Church Educational System (CES) Continuing Education course on strengthening marriage, as well as a Sunday School course on Marriage and Family Relations. These opportunities led me to ponder even more deeply the topic of sexual intimacy, as I became aware that many other couples also faced sexually unfulfilled marriages.

Having dealt with and overcome my own challenges regarding intimacy in marriage through careful and intensive study and effort, I felt that my own experience in overcoming my struggles provided valuable "in-the-trenches" insights. While many books are written from the outside looking in, this book has the added perspective of being written from someone who's been there.

Learning of the personal struggles and heartaches of many people in the marriage classes I taught, and through personal associations and church callings, my desire to provide help increased. Personal feedback from the marriage classes, as well as discussions with many people, confirmed the significant need for good sexual information and helpful answers. When the time came to decide if I would teach the CES course again the following semester, I instead felt directed to put the information into a book that could benefit a larger audience. I was somewhat surprised by these feelings, because I thought the first book I would write would be about overcoming depression.

The Lord, apparently, had other plans.

One friend shared with me some frustrations that she had felt in her marriage for many years. She made it perfectly clear that if I wrote this book for no one else but her, it would be worth it. Another woman told me that her husband had reached the end of his rope with her aversion to sex. Suggestions I shared from this book stopped their downward spiral and put their marriage on a course toward sexual fulfillment.

Needs That This Book Addresses

Certain challenges plague couples as they seek to overcome barriers to sexual fulfillment in marriage. I have identified the following key issues couples face in their attempts to create a fulfilling and intimate relationship in marriage:

1. The need to reaffirm the sanctity and power of sexual relations in marriage through reverent and open discussion. The first and most apparent stumbling block regarding sexual difficulties is the mistaken view that sex is inherently ungodly, evil or wrong. Couples need to know that sex in marriage is wholesome, good and ordained of God. Even after marriage, discussion of sex as a sanctifying experience is essentially nonexistent. Couples need to be able to discuss God's approval of and divine purposes for sexual relations within marriage.

2. The need for effective gospel-centered sexual self-help resources. Gospel-centered, self-help books on such a sensitive and delicate subject as sex are essential to the process of creating the kind of joy and fulfillment in marriage God intended. With self-help books, couples can privately seek solutions to their struggles.

3. The need for more comprehensive sexual solutions. Though most LDS books focus on emotional and spiritual aspects of sexual relations, few have been sufficiently thorough regarding the sexual dimension to make a substantive difference. Dr. Brent Barlow, LDS author and BYU professor, stated, "Most books . . . on sexuality in marriage are either so blatant that they are offensive or so bland that they are not helpful."[1] This book deals with complex sexual matters within the context of all dimensions of the relationship in an in-depth manner that includes gospel principles and practical solutions. In this book I balance boldness with respect and reverence while I appropriately address the sacred nature of sexual intimacy in marriage.

4. The need to validate couples with otherwise good relationships who have problems with physical intimacy. The common myth that "if the marriage is good, then physical relations will be good," is a cause for concern. This book counters this mistaken premise and validates couples who in other respects have good marriages. Many couples endlessly wonder why they experience sexual difficulties when they try so hard to love each other. This book frees them to seek the specific help they need, while allowing them to find strength in what is good about their marriage. Emotional and spiritual intimacy is an important foundation for sexual fulfillment and oneness in marriage. But weakness in those areas alone does not cause sexual dissatisfaction, nor is a good marriage a guarantee of good sexual relations.

5. The need for greater vision regarding oneness in marriage. To reach the pinnacle of complete oneness in marriage, as God intended, couples must understand the importance of emotional, spiritual and physical intimacy. This book provides comprehensive solutions by teaching couples how to strengthen all three dimensions of marital oneness.

6. The need for the female perspective regarding sexual frustrations and solutions. Many women hunger for help with sexual intimacy in marriage but want that help to come from women. Good Christian books about sexual intimacy in marriage by women and for women are needed. This book, though primarily directed to women, is also for men who want to better understand their wives, and learn how they can work together to create sexual fulfillment and oneness in marriage. If men never hear the female perspective on sexual intimacy issues, they will be at a disadvantage in understanding their wives, and hampered in achieving mutual fulfillment. This book is intended as a resource for women to share with their husbands, but also as a source of insight for men who want to create a better sexual relationship with their wives.

7. The need to understand the significance of negative sexual conditioning as an underlying and oft-ignored cause of the lack of sexual fulfillment in marriage. Few books recognize the significance of negative sexual conditioning and the resulting inhibited sexual response. This conditioning, which I call the "Good Girl Syndrome," inhibits the ability to relax and allow full sexual fulfillment to occur due to the negative thoughts and beliefs about sexuality acquired from parents, church and society. This book counters the negativity and shame surrounding sexuality by presenting a godly perspective of the sanctity of sexual relations within marriage.

8. The need to counterbalance the distorted and deceptive view of sexuality promoted by the world. We live in a world saturated by Satan's view of sexuality. His preeminence in this arena allows him to spread his perspective like wildfire without much hindrance. The world generally rules the dialogue on sexuality. Satan gets 100 hours of his sexual programming to every 1 hour of God's perspective. A healthy and godly perspective on sexual relations in marriage needs more airtime. Books that promote a gospel perspective of sex are few compared to the number of books that do not. Likewise, how many examples of a healthy, godly perspective of sexual intimacy do we get in the media, compared to countless examples of the world's perspective?

President Harold B. Lee stated, "The day will soon be dawning when the whole world will come to our doors and will say, 'Show us your way that we may walk in your path.'"[2] President John Taylor prophesied, "You will see the day that Zion will be far ahead of the outside world in everything pertaining to learning of every kind as we are today in regard to religious matters."[3] Members of The Church of Jesus Christ of Latter-day Saints have a responsibility to let their light shine regarding all truth. This book represents my desire to shine the light of truth on the too-little-understood area of strengthening marriage through sexual fulfillment and oneness.

This book is written for all who seek light and truth on the subject of sexual intimacy in marriage. This book is especially for women in The Church of Jesus Christ of Latter-day Saints and their husbands, as well as for those preparing for marriage. Parents and youth leaders can also learn from this book how to better teach and prepare future generations for fulfillment in marriage. This is a gift to bless their lives with help and lift their hearts with hope. I pray that good men and women everywhere who are searching for light and truth on the sacred subject of sexual relations in marriage, and who want to improve their own relationships, will be led to this book.

Sexual fulfillment and oneness in marriage is an individual and ongoing process for every couple. I believe in the power of the teachings and principles I have shared here to bless lives, strengthen marriages and build strong families.

NOTES

Preface

[1] Barlow, *Just for Newlyweds*, 56.
[2] Lee, *Teachings of Presidents of the Church*, 149.
[3] Kimball, "The Gospel Vision of the Arts," *Ensign*, July 1977, 3.

INTRODUCTION

Sex Isn't Bad

Sexual intimacy in marriage—it need not be a forbidden subject. Many can't even say the word *sex* without a flood of suspicion or negative connotations sweeping over them. In this book, I emphasize that sex itself is not bad or evil and draw upon scripture and gospel teachings to assert that sexual intimacy within marriage is divinely ordained. Satan spends a lot of time trying to erode its divinity. Elder Parley P. Pratt addressed this notion, saying, "Some persons have supposed that our natural affections were the results of a fallen and corrupt nature, and that they are *'carnal, sensual, and devilish,'* and therefore ought to be resisted, subdued, or overcome as so many evils which prevent our perfection, or progress in the spiritual life. . . .Our natural affections are planted in us by the Spirit of God, for a wise purpose. . . ."[1]

And They Were Not Ashamed—Strengthening Marriage through Sexual Fulfillment places sex in its rightful position as ordained of God. God has stated through his living prophets that sexual relations in marriage are "divinely appointed."[2] President Spencer W. Kimball affirmed the righteousness of sexual relations within marriage when he declared, "In the context of lawful marriage, the intimacy of sexual relations is right and divinely approved. *There is nothing unholy or degrading about sexuality in itself,* for by that means men and women join in a process of creation and in an expression of love."[3]

God has commanded couples to multiply and replenish the earth[4] and to become "one flesh."[5] President Kimball stated, "Husband and wife. . .are authorized, in fact they are commanded, to have proper sex when they are properly married for time and eternity."[6]

God intended couples to find pleasure and enjoyment within the intimate embrace of holy matrimony. In Genesis, after Adam and Eve were commanded to be "one flesh," the scriptures reveal they were naked but "were not ashamed."[7] In a similar fashion, God never intended shame to exist within the sacred, intimate relations of marriage. Nevertheless, it is hard even after marriage for some to shake the feelings of shame and sinfulness they have learned to associate with sex. These negative feelings too often manifest themselves through inappropriate sexual inhibitions and a suppressed sexual response.

Many religious couples, especially where one or both struggle with negative feelings about sex, feel a need for doctrinal permission to even discuss or study such things. My purpose in writing this book is to assure you that it is permissible and even essential to study to improve the sexual dimension of marriage. It is important to intimately discuss sex with your spouse and it can be helpful to discuss it generally with others.

Sexually Dissatisfied? You're Not Alone

If you struggle with sexual frustrations in your marriage, you are not alone. *The American Family Physician*, a peer-reviewed journal of the American Academy of Family Physicians, reports a notable prevalence of sexual problems, "Sexual dysfunction, difficulties, and concerns are common. The estimated prevalence of sexual dysfunction in the general population is as high as 52 percent in men and 63 percent in women. Sexual concerns have been reported in 75 percent of couples seeking marital therapy and are nearly universal in women seeking routine gynecologic care."[8]

Did you get that? Over *50 percent* of all couples experience sexual difficulties, and LDS couples are certainly included in these statistics. The success of the LDS book *Between Husband and Wife: Gospel Perspectives on Marital Intimacy* by Drs. Lamb and Brinley attests to the hunger of LDS couples for appropriate, gospel-based sexual information.

A less scientific look at sexual dissatisfaction comes from the experience of columnist Ann Landers. In an article in the January 15, 1985, edition of *The Washington Post*, Kevin Klose reported the unfortunate sexual state of many women, as revealed to this popular columnist:

> In an unprecedented torrent of unhappiness that has surprised and saddened her, more than 60,000 women have written columnist Ann Landers to say emphatically that they far prefer being hugged and treated tenderly by men to having sexual intercourse with them.
>
> "It makes me unhappy that there are so many unfulfilled women out there who have really given up," said Landers.

Ann Landers asked women to respond "Yes" or "No" to the question, "Would you be content to be held close and treated tenderly, and forget about 'the [sex] act?'" More than 90,000 women responded and 72 percent of them declared, "Yes." If you, too, could forego sexual relations in your marriage, you are not alone. But it isn't just women who are unfulfilled. When wives are unfulfilled, husbands are also unfulfilled.

The ultimate sexual experience is one where pleasure and enjoyment are shared by both husband and wife.

Dangers of Sexual Dissatisfaction

Divorce, parallel marriage, emotional and physical ailments, and vulnerability to temptation are some of the dangers faced in sexually dissatisfied marriages. While divorce destroys about five in ten marriages, many of those couples who stay married settle into the emotional emptiness of marital mediocrity, creating what is called "parallel marriage." Couples in parallel marriages may share a house and a life, but they don't share their hearts. These couples often appear to be doing fine from the outside, but they are merely going through the motions. Parallel marriages are a particular tragedy due to the loss of personal happiness, potential and power in building God's kingdom.

President Kimball warned of the danger of divorce when sexual problems go unattended stating, "Divorces often occur over sex. . . .If you study the divorces, as we have had to do in these past years, you will find there are [many] reasons. Generally sex is the first. They did not get along sexually. They may not say that in the court. They may not even tell that to their attorneys, but that is the reason."[9]

When a husband or wife feels unfulfilled or dislikes sexual intimacy, the sexual relationship becomes a source of accumulating bitterness, frustration and contention. Couples either resign themselves to a physically unfulfilling relationship or allow anger to erupt into ongoing arguments about sex. Others try to ignore sex, endure it or hope it will go away.

Sexual intimacy is a critical component in a fulfilling marriage, and the emptiness of an unsatisfying sexual relationship may result in divorce. While one spouse may feel the physical pleasure of the sex act, it becomes hollow when it is not shared or experienced as an emotional experience as well. The spouse who does not experience sexual pleasure is likely to experience emotional emptiness as well. But even the spouse who experiences physical pleasure, when it is not shared, may also experience emotional emptiness.

Dr. James Dobson, respected Christian author and founder of *Focus on the Family*, believes sexual frustration is one of the sources of depression in women. He asserts, "Ultimately, the emotional pressure of [sexual] conflict often threatens to produce a physical blowout somewhere within."[10] Dr. David Hernandez expressed his opinion that "patients are under such pressure to perform in bed, and they experience such anxiety over their orgasmic inadequacies, that their physical health is adversely affected by the resulting stress."[11] He identified some of the common ailments as gastrointestinal (stomach) disorders, migraine headaches, high blood pressure, colonitis and general fatigue.

A study published in *The Journal of the American Medical Association* confirms this connection between sexual problems and emotional and physiological problems. It states, "Emotional and stress-related problems among women and men generate elevated risk of experiencing sexual difficulties." It adds a caution regarding which condition causes the other, stating, "While we caution that the causal order of this relationship is uncertain, these results suggest that psychosocial disturbances affect sexual functioning."[12] Whether sexual problems cause emotional and physical ailments or emotional and physical ailments cause sexual problems is yet to be determined scientifically. But they are definitely related.

Living below God's plan for sexual fulfillment and oneness in marriage leaves spouses vulnerable to temptation and tragedy. Divorce, unhealthy habits, addictions and moral transgression mar many marriages. Dr. Homer Ellsworth referred to Paul's counsel in 1 Corinthians 7:4-5 (JST), saying that couples need to strive to keep each other fulfilled sexually. "Abstinence in marriage," he says, "can cause unnecessary temptations and tensions."[13]

Couples need not live with these threats any longer. As sexual intimacy in marriage improves, the dangers that sexually dissatisfied couples face are reduced. This book provides the answers that will help couples find mutual sexual fulfillment, if they will seek the guidance of the Spirit and invest the time and effort needed to strengthen their sexual relationship.

God Intends Sexual Fulfillment in Marriage

There was a time I feared I would never enjoy sex. No matter how I tried, I just couldn't seem to relax and enjoy the experience. I wasn't sure God even cared about such things as sexual enjoyment in marriage. I have since learned that He does care. Heavenly Father wants me, my husband, and every couple to enjoy this gift within marriage. God cares about the sexual relationship you have with your spouse. He has commanded sexual relations within marriage and wants couples to experience the full potential of the godly gift he has given them.

President Kimball promised, "Marriage can be more an *exultant ecstasy* than the human mind can conceive. This is within the reach of every couple, every person."[14]

Elder Pratt revealed the divine purposes and potential of sexual intimacy within marriage:

> Our natural affections are planted in us by the Spirit of God, for a wise purpose; and they are the very main-springs of life and happiness—they are the cement of all virtuous and heavenly society—they are the essence of charity, or love. . . . There is not a more pure and holy principle in existence than the affection which glows in the bosom of a virtuous man for his companion. . . .The fact is, God made man, male and female; he planted in their bosoms those affections which are calculated to promote their happiness and union.[15]

God designed sexual relations to be a divine privilege and a glorious experience between husband and wife. Fulfilling sexual relations can ignite and enliven a marriage in a way nothing else can.

What this Book Is About

And They Were Not Ashamed—Strengthening Marriage through Sexual Fulfillment is the ultimate how-to handbook, power-packed with hope and help for creating a mutually fulfilling emotional, spiritual and physical relationship in marriage. *And They Were Not Ashamed* provides more than just insight into marital intimacy issues, it offers ways to address and overcome them. The focus of this book is to:

- Reaffirm the sanctity of sexual relations in marriage by restoring light and truth to the subject, while freeing couples from unnecessary and inappropriate sexual embarrassment, guilt and shame.

- Provide hope and help to couples using a fresh and frank approach on how to overcome negative sexual beliefs and inhibitions.

- Teach couples how to create marital oneness as the peak experience of emotional, spiritual and physical intimacy in marriage.

- Help parents and youth leaders better teach future generations to be morally clean while preparing them for intimacy and lasting fulfillment within marriage.

While all couples can improve in each area of their relationship, some may want to focus on just one dimension at a time. As their relationship grows, this book can help them move on to another dimension.

Sexual fulfillment has many definitions and dimensions. It is defined here as a sacred and symbolic union in marriage—a symphony of emotional, spiritual and physical intimacy and oneness. Sexual fulfillment signifies mutual enjoyment, passion, fun and—where physically possible—regular orgasms for both husband and wife.

With the ultimate purpose of marriage being total marital intimacy and oneness, not only can couples find help for improving *physical* intimacy, but they can also find help for improving *emotional* and *spiritual* intimacy as well. This book builds a vision of the glorious potential of complete oneness in marriage, and provides effective solutions for overcoming sexual dissatisfaction. Complete marital oneness provides an ultimate satisfying sexual relationship, as designed and ordained by God.

NOTES

Introduction

[1] Robinson, *Writings of Parley Parker Pratt*, 52–54.

[2] "The Family: A Proclamation to the World," *Ensign*, Nov. 1995, 102.

[3] Kimball, *Teachings of Spencer W. Kimball*, 311 (emphasis added).

[4] *See* Genesis 1:28.

[5] Genesis 2:24.

[6] Kimball, *Teachings of Spencer W. Kimball*, 312.

[7] Genesis 2:25.

[8] Nusbaum and Hamilton, "Proactive Sexual Health History," *American Family Physician*, 1706.

[9] Kimball, *Teachings of Spencer W. Kimball*, 312.

[10] Dobson, *What Wives Wish Their Husbands Knew About Women*, 122.

[11] Dobson, *What Wives Wish*, 122–23.

[12] Laumann, Paik, and Rosen, "Sexual Dysfunction," *Journal of The American Medical Association*, 543.

[13] Ellsworth, "I Have a Question," *Ensign*, Aug. 1979, 24.

[14] Kimball, "Oneness in Marriage," *Ensign*, Oct. 2002, 42 (emphasis added).

[15] Robinson, *Writings of Parley Parker Pratt*, 52–53.

CHAPTER VIEW

✤

Chapter 1

THE GOOD GIRL SYNDROME

Sex, to Janet, was dirty, immoral and wrong, something she'd been taught NOT to do. She wondered about the appropriateness of sexual relations even within marriage. Sex was okay if she and her husband were trying to have a baby, but any "extra-curricular" or "recreational" sex for pleasure felt dirty and unrighteous.

An LDS bishop and his wife went to see a marriage counselor because their marriage was falling apart. "Sex had been a disaster from the beginning of their marriage. What made it worse was the husband felt that good Latter-day Saints shouldn't have such problems. He believed that if anyone should have a model marriage, the bishop and his wife should. In fact, virtually everyone in the ward assumed that they were the perfect couple, and he felt both hypocritical and a little bitter that the image was false."

The bishop said to the counselor, "Show me the justice of it. We keep all of the commandments. We pay a full tithe and a lot more. We keep the Word of Wisdom. We were chaste before our marriage and have been faithful since. Neither of us has ever refused a call. We attend the temple regularly. We try to be missionaries to our neighbors. And despite all of this, we are miserably unhappy with each other and have a lousy sex life. That's not the way it's supposed to work out."[1]

The "Good Girl Syndrome"

For each couple who enter marriage, expecting bliss and joy, it is a shock and a disappointment to encounter frustrations and problems with sexual intimacy that leave each of them feeling hurt and misunderstood. There is an unnamed factor that has a powerful influence on the challenges couples face regarding sexual intimacy in marriage. I call this factor the "Good Girl Syndrome." It is the significant impact of the negative sexual conditioning that many receive, especially women, regarding their own bodies and the purposes of sexuality. The Good Girl Syndrome refers to the deeply internalized feelings and attitudes that rigidly emphasize only the negatives associated with sexuality. When such negative attitudes and beliefs harden and persist into marriage, they affect the ability of husbands and wives to express and enjoy sexual fulfillment in marriage.

The Good Girl Syndrome is a result of the negative conditioning that occurs from parents, church, and society as they teach—or fail to teach—the goodness of sexuality and its divine purposes. This conditioning leads to negative thoughts and feelings about sex and the body, resulting in an inhibited sexual response within marriage. Although physical problems and relationship issues can also cause sexual dissatisfaction, the negative effects of the Good Girl Syndrome are so pervasive that efforts to address other causes may be inadequate until deeper issues have been overcome. *The Good Girl Syndrome may be the great underlying and underestimated cause of sexual dissatisfaction in marriage.*

The Good Girl Syndrome does affect men, but is generally more prevalent and pronounced in women. For this reason I refer to it as the Good *Girl* Syndrome.

The Good Girl Syndrome represents a distorted image of what a "good girl" really is or should be. The good girl should be applauded for her desire to do what is right, but the unintentional overemphasis on the negative consequences of immodesty and immorality and the negative images in society lead many to incorrectly internalize negative teachings regarding sexuality.

The good girl would rather err on the side of right than make a mistake, which is a good thing. But the sometimes unfortunate, unintended consequences are that she distances herself from anything perceived as bad or sinful to the point of not letting herself learn about or enjoy sexual relations even within marriage. For example, the good girl would rather avoid learning about sexual intimacy in marriage altogether if she thinks she has to wade through smut to get there. Negative internalization regarding sex and the body is one of the primary roadblocks to sexual satisfaction and fulfillment in marriage.

The Good Girl Syndrome affects many couples. Dr. James Dobson, Christian leader and president of *Focus on the Family*, identified the problems associated with the Good Girl Syndrome:

> Adult attitudes toward sexual relations are largely conditioned during childhood and adolescence. It is surprising to observe how many otherwise well-adjusted people still think of married sex as dirty, animalistic, or evil. Such a person who has been taught a one-sided, negative approach to sex during the formative years may find it impossible to release these carefully construct[ed] inhibitions on the wedding night. The marriage ceremony is simply insufficient to reorient one's attitude from "Thou shalt not" to "Thou shalt—regularly and with great passion!" That mental turnabout is not easily achieved.[2]

Parents, church leaders, teachers, and society in general contribute to the development of the Good Girl Syndrome. Society inundates us with highly sexual, anything-goes messages and images. Parents and church leaders counter by teaching the ugly and pernicious evils of sexuality, failing to include that sex has godly purposes in marriage and is a gift from God. Marriage therapist Michele Weiner Davis acknowledged the negative sexual conditioning of children in her book *The Sex-Starved Marriage*:

> Children are like sponges, absorbing and believing much of what adults tell them about the world. If you were taught that sex is bad or dirty or that you're a bad person for thinking about sex, chances are that these ideas have become a part of you. Many adults have to unlearn their childhood lessons in order to relax and truly enjoy themselves.[3]

The Good Girl Syndrome is caused by ignorance as well as distorted and incorrect beliefs, perceptions, attitudes and associations accumulated over time. We are told "No!" and "Don't!" so often regarding sexual relations, and with such emphatic condemnation, that we come to believe sex is wrong and immoral, PERIOD!

Silence about the positive aspects and the blessings of the expression of sex and the appropriate use of the body adds fuel to the well-advertised negatives. The result is people who feel uncomfortable, even shameful, with the whole sexual experience. Instead of entering the marriage relationship with awe and wonder regarding the body and its glorious purposes, they feel nervous, shameful, embarrassed and uncomfortable and view sex as wrong except for procreative purposes. The consequent sexual problems are not simply marital adjustment issues, but are deeply internalized, unproductive beliefs and emotions associated with sex and the body.

Symptoms of the "Good Girl Syndrome"

Listed below are some of the symptoms of the Good Girl Syndrome. Rate on a scale of zero (none) to ten (a lot) the effect of each issue in your life. This exercise can help you become aware of the negative conditioning you may have unconsciously internalized.

- Discomfort, embarrassment or inability to appropriately discuss sexual matters.
- Underlying belief that sex is bad, wrong, dirty or sinful.
- Lack of understanding of the divine purposes of sex—particularly that God intended it for pleasure, as well as procreation.
- Inability to relax and let go within the sexual experience.
- Lack of enjoyment of sexual relations—participation out of duty.
- Lack of sexual understanding and "know-how"—a simplistic perception that if I just "do what's right" I will have marital bliss.
- Inappropriate inhibitions, guilt, shame or awkwardness associated with sexual relations within marriage.
- Discomfort or distaste with sexual parts of the body and body functioning.

Sexual Conditioning from Parents

The negative conditioning may begin when young children begin to explore and discover their bodies. Parents' strong reactions can cause feelings of shame and guilt, creating the impression that the body is bad or dirty, or that behavior involving certain body parts is sinful. In *A Parent's Guide,* published by the The Church of Jesus Christ of Latter-day Saints, parents are counseled to be aware of their reactions to their children's sex-related learning and exploration. The Church counseled, "Male and female children will naturally discover and explore their genitals just as they do the rest of their bodies. . . . Your reaction to these natural explorations will influence the way a child later feels about his procreative powers. . . . Remain neutral, and the child will accept that these parts of his body are good, just as all the other parts are."[4]

Shaming can lead a child to think she is fundamentally bad. Young children readily internalize shame. Dr. John Gray shed some light on the unforeseen shame children may accumulate regarding their bodies and themselves, "Young children, up to nine years old, are not capable of dealing with shaming messages without assuming too much blame. Any kind of punishment, disapproval, or emotional upset in reaction to your child's mistakes ultimately gives a shaming message. . . . Before the age of nine, a child cannot discern the difference between I *did* something bad and I *am* bad."[5]

In an effort to encourage premarital chastity, parents may send condemning messages about the body and its sexual functions. Instead of teaching that the body—all of it—as well as sexual relations in marriage, are good gifts from God, parents send messages like, "You shouldn't touch your body," "Your body is dirty," or "Sex is bad / sinful." When parents focus only on premarital chastity and forget about preparing their children for the joys of sexual fulfillment in marriage, their message is skewed to the negative with mostly warnings and consequences rather than filled with the blessings and godly purposes of sex.

The challenge parents face is to communicate love to the child while discouraging certain behaviors. Parents' reactions generally have more to do with *their* own sexual issues than with the child's behavior. Parents, unaware of their own negative conditioning, can frustrate their impressionable children who are building their own sexual identity and beliefs.

Parents without their own understanding and personal conviction of the sanctity of sex may unintentionally send negative messages about sex—even sex within marriage. An interchange between one young woman and her mother illustrates this point.

Rhonda had just had a bridal shower. The next day, she and her mom were at the mall together doing some shopping. Rhonda was planning to exchange some lingerie she had received at the shower, but her mother suggested that she instead buy something "useful." Rhonda was dismayed that her mother seemed to feel that pleasing her new husband was something fruitless and unimportant.

Parents who do not affirm sex as important, fun and vital to a happy, satisfying marriage do their children a disservice. Even seemingly unimportant, passing comments can have profound effects on children. This contributes to the Good Girl Syndrome. In speaking to her daughter about sexual relations, another mother contributed to her daughter's negative conditioning. She referred to sex in a foreboding manner, and her tone indicated to her children that even within marriage, sex was a chore, a burden and a wifely duty. Daughters aren't the only ones to absorb a mother's negative attitudes. Sons, too, may learn that it is normal for a wife to dislike sex. Thus, they may not recognize that their wife's attitude needs to be addressed.

Parents also contribute to the Good Girl Syndrome when they do not, or will not, talk about sex at all. Carol related her experience of finding a book about sex on her bed. Though she knew it came from her mother, nothing was ever said about it. Carol wondered if there was something wrong with sex because her parents never talked about it and became uncomfortable if the subject ever came up. The whole subject of sex was taboo.

Many parents provide little or no sexual education to their children. And some well-intentioned parents may make matters worse. Parents who do teach about sex, but without preparation or a personal conviction of the sacredness of sex, may be uncomfortable with the subject and cause negative feelings and memories for their children.

During one family home evening, the King family had gathered together for "the big talk." The discomfort in the air was considerable. Children of all ages, personalities, and maturity levels sat in paralyzed silence as their father spoke about sex. The experience was an uncomfortable fiasco—one none of them hoped to experience again.

Children may hear the right words, "Sex is sacred. It is beautiful. It is a wonderful experience." However, if the words are spoken without personal conviction and a spirit of reverence, they are meaningless. Children are very perceptive; the right words won't hide parents' negative feelings.

Jan shared her feelings of futility in teaching her children the sanctity of sex. She wondered how she could tell her daughter that sex was special when that was not how she herself felt. She described the sexual experience as one of guilt, frustration, dirtiness, worldliness and unladylike behavior. How could she teach the sanctity of sex when she did not believe in it herself?

Hollow, incorrect or nonexistent teaching about sex and the body plays a significant role in the development of the Good Girl Syndrome. Parents need to become aware of their own sexual inhibitions, negative feelings and beliefs, and strive to overcome them, so that they can be more effective in teaching their children about sex.

Sexual Conditioning from Church

During the teen years, teachings regarding human intimacy often fall into the same category as teachings regarding drugs, alcohol, and tobacco. The "fine print" may indicate that sexual relations are acceptable after marriage, but the message comes across as "Stay away from 'drugs' (until you're married)." Such teachings may keep kids morally clean in the short run, but do little to support the concept of sex as something good and wholesome after marriage.

We teach the best way we know to help youth refrain from immoral behavior. It is not so much what's being taught that is a problem, but *how* it is being taught. One youth leader, a Young Women's president, referred to lovemaking as "the big nasty." Her choice of words challenge the belief that sex within marriage is sacred and sanctioned by God. References such as this contribute to a sense of sexual shame and to a difficult transition after marriage.

When teaching chastity or sexual abstinence, the message is often, "Good girls don't." This is true prior to marriage. However, the message should also be, that, once married, GOOD GIRLS DO! Perhaps youth leaders at times have gone too far in trying to prevent premarital sexual relations to the point that some young women come to believe good girls *never* do. Young women must be taught correctly, so that they can enjoy sexual relations within marriage and *still* consider themselves good girls.

When teaching chastity or sexual abstinence, the message is often, "Good girls don't." This is true prior to marriage. However, the message should also be, that, once married, GOOD GIRLS DO!

Sexual feelings in some circumstances have been so condemned that good girls go the extra mile—nearly extinguishing these feelings altogether. The goal of making it to the temple morally clean is achieved, but a price is paid in marital happiness and sexual fulfillment. Both premarital chastity and marital sexual fulfillment can be achieved through a renewed emphasis on teaching the light and truth regarding the gift and blessings of sexual relations within marriage.

The lack of godly perspective and the abundance of negatives and warnings regarding sex lead some to believe sex is not of God at all—but of Satan. As some youth internalize the notion of sexual intimacy as carnal, sensual and devilish, feelings of shame and embarrassment arise as their own God-given sexuality blossoms. Rather than welcoming and guiding this developing sexuality, parents and teachers censure it. Thus, this negativity often extends into marriage.

Modesty is an area of particular concern for young women in the development of negative sexual attitudes. Young women may be taught, "You have no idea what it does to a boy if you are immodest." Some young women come to feel more responsible for the behavior of the young men they associate with than to God and themselves to be modest.

Tami was one of these young women who felt that her dress and appearance were more responsible for young men's behavior than were the young men themselves. As an adult, Tami was still bothered any time a discussion of modesty ensued, as she recalled the heavy responsibility she felt for young men's sexual behavior.

When scare tactics and misplaced responsibility are used to teach modesty, the message received may be, "Young men are unable to control themselves." Modesty should be something a young woman does for herself and for God—not because boys can't control themselves.

The notion that boys are unable to control themselves is a scary message. If men can't control themselves, they must be dangerous. This negative perception is a heavy burden for young women. Young men may also learn to doubt whether they really can control their sexual feelings. In this way, well-intentioned teachers and leaders remove from these young men the responsibility that is rightfully theirs.

Modesty is so impressed into young girls' minds that appropriate occasions of revealing and sharing their bodies within marriage may be difficult, if not impossible, without great embarrassment and reservation. Joni reported her discomfort with being undressed in the presence of her husband even after many years of marriage. Being naked went totally against her grain—and against all she'd been taught throughout her life. However, it is God's intention that we, like Adam and Eve, be UNashamed, though naked,[6] when within the privacy of the marital relationship—our own little Garden of Eden.

In gospel teachings we often refer to the commandment Adam and Eve received to "cleave" unto each other and become "one flesh."[7] Becoming "one flesh" is rarely emphasized as being a God-given commandment to have sexual relations within marriage. The next verse is often ignored altogether, "And they were both naked, the man and his wife, and were not ashamed."[8] Applying this idea to the couple relationship, sexual relations within marriage were never intended to cause feelings of shame, guilt, disgust or embarrassment.

Church leaders primarily provide positive, uplifting counsel. But regarding sexual intimacy in marriage, they sometimes inadvertently discourage young people who are preparing for marriage or couples who are struggling with sexual problems within marriage. Unfortunately, some ecclesiastical leaders or well-meaning adults may contribute to the fear and apprehension many already feel, making it difficult for a "good girl" to relax and enjoy the sexual experience in marriage without being focused on doing anything "wrong."

When Sandy was preparing for marriage she met with a member of the stake presidency for her temple recommend interview. He proceeded to share his beliefs about some things he felt were improper in the sexual dimension of marriage. He then identified various inappropriate behaviors and strongly cautioned her against them. Already nervous and uptight about the honeymoon experience, Sandy found it difficult to relax and enjoy the sexual pleasures of marriage with the sting of shame filling her mind. She continued to harbor feelings of apprehension about committing sexual sin within marriage for many years.

Another woman, Kate, had been unhappy with sexual relations for many years. In other ways she and her husband had a wonderful relationship, and they had even tried to address their sexual problems, but sex continued to cause frustration. Kate finally decided to talk to a priesthood leader. She told him, "I don't like sex. I think it's dirty and gross and my husband wants it more than I do. I could probably go without it for the rest of my life. I have never enjoyed it, and yet I know my husband needs it." The leader was silent, perplexed about what to say. Finally he responded that sex was overrated, and that it shouldn't be so important to her husband. Kate left this encounter frustrated and with little hope.

Christian author Joe Beam expressed his frustration with the negative teaching of Christian parents and church leaders:

We're weary of dealing with young women who were taught for years, "Sex is bad. Sex is bad. Sex is bad . . . " and then later, "Oh, you're getting married tomorrow, then sex is good!" You can't undo a life of teaching in a couple of days, weeks, or months. We see too many young women, especially from Christian homes, who've been given such conflicting information about sex from their parents and church that they enter marriage with conflicting emotions about the sexual union they're about to have with their husbands. They want to enjoy lovemaking but feel somehow that they're doing something wrong, something shameful.[9]

LDS authors Stephen E. Lamb and Douglas E. Brinley, a physician and marriage counselor, respectively, are not surprised that many youth enter marriage with anxiety and inner conflict about sex. It's quite a transition from saying "No" all your life to now being able to say "Yes." Drs. Lamb and Brinley wonder if perhaps parents and other adults in their attempt to encourage chastity have sent an unbalanced message about sexual relations, causing many to struggle when sexual expression becomes permissible in marriage.[10]

To answer their question, we *have* failed to send the message of a proper time and place for the exultant joy of sexual intimacy in marriage. We have not spoken positively of sexual matters frequently enough. We haven't fully explained and made clear the righteousness of sexual relations within marriage nor of the blessing God has bestowed upon it. We have not said it with enough confidence or conviction. The inner conflict about sexual matters that Drs. Lamb and Brinley describe continues to haunt many marriages. We must clearly send the message that after marriage chastity is not abstinence.

Sexual Conditioning from Society

Society bombards us with sex. Television programs, videos, the Internet, books, magazines, movies and music are filled with lust-driven sex. Satan has 24-hour access to our hearts and minds through society's swamp of sexual sensualization.

Sex is everywhere in society, but at home or at church, discussion of it is often taboo. It's a "forbidden subject." Few are willing to talk openly and honestly enough to adequately answer the questions and concerns that abound. Satan's sexual programming strives to overshadow a more godly perspective of sex. When youth are inundated with incorrect sexual teachings and their parents fail to teach them correctly, where can they go to get their questions answered appropriately?

With the mass of illicit and self-centered sex in the media, many also receive the message from society that sex is bad—something only "bad girls" do. Good girls and good boys shouldn't be interested in that kind of stuff. While boys get a lot of the same messages girls do, they may have an easier time overcoming negative messages because of their different physiology. Nevertheless, they too can become inhibited by the idea that sex is bad or come to believe that only bad boys think about it. When they marry, they may receive "approval" to engage in sexual relations, but the negative internal programming remains.

To add to the confusion, the news and other media are filled with sensational stories of sexual aberrations. These images of sexual predators, abuse, exploitation and deviance affect one's ability to perceive sex as sacred and respond accordingly. Thus, it can be a struggle to enjoy wholesome lovemaking in marriage.

Victims of sexual abuse may have a particularly difficult time building a positive foundation for healthy sexual relations within marriage. They often have no reference for sex as a sacred experience, and wonder if sex is only something people do to hurt someone else. Professional counseling may be needed to heal from the wounds of abuse and help the victim find sexual fulfillment in marriage.

In spite of the sensational headlines that attract attention, we must remember that those who sexually abuse others are in the minority. Elder Boyd K. Packer stated, "Remember that trouble attracts attention! We travel the highway with thousands of cars moving in either direction without paying much attention to any of them. But should an accident occur, we notice immediately. If it happens again, we get the false impression that no one can go safely down the road. One accident may make the front page, while a hundred million cars that safely pass are not regarded as worth mentioning."[11] We need to spend more time focusing on the millions who travel safely instead of on the accidents.

Movies and magazines add to society's negative conditioning regarding sex. One young man described the negative sexual impressions he had gained during his teen years from movies he had seen and magazines he had run across that portrayed sex as ugly, sinful and selfish.[12] Too often this understanding of sexuality is broadcast as the only reality. Unfortunately, there is no shortage of examples supporting this belief. We must concentrate instead on the divinity of sexual relations in marriage rather than on the deceptions, distortions, and abuses.

Another pervasive message about sex is that sex is a painful experience. While there can be some initial discomfort for some brides, the suggestion of pain itself can be a self-fulfilling prophecy. The ability to relax during sexual relations is critical. Sexual consummation and climax require that a woman be at ease mentally and relaxed physically. If a woman is fearful and concerned about possible pain, her vaginal muscles may constrict making penetration difficult. It's pretty hard for a young bride to relax when her internal programming tells her she is doing something sinful. The concept of sexual pain simply intensifies the fear, shame and guilt already being experienced.

Stories of sexual pain, without medical, physiological and psychological information do little to instill confidence and eager anticipation of the sex act, especially in young people who are uneducated about sexual functioning. Suzanne was one of these women whose descriptions of her early marital experiences caused apprehension for her naive friends. Her eyes filled with tears as she told her single friends of the terrible pain she experienced every time she and her husband had sex. Her friends listened in stunned silence, shedding their own tears of sympathy, and wondering if their experience would be the same.

It's pretty hard for a young bride to relax when her
internal programming tells her she is doing something sinful.

One couple, Matt and Lisa, shared their experience and struggles with the Good Girl Syndrome. Even though Lisa had parents who were fairly open about sexual matters and had been available for questions, ultimately the conditioning of church and society accumulated to create sexual dissatisfaction and frustration within their lives.

As Lisa had prepared for her upcoming marriage, she had no reason to assume she wouldn't enjoy sexual relations. She had tried to do all the right things and had kept herself morally clean. As a good girl, she assumed that since she had done everything "right," God would bless her, and her life would turn out great.

Lisa was caught off guard when at her premarital exam her LDS doctor told her that after marriage she could go ahead and "be sexy." Taken aback she thought, "How do I do that?" She'd never had any Young Women's classes on that. She was also unprepared to learn how painful sex might be. After her appointment she thought to herself, "If sex is anything like that, then no thank you!"

Her husband, Matt, had done all the right things too. He had gone on a mission and kept the commandments. He was raised in a good family—although there was not much discussion about sex.

While Matt had some sexual knowledge from school and friends, it wasn't enough to know how to create a fulfilling sexual experience for both of them. After all, good boys aren't supposed to think about, read about or talk about sex. Matt and Lisa had no way of knowing that what works for a man may not necessarily fulfill a woman. Many young men like Matt enter marriage with the expectation that sex will be pure pleasure and fireworks. Lisa assumed that, too, although she didn't know much about her own body and how it worked. Many men have dreamed of having sex every day since they entered puberty, and assume it will happen just like in their dreams. Matt and Lisa had been told sex might not happen perfectly in the beginning, but they assumed *they* would be different.

Things didn't go quite as expected. Matt wasn't sure what to do other than what was natural for him, and Lisa spent most of her time trying not to be too anxious about the pain. They both wondered, "Is this it?" They talked about why things weren't working as well as they'd hoped. His "good boy" conditioning led Matt to wonder if they were being cursed for not having children right away. "Good girl" Lisa wondered if he might be right.

After a while sex seemed fine for Matt, but Lisa never had much desire and didn't get very aroused. After a while of trying to enjoy it, she sought help from books. But more knowledge and technique didn't help. Wondering if something was wrong, they went back to the doctor. His suggestions didn't help either.

When Lisa asked her mom about it, her mother told her that sex needs to happen in the mind as well as the body—especially for a woman. Lisa agreed that she was definitely having a hard time focusing on sex or being turned on mentally. Her mind always wandered to other things. How could she let herself get turned on when the conditioning she'd received told her sex was wrong? Lisa didn't realize that even though she had never been abused sexually, she had nevertheless accumulated the notion of men as sexual predators. This contributed to her growing feelings of disgust with sex in general, and the feeling men were creatures unable to control themselves. Sex became a chore for Lisa—something that had to be tolerated for the sake of her husband. Babies and motherhood came along, and sex was simply relegated to the back burner as another item on her "to do" list.

Challenging the Good Girl Syndrome

Since it significantly affects sexual fulfillment, the Good Girl Syndrome must be challenged. Causes of the Good Girl Syndrome are summarized here:

- Lack of divine conviction of the sacred nature of sex and the body by those who teach children.

- Unwillingness or inability of parents to sufficiently and correctly teach their children about the body and sex.

- Overemphasis on the negative aspects and consequences of immodesty and premarital sex.

- Lack of understanding of the blessings of premarital chastity and sexual relations within marriage.

- Belief that "good girls don't," which persists into marriage.

- Distorted perceptions that men can't control themselves sexually.

- Accumulation of society's distorted sexual messages without an avenue of appropriate and sufficient sexual discussion to counter them.

Within this book are many affirming scriptures and statements from LDS Church leaders and others providing the divine permission many need to relax enough to allow themselves to think about, talk about, read about and *do something about* improving sexual intimacy within their marriages. Christian physician, Ed Wheat, in his book, *Intended for Pleasure,* affirmed the divine permission sex has been given, "You have God's permission to enjoy sex within your marriage. He invented sex; He thought it up to begin with. You can learn to enjoy it, and . . . can develop a thrilling, happy marriage."[13]

Being a good girl is a great thing. But good girls can read about, discuss and participate in marital sexual relations and still BE good girls in the sight of God. Overcoming the Good Girl Syndrome does not mean you become a *bad* girl, but that you develop a healthy and accurate understanding of the godly purposes and potential of sexual relations in marriage.

Sacred help from a loving God is available and absolutely essential. Sexual fulfillment can be developed through positive premarital sexual education along with an understanding that time, effort and intimate education between husband and wife will be needed after marriage as well.

The path to marital oneness and bliss is an individual, yet shared, sacred journey. As you read this book, prayerfully seek divine counsel from Him who knows all things. Your personal, omnipotent Physician is there to help you. "Christ is the Great Physician who rose from the dead 'with healing in his wings' (2 Nephi 25:13)."[14] He can and will heal you and make you whole, but He often does so with the help of his earthly angels. Hope and help for couples will come in the form of knowledgeable friends, mentors who are willing to share what they've learned, and professional counselors, as well as from books and other resources.

Creating Awareness

Step 1. To overcome the Good Girl Syndrome, become aware of your own negative sexual conditioning. Quiet reflection can help you make conscious the unconscious, so you can challenge and address those feelings and beliefs. Elder Neal A. Maxwell stated, "Transformation follow[s] introspection."[15] Consider what concepts or symptoms of the Good Girl Syndrome (listed at the beginning of this chapter) you can relate to. Self-revelation takes time—be patient and gentle with yourself as you progress. Pray for help, and it will come.

Quietly reflect on what you think about sex—be completely honest with yourself. If you deny what you really feel in order to give the "correct" answer, you will only be delaying the growth you need to attain sexual fulfillment and marital happiness. What are your thoughts and feelings? The Holy Spirit can teach you about yourself. "The Comforter, which is the Holy Ghost, whom the Father will send in my name, he shall teach you all things, and bring all things to your remembrance."[16] The Spirit can help you become aware of incorrect beliefs you may have regarding the sacred sexual union in marriage. If this exercise brings up any disturbing emotions, please seek the assistance of a professional counselor. Appendix II at the end of this book includes information to help you find a good counselor.

Step 2. Dig deep into the heart of the matter. Commit to writing your thoughts and feelings about sex. Use your left hand, or non-dominant hand to do this writing. Though this concept may be new to you, it is a common practice among therapists. The idea behind writing with your non-dominant hand is that it allows greater access to your core beliefs and truest emotions, bypassing the culturally conditioned filter of the intellect. Lucia Capacchione's book *The Power of Your Other Hand* described how this tool of self-revelation works.

A person's non-dominant hand is a direct channel to inner potential. . . . [Through her research and fieldwork] Lucia has . . . noticed people improving their health, developing inner healing powers, and receiving greater fulfillment in their relationships. . . .

The exercises [using your other hand] will help you explore and understand your thoughts and feelings on a completely different level, finding out things about yourself that have been buried or concealed for quite some time.[17]

You need to know what your *heart feels*, not just what your *mind thinks* about the following questions. Let your heart, not your intellect, do the answering. Pay attention to your emotions. If tears begin to flow, identify the underlying thoughts and feelings, and write them down. Record all these impressions as you answer the following questions:

1. What do I think about sex? How do I feel about it?

2. What do I think about the body . . . all parts of it? Are there any parts I am uncomfortable with?

3. How did I learn about sex? What was I taught?

4. What do I really believe God feels about sex? (No "Sunday School" answers here.)

5. How important is the sexual relationship in my marriage?

Step 3. Share this writing with your spouse. Read it to him, or let him read it himself before discussing it. Each of you should share and discuss what you've learned from the writing exercise. This sharing may be difficult. Pray for help. Healing awaits not only in the process of writing, but also in the process of sharing. If you are honest in this exercise, you will uncover some of the sacred ground of your soul.

Step 4. Consider visiting with a counselor to help you through this process. A therapist is trained to help you correct and overcome negative beliefs and experiences. This is a wise and helpful step for many people. It may not be an easy process, but it can be very worth it.

Dana's experience provides insight into the counseling experience. She was sick and tired of hating sex, and she was at the point where she knew she'd exhausted all her own ideas. She knew this couldn't be how marriage was supposed to be. She knew she needed professional help. She took the matter to the Lord, and He helped Dana and her husband find a counselor who was just right for them.

She had written down her beliefs and feelings, and was surprised to learn she had some seriously negative beliefs about sex and men. She shared them with her husband, and took them to their counseling sessions. Dana told the counselor about her writing. He asked if she would share it with him.

Throughout the next few counseling sessions they addressed each issue. As they continued through this process, Dana overcame the negative power of those beliefs. What she had written was no longer true for her. An unseen spell had been broken. She was freed from the belief that sex was bad and dirty, and that men were uncontrollable monsters. She learned that sex was ordained of God, and that He wanted her to fully enjoy it.

While the negative beliefs were now gone, there was still work to do to remove the inhibitions that had resulted. But Dana now knew the effort she was making to improve sexual relations for herself and for her husband was as important to the Lord as it was to her. She had a new conviction of the sanctity of sexual relations and knew her efforts would make a difference.

Every couple's experience in counseling will be different. Everyone has different issues and depths of difficulty to address. Becoming aware of these beliefs and beginning to address them is the first step in overcoming the Good Girl Syndrome, and working toward creating sexual fulfillment in marriage. Sexual fulfillment in marriage is a worthy goal. God intended sexual relations to be enjoyable for both husband and wife, and wants every couple to achieve happiness therein.

The next chapter addresses the second step in overcoming the Good Girl Syndrome. Couples must attain a personal conviction, like a testimony, that God has ordained—and approves of—sex, and wants them to find sexual fulfillment in marriage. Scriptures and inspired statements from Church leaders and others will help couples create a firm foundation of faith upon which to build sexual fulfillment in marriage.

Chapter 1—"Home" Work

This section provides a convenient summary of the suggestions and applications found throughout the chapter. These "home" work assignments can be applied within the privacy of the home.

- Review the list of symptoms of the Good Girl Syndrome. Rate on a scale—zero (none) to ten (a lot)—how much each symptom affects your life.

• To overcome the Good Girl Syndrome:

Step 1. Reflect on the sexual conditioning you've received. Pray for the Spirit to guide you to the people and resources you need to help you.

Step 2. Write your thoughts and feelings about sex using your non-dominant hand. Pay attention to your emotions and be completely honest as you answer the following questions: (1) What do I think about sex? How do I feel about it? (2) What do I think about the body . . . all parts of it? (3) How did I learn about sex? What was I taught? (4) What do I really believe *God* feels about sex? (5) How important is the sexual relationship in my marriage?

Step 3. Schedule time to share your writing with your spouse. Discuss what you have learned.

Step 4. Consider seeking professional help to work through the issues you may have uncovered.

NOTES

Chapter 1—The Good Girl Syndrome

[1]Broderick, *One Flesh, One Heart,* 2–3.

[2]Dobson, *What Wives Wish Their Husbands Knew About Women,* 120.

[3]Weiner Davis, *Sex-Starved Marriage,* 50.

[4]*Parent's Guide,* 21.

[5]Gray, *Children Are from Heaven,* 218.

[6]*See* Genesis 2:25.

[7]Genesis 2:24.

[8]Genesis 2:25.

[9]Beam, *Becoming One,* 134.

[10]*See* Lamb and Brinley, *Between Husband and Wife,* 18.

[11]Packer, "Marriage," *Ensign,* May 1981, 14–15.

[12]*See* Lamb and Brinley, *Between Husband and Wife,* 58.

[13]Wheat and Wheat, *Intended for Pleasure,* 14.

[14]Faust, "Strengthening the Inner Self," *Ensign,* Feb. 2003, 5.

[15]Maxwell, "Care for the Life of the Soul," *Ensign,* May 2003, 68.

[16]John 14:26.

[17]Capacchione, *Power of Your Other Hand,* back cover.

CHAPTER VIEW

Chapter 2

THE SANCTITY OF SEXUAL RELATIONS IN MARRIAGE — BUILDING A FOUNDATION OF FAITH

Adam and I have been married for five years, and I've never liked sex. I dread Valentine's Day and our anniversary. It's just a "sex fest" for Adam. I feel like a piece of meat. He wants me all the time and I feel he is only nice to me when he wants something in return. On days he knows he probably won't get any sex, he barely pays attention to me.

He generally gets sex when and how he wants it. It makes me so mad. He doesn't meet my needs, so why should I meet his? It's never for me. He is so selfish. This makes me want sex even less. I feel he manipulates me into bed, and it infuriates me.

I'm mad, but I'm also sad that I don't like sex with Adam. I know he really wants me to enjoy it, but mostly I don't, and then I worry about disappointing him. How can I enjoy something that seems sinful to me? Is it normal to dislike sex after having a baby, or do I have so much resentment toward him that I can't enjoy being with him?

I have a great fear of becoming like my parents, because I know they have issues with sex. I know my mom feels like a sex object. I feel like that, too, at times. Are we headed down that same terrible path? I don't want my daughter to go through the hell I've been through. I want to get it figured out now, because I think Adam and I can have a wonderful marriage. I want Adam to know that I care for him and I want to give him everything he wants, but I just can't right now. I'm so tired of not getting anything in return. I give and give, but nothing comes back.

———

After 35 years of marriage and eight children, Bernice announced to her husband that there would be no more bedroom activity. "I'm not going to corrupt myself with any more of this. Sex is an ugly, unholy, carnal act and I'll have no more of it."

———

I've been gypped. She pulled a bait and switch on me. My wife was so affectionate and sexy before marriage. Now she won't even let me touch her. Our lovemaking happens only occasionally, and it's very empty. Her body is there, but her spirit isn't. I feel deprived and neglected. I'm an easy-going guy, but my wife makes me feel like an evil sex maniac.

We've been married over 15 years. I don't know how much longer I can take this. I don't know what's wrong. It's like she's turned stone cold. I feel like I'm walking on eggshells all the time and I never get my needs met. Surely this isn't how marriage is supposed to be. I always dreamed sexual relations would be part of a happy and healthy marriage. Now I'm married, but it's nothing like I thought it would be.

Sex Is Good and a Gift from God

The stories shared above identify some of the heartache, distorted beliefs, and difficulties couples face in the sexual dimension of marriage. For some, sex is positive. Others understand this intellectually, but don't really feel it in their heart. Shame, guilt, and other negative feelings remain associated with sex even though they "know" it is approved within marriage.

Our intellectual knowledge must go deeper. We must shift our focus from the evils and warnings regarding sex to the proper and divine role of sexual intimacy in our lives. Gaining this heavenly perspective can be an absolutely transforming experience.

To overcome the negative effects of the Good Girl Syndrome and to create the oneness in marriage that God intended, husband and wife must come to know that sex is good—and of God. To those who are married, sexual intimacy is a "rightful gift of God."[1] You must come to feel the divine permission, power, and potential of pure and virtuous sexual relations within marriage—the way God designed them to be.

Traci "knew" sex was approved and necessary in marriage, but she didn't really believe it. After attending a few marriage classes filled with affirming scriptures and statements on the sanctity of sexual relations in marriage, she began to feel a change of heart. She realized that sex is a vital aspect of a happy and healthy marriage. She began to see that sex can—and should be—wonderful. She acknowledged that sexual relations are APPROVED by God and necessary to achieve the marital oneness she sought. This knowledge transformed her attitude, filled her heart with renewed hope, and encouraged her to seek improvement in this area of her marriage.

Dr. Ed Wheat provided assurance to struggling couples when he declared, "As a Christian physician, it is my privilege to communicate an important message to unhappy couples with wrong attitudes and faulty approaches to sex. The message, in brief, is this: You have God's permission to enjoy sex within your marriage. He invented sex; He thought it up to begin with. You can learn to enjoy it, and…you can develop a thrilling, happy marriage."[2]

In this chapter, faith-promoting statements and scriptures will be shared to restore light and truth to sexual relations in marriage, building a foundation upon which sexual fulfillment can flourish. As you read and ponder the affirming scriptures and statements, they will strengthen your belief in the sanctity, holiness, purity, and virtue of sex, and wash over you like a flood of pure and living water. As we begin to change the collective energy about sexuality to a more healthy and positive force, great blessings will result.

Knowledge alone has the power to awaken dormant seeds of growth and change. Gaining awareness of new and more productive attitudes and beliefs brings about a spontaneous awakening as the mind and body begin to process and integrate the new information.

Couples will also be shown *how* to attain a personal conviction that sexual fulfillment in marriage is ordained of God. As you awaken to your deepest beliefs, you can begin to challenge and reprogram them to be completely aligned with how God feels about sexual relations in marriage. If you already have a healthy and vibrant belief that sex is good and blessed by God, this chapter will serve to fortify your faith.

Most people have heard newlyweds express concern about having sexual relations even after they are married. Referring to their honeymoon, young couples have been known to wonder, "Are we in trouble for what we did last night?" or "Are you *sure* what we did was okay?" In response to these types of concerns, President Spencer W. Kimball stated, "Husband and wife . . . are authorized, in fact they are commanded, to have proper sex when they are properly married for time and eternity."[3]

One reason some may not have a solid conviction of the sanctity of sex, much less an understanding that it really is okay after marriage, is that they haven't been taught, nor have they sought the Lord's wisdom on it. Some may think sex doesn't need any further discussion, but experience suggests otherwise. One member wondered if she was worthy to attend the temple if she and her husband had had sex the night before.

John and Brenda had been married early in the morning. Later that day John walked into the church alone to help set up decorations for the evening reception. His uncle was surprised to see him there alone. The uncle inquired as to where his new bride was, and the young groom confided that they had planned to arrive separately so that no one would think anything inappropriate was going on. The uncle shook his head in disbelief. "You're married now," he said. "It's a commandment."

Sex and sexual pleasure within marriage are not bad, nor forbidden. Sexual relations are good and wholesome. Unfortunately, Satan's preeminence on this topic allows him to spread his perspective like wildfire without much hindrance. There is barely a faint whisper to counterbalance the world's distorted perspective. Great is the need for God's plan and purposes for physical intimacy within marriage to be heard above the roar of the world's view. The Lord's divine design of marital sexuality needs more airtime.

People don't talk much about sex. Even appropriate dialogue between parents and children, husband and wife, or adults in general is rare. Some reasons for this may include discomfort and embarrassment with the subject, not knowing what to say, or thinking sex is too private and sacred to discuss even in general. Many young people grow up wondering if sex is bad or if something is wrong with it because adults never seem to talk about it. It all seems very hush-hush. And if the subject ever surfaces, it is usually quickly and uncomfortably shut down.

Have you ever asked a parent or church leader a question about sex and then felt the air cool suddenly while they squirmed and stuttered before stammering out a quick statement? Many imitate the discomfort and embarrassment they observed in their parents and leaders when they were younger.

The professor of a child development class at BYU Idaho was lecturing on the importance of using correct terms for parts of the body when teaching children about sex and morality. He went on to identify the correct terms of the reproductive parts of the body. During this portion of the class, a returned missionary raised his hand to indicate he believed the Spirit was offended by the words being used. He had confused his discomfort and negative conditioning associated with the words, with the Spirit being offended. Church leaders have counseled us on the importance of using correct terms:

> Slang terms are not in keeping with the divine origin of our bodies. We are forbidden to refer to Deity with disrespect. Would it be pleasing to the Lord to refer to our bodies made in his image with disrespect? Neither should we be silly and use ridiculous words or terms. Teach sexuality by using correct, respectful language, information, and example.[4]

" AND THEN HE SAID; SON,, SEX IS NOT SECRET IT'S SACRED AND TALKING ABOUT IT MAKES YOUR MOTHER FAINT." [5]

Another reason some may not talk much about intimacy in marriage is the notion that sex is too sacred or private to discuss. But we can discuss the sanctity of sexual relations respectfully and reverently without divulging private information. There is much that can and should be openly and confidently discussed about the godly gift of sexuality to counter the negative and deceptive messages that surround sex in our society.

In our zeal to keep sacred things sacred we hesitate to talk about them at all. Thus, the sacredness slips into a secretness that can shut the door to needed light and understanding. Sex needs to be taken out of the darkness and brought into God's light. Respectful and appropriate sexual discussion need not be so private that we fear to discuss it openly, frequently, or comfortably with our children, our spouse, or other adults.

While there are many reasons for the reluctance to discuss sexual matters, it is critical that we overcome our reservations. Dissatisfaction with sex as a primary cause of divorce should compel couples to spend time and effort learning to discuss sexual issues and to come to know that sex is good and of God.

The sacredness [of sexual relations] slips into a secretness that can
shut the door to needed light and understanding. Sex needs to be
taken out of the darkness and brought into God's light.

In preparing a marriage class on physical intimacy, I was pleasantly surprised at the abundance of scriptures and statements affirming the sanctity of sex in marriage. As I read and pondered them, light and truth flooded my spirit. My own understanding and conviction of the godliness of sex was strengthened. To confirm sexual relations as a gift from God, take a few moments to savor each of the following statements.

- President Kimball provided insight into God's plan and purposes for the goodly desire He gave husbands and wives, "The sexual drives which bind men and women together as one are good and necessary. They make it possible to leave one's parents and cleave unto one another."[6]

- Elder Boyd K. Packer identified the goodness of the gift of sexual relations in the following statement, "This power [of creation] is good. . . . It is a sacred and significant power, and I repeat . . . that this power is good. . . . It is a gift from God our Father. In the righteous exercise of it, as in nothing else, we may come close to Him."[7]

- Elder Packer further identified this sacred power as the very key to happiness—*the very key*! "Eternal family life . . . can be achieved because our Heavenly Father has bestowed this choicest gift of all upon you—this power of creation. It is *the very key* to happiness. Hold this gift as sacred and pure."[8]

- Dr. Victor B. Cline identified sex as one of God's great gifts and blessings to married couples, "The human reproductive drive is one of God's great gifts to mankind. It allows us to participate in the act of creation. . . . Sexual intimacy with genuine affection may also bond the husband and wife together, heal wounds in the relationship, and bless the man and woman with a special kind of joy and caring for each other. Indeed, the physical union of husband and wife is not only a commandment of God, but it is also a great blessing for us."[9]

- Dr. Brent Barlow, BYU professor, LDS marriage counselor and author, shared his conviction, "Sexuality is a beautiful power given to mankind from God."[10]

- Dr. Barlow said further, "We also believe in the good that can be derived from the appropriate use of intimacy in marriage. We are well aware of the joy and unity that can come to a married couple when this particular dimension of the marital relationship is nurtured."[11]

- Dr. Homer Ellsworth, former member of the Melchizedek Priesthood General Committee, stated, "Prophets have taught that physical intimacy is a strong force in strengthening the love bond in marriage, enhancing and reinforcing marital unity. Indeed, it is the rightful gift of God to the married."[12]

- President Kimball made a powerful and profound statement that not only speaks of the physical aspect of intimacy in marriage but also speaks of the potential for marriage as a whole. He said, "Marriage can be more an *exultant ecstasy* than the human mind can conceive. This is within the reach of every couple, every person."[13]

Ponder the thought of marriage as an "exultant ecstasy" not only sexually but also in all dimensions. This opens a whole new world of possibilities. I hope you are beginning to feel the assurance and conviction that God really approves of sex and wants you to find the joy and pleasure He intended.

Sex Is Sacred and Ordained of God

The word *sacred* describes something "regarded as holy; consecrated to God; worthy of or regarded with reverence."[14] We know "marriage is ordained of God."[15] But do we believe *sexual intimacy* within marriage is also ordained of God? In the Proclamation on the Family, God's living prophets have confirmed this truth, "We declare the means by which mortal life is created to be divinely appointed."[16] This is an important principle to understand and believe.

Let's look more closely at the words used in the Proclamation. *Means* is the "method" or "way"[17] something is brought about; *divinely* means "godlike, holy, sacred, spiritual, exalted;"[18] *Appointed* is defined as "determined, established, prescribed, commanded, decreed, directed, ordered, required."[19] If we put this together, we see that the means (or way) that mortal life is created (the sex act) is divinely appointed (prescribed, decreed or required by God) making it sacred, godly, holy, and even sanctifying. In other words, God approves.

President Ezra Taft Benson stated, "Sex was created and established by our Heavenly Father for sacred, holy, and high purposes."[20] Note that he says *purposes* (plural)—not just one purpose. Procreation is understood as the primary purpose for sex, but there are other purposes as well. Some of the purposes of sexual relations in marriage beyond procreation include expressing love, providing mutual pleasure and enjoyment, experiencing physical, emotional, and spiritual bonding, and oneness, healing wounds in the relationship and rejuvenating the mind, body, and spirit.

Couples have been told to become "one flesh" and fill the measure of their creation,[21] and have *joy* therein. In 2 Nephi 2:25 we read that we exist that we might have joy. In Moses 5:10 we read, "My eyes are opened, and in this life I shall have joy." If we can open our eyes to the light God shines on sexual intimacy in marriage, we can accept sex as a way to experience joy in this life. Not only are we to have joy in our posterity, but we are also to have joy in the "means by which mortal life is created."[22]

Sex is a sacred blessing and gift from God to husbands and wives. It is a means of strengthening marriage. It is a spiritual gift. The Lord tells us in D&C 29:34 that to Him all things are spiritual (including sex), and that no law He has given is merely temporal. The light of God can transform sex from something seemingly inappropriate to something holy and ordained of God. The following statements of support for the sanctity of sexual relations in marriage can help settle the conscience and secure a conscious confirmation that marital sex is of God.

President Kimball stated, "In the context of lawful marriage, the intimacy of sexual relations is right and divinely approved. *There is nothing unholy or degrading about sexuality in itself,* for by that means men and women join in a process of creation and in an expression of love."[23]

Elder Dallin H. Oaks stated, "The power to create mortal life is the most exalted power God has given his children. Its use was mandated in the first commandment. . . . The expression of our procreative powers is pleasing to God."[24]

Elder Parley P. Pratt provided a powerful statement on marital sexuality, "Our natural affections are planted in us by the Spirit of God, for a wise purpose; and they are the very main-springs of life and happiness— they are the cement of all virtuous and heavenly society—they are the essence of charity, or love. . . . There is not a more pure and holy principle in existence than the affection which glows in the bosom of a virtuous man for his companion. . . . The fact is, God made man, male and female; he planted in their bosoms those affections which are calculated to promote their happiness and union."[25]

In his April 1974 General Conference address, President Kimball quoted a popular evangelist, Billy Graham:

> The Bible celebrates sex and its proper use, presenting it as God-created, God-ordained, God-blessed. It makes plain that God himself implanted the physical magnetism between the sexes for two reasons: for the propagation of the human race, *and for the expression of that kind of love between man and wife that makes for true oneness.* His commandment to the first man and woman to be "one flesh" was as important as his command to "be fruitful and multiply."
>
> The Bible makes plain that evil, when related to sex means not the use of something inherently corrupt but the misuse of something pure and good. It teaches clearly that sex can be a wonderful servant but a terrible master: that it can be a

30

creative force more powerful than any other in the fostering of a love, companionship, happiness or can be the most destructive of all of life's forces."[26]

———

President Harold B. Lee also affirmed that sex is of God, "Marriage is fraught with the highest bliss. . . . The divine impulse within every true man and woman that impels companionship with the opposite sex is intended by our Maker as a holy impulse for a holy purpose—not to be satisfied as a mere biological urge or as a lust of the flesh in promiscuous associations, but to be reserved as an expression of true love in holy wedlock."[27]

President Lee calls sex a "divine impulse" and a "holy impulse." He also provides insight into a common misconception of the male sex drive. It *is* a physiological function for men, but, as he states, it is not a "mere biological urge." Men not only need sexual relations to satisfy their divinely created sex drive, but this sacred sexual union between husband and wife is also an important means for expressing and receiving the highest form of love.

———

Elder Hugh B. Brown said, "The powerful sex drives are instinctive, which is to say, God-given, and therefore are not evil."[28]

———

Elder Brown also stated, "When the Lord established marriage—and He is its author—He made sex union lawful within that relationship, and it becomes both honorable and sanctified."[29]

———

President Joseph F. Smith added insight to the godly purposes of sexual relations. He stated, "The lawful association of the sexes is ordained of God, not only as the sole means of race perpetuation, but for the development of the *higher faculties* and *nobler traits* of human nature, which the love-inspired companionship of man and woman alone can insure."[30] What are these "higher faculties" and "nobler traits"? It is something worth pondering.

Sexual relations have a symbolic, even sacramental sacredness, providing a means for husband and wife to be sanctified as they become one. Elder Jeffrey R. Holland gave an entire talk on this topic entitled, "Of Souls, Symbols, and Sacraments" that is well worth reading.[31] Understanding sexual intimacy as an ordinance in marriage helps couples view sexual union as a more vital and sacred part of their relationship.

Dr. Wendy L. Watson, LDS therapist and BYU professor, shared the following perspective, "Have you ever considered that marital intimacy might have something in common with baptism, confirmation, temple sealings, baby blessings, and even the Sacrament? Such a perspective helps us begin to understand the exquisite sacredness of physical intimacy and the profound significance and influence of co-creating love in marriage!"[32]

The sexual relationship of marriage has a power and potential that we do not yet understand. With the right intent, physical intimacy in marriage can heal and bind hearts together—unifying body and spirit—creating oneness in a profound and powerful way.

And They Were Not Ashamed—What the Scriptures Teach about Physical Intimacy in Marriage

Satan has surrounded sexuality with mists of darkness clouding our vision and that of our children. Even within the divinely ordained sexual relationship of marriage darkness remains. The scriptures can pierce the darkness with light and truth.

*Satan has surrounded sexuality with mists of darkness
clouding our vision and that of our children. . . .
The scriptures can pierce the darkness with light and truth.*

We've discussed many inspiring statements affirming sexual relations in marriage. But there is even more light and truth we can glean from the scriptures on the sanctity of sex. Let's go on a scriptural journey to see what we can find. Let's begin in Doctrine and Covenants 49:15.

1. We know that marriage is ordained of God.[33] God created marriage. God approves of marriage. The footnotes of D&C 49:15 lead us to Genesis.

2. In Genesis 2:18 we read, "And the Lord God said, It is not good that the man should be alone." Why? Is there something eternally important about a man and woman being together in marriage? In Ecclesiastes 4:9-12 it says that two are better than one because they have "reward [blessings, an inheritance] for their labour." And if one spouse stumbles or falls, the other will lift him up. In verse 11 it says that two, together, create warmth. And if one spouse should be prevailed upon, then husband and wife shall withstand him. Think of all the learning, growth, and blessings that come from the combining of two lives in marriage. After declaring that man shouldn't be alone, God took one of Adam's ribs ("bone of his bones, flesh of his flesh") and made a woman.[34]

3. In Genesis 2:24 we are told that man and woman are to leave their parents and cleave (or join) unto each other and become ONE—one flesh. This same phrase is repeated six other times in the scriptures.[35] These scriptures in which we are commanded to leave our parents and "become one flesh" are confirmation of the importance of the marital unit.

A temple sealer emphasized this fact during a marriage sealing where he reminded those present that in eternity we will not be grouped in family units of father, mother, and children as we commonly assume, but in units of husbands and wives. This does not mean parents and children will have no association, but rather it places a high emphasis on the primary importance of the marital relationship. Elder Bruce R. McConkie declared, "Our marriages will continue in the realms that are ahead. We shall get into the paradise of God, and we shall be husband and wife. We shall come up in the resurrection, and we shall be husband and wife."[36]

Notice that the scripture in Genesis doesn't say we should become "one heart" or "one mind," though those are also important. It clearly says "one flesh" which means we cannot and must not gloss over the fact that God is talking about something physical. We are commanded to become one flesh, that is, to participate in physical intimacies with each other. This is a vital component of husbands and wives becoming ONE. So, how did the Lord plan to accomplish this?

4. In Abraham 4:28 we read, "And the Gods said: We will *bless* them. And the Gods said: We will *cause* them to be fruitful and multiply, and replenish the earth." Notice the phrases "We will *bless* them"; and "We will *cause* them." God apparently felt it was a blessing not only to have the power to procreate, but also to give husbands and wives sexual desires for each other. This suggests God purposefully planted within husband and wife the attraction they feel for each other. He gave us these feelings on purpose to bless us and "cause" us to desire each other. This scriptural insight into the origin and purpose of our desires for each other sheds light on how God intends sexual intimacy to bless us both as the means of procreation and as an expression of marital love.

5. Remember the seven scriptures commanding us to be "one flesh"? As if the words "one flesh" are not descriptive enough, following three of those scriptures is the statement, "And they were both naked, the man and his wife, and were not ashamed."[37] At this point Adam and Eve have become husband and wife (since the scriptures refer to the "man and his wife"). In other words, after blessing us with this physical desire, God then commanded us to follow through on those desires within marriage.

Perhaps we may apply the response of Adam and Eve at this point to our own orientation toward physical intimacy in marriage. That is, we need not be ashamed of our nakedness, and more specifically, of sexual relations within marriage.

Shame is usually associated with sin, but shame continues to surround sexuality even when there is no sin. It can be very challenging in the marital relationship if spouses have a sense of shame, embarrassment, or fear of sharing their bodies as God intended. We might ask how shame and fear became associated with that which the Lord has approved in marriage—the sexual oneness of husband and wife?

6. We know that the glory of God is intelligence or light and truth.[38] God's light and truth are needed for us to understand His intended role for physical intimacy in marriage. Furthermore, we know that light and truth forsake the evil one.[39] If we ask why shame is associated with sex—even sex within marriage—we can see in the verse 39 that Satan has removed light and truth from sexuality, causing many to confuse sex with sin.

In verse 38 we read, "Every spirit of man was innocent in the beginning; and God having redeemed man from the fall, men became again, in their infant state, innocent before God."[40] And in the next verse, "*That wicked one cometh and taketh away light and truth.*"[41] God's light and truth surrounded sexuality in the beginning, when Adam and Eve were in a state of innocence. But look at the scripture again. Even after the fall, because of the Savior's atonement, man became again innocent before God.

From the footnotes in verse 39 we learn that it was through the following: lack of understanding,[42] unbelief,[43] hardened hearts,[44] disobedience,[45] false traditions or lies passed down through generations[46] and treating lightly that which we have received[47] that light and truth were taken away. Satan left in their wake shame, embarrassment, and discomfort as inhibitors of the exultant ecstasy God intended in marriage. When

God's truth about physical intimacy is not fully understood and internalized, it inhibits the natural God-given response intended.

We can restore light and truth to physical intimacy in marriage by following God's command to "bring up [our] children in light and truth."[48] God's perspective provides a healthy and divine understanding of physical intimacy in marriage, in which there is no shame or embarrassment.

7. In Hebrews 13:4 we read, "Marriage is honourable in all. . . . " I interpret that to mean ALL parts of marriage are honorable—including sexual relations. Honorable means "noble, admirable, upright, virtuous, proper, right."[49] The scripture continues, ". . . and the bed undefiled." The word *bed* translated in the Greek New Testament is actually *coitus,* or another term for sexual intercourse.[50] Undefiled means "clean, spotless, unsullied, innocent and pure."[51] Therefore, the marriage bed, representing sexual intimacy in marriage, is clean and pure.

8. Perhaps the most explicit scriptures God has given are found in Proverbs 5:18-19 where husband and wife are assured of God's divine favor in finding joy in their sexual relationship. We read, "Rejoice with the wife of thy youth. . . . Let her breasts satisfy thee at all times; and be thou ravished always with her love." These scriptures suggest that husband and wife are to enjoy each other, their bodies, and even have fun together sexually. Being ravished with each other's love suggests we are to love each other fervently and passionately. The footnote to verse 19 refers to D&C 42:22, which reminds couples to love one another with all their heart and to cleave unto each other and none else.

In the scriptural context of Proverbs 5 men and women are counseled to find joy in their spouse in order to avoid immorality. This suggests that as husband and wife learn to find joy and fulfillment within their intimate relationship, they will be blessed and the allure of sexual temptations will be avoided.

9. There is even more to the intimate act of joining our bodies during sexual relations than we may realize. In 1 Corinthians 6:19-20 we read, "Know ye not that your body is the temple of the Holy Ghost which is in you, which ye have of God . . . therefore glorify God in your body, and in your spirit, which are God's." Is it possible that as husbands and wives keep God's command to be "one flesh" and to be "naked and not ashamed," they will increase their understanding and be able to transcend the physical into the spiritual? Is it possible that in becoming one flesh they glorify God with their bodies and their spirits?

Surely a husband and wife, both possessing the Holy Spirit of God, when they join their bodies together physically not only become one body and one flesh but also one in spirit—one spirit "joined unto the Lord."[52] God's command to cleave unto each other and become one flesh[53] allows husband and wife to become ONE spiritually with God through the intimate act of joining their bodies, which is where their spirits reside.

10. Look again at Matthew 19:5, which is one of the seven scriptures that refers to man leaving his father and mother and cleaving to his wife to become one flesh. We read in the following verse, "Wherefore they are no more twain, but one flesh. What therefore God hath joined together, let not man put asunder." *Asunder* means to tear apart or into pieces.[54] We know God wants us to remain together as husband and wife. It appears that we should also refrain from letting Satan or man put asunder or defile that which God has created and called good—such as sexual relations in marriage.

Satan does not want us to seek or understand light and truth. He does all he can to keep us in darkness away from happiness. "Because he had fallen from heaven, and had become miserable forever, he sought also the misery of all mankind . . . "[55] "that all men might be miserable like unto himself."[56] Satan has found that distorting the divinity of sexual relations in marriage is an effective way to destroy happiness, marriages, and families.

Sexual togetherness is good and is of God—correctly associated with light and truth, which have always been there—from the beginning. Miraculous things will happen as we put light and truth back into sex.

"We Believe in It"

These scriptures provide powerful evidence of the sanctity of sexual relations in marriage. Dr. Barlow shared a classic but simple story that expresses this very clearly:

> Several years ago when I was a young missionary and had just received a new companion, we met a Protestant minister who invited us in out of the cold. After exchanging points of view on various topics, he asked us, "And what is the Mormon attitude towards sexuality?"
>
> I choked on my cup of hot chocolate, but my new companion seemed unmoved. "Well," said the minister after a moment of silence, "could you please tell me the Mormon philosophy toward sexuality?" I was tongue-tied and believed my new companion knew next to nothing on the matter. However, when my companion realized that I didn't have an answer, he finally said, "Sir, we believe in it."
>
> It has been more than twenty years since that time, and I have been asked the same question by numerous students, friends, professional people, and LDS

members and nonmembers alike. And still, I haven't yet been able to come up with a better answer than the one given by my supposedly naive companion: "We believe in it."[57]

The important question is, "Do YOU believe in it?" We need to believe in the goodness and righteousness of sexual relations in marriage. We must each be committed to our personal growth. Our foundation of faith must be strong to sustain us as we learn how to enjoy the exquisite intimacy possible in marriage. But gaining a conviction of the sanctity of sex must not be merely another item on a "to do" list. It must come from the heart.

Attaining a Conviction That Sex Is of God

Wise couples build their house and their marriage upon a rock, so it can withstand the "mighty winds."[58] Attaining a firm foundation of faith in the sanctity and godliness of sexual relations is the rock upon which to build. *To attain* means "to succeed in getting or arriving at; to achieve; to come to or arrive at by growth or effort."[59] To attain a conviction of the sanctity of sex may seem like a silly thing to some, but it is a necessary step. The negative conditioning and beliefs some may have about sex create a very shaky foundation for the marital bed.

Once you *know* God created sex within marriage for high and holy purposes you can begin to reduce and even eliminate further accumulation of negative assaults on your beliefs, and you will be less influenced by derogatory comments from others. Others' disgust with or feelings of duty, dirtiness or drudgery about sex will have little or no impact on you because you will know the truth. Negative remarks will no longer fit within your belief system and will roll off your back, instead of adding fuel to the fire of marital frustration. But developing godly beliefs in sex will not immediately undo all the damage previously done. Additional time and effort will be needed to overcome internalized inhibitions.

Both husband and wife need to know in their hearts and in their whole beings that sex is good, that sex is okay. Sex isn't dirty or evil. It is (or should be) a glorious experience between husband and wife. God not only approves of sex, but He has commanded us to participate in it and not feel ashamed. His command to BE ONE as husband and wife is not just a nice idea, *it is a commandment*. It is also our exalted opportunity.

We know from James 1:5 that if any of us lacks wisdom, we can ask of God. Do you lack wisdom regarding sex within marriage? Do you lack wisdom regarding God's blessing upon sexual relations? Do you believe God will answer your questions regarding something such as sex? He will. You may already have a testimony of tithing. You may already have a testimony of prayer. Why not seek a divine conviction of the godliness and holiness of sexual intimacy in marriage?

The knowledge that God blesses and approves of sex in marriage must be in place before we begin a serious search for solutions to strengthen this vital element of marriage. For some, this foundation is already in place. However, if the concept of sex being sanctioned by God feels foreign to you, I urge you to reflect on your beliefs and see if there are some adjustments you can make in this area so that you can attain a divine conviction that God approves of sex:

Step 1. Re-read the scriptures and statements quoted above. Re-program any negative or incorrect beliefs to include God's light and truth. Write down what you are learning. Note any thoughts, feelings, or negative and incorrect beliefs that need to be changed.

Step 2. Liken the scriptures and statements to yourself and your situation. We learn from 1 Nephi 19:23 that we are to liken all scriptures unto ourselves that they might be for our profit and learning. As we apply the scriptures to ourselves, we can find great counsel on any subject—even sex. One woman learned how she could find personal answers in the scriptures to any question. After she was diagnosed with leukemia she was counseled to search the scriptures seeking answers regarding her battle with this disease. She thought to herself, "Why would I search the scriptures about my illness? There's nothing in the scriptures about leukemia."

Nevertheless, she followed this counsel and even kept a "leukemia journal" throughout her treatment. There she recorded the insights and comfort she received through her study of the scriptures. She came to realize that the scriptures really are about leukemia. Just as the scriptures taught her about her battle with leukemia, you can use the scriptures to learn about sexual relations in marriage.

Step 3. Ponder each statement and scripture to let them sink deep into your soul as building blocks toward a firm foundation of the sanctity of sexual relations. What do you think about what you have read? Does it make sense? Does it seem to be what the Lord would say regarding intimate relations in marriage?

Step 4. Pray with real intent and sincerity of heart. Moroni 10:3-5 describes this process in gaining an assurance, "And when ye shall receive these things, I would exhort you that ye would ask God, the Eternal Father, in the name of Christ, if these things are not true; and if ye shall ask with a sincere heart, with real intent, having faith in Christ, he will manifest the truth of it unto you, by the power of the Holy Ghost. And by the power of the Holy Ghost ye may know the truth of all things." Though Moroni is speaking specifically about reading, pondering, and praying about the Book of Mormon, this counsel can apply to your need to have God's assurance on any matter, including sexual relations in marriage.

Step 5. Read and discuss this chapter with your spouse if possible. Share your thoughts and discuss how you can apply this information to improve sexual intimacy within your marriage. Maybe your spouse already has a healthy attitude and godly understanding of the sanctity of sexual relations in marriage. Help him to understand your struggle to internalize those beliefs, and invite his faith and prayers on your behalf.

Step 6. Fast for added power. In the scriptures, Jesus taught his disciples that both prayer AND fasting were needed to cast out devils.[60] Removing negative or incorrect beliefs may be likened to casting out devils and restoring light and truth.

Step 7. The last step of attaining a conviction of the godliness of sex is to have the power of the Holy Ghost confirm its truth to you. It is by the power of the Spirit as you read, study, ponder, and pray that you learn truth in such a way as to touch your heart, "But the Comforter, which is the Holy Ghost . . . shall teach you all things, and bring all things to your remembrance."[61] This can and will happen as you open your heart and seek for truth. Repeat the above steps until God's Holy Spirit confirms to you the truthfulness of the sanctity and importance of sexual relations in marriage.

What might your understanding be once you have gained this conviction of the sanctity of sex? Elder Loren C. Dunn describes the experience of gaining a testimony that may have relevance. He described it as " . . . an experience that defies description. . . . It is the awakening of the mind and spirit to absolute truth. It is a revelation from God. It goes beyond what we can know and understand with our mortal senses."[62] Imagine having this profound experience and knowledge concerning sex in your marriage. With desire, determination, and dedicated effort, you can.

For some, the negative conditioning of the Good Girl Syndrome makes the transition from "sex is wrong" to "sex is sanctioned" after marriage very difficult. This is why gaining a conviction of the sanctity of sex is an essential step in creating a foundation of faith for sexual fulfillment in your marriage. It will be important that you have this foundation to lean upon when the road gets rough or when you become frustrated as you seek to apply solutions. Knowing that God approves of sex and wants you to enjoy it will help you to be able to find the desire, motivation, time, and energy to make necessary changes.

Challenging old beliefs and gaining a firm testimony of the sanctity of sex will not immediately solve *all* sexual issues. Negative feelings and inhibitions will not necessarily melt away once you know sex is good and of God. There are many layers and issues that will need to be addressed and worked on to achieve the sexual oneness and intimacy you are meant to have.

Chapter 1 gave you the steps to help create awareness of the negative conditioning and attitudes that may be holding you back sexually. In Chapter 2, I have encouraged you to seek a conviction of the sanctity of sexual relations. Both of these steps are essential to form a firm foundation of faith upon which you can continue to build. Once your personal conviction is received it can be translated into action. Elder James E. Faust reminds us, "Conviction . . . is worthless till it convert itself into conduct."[63]

There is an untapped potential power in the realm of fulfilling physical intimacy for both husband and wife. A strong and sanctifying sexual relationship in marriage can fortify, illuminate, and ignite a marriage in a way nothing else can. God intends sex in marriage to be exquisitely enjoyable, enlightening, and edifying. He wants you to find joy in this dimension of your marriage and not be ashamed. As you do your part He will show the way—whatever it takes—whether it be through this book, other books or through professional help. It may not be easy. It may not be quick. But if you will persevere you will find the answers and the marital joy you seek.

Chapter 2—"Home" Work

Step 1. Re-read the affirming scriptures and statements regarding sex found in this chapter to attain a conviction that sex is of God. Write down your thoughts.

Step 2. Liken the scriptures and statements to yourself and your marriage.

Step 3. Ponder each statement and scripture regarding sexual intimacy in marriage.

Step 4. Pray with real intent to know that sex is of God.

Step 5. Read and discuss this chapter with your spouse.

Step 6. Fast for added spiritual power to attain a conviction of the sanctity of sex.

Step 7. Repeat these steps until the Holy Spirit confirms to you the sanctity and importance of sexual relations in marriage.

NOTES

Chapter 2—The Sanctity of Sexual Relations in Marriage—Building a Foundation of Faith

[1]Ellsworth, "I Have a Question," *Ensign*, Aug. 1979, 24.

[2]Wheat and Wheat, *Intended for Pleasure*, 14.

[3]Kimball, *Teachings of Spencer W. Kimball*, 312.

[4]*Parent's Guide*, 30.

[5]Grondahl, *Freeway to Perfection*, 23.

[6]Kimball, "Privileges and Responsibilities of Sisters," *Ensign*, Nov. 1978, 102.

[7]Packer, *Teach Ye Diligently*, 259-61.

[8]Packer, "Why Stay Morally Clean," *Ensign*, July 1972, 113 (emphasis added).

[9]Cline, "Obscenity: How It Affects Us," *Ensign*, Apr. 1984, 34.

[10]Barlow, "They Twain Shall Be One," *Ensign*, Sept. 1986, 50.

[11]Barlow, "They Twain," *Ensign*, Sept. 1986, 50.

[12]Ellsworth, "I Have A Question," *Ensign*, Aug. 1979, 24.

[13]Kimball, "Oneness in Marriage," *Ensign*, Oct. 2002, 42 (emphasis added).

[14]*Webster's Universal Dictionary*, 456.

[15]Doctrine & Covenants 49:15.

[16]"The Family: A Proclamation to the World," *Ensign*, Nov. 1995, 102.

[17]*Webster's*, 699.

[18]*Webster's*, 634.

[19]*Webster's*, 594.

[20]Benson, *Teachings of Ezra Taft Benson*, 409.

[21]Doctrine & Covenants 49:16.

[22]*"Family: A Proclamation," Ensign, Nov. 1995, 102.*

[23]Kimball, *Teachings*, 311 (emphasis added).

[24]Oaks, "Great Plan of Happiness," *Ensign*, Nov. 1993, 74.

[25]Robinson, *Writings of Parley Parker Pratt*, 52-53.

[26]Kimball, "Guidelines to Carry Forth the Work of God in Cleanliness," *Ensign*, May 1974, 4. *See also* Graham, "What the Bible Says About Sex," *Reader's Digest*, May 1970, 118 (emphasis added).

[27]Lee, *Teachings of Presidents of the Church*, 112.

[28]Brown, *You and Your Marriage*, 83.

[29]Brown, *You and Your Marriage*, 77.

[30]Smith, "Thoughts on Marriage Compatibility," *Ensign*, Sept. 1981, 45 (emphasis added).

[31]Holland, "Of Souls, Symbols, and Sacraments," BYU Devotional, Jan. 12, 1988.

[32]Watson, *Purity and Passion*, 135.

[33]*See* Doctrine & Covenants 49:15.

[34]*See* Genesis 2:21-23.

[35]*See also* Matthew 19:5-6, Mark 10:8, Ephesians 5:31, Doctrine & Covenants 49:16, Moses 3:24, and Abraham 5:18.

[36]McConkie, "Celestial Marriage," *New Era*, June 1978, 17.

[37]*See* Genesis 2:25, Moses 3:25, Abraham 5:19.

[38]*See* Doctrine & Covenants 93:36.

[39]*See* Doctrine & Covenants 93:37.

[40]Doctrine & Covenants 93:38.

[41]Doctrine & Covenants 93:39 (emphasis added).

[42]*See* Matthew 13:19.

[43]*See* 2 Corinthians 4:4.

[44]*See* Alma 12:10.

[45]*See* Doctrine & Covenants 93:39; and Alma 12:9.

[46]*See* Doctrine & Covenants 93:39; and Jeremiah 16:19.

[47]*See* Doctrine & Covenants 84:54.

[48]*See* Doctrine & Covenants 93:40.

[49]*Webster's*, 669.

[50]Wheat and Wheat, *Intended for Pleasure*, 83.

[51]*Webster's*, 775.

[52]1 Corinthians 6:17.

[53]*See* Genesis 2:24.

[54]*Webster's*, 47.

[55]2 Nephi 2:18.

[56]2 Nephi 2:27.

[57]Barlow, "They Twain," *Ensign*, Sept. 1986, 49.

[58]Helaman 5:12.

[59]*Webster's*, 48.

[60]*See* Matthew 17:21.

[61]John 14:26.

[62]Dunn, "How to Gain a Testimony," *Ensign*, Jan. 1973, 84.

[63]Faust, "Strengthening the Inner Self," *Ensign,* Feb. 2003, 4.

CHAPTER VIEW

❧

Chapter 3

THE SYMPHONY OF THE FEMALE
SEXUAL RESPONSE, PART I

Janie wanted to know if it was okay for her husband to manually stimulate her clitoris during sex. She was concerned that they were doing something inappropriate. I asked if she knew the physiological purpose of the clitoris. She didn't. I told her the clitoris has no other purpose than for pleasure. I asked if she believed God created our bodies. She said she did. I reminded her of the scriptures affirming that our bodies were created in God's likeness, and that God declared what He had created to be "very good."[1] Janie had been married for over seven years, yet she did not understand the full function and response of the sex organs, nor God's approval of their righteous use within marriage.

The Symphony of the Sexual Response

The ultimate sexual experience occurs when sexual fulfillment is harmoniously created and shared by both husband and wife. Though the sexual response varies from person to person and from male to female, attaining feelings of sexual pleasure, emotional and physical buildup, and complete sexual release is like a marital symphony. Typically for men, the creation of "sexual music" might be likened to pressing "play" on a CD player. But for women, sexual music is more like that of an instrument that must be tuned, warmed up and played masterfully—as in a symphony of sexual interludes. The female body is capable of extraordinary sexual ecstasy. The body is our greatest earthly "instrument."

The goal of this chapter is greater understanding of the symphonic process, or phases, of the sexual response. You must master how sensual music is created within yourself, as well as understand and appreciate how sexual fulfillment occurs for your spouse. With desire, time and effort husband and wife together can create harmony— a sacred symphony of sexual fulfillment—blessed by God. This symphony of sexual fulfillment will bless marriages immeasurably.

While this chapter focuses on sexual technique and the human sexual response, particularly of women, techniques alone will not ensure sexual fulfillment. Dr. Wheat, a Christian physician, and his wife Gaye stated, "Mastery of physical techniques is only part of the answer. . . . A couple cannot separate sex from the rest of the marriage. . . . Everything that happens in a marriage has its effect on the lovemaking experience."[2]

Sex Education Needed

Women generally have a significant sexual learning curve once they enter marriage, whereas men have a head start on their sexual awareness due to the external nature of their sexual organs. Sexual fulfillment for women is a learned physiological response requiring time, experience, communication and information about the body and the sexual response. If couples have sexual difficulties, often their solution is to back away and avoid straightforward efforts to learn about and resolve their issues. While patience and understanding are critical, and should be part of overcoming sexual concerns, it is also important to dedicate specific time and effort to sexual learning.

To fully partake of God's plan for physical pleasure in marriage, couples must understand male and female anatomy, physiology and the stages of the sexual response. They must learn what is pleasurable to themselves and to each other. The body is an amazing creation, but much of its territory is yet uncharted by many couples.

Though lovemaking is a natural process, what comes naturally will not ultimately satisfy both husband and wife sexually. Additional education is needed. "If you do what comes naturally in lovemaking, almost every time you will be wrong,"[3] comments Ed Wheat. Referring to Dr. Wheat's comment, Christian pastor Tim LaHaye and his wife, Beverly, went on to say, "In reality [Dr. Wheat] was cautioning his male audience that each 'natural' or self-satisfying step in gaining sexual gratification for a man would probably be incompatible with his wife's needs. For that reason, a couple must seriously study this subject just prior to marriage, and then after their marriage they can begin their practice to learn the most satisfying techniques."[4]

The only sex education Steven received was when his dad told him that since he had grown up on a farm he should already know how "it" worked. Human sexuality is a lot different than animal mating behavior. With premarital sex education like that it's easy to see how couples can run into sexual problems in marriage.

The body is a miracle—a gift from God. We must master our bodies and their sexual potential through study and intimate instruction to fully experience the exultant ecstasy that is possible in marriage. Dr. Wheat proclaimed, "When we discover the many intricate details of our bodies that provide so many intense, wonderful physical sensations for husbands and wives to enjoy together, we can be sure that [God] intended us to experience full satisfaction in the marriage relationship."[5]

Factual knowledge about how an orgasm is created is important, but so is having an idea of what it feels like. Many couples don't really know what they are trying to accomplish sexually—especially when it comes to female orgasm. It can be frustrating to wonder if the wife has even had an orgasm. Couples may try to discuss the situation, but often they simply don't have enough knowledge to do anything differently. It can be even more frustrating if they don't know where to go for help. This book as well as the following books can be helpful resources to teach couples more about techniques as well as problems and solutions of the human sexual response:

- *Intended for Pleasure: Sex Technique and Sexual Fulfillment in Christian Marriage*, Ed and Gaye Wheat, 1997.

- *The Act of Marriage: The Beauty of Sexual Love*, Tim and Beverly LaHaye, 1998.

- *Between Husband and Wife: Gospel Perspectives on Marital Intimacy*, Stephen E. Lamb and Douglas E. Brinley, 2000.

- *And They Shall Be One Flesh: A Sensible Sex Guide for the Bride and Groom*, Lindsay R. Curtis, 1968.

- *The Sex-Starved Marriage: A Couple's Guide to Boosting Their Marriage Libido*, Michele Weiner Davis, 2003.

Three Considerations

The following information provides important context to better understand the symphony of the sexual response:

Sex Is a Decision. For men sex is more of a reaction. For women sex is more of a decision. Men's bodies can become sexually ready even when their intellect tells them "No." Women must mentally agree to sex before their bodies can begin to respond sexually. They often need to be turned on before they feel sexual desire, and in order to do this they must be willing to engage in the experience, having faith that their feelings will follow. Making a conscious decision to engage in sex permits the female mind and body to begin the natural unfolding of the sexual response.

Natural Unfolding. While the hope is that husband and wife will both regularly experience orgasm, it is important to keep in mind that the sexual response should be a natural unfolding—even a divine unfolding. Couples should force nothing, pretend nothing, judge nothing, require nothing and have nothing to prove. No-expectation sex is the best sex. The focus should be on simply enjoying every touch, every kiss and every caress, basking in the sexual energy you are sharing.

Sex provides the greatest emotional and physical harmony when a relaxed approach is taken. Planning to just enjoy each other no matter what happens removes the pleasure-killing performance pressure. Relax and have fun. Bring laughter and playfulness to your sexual interactions. Let go of any pressure to perform. It is more likely you will knock the stars out of the sky if you simply relax and enjoy than if you set up incredible expectations.

Husbands shouldn't go after the clitoris, the G-spot or her orgasm like they would a touchdown. If a wife feels like a bystander as her husband rushes on to victory, it is likely she will not find sex very satisfying, nor will there be many mutual "touchdowns."

Sex without expectations may be difficult. Some may unconsciously write, "must achieve orgasm" on their mental "to do" list. The likelihood of sexual fulfillment increases with an attitude of letting go instead of achieving. Sexual fulfillment is not achieved simply by exerting willpower. Learning to let go is addressed in the warm-up/ preparation phase discussed below as well as in Chapter 7, which deals with overcoming negative beliefs and inhibitions.

Focus on Self. Women are taught to be selfless and giving. This may be especially true when it comes to sex, where they may have a hard time receiving or allowing themselves to "selfishly" enjoy physical pleasure. Husbands need to be aware that wives may be more concerned about his pleasure than her own. This can result in a diminished response from her, and reduce his enjoyment as well. Wives must be willing to receive during lovemaking if they want to give the greatest pleasure to their husbands.

While sex is about giving and receiving love and pleasure, it is also about taking turns being "self" focused. Selfishness is generally identified as a negative attribute, but to achieve sexual fulfillment there must be a healthy degree of being centered on the self—centered on our own pleasure and sensations. Being self-focused sexually can help women achieve orgasm—which is also a great turn-on for most husbands. Speaking to women, Dr. Wheat stated:

> The concentration must be on your own feelings, your own sensations, your own desires, as you move with them and let them take you where they will. . . . As you learn to respond by concentrating on your sensations, you *are* learning to please your husband! You cannot imagine how devastating an indifferent response is to a man who tries time after time to arouse his wife with lovemaking. You also cannot imagine the ecstatic thrills that come to a man when he sees his wife responding totally, enjoying every moment of their time together with a lovely abandon.[6]

So, women, it's okay to focus on your own pleasure. You have permission to see that *your* sexual needs are met as well as your husband's. In this context, sexual selfishness is not selfishness at all, because the greatest gift wives can give their husbands is to be sexually satisfied. A husband's greatest sexual fulfillment comes from lighting the fire of desire in his wife and watching it roar into flames of passion and pleasure.

New Insights on the Female Sexual Response

Four phases are frequently identified regarding the human sexual response. They generally follow some variation of: (1) Desire; (2) Excitement / arousal / plateau / foreplay; (3) Intercourse / orgasm / climax; and (4) Recovery / resolution / afterglow. To more accurately reflect the sexual response of women and to place needed emphasis I have added a phase, Phase 1: Warm-up / Preparation, and have also reversed the order of two phases, Arousal before Desire. My description of the sexual response is as follows:

1. Warm-up / Preparation

2. Foreplay / Arousal

3. Desire

4. Orgasm / Climax / Intercourse

5. Afterglow

This re-ordering of the sexual response phases and the addition of the Warm-up / Preparation phase reflects a unique approach and adds significant insight to the female sexual response. Understanding this pattern can be a key for both husbands and wives in comprehending how to improve their lovemaking.

PHASE I—WARM-UP / PREPARATION

"I'm just not in the mood" is a frequent response to sexual advances in marriage. Since men are like light switches and women are like slow-warming irons, it is understandable that the "Warm-up / Preparation" phase is often overlooked or completely ignored, particularly by men. Because of their physiology, "for the most part, men are in a constant state of sexual readiness."[7] Women are not. Men may wish they could skip this nonsense of a "warm-up phase" and get to the "good part." But their wives need preparation before they can get to the good part.

As couples learn how women prepare mentally and physically for lovemaking with talk, touch and time (the three "T's") they are empowered to create the mood rather than waiting for the mood. Waiting for that magical mood to strike will no longer be necessary.

Purpose of the Warm-up Phase

The Warm-up / Preparation phase is needed before some women can even begin to participate sexually. The Warm-up / Preparation phase allows women to mentally transition from mommy mode to wife and intimate-companion mode. She may still be thinking about the kids' homework and what she has to do tomorrow, when her husband is ready to go. For a wife to start on equal footing with her husband sexually she must be given sufficient time, touch and attention, otherwise he may be off and running, scoring a homerun before she even gets up to bat.

The Warm-up phase allows both husband and wife to focus mentally and connect emotionally before connecting physically. The talk, touch and time devoted to this phase provide the opportunity for her to get in the mood and be an *active* participant in lovemaking.

How Husbands Can Help Prepare for the Warm-up Phase

Women may not have the time, energy or interest to even allow themselves to enter the Warm-up phase without their husband's willing and loving assistance with household responsibilities. Continuing to court and woo their wife also helps provide an atmosphere conducive to intimate relations.

Share Household Responsibilities. Husbands play a pivotal part in providing their wives sexual warm-up and preparation time by sharing household responsibilities. With endless household demands on women's time and attention, a husband's active participation in the home makes it easier for his wife to decide to engage in sexual relations. In fact, one woman wanted me to be sure to list housework as a powerful aphrodisiac. As men learn to view their active interest and participation in the home and family as an integral part of their wives' ability to engage sexually, both spouses' needs will be better fulfilled.

To help his wife with this important phase of sexual preparation the husband might consider regularly taking on some of the evening responsibilities, such as cleaning the kitchen, helping with homework, preparing the next day's lunches or doing the children's bedtime routine. President Boyd K. Packer encouraged men's participation in the home when he said, "There is no task, however menial, connected with the care of babies, the nurturing of children, or with the maintenance of the home that is not [a husband's] equal obligation."[8] This assistance can ease a wife's load and free her to relax and engage in some of the warm-up / preparation activities suggested below. The following story provides a humorous look into the issue of intimacy, husbands and housework.

Tom used to fuss all the time to Teresa that she was never in the mood, even when he brought home flowers or did something special for her. With two little children and a new baby, Teresa was always busy caring for the children, cooking, cleaning and running errands or making a meal for the neighbor who just had a baby or who was in the hospital. Teresa would jokingly tell him, "If you had all this to do, you wouldn't have the energy for 'you know what' either." This went on for months.

Their sex life was okay, but not often enough for him. Once a month was the average. Tom used to complain to his friends that Teresa was not aware of his needs. One day a friend suggested he do the housework for her as a surprise. When Teresa walked in the door late one night she was in for a shock! The living room was picked up and the floor had been vacuumed. She couldn't hear the kids screaming and realized they must be in bed. She went into the kitchen knowing there were dishes to be done and found the kitchen spotless. The garbage had been taken out, and the cat had food and water. Tom was working on the laundry that was neatly folded in baskets ready to be put away in each bedroom.

She was delighted and touched by this act of love. Lovingly she walked over to him, gave him a kiss and said, "I'll meet you upstairs." After he was done he came upstairs and crawled into bed next to her. She reached over for him and he said, "Honey, not tonight. I am too tired."

Men often underestimate the power of their participation in the home and family as an aphrodisiac. Marriage therapist Michele Weiner Davis emphasized how a husband's household help can increase his wife's sexual desire:

> Show me a woman who feels as if she's doing more than her fair share of housework or child care and I'll show you a woman who has more than her fair share of "headaches." Nothing turns a woman off quite as effectively as the feeling that she's doing most of the work at home. . . . I can guarantee that you won't find her burning the midnight oil dreaming up ways to please her husband sexually. . . . When a low-desire woman feels burned out, the first thing to go on her to-do list is sex.[9]

A word of advice to husbands: Your willingness to be a partner in the household responsibilities must be constant and genuine to be effective. It won't work if you only give your wife your undivided attention and extra help with household responsibilities when you are hoping for sexual favors in return.

Woo Your Wife. Romantic gestures such as roses and candlelight dinners can be important to a wife, but a husband's understanding that foreplay occurs throughout the day is even more vital. The wooing, courting, and emotional intimacy men are willing to share help provide an atmosphere conducive to thrilling intimate relations. The importance of husbands wooing and romancing their wives and winning them over cannot be overstated. LDS physician, Lindsay R. Curtis, stated, "The woman longs for and looks forward to being courted and is so designed that she may require some little time to respond adequately to the wooing of the man. But although this desire in a woman is slow in awakening, once awakened, it is often capable of greater expression."[10]

The wise husband understands that foreplay for his wife begins the moment one session of lovemaking ends and weaves its way through all aspects of their lives. Dr. Wheat gave husbands insightful counsel on the importance of attention to the whole relationship:

> Because your sexual relationship will tend to reflect your emotional relationship, it is important to realize that every meaningful, fully enjoyable sex act really begins with a loving, attentive attitude hours or even days before. Husband, you should be aware that your wife views the sex act as part of her total relationship with you, even though you, like other men, may think of it separately. When both partners assume the responsibility for giving of their total selves—physically, emotionally, and spiritually—sexual interaction becomes a dynamic way of fully expressing love for each other. *It is your daily behavior toward each other* that will measure the extent and depth of the pleasure you find in making love sexually.[11]

Household help and a loving atmosphere are important aspects of helping a woman prepare for lovemaking, but women have a responsibility as well. Orgasm isn't just something that a man with intimate knowledge and skillful stimulating techniques provides a woman—it is something she must also be *willing* and *able* to let herself experience. The Warm-up phase is an important part of her preparation, with five components of preparing for sexual relations: (1) preparing the environment; (2) relaxing; (3) preparing mentally; (4) connecting emotionally; and (5) getting a head start on sexual arousal.

So what might women do during this Warm-up / Preparation phase? Some ideas will be given here, but each woman must become the expert on what turns her on and helps her to fully engage in the sexual experience—mentally, emotionally, spiritually and physically.

Orgasm isn't just something that a man with intimate knowledge
and skillful stimulating techniques provides a woman — it is
something she must also be willing *and* able *to let herself experience.*

❧

1. Prepare the Environment. Preparing the environment for romance and relaxation is instrumental in creating a sexually fulfilling experience. Experiment until you find the right ambience to assist you in transitioning and "letting go." Ambience can be enriched with soft music, scented candles, special silky bedding, dimmed lights, or sexy lingerie. Don't forget to lock the door. Attention to personal hygiene can make a huge difference between a subdued response and passionate participation. If it matters to you, let your husband know you prefer clean-shaven softness or the rough and rugged look, and he will likely oblige you. Suggest lotion to smooth his skin (offer to apply it), reducing any discomfort or distraction from his caresses. Freshly brushed teeth rinsed with mouthwash can also reduce sexual reservations and increase intimate enjoyment. His willingness to please you can be great foreplay.

2. Relax. The need to relax prior to making love may seem foreign to men. One man remarked, "Interestingly enough, most men use sex for de-stressing, whereas most women have to be relaxed before engaging! Some cosmic joke!" In the evening (or whenever lovemaking occurs), take a few minutes to slow down. Breathing deeply and being loving and gentle with yourself can pay rich dividends. Relaxation can help you let go of your day so you can BE in the moment.

Relaxation Breathing. Close your eyes and focus inside yourself. You might try imagining you are standing inside your heart. Breathe normally for a few breaths, then inhale deeply (filling your diaphragm) to the count of four; hold for four; then exhale to the count of eight. Continue these cleansing breaths for a few minutes. Use this relaxation breathing any time.

Nurturing Touch. Another helpful way to slow down and relax is to give yourself the gift of nonsexual physical touch. This can be done by gently stroking the back or inside of your hands, arms, face and neck or individually caressing each finger as if affirming love and tenderness to the self. Like the gentle touch you receive from those you love, you can provide loving touch to yourself. You may want to express your love and unconditional acceptance toward yourself during this time. This may be new to you but can be valuable preparation for sexual intimacy with your spouse.

3. Prepare Mentally. To get in the mood and to transition into lovemaking mode, clear your mind of everything but the lovemaking experience. Michele Weiner Davis, author of *The Sex-Starved Marriage*, calls this "clearing out the mental clutter."[12] Shifting the mind from kids, kitchen and kitty litter to romantic overtures doesn't happen quickly or easily. But with concerted effort you can learn to choose what you think and feel. One way to quiet the mind and train it to stay focused on sexual sensations is to pay attention to the rise and fall of your breathing. Breathe slowly and deeply as you let yourself slip into the world of arousal. In time, less effort will be needed as you naturally melt into the moment.

If you did the homework from Chapter 1, you already know what some of your negative thoughts and beliefs are regarding sex. These are the thoughts you will have to remove from your mind in preparation for satisfying physical relations. Overcoming mental and emotional barriers and inhibitions will be addressed in Chapter 7.

Thoughts are instructions to the brain. If negative thoughts about sex or your husband creep in they become instructions—telling your body how to feel. What are the thoughts you have during sex? Are your thoughts conducive to enjoyable and passionate relations, or are they detrimental and distracting—diverting you from feelings of love and pleasure?

With practice you can eliminate negative or unproductive thoughts. For example if the thought comes to mind, "I don't have time for this," or, "I don't like sex," you can challenge your thoughts by talking back to them and replacing them with something positive. You can say, "I DO have time to share love and experience ecstasy with my husband"; or, "I want to enjoy sex. I do enjoy sex." During lovemaking, rehearse the thought, "Touch is the dessert of life."

Record negative thoughts and feelings in a private sexual learning journal, so they can be addressed and overcome with the skills taught in Chapter 7. For example, thinking and verbalizing romantic or sexy statements during lovemaking can heighten your sexual arousal and draw your focus to pleasure and to positive thoughts.

4. Connect Emotionally. Sexual relations can be more satisfying for both husband and wife when emotional connection is an integral part of lovemaking. "Pillow talk" and "positive flooding" are two ways to connect emotionally and provide emotional arousal prior to lovemaking.

Pillow Talk. Regularly taking time for Pillow Talk to share thoughts and feelings can be great foreplay. During pillow talk don't discuss children, finances or other potentially contentious topics—discuss hopes, dreams, feelings or study and discuss this and other helpful books.

Positive Flooding. Dr. Harville Hendrix created an exercise called "Positive Flooding," which is another excellent emotional connector.[13] It is a wonderful beginning to any sexual encounter. Husband and wife take turns expressing the following:

a. Share at least five positive statements about your spouse's body;

b. Acknowledge at least five positive characteristics in your spouse;

c. Complete the statement, "I love it when you . . . " identifying at least five positive behaviors your spouse does; then

d. Say "I love you" with all the genuine feeling you can muster.

Positive flooding can create a strong and secure connection between you and your spouse. If your spouse is currently unwilling to participate in this flooding for any reason, you may ask if he would mind you doing the exercise. Assure him there is no pressure for him to do it in return (and mean it). There are positive benefits even if only one spouse does the flooding.

5. Give Female Sexual Arousal a Head Start. Since it generally takes a bit longer for women to get their sexual motors running women need a head start. Wives have a chance to catch up as couples focus on building her pleasure before her husband's. If the husband is quickly aroused and expecting to do something about it, it may be difficult for him to be sufficiently patient and attentive to his wife for her to become aroused enough to experience orgasm; therefore, keep the focus on her until she is fully aroused. Just before or after her orgasm, he too can let go and join her in the ecstasy of orgasm.

Some couples have the mistaken perception that once the man is aroused they need to move right into intercourse. To remove this perception couples may need to experiment with multiple cycles of male arousal to gain experience and confidence that his arousal can subside and reoccur several times during lovemaking. As the husband gains greater understanding of and mastery over his arousal and the wife provides sufficient stimulation, they can rest assured that their focus on her arousal won't inhibit mutual sexual fulfillment.

Stimulation of the clitoris is the key to the feminine sexual response. In the beginning as couples are both learning it may take up to an hour of direct and/or indirect stimulation of the clitoris to reach orgasm. A husband should wait until his sweetheart is very near climax and gives her go ahead before he penetrates.

To give the wife a head start sexually, one idea may be to go into the bedroom together, prepare for lovemaking, but plan to engage in twenty minutes or so of pillow talk or positive flooding to engage her in emotional arousal. After some foreplay, stimulate the wife's clitoris to help feelings of sexual arousal begin to flow. For those women who require a fair amount of direct clitoral stimulation, this allows sufficient time to prepare sexually and become aroused before her husband is ready to go.

"Kegel" exercises—contracting or tightening the pubococcygeus (P.C.) muscle—can also intensify sexual arousal. Tim and Beverly LaHaye, in their book *The Act of Marriage,* have a chapter entitled, "The Key to Feminine Response" which is an excellent and thorough explanation of this P.C. muscle and the benefits of strengthening it.[14] Coupled with communication and sufficient clitoral stimulation contracting the P.C. muscle can help increase sexual arousal and intensify orgasms.

PHASE 2—FOREPLAY / AROUSAL

A woman's arousal is like a gift, delicately wrapped in layers of tissue paper each needing to be carefully unwrapped. If there has been sufficient warm-up or mental preparation, foreplay can increase arousal and create sexual desire within the wife. The gradual buildup and intensifying of sensations and emotions with gentle caressing, kissing, stroking and fondling serve to prepare the mind and body for intercourse and orgasm. Dr. Wheat described foreplay as a luxurious time of unrushed love play. He stated:

> This time of sexual stimulation, often called foreplay, can be delightful for both husband and wife, if the husband realizes that his tender skill at this point will prepare his wife for the love act itself. Most women like to be wooed and won. Let the man indicate by the way he approaches his wife that he is demonstrating his love for her, not claiming sex as his right. The husband must be careful not to appear hurried, crude, rude, mechanical, or impatient![15]

Foreplay is not "one size fits all." It comes in as many varieties as there are individuals, and it can change with circumstances and moods. For most women the ideal foreplay includes a delicate mix of physical pleasure and emotional intimacy. Physical pleasure and emotional intimacy need not be mutually exclusive experiences. Husband and wife can combine pleasure with intimacy by maintaining eye contact, expressing verbal affirmations of enjoyment and pleasure or by breathing in sync for an exquisite emotional rush.

Every person has erogenous areas on their body that when touched or stimulated increase sexual arousal. It is the opportunity and responsibility of husband and wife to embark on a lifelong treasure hunt to learn and develop each other's sexual hot spots. This intimate knowledge is necessary for maximum sexual fulfillment as a wrong move can derail the pleasure train for some women.

The search for these sacred areas may take an excitingly long time. Maybe that's why in biblical times[16] newlywed husbands were released from all military responsibilities for a whole year, presumably so couples could get to "know"[17] each other and learn how to become "one flesh."[18] Dedicating the first year of marriage to getting to know each other intimately—physically, emotionally and spiritually—creates a solid foundation upon which to build a family.

While you will likely find stimulating each other's sexual hot spots exciting, foreplay can be even more sensual when attention is given to the whole body or the whole person. The body has an amazing ability to be erogenous to one whose sexual senses are awakened. Dr. Wheat encouraged this all-encompassing sensual foreplay by stating, "Relaxed love play begins with kissing, embracing, petting, and fondling. The most effective touching for both man and wife in the early part of sex play is a gentle caressing of *all* the body. All includes everything and excludes nothing. Do not touch only those areas that seem directly related to excitement."[19] When all parts of the body are included in lovemaking a message is sent that all parts of the person are loved and accepted by the other. The feeling of being just an object of sexual gratification is diminished when all parts of the body are loved and given attention.

Another important factor in foreplay is for both husband and wife to become expert at reading each other's responses and sexual state of being. This comes with time, practice and communicating your wants and needs. Couples must share what they find pleasurable and what is a turnoff. Couples must also become expert regarding their own body and sexual desires. It will take some trial and error so be patient with yourself and each other as you learn and experiment together.

If Good Girl conditioning is still an issue, some of the love play of sexual intimacy may create anxiety, embarrassment or discomfort. Necking and petting are terms that have been most often used in connection with sinful premarital sexual behavior. The adversary uses such misunderstandings to drive a wedge between husband and wife. But sin does not apply to these sacred pleasures within marriage. Be assured that within the bond of marriage these intimate activities are appropriate, proper, and vital to sexual fulfillment. Couples may need to be attentive to and address any negative feelings that foreplay induces.

The Clitoris. While there are many different parts of the body that can sexually arouse a woman, the clitoris, not the vagina, is considered the center of feminine response.[20] The clitoris is one of the highly erogenous parts of the body. Dr. Curtis, an LDS physician, described the clitoris as "a small, elongated, highly sensitive body, usually about three quarters of an inch long, situated at the top of the vulva, just above the urethra. In essence it is a miniature penis without a urinary opening. Composed of erectile tissue, it becomes rigid upon stimulation and if titillated long enough, it will eventuate in an orgasm."[21]

Women who are unaware of their sexual anatomy and the pleasurable purpose of the clitoris may be missing out on exquisite sexual enjoyment. Like Janie, who was unsure if it was okay for her husband to manually stimulate her clitoris, other wives, still under the influence of the Good Girl Syndrome or through sexual ignorance, may have similar questions and reservations that keep them from enjoying sexual fulfillment in marriage. But again, we know God created our bodies in his image, "In the image of his own body, male and female, created he them, and *blessed* them."[22] Remember the clitoris has no other known function than creating pleasure. God apparently made it that way—and called it a *blessing.*

In addition to the Good Girl Syndrome, insufficient sexual education regarding the clitoris and the feminine sexual response can keep many women from understanding, experiencing and delighting in their God-given sexuality. Dr. Brent Barlow, LDS counselor and BYU professor, stated regarding the clitoris, "Some young women I have talked to have never heard about it or do not know where it is located. It is one of the little organs . . . that God created in the female and that has no reproductive function whatsoever. It is there for one purpose only: to produce pleasure."[23]

Insufficient sexual education regarding the clitoris and the feminine sexual response can keep many women from understanding, experiencing and delighting in their God-given sexuality.

This lack of knowledge regarding the clitoris is not limited to young women. Dr. Romel W. Mackelprang described the conditioning that leads grown women, even mothers, to be unaware of this important pleasurable part of the body:

> Boys and girls are taught to not touch themselves and are sometimes told that their genitals are undesirable or "nasty." This may be especially true for girls who, unlike boys, have no "legitimate" reason to regularly touch or view their genitalia. Girls may grow to womanhood without learning what their genitals look like or even the proper names of their sexual organs. An example of this was related to me by the nurse of a young, acutely disabled woman I was counseling. As the

nurse began to teach this woman and her mother how to insert a catheter into the bladder, the mother asked about the "little mound of tissue" that was her daughter's clitoris. When the nurse offered an explanation, this mother of five adults expressed surprise, having always assumed that the clitoris was inside the vagina.[24]

As the center of feminine sexual response, stimulation of the clitoris is critical to sexual fulfillment. Tim and Beverly LaHaye stated:

> The reluctance of many loving partners to incorporate clitoral stimulation as a necessary and meaningful part of their foreplay has probably cheated more women out of the exciting experience of orgasmic fulfillment than any other one thing. . . . To highlight the significance of the clitoris to the woman's sexual enjoyment, many researchers have compared [the clitoris] with the penis. It has been called the 'most keenly sexual part of a woman's body' and is still regarded by many as "the seat of all sexual satisfaction."[25]

For many, the intercourse of penis and vagina does not provide sufficient stimulation of the clitoris. Some sexual positions may make direct stimulation more possible, but they are often uncomfortable and may provide too much stimulation for the man to maintain control long enough for the wife to reach her orgasm. Additional direct stimulation of the clitoris may be needed. Christian professor Dr. Herbert J. Miles agreed. He stated:

> Since the clitoris is the arousal trigger of the wife, and since the penis does not contact the clitoris in normal intercourse, marriage counselors recommend what is called "direct" stimulation. That is, the husband, in the process of love-play before intercourse starts, will gently stimulate all the erotic zones of his wife's body . . . and finally her clitoris. He will continue stimulation of the clitoris for . . . whatever time it takes, until he is certain she is fully aroused sexually and ready for intercourse. There is nothing wrong in this procedure. . . . A couple must do the right thing at the right time in the right attitude for full arousal and complete love harmony. It is normal in the love-play and arousal period for a couple to touch and handle each other's sexual organs. This is a pleasant and meaningful part of love expression. It was planned this way by the Creator.[26]

For learning purposes you might consider being in charge of clitoral stimulation to become expert on the functioning of your own body, then you can teach your husband. If you have questions regarding the appropriateness of clitoral stimulation or any other aspect of sexuality, discuss them together and take them to the Lord, so you can rest assured that God approves of the righteous use of the magnificent bodies He created for us. If any of the suggestions throughout this book cause some inner resistance you may want to see Chapter 7 about overcoming inhibitions and distinguishing between inappropriate sexual behavior and inhibitions caused by negative sexual conditioning.

The Grafenberg Area. In the 1950's a German obstetrician and gynecologist by the name of Ernest Grafenberg discovered an erotic zone inside the vagina that was particularly sensitive to sexual stimulation. This area has become known as the G-spot, though it is more of an "area" than an exact "spot." When stimulated during arousal, it swells in size and is reported to create a different quality and greater intensity of orgasm than that which emanates from clitoral stimulation. One woman described the feeling of a G-spot orgasm as, "an orgasm—times 10!"

There has been some debate about the G-spot. For some it can be difficult to find, as the size and location of the G-spot vary from woman to woman. For others it may be dormant and require much direct stimulation to arouse any response. Still others find it no more erogenous than any other area of the vagina. While most of the vagina isn't necessarily sensitive to stimulation, the raised area of tissue in the vagina known as the G-spot is believed to have a higher concentration of nerve endings.

The G-spot is a mound of nerve tissue about the size of a bean when not aroused, and about the size of a quarter when aroused. It is generally located about one and a half to three inches inside the vagina directly behind the pubic bone on the front side of the vagina (toward the abdomen). The G-spot may be easier for your husband to find and may feel more pleasurable when you are already aroused from clitoral stimulation. Because the G-spot is deep within the tissue, firm strokes and pressure are needed to deeply press the spongy mass of the vagina against the pubic bone. It may be easier to find with the wife lying on her stomach and the husband inserting one or two fingers, palm down, into the vagina and stimulating with small circles or an upside-down "come here" motion. The angle and pressure of the penis inside the vagina would have to be just right to be effective.

Because pressure on the G-spot pushes the urethra against the pubic bone, the initial sensation some women may feel is the need to urinate. (It's always a good idea to urinate before lovemaking anyway.) Others may initially feel some discomfort or a sensitive raw feeling. The sensation of needing to urinate passes and is replaced with a feeling of increased pleasure and arousal. The wife will know when the right spot is found. Continued stroking may produce increased pleasure—resulting in an intense orgasm.

The G-spot should be approached with the utmost reverence and respect rather than simply seeking a bigger sexual thrill. Awakening the G-spot may take time, patience and practice; nevertheless, couples may want to make it part of their sensual explorations for erogenous zones as they investigate its potential for pleasure. For additional information, you might check out the Christian site, "The Marriage Bed: Sex and Intimacy for Married Christians" at www.TheMarriageBed.com.

Communicating Increased Arousal. With escalating arousal the desire for stronger and more passionate or focused caresses may increase. Again, it is your responsibility to communicate your desires to your husband. Even a simple and slow, "Mmmmm!" when something feels good can help your spouse learn what works and what doesn't. It is equally important that the husband be exquisitely attentive to the wife to learn what she wants and needs—and when. Wives can help husbands learn to read their responses and sexual state by communicating their pleasure instead of keeping it inside. How will he know what you're feeling or what you want him to do if you don't tell him or show him?

Women can also teach without words as they guide their husband's hands, or moan their approval of particularly pleasing caresses or activities. Dr. Wheat admonished wives when he said, "As [a wife] concentrates on her physical feelings, she should learn to communicate her level of sexual excitement to her husband with looks, touches, and sometimes loving words. This helps the husband to properly time his lovemaking. One of the most common sources of sexual unhappiness is the failure of a woman to tell her husband frankly and clearly what stimulates her and when she is ready for a particular stimulation."[27]

You may prefer to discuss this later, at another time and place, telling your husband that when he did "such and such" you really liked it, or when he did something else it wasn't as arousing. You are the foremost sexual teacher for your spouse. Only you can teach him what you want. You are, or should be, the authority on your body and its sexual functioning, as well as the expert on your husband's sexual desires. The astute husband makes it a priority to be the world's greatest authority on how to please his wife. With intimate knowledge and pure love, husband and wife can both stretch to give the personalized sexual love each wants and needs.

The Transcendent State of Arousal. The state of arousal is a magical state of being. It represents a mental and psychological letting go of earthly cares and slipping into the sexual sphere where uninhibited pleasurable sensations reign. Arousal commands your full attention. You will feel no desire to discuss the day's events or schedule your week with your husband while in the state of sexual arousal. It is an altered state—different from anything you regularly experience in day-to-day life. With a solid understanding of the godly purposes and sanctity of sexual relations, arousal becomes a magical, uninhibited "never, never land." Some of the physical indicators of arousal include:

- Increasingly rapid breathing

- Skin that becomes warm and sensitive to the touch

- Wetness or lubrication of the vagina

- Engorgement or swelling of the outer lips (labia majora)

- Flared inner lips (labia minora)

- Erect nipples

The arousal phase is a unique state of being. What might seem embarrassing or out of character in a regular state may seem desirable, even pleasurable and enjoyable, during the state of sexual arousal. Full sexual arousal provides a state of uninhibited abandon that allows you to let go and surrender to the sexual experience and sensations.

Another appeal of the state of sexual arousal is that any of your perceived flaws and imperfections are heartily overlooked by your husband during arousal. In this state, to him you are the most beautiful creature ever created. It is wise for husbands to reinforce this concept by willingly, genuinely and generously communicating their adoration of you and your body.

The harmonious symphony of the sexual response is evident throughout the Warm-up / Preparation phase as well as the Foreplay / Arousal stage. In the next chapter the symphony continues with the phases of Desire and Orgasm / Climax / Intercourse, and ends with Afterglow, like a beautiful sunset on a warm summer night.

Chapter 3—"Home" Work

- Get educated sexually. Learn about your sexual anatomy and the importance of the clitoris in female sexual arousal. Read and discuss this and other helpful books with your spouse.

- Understand that you must consciously decide to enjoy sex if it is to be a fulfilling experience.

- Allow yourself to focus on your own sexual needs during lovemaking.

- Discuss with your husband the importance of his active interest and participation in home and family responsibilities to help you have time and energy to willingly engage in lovemaking.

- Make time for sexual warm-up and preparation by preparing the environment, relaxing, preparing mentally, connecting emotionally and giving your sexual arousal a head start.

- Commit to communicate your feelings, wants, needs, likes and dislikes during lovemaking.

NOTES

Chapter 3—The Symphony of the Female Sexual Response, Part I

[1] *See* Genesis 1:26–27, 31.
[2] Wheat and Wheat, *Intended for Pleasure*, 19.
[3] LaHaye and LaHaye, *Act of Marriage*, 93.
[4] LaHaye and LaHaye, *Act of Marriage*, 93.
[5] Wheat and Wheat, *Intended for Pleasure*, 16.
[6] Wheat and Wheat, *Intended for Pleasure*, 113–14.
[7] Curtis, *And They Shall Be One Flesh*, 54.
[8] Packer, "Tribute to Women," *Ensign*, July 1989, 78.
[9] Weiner Davis, *Sex-Starved Marriage*, 144–45.
[10] Curtis, *And They Shall Be One Flesh*, 54.
[11] Wheat and Wheat, *Intended for Pleasure*, 81.
[12] *See* Weiner Davis, *Sex-Starved Marriage*, 99.
[13] *See* Hendrix, *Getting the Love You Want Manual*, 1993, 121.
[14] *See* LaHaye and LaHaye, *Act of Marriage*, 195–217.
[15] Wheat and Wheat, *Intended for Pleasure*, 81.
[16] *See* Deuteronomy 24:5, *See Also* Bible Dictionary: Marriage.
[17] *See* Moses 5:2.
[18] Matthew 19:5.
[19] Wheat and Wheat, *Intended for Pleasure*, 81–82.
[20] Wheat and Wheat, *Intended for Pleasure*, 85.
[21] Curtis, *And They Shall Be One Flesh*, 56.
[22] Moses 6:9 (emphasis added).
[23] Barlow, *Just for Newlyweds*, 51.
[24] Mackelprang, "They Shall Be One Flesh," *Multiply and Replenish*, 49.
[25] LaHaye and LaHaye, *Act of Marriage*, 112.
[26] Miles, *Sexual Happiness*, 71.
[27] Wheat and Wheat, *Intended for Pleasure*, 84.

CHAPTER VIEW

❧

Chapter 4

THE SYMPHONY OF THE FEMALE
SEXUAL RESPONSE, PART II

Karen, a lovely twenty-nine-year-old mother of three, came for counseling. She was obviously distressed: "Pastor, I really love my husband, but lately I have noticed that my resentment toward him is growing something fierce. If something doesn't happen pretty soon, I'm going to end up hating him!" Although it was hard for her to express it, she finally admitted that the problem concerned their love life. "He is the only one who gets satisfaction out of it! I have always considered myself an affectionate woman and have rarely refused to make love to him; but just about the time I really get excited, he comes inside me and it's all over. He flops over on his side of the bed and falls sound asleep—and that's

when I get mad! It takes me over an hour to unwind enough to go to sleep. . . . "

Like many other unfulfilled wives, [Karen] knew very little about sex, and much of her information was wrong. Unfortunately her husband, Jeff, knew less than she did. . . . These two Christian young people had entered marriage with the naive idea that their love was so powerful that "everything will just work out naturally. . . . " [This] certainly isn't true of female orgasm.[1]

As couples travel through Phase 1—Warm-up / Preparation, and Phase 2—Foreplay / Arousal, the wife can begin to experience the exhilarating emotions of sexual desire. The symphony of the sexual response flows from Desire into Orgasm / Climax / Intercourse, then ebbs into the heavenly ambience of the Afterglow.

PHASE 3—DESIRE

Desire, or *libido*, is the yearning, want or interest in initiating or responding to sexual advances. Desire is a complex phenomenon that is a by-product of many factors, such as current marriage dynamics, past experiences, body image, physiological issues (such as pregnancy or illness), and even spiritual factors.[2] Differing degrees of sexual desire is the most common sexual problem couples encounter. While many define the desire gap between husband and wife as high libido versus low libido, it is in reality an issue of misunderstanding how men and women experience desire differently.

Phase 3—The Desire phase—is commonly identified as the first phase in the human sexual response. This ignores the important Warm-up / Preparation phase that women need and assumes desire always comes first. It may be true that most "men are in a constant state of sexual readiness [and desire],"[3] but women are generally *not* nor do they easily or quickly get into that state of readiness. The additional needs of women require switching the Desire phase from the first phase to the third phase, after the Warm-up and Arousal phases.

Desire Follows Arousal

Before most women begin to feel sexual desire they must be "talked" into it and "touched" into it. Couples must remember the three "T's" of female sexual desire and arousal—talk, touch and time. For many women sexual desire doesn't manifest itself until *after* sexual arousal. Marriage therapist Michele Weiner Davis explained, "When [women] decide to be receptive to their partners' advances or initiate sexual contact themselves, not to quell a sexual hunger but for other, equally valid reasons such as the desire for intimate connection, being touched in stimulating ways often leads to arousal. Arousal triggers a strong desire to continue being sexual. Hence, desire follows arousal."[4]

Couples must remember the three "T's" of female
sexual desire and arousal—talk, touch and time.

So, for those who thought they just weren't sexual, it may be that they have always been sexual, but just didn't understand that they needed sexual stimulation and arousal before sexual desire could occur. Weiner Davis went on to say, "Have you ever noticed that although you might not have been thinking sexual thoughts or feeling particularly sexy, if you push yourself to 'get started' when your spouse approaches you, it feels good, and you find yourself getting into it? If so, this upside-down view of sexual desire can be incredibly liberating. It's not that you lack sexual desire, it's just that for you, desire doesn't happen until you've been physically aroused."[5]

If you realize you need sexual arousal prior to experiencing desire, you may need to adopt what Weiner Davis calls "The Nike Solution"[6]—Just do it! If you push forward with faith, arousal and desire will follow.

Gail noticed she really had to work at getting in the mood for sex, even though she ultimately got into it and enjoyed it. She said, "Sometimes I just need to go forward with the sexual experience committing myself mentally to it. I have to remind myself that I got into it last time, and I liked it. Once the stimulation is sufficient, I get swept up in the ecstasy of the experience. You'd think the need for a conscious choice would go away, but sex is still a decision I have to make nearly every time. It's like an 'act of faith' to embark on the sexual experience without the sexual desire in hand."

Love is a choice. For many women, engaging in sexual relations may also have to be a conscious choice. With the information and suggestions in this book, sex need not be begrudgingly and hesitatingly endured, but become a source of boundless pleasure and intimacy.

Causes of Low Sexual Desire

If low sexual desire is the most common sexual problem in your marriage, it is worth some time and effort to understand why. Below is a compilation of problem areas couples may face. The issues that attract your attention may indicate areas that need to be addressed.

While there are physiological or medical causes of low sexual desire, there "is almost always an emotional overlay when it comes to problems with sexual desire."[7] Low sexual desire may result from (1) physiological causes, (2) psychological / emotional factors, or (3) relationship issues that affect your ability to achieve God-ordained sexual fulfillment in marriage.

Physiological Causes

1. Fluctuating hormones and imbalances

2. Illnesses

3. Medications

4. Physical pain during intercourse

5. Premature ejaculation (which can also be psychologically based)

6. Weak vaginal muscles (P.C. muscle)

Psychological Factors

1. Sexual, physical or emotional abuse or neglect as a child

2. Depression (also physiological)

3. Poor self-esteem

4. Poor body image

5. Motherhood ("I'm a mother, not a lover.")

6. Fatigue (children and household responsibilities)

7. Inhibitions from cultural conditioning, teachings, and expectations—seeing sex as sin (the Good Girl Syndrome)

8. Negative or painful sexual experiences (including frustrating and fearful honeymoon experiences)

9. Feelings of sexual failure (prolonged periods of disappointment and infrequent or nonexistent orgasmic experiences)

10. Stress

11. Grief over a loss

12. Midlife crisis

13. Fear (of pain, of something new, of the unknown, of losing control)

14. Guilt over past sins (resolved or unresolved)

Relationship Issues

1. Emotional versus physical intimacy dilemmas (he wants physical intimacy, she wants emotional intimacy)

2. Insufficient nonsexual physical touch and affection

3. Insensitive or mechanical, predictable and routine sex

4. Time constraints (fulfilling lovemaking takes time)

5. Intimacy diversions and drains (too much television, work, reading, computer time)

6. Reluctance to discuss sex and communicate wants and needs

7. Sexual ignorance (poor preparation for marriage)

8. Sexual passivity

9. Aggressive, coercive behavior in marriage (nagging, dominating, criticizing)

10. Going along to get along (avoiding conflict)

11. Lack of sexual surrender (which is difficult for the strong-willed woman)

12. Lack of forgiveness

13. Bottled-up anger, resentment and feelings of revenge

Gaps in His and Her Sexual Desire Can Diminish

Beth told me that she and her husband didn't need to *improve* their sexual relationship; they just wished they both had similar levels of desire. When couples experience sexual fulfillment and marital oneness as God intended, the gap between his and her desire for sex significantly diminishes. Although a husband and wife may never *completely* desire sexual relations equally, some basic economic principles apply.

According to the law of supply and demand, when something is scarce, the demand for it increases. When the high-desire spouse waits for sexual intimacy, and those opportunities are rare and reluctant, he may be on watch 24 / 7. Because the supply is low, the demand for it increases. He waits and watches for his next sexual nourishment like a hungry animal. Conversely, when the supply of sexual relations is bounteous and enjoyed by both husband and wife, his desire may remain strong, but the feelings of hunger and emptiness are abated.

The concept of quality versus quantity also applies to sexual relations. Going through the motions sexually does little to satisfy. It's like eating a Twinkie instead of a healthy home-cooked meal. The Twinkie may provide initial appeasement, but satisfaction is short-lived—leaving emptiness and a hunger for more and more. The consumer keeps hoping it will someday satisfy, but it never does. A truly satisfying sexual relationship is like a home-cooked meal—it fulfills both participants in a substantive way. There is less need for the higher-desire spouse to obsess about the next sexual "Twinkie," when he knows he'll have regular healthy home-cooked meals. As the quality of the sexual experience increases for the wife (she enjoys full arousal and regular orgasm), her desire for sexual relations may also increase.

Kirsten would have questioned anyone's assertion that husbands' and wives' desire gaps could diminish. But, as she worked to improve their sexual relationship, she began to feel deep inside that it would one day be all she hoped for. During the process of learning and improving their sexual relationship, she teased her husband that when they got this all figured out, she'd probably want sex more than he did. After ten years of having a less-than-enthusiastic wife, he gave her a look of, "Yeah, right! That will be the day!" The day did come. After they had significantly improved the quality and quantity of their sexual encounters she was actually more eager one night than he was. She reminded him that she had predicted this day would come!

As the marital and sexual relationship improves, knowledge is gained, and problems are overcome, sexual fulfillment will increase. This increase in quality, even quantity, creates a balancing of the husband's and wife's sexual desire to the point that the desire gap can close quite comfortably.

PHASE 4—ORGASM / CLIMAX / INTERCOURSE

While sexual relations can be enjoyable just for the intimacy—the closeness and physical touch that is shared—the general hope is that both husband and wife will regularly experience the ecstasy of orgasm during lovemaking. Regular orgasms for both husband and wife should be a high priority due to the physiological, psychological, emotional and spiritual benefits orgasmic release affords.

I have purposely listed "orgasm" before "intercourse" in the fourth phase of the sexual response. For the sake of feminine fulfillment, her orgasm needs to have first priority during lovemaking. A woman's sexual response is slower to build and be resolved, and since it is difficult for men to keep the fire burning after they've climaxed, women are more likely to achieve orgasm if it is reached before the husband's ejaculation. When the focus is first on the wife's fulfillment, there is less of a problem with the husband climaxing before her, leaving her behind where she is likely to be unsatisfied.

Since women take longer to climax and require passionate attentiveness to reach this point, a husband needs to have self-discipline and lots of patience—even endurance. Whereas orgasm in women ignites their sexual energy, ejaculation exhausts a man and extinguishes his passion, making him susceptible to rolling over and falling asleep. After his climax, it's difficult to provide the attention and passion needed for his wife to be whisked away into the ecstasy of the experience.

Some women regard orgasm as unnecessary because of their difficulty or inability to experience it, or because of the skill, time and effort it may require. But the Lord surely intended orgasm to be a regular part of lovemaking, not only for the husband, but also for the wife. God created women with the capacity not only for orgasmic expression, but also the capacity to experience multiple orgasms. This may seem like an unimaginable luxury to those still struggling to experience one orgasm, but multiple orgasms are physically possible, nonetheless.

The Orgasm

An orgasm is the natural response to complete physical, emotional and mental arousal. It is a psychological "letting go." The best way to comprehend orgasm is certainly to experience it, since the nuances of the emotions and sensations are difficult to describe. If you have no idea what you're striving for, it can be even more difficult to experience. The following descriptions may be helpful.

Dr. Marie Robinson, psychiatrist, medical doctor and wife, described the female orgasm as follows:

> Orgasm is the physiological response which brings sexual intercourse to its natural and beautiful termination. . . . In the moment just preceding orgasm, muscular tension suddenly rises. . . .
>
> At the moment of greatest muscular tension all sensations seem to take one further rise upward. The woman tenses beyond the point where, it seems, it would be possible to maintain such tension for a moment longer. And indeed it is not possible, and now her whole body suddenly plunges into a series of muscular spasms. These spasms take place within the vagina itself, shaking the body with waves of pleasure. . . .
>
> If a woman is [sexually] satisfied by her orgasmic experience she will discharge the neurological and muscular tension developed in the sexual buildup.[8]

Dr. Ed Wheat, Christian physician and sex therapist, provided another good description of orgasm in women. He stated:

> [Orgasm] has been described as a momentary feeling of suspension, followed by a sensation of warmth starting in the perineal area and pervading the entire body. Rhythmic contractions of the lower third of the vagina follow. There may be from three to ten contractions over the period of a few seconds. She can increase the intensity of the physical sensations by voluntarily strengthening her P.C. muscle contractions . . . as she lets herself go in seeking release. As her physical movements, her response to her partner's stimulation and her own mental concentration blend into a total reaching for satisfaction, she comes to climax—often an emotional mountain-peak experience, when the rest of the world recedes and seems to stand still—a high point of feeling, best described as ecstasy.
>
> Sometimes a woman does not know if she has experienced an orgasm. If you feel your vagina contracting involuntarily, if you feel excited at first, and later feel

calm and physically satisfied, you can take this as evidence that you have had an orgasm even though perhaps a weak one.[9]

———

Orgasm might also be described as pleasurable sensations that slowly build, until the sexual tension bursts into a shooting star throughout the body. Rapid involuntary contractions or spasms radiate from the vagina and genitals. What began with some concentration on your part builds into a sexual crescendo until the sensations overtake you, reaching a fevered pitch. The sensations surge in intensity, momentarily transporting you from the present to an uninhibited wonderland. Like a sunburst of warmth and energy, the feelings penetrate your body, mind and spirit—coursing through you like an overwhelming, yet tangible feeling of love and ecstasy. The rush of blood to the genitals creates pleasurable pulsations and a soft fulness. It may even feel as if your heart is beating and pulsating in the genital area.

Orgasms can be created by clitoral, vaginal or G-spot stimulation (see Chapter 3). While some women may experience orgasm from vaginal stimulation or intercourse, many women find it necessary to have direct clitoral stimulation. With the clitoris as the center of the female sexual response, the stimulation from intercourse alone is often insufficient, since there is minimal direct contact with the clitoris (or with the G-spot).

The important question for many couples is not so much *what* an orgasm is, but *how* to create it. It is not a mechanical, step-by-step procedure that works the same every time. Lovemaking is an art that requires knowledge, practice and skillful application of what is pleasurable and sexually arousing. In the same way that a musician can become more knowledgeable and skillful, a couple can learn to freely and frequently experience the ecstasy of orgasm.

The underlying factor in experiencing orgasm is the ability to relax, let go, and enjoy. While this sounds deceptively easy, letting go requires a foundation of healthy beliefs and attitudes regarding sex, as well as the ability to minimize mental distractions that can keep a woman from focusing on pleasure. Removing inhibitions, reprogramming herself positively, developing mental discipline and focusing on her breathing are the keys that unlock the door to uninhibited enjoyment and fulfillment in lovemaking. Women will find that "trying" to experience an orgasm is counterproductive; the harder they try, the less likely they are to relax and enjoy the experience, which is necessary to achieve orgasm.

Letting go requires a foundation of healthy beliefs and attitudes regarding sex, as well as the ability to minimize mental distractions that can keep a woman from focusing on pleasure.

There are as many paths to orgasm as there are women. Just as every day is different, a woman's mood and her circumstances may differ. But as knowledge and experience are gained, each couple will be better able to find the path that works best for them. Couples may find it helpful to have an understanding of one way to reach orgasm to begin with. LDS medical doctor Lindsay R. Curtis provided the following road map as a guide:

> Normally the clitoris is manually stimulated along with caresses upon the lips and the breasts, hopefully arousing the wife to a pre-climatic state, at which time the male mounts and effects penetration. However, many women find it necessary to continue the stimulation of the clitoris in order to come to a complete climax. In this case, it is advisable for the husband or the wife (some find it easier for the wife to accomplish this) to maintain a titillating finger upon the clitoris even though the husband has penetrated. This is done until climax in the wife is complete and emotional relief has been achieved.
>
> In some cases there is sufficient stimulation of the penis to the vagina or even to the clitoris to bring the wife to a climax. But where this is not the case, it is better to keep a finger (husband's or wife's) upon it, either to press it against the penis or actually to continue to titillate it until climax is achieved and completed. . . .
>
> Too often, if the husband penetrates the vagina too early, i.e., before the wife is sufficiently aroused, he will ejaculate too soon, leaving her in an unsatisfied, highly keyed-up, completely frustrated condition. If this occurs, the husband should manually titillate the clitoris while continuing other caresses until his wife has reached her climax and finds welcome relief from the emotional build-up.[10]

Orgasmic Difficulty

Many couples experience difficulty reaching orgasm. According to Dr. David Reuben, women who have orgasmic difficulty "are simply under-stimulated sexually."[11] When orgasm is not attained, the primary physiological cause is insufficient and incorrect clitoral stimulation. Just as men need sufficient stimulation of the penis to climax or ejaculate, women need sufficient stimulation of the clitoris to reach orgasm. No one would insist a man should be able to have an orgasm without stimulation of the penis; neither should a woman be expected to have an orgasm without stimulation of the clitoris.

Other causes of orgasmic difficulty may be found by reviewing the causes of low sexual desire. The female orgasm is a complex phenomenon. Many conditions need to be met to create this peak experience. Dr. Wheat shared his perspective of the underlying causes of the lack of orgasm in marriage, "Most cases of failure to attain orgasm that I have seen began with poor preparation for marriage, a frustrating and fearful honeymoon, followed by a prolonged period of disappointment, blundering, and boredom in marriage that conditioned the wife to feel there was no hope for fulfillment."[12]

By obtaining sexual knowledge, overcoming barriers and inhibitions, practicing and having patience, couples can learn the art of orgasmic expression as intended by God. For those women who "desire to have an orgasm, because you know it is your right, your provision from God, and because you want to keenly enjoy the most intimate times with your husband, then there is no reason why you cannot experience an orgasm. It will come."[13]

Some women have come to believe orgasm is not really necessary for them. But what if we were to suggest that a man only have an orgasm "once in a while" during lovemaking. The thought is laughable, yet women have learned to accept the idea that only men are entitled to regular orgasm. According to Dr. Curtis, female orgasm is possible *every* time, even multiple times, if sufficient conditions are met. A woman, he says, may learn "either from misdirected or maladjusted parents or from well-meaning but misinformed friends . . . that it is uncommon for a woman to achieve an orgasm or climax. Nothing could be farther from the truth . . . it is rare to find a woman who is incapable of an orgasm when she is properly stimulated."[14]

Does Orgasm Really Matter?

God created lovemaking. He cares about sexual fulfillment in marriage. He commanded husbands and wives to "be one" in order to be His.[15] He left little doubt as to his meaning when He commanded husband and wife to "cleave" unto one another and "be one flesh."[16] The scriptures tell us that the joyous sexual expression of love between husband and wife is God's plan. God has told us we "are" (that is, we exist) "that [we] might have joy."[17] One of the greatest joys God has given husbands and wives is the exquisite ability to make love and experience sexual pleasure, passion, joy and oneness. He intends for women to experience all the ecstasy of which they are divinely capable. We must not ignore such a gift. Orgasm is worth the time, effort and even the reprogramming it may take.

It is not surprising that someone who has never or rarely experienced orgasm dislikes or has little interest in sex. After nearly eleven years of feeling this way, I decided that "enough was enough." I knew deep in my heart that God never meant for His gift of sexual intimacy to be so poorly used. With the help of the Lord, my husband and I have found greater marital fulfillment. With God's help and the help of this book, you too can find the sexual fulfillment God intends.

A Compelling Interest for Complete Sexual Fulfillment

Most people acknowledge a man's physiological need for sexual release; yet we don't recognize a woman's sexual needs as having comparable importance. Women might be less uptight and stressed if they were to experience regular "discharge [of] neurological and muscular tension"[18] available only through orgasmic release. One woman discovered this for herself.

After much time and effort to improve her sexual relationship with her husband, Julie was thrilled to reach a point where she not only desired sexual relations with her husband, but also felt a physiological need being fulfilled. She shared this experience with me:

> I had gone to bed very late one night, uptight and stressed from a busy day. My husband was already asleep, and had been for some time. I lay there restlessly struggling to fall asleep with thoughts of the day and other worries swirling in my mind. I knew if I made love to my husband it would help me clear my mind and de-stress, so that I could fall into a peaceful sleep. I woke up my husband and said, "Let's go for it." Thankfully, he was happy to oblige. I was able to drift off to sleep.

It's been a long time coming to get to this point sexually for me, but I am beginning to wonder if there is a physiological need for sex in women just as there seems to be in men. I almost feel about sex the way I know my husband does. I want it. I enjoy it. I even feel a physical, emotional and psychological need for it. It's amazing. I would have never believed I could feel this way.

Remember Karen, the sexually unsatisfied and frustrated woman in the opening story? She stated, "Just about the time I really get excited, he comes inside me and it's all over . . . and that's when I get mad! It takes me over an hour to unwind enough to go to sleep."[19] Her feelings provide some insight into the potential physical and emotional distress that might occur when a woman goes unsatisfied for long periods of time.

Dr. Curtis characterized this problem of female sexual frustration when he identified this state of being, " . . . leaving her in an unsatisfied, highly keyed-up, completely frustrated condition . . . [needing] relief from the emotional build-up."[20] When sexual energy and tension are not satisfactorily or fully released, this can cause anger and frustration, a dislike of lovemaking, and resentment toward the spouse. Most women don't realize there is a relationship between the lack of sexual release during lovemaking and the risk of physical and emotional "dis-ease."

An understanding of what occurs physiologically during orgasm may help couples understand the importance of the female orgasm and encourage them to seek for it regularly. Dr. Wheat's explanation of the physiological response during orgasm may be helpful to understand the negative effects on the woman's body when full sexual release does not occur regularly:

> In the plateau phase, the time of increasing sexual arousal, all of the wife's pelvic structures become engorged with blood under a significant amount of pressure. If she proceeds to a good strong orgasm, the involuntary muscular contractions close off the small arteries and open the venous system to produce drainage of this pooled blood in a matter of minutes. This leaves a distinct, pleasantly overwhelming sensation of comfort and warmth in the pelvic area, followed by a feeling of relaxation.
>
> Each time the stimulated wife fails to reach orgasm, this represents some injury to the pelvic organs and to her emotions, often leaving her with nervousness, weakness, fatigue, and moderate to severe pelvic pain and low-back pain.[21]

To prevent this from happening, and to strengthen a wife's relationship with her husband, Dr. Wheat proposed that husbands and wives make "every effort to learn how to achieve full orgasm on a regular basis."[22]

Questions to Ask Yourself Regarding Sexual Fulfillment

If you have not yet experienced, or rarely experience orgasm, you may want to ask yourself the following questions:

1. Do I have a conviction or testimony of the sanctity of sex? Do I know God approves of it? Do I have a healthy attitude and respect for sexual relations in marriage?

2. Have I removed inappropriate inhibitions and psychological barriers resulting from negative conditioning and/or negative past experiences?

3. Does my husband know what kind of emotional intimacy and foreplay I need to become fully aroused? Have I given him this information?

4. Do I understand the female anatomy and function? Do I know what and where the clitoris is? Do I receive sufficient stimulation to reach orgasm?

5. Do I know what turns me on? Do I know what works best for stimulating my clitoris? Have I determined what kind of touch or stimulation is needed? When? What intensity, quantity, or speed is most arousing?

6. Does my husband know what kind of clitoral stimulation works for me? Do I know what else arouses me sexually? Have I explained, shown and taught my husband?

7. Do our sexual encounters focus first/only on satisfying my husband? Do I often just take care of his needs to get it "over with"?

8. Do I have inhibitions or do I get so concerned about having an orgasm or other performance pressures that I have a hard time letting go and just enjoying sex?

9. Do I know what turns me off? Does my husband know what turns me off (not showering, not brushing his teeth and/or using mouthwash, scratchy hands, rough caresses)? Have I gently told him?

10. Do we plan for enough time for sex, especially in the beginning as we learn to create regular orgasms?

11. Have I addressed any other psychological barriers I may be dealing with?

12. Have we addressed any relationship issues (personally or with professional help) that may be standing in the way of full sexual sharing and satisfaction?

If you answered no to any of these questions, it's time to say, "Enough is enough."

Now is the time to make this important change in your life. Heavenly Father wants you to enjoy sexual relations with your husband to the utmost. The issues above are addressed throughout this book.

A Word About "Quickies"

Couples should work toward complete mutual fulfillment in every lovemaking experience, but sometimes that may not be possible due to time and/or energy constraints. You may both decide to enjoy a "quickie" together when only a few moments are available or when one of you isn't in the mood for "gourmet" sex. A quickie most likely will not provide sufficient time and/or stimulation for the wife to reach orgasm, but if your attitude is right and circumstances are such, a quickie can be like a little gift. Quickies can be okay, as long as they are mutually agreed upon and do not become the regular fare.

PHASE 5—AFTERGLOW

The Afterglow phase provides a little bit of heaven on earth. If the afterglow is not rushed or ignored, it can provide precious moments for both husband and wife. The Afterglow phase is a time when couples can bask in the glow of love and pleasure, and share tender feelings for each other. Dr. Marie Robinson said of the afterglow, "Full sexual satisfaction is followed by a state of utter calm. The body feels absolutely quiescent. Psychologically the person feels completely satisfied, at peace with the world and all things in it. The woman in particular feels extremely loving toward the partner who has given her so much joy, such a transport of ecstasy. Often she wishes to hold him close for a while, to linger tenderly in the now subdued glow of their passion."[23]

While the husband may be tempted to roll over and fall asleep, he needs to remain attentive and loving throughout the afterglow, sharing this moment of closeness with his wife. Just as a woman's sexual desire is aroused more slowly, her sexual arousal dissipates more slowly, in contrast to a man's, whose arousal peaks and diminishes quickly. Dr. Curtis provided a beautiful description of the afterglow phase:

> After the orgasm both husband and wife feel a certain relaxed serenity. Each has a distinct feeling of satisfaction at having brought great joy to the other. They feel a lovely languor that eventuates in a deep, relaxed, refreshing sleep. However, there are a few precious moments just before they sleep when all is well between them.

Never have they felt closer to each other than they do now. Never has their marriage meant more to them than now.

This is the sacred opportunity when a husband can embrace his wife firmly yet tenderly as he reaffirms his love for her and reassures her importance in his life. Generally the expression is mutual. To miss this afterglow is to pass by some of the finest moments of life. To experience them, is to live the fuller life.[24]

Imagine the most breathtakingly beautiful sunset, drawing a delightful summer's day to a close. Such is the afterglow experience. After orgasm, as the rush subsides, the tingling lingers, until it slowly fades, leaving a warm glow. Its embers flicker as one languishes in the arms of his or her beloved spouse. All is well. You are emotionally, spiritually and physically content—even if only for a few moments. There has been a symbolic rebirth—a cleansing, purging and healing of body and soul—clearing mental and physical tensions and leaving you feeling alive, complete and whole. You've just experienced a recommitment of love and trust, reuniting husband and wife as *one* in one of the most sacred and spiritual experiences God created within the covenant of marriage.

Chapter 4—"Home" Work

- If sexual desire is slow to occur, make the effort to get started sexually, accepting that the sexual desire may not awaken until after arousal occurs.

- Review the physiological, psychological and relationship factors of low sexual desire and orgasmic difficulty. Seek God's assistance as you address factors you may be struggling with.

- Recognizing the physiological, psychological, emotional and spiritual benefits of orgasmic release, strive to create mutually satisfying sexual relations that include regular orgasmic expression. Know that orgasm is your divine right and gift from God.

- Ask yourself the questions suggested on page 78 as you seek to identify what may be keeping you from experiencing the complete sexual fulfillment God intended.

NOTES

Chapter 4—The Symphony of the Female Sexual Response, Part II

[1]LaHaye and LaHaye, *Act of Marriage,* 148–49.
[2]*See* Lamb and Brinley, *Between Husband and Wife,* 34.
[3]Curtis, *And They Shall Be One Flesh,* 54.
[4]Weiner Davis, *Sex-Starved Marriage,* 29.
[5]Weiner Davis, *Sex-Starved Marriage,* 29.
[6]*See* Weiner Davis, *Sex-Starved Marriage,* 99.
[7]Weiner Davis, *Sex-Starved Marriage,* 42.
[8]Robinson, *Power of Sexual Surrender,* 25–26 or Lahaye and Lahaye, *Act of Marriage,* 154-55.
[9]Wheat and Wheat, *Intended for Pleasure,* 88.
[10]Curtis, *And They Shall Be One Flesh,* 56–57.
[11]LaHaye and LaHaye, *Act of Marriage,* 157.
[12]Wheat and Wheat, *Intended for Pleasure,* 121.
[13]Wheat and Wheat, *Intended for Pleasure,* 113.
[14]Curtis, *And They Shall Be One Flesh,* 52.
[15]*See* Doctrine & Covenants 38:27.
[16]*See* Genesis 2:24.
[17]2 Nephi 2:25.
[18]Robinson, *Power of Sexual Surrender,* 25–26.
[19]LaHaye and LaHaye, *Act of Marriage,* 148.
[20]Curtis, *And They Shall Be One Flesh,* 57.
[21]Wheat and Wheat, *Intended for Pleasure,* 120.
[22]Wheat and Wheat, *Intended for Pleasure,* 120.
[23]Robinson, *Power of Sexual Surrender,* 25–26.
[24]Curtis, *And They Shall Be One Flesh,* 58.

CHAPTER VIEW

1. Stronger Sex Drive / Weaker Sex Drive

2. Fast and Furious Passion and Fireworks / Slow and Satisfying Romance and Loving

3. Ready to Go / Need Time to Warm up

4. Sexual Desire Is Primarily Physical / Sexual Desire Is Primarily Emotional

5. Stimulated by the Body Before the Person / Stimulated by the Person Before the Body

6. Need Sex to Feel Love / Need Love to Desire Sex

7. Sex as a Reaction / Sex as a Decision

8. Stimulated Visually / Stimulated Mentally and through Touch

9. Direct Stimulation / Indirect Stimulation

10. Excited Quickly / Excited Slowly

11. Pleasure as a Release / Pleasure from Gradual Buildup

12. Constant Sexual Desire—Orgasm Is Predictable / Variable Sexual Desire—Orgasm Is Unpredictable

13. Limited to One Orgasm / Capable of Multiple Orgasms

14. Penis as Sexual Center / Clitoris as Sexual Center

15. Sexual Peak in the Morning / Sexual Peak in the Evening

16. Lovemaking Ends with Orgasm / Lovemaking Ends with Afterglow

17. Need to Control Sexual Energy / Need to Awaken and Free Sexual Energy

18. Simple Sexual Fulfillment / Complex Sexual Fulfillment

Chapter 5—"Home" Work

Chapter 5

CREATING UNDERSTANDING AND EMPATHY FOR SEXUAL DIFFERENCES

And God said, Let us make man in our image, after our likeness. . . . So God created man in his own image, in the image of God created he him; male and female created he them. . . . And the Lord God said, It is not good that the man should be alone; I will make him an help meet for him. . . . And the Lord God caused a deep sleep to fall upon Adam. . . and he took one of his ribs. . . . And the rib, which the Lord God had taken from man, made he a woman. . . . And Adam said, This is now bone of my bones, and flesh of my flesh: she shall be called Woman, because she was taken out of Man.[1]

God created man and woman in His image after His likeness. He acknowledged that it was not good for man to be alone, so He took part of man and created woman, uniting them as one—each a part of the other, yet different from each other. You can hear the reverence in Adam's words as he acknowledges that she is created from within him. He said she is "bone of my bones, and flesh of my flesh."[2]

Physiologically man and woman are different, but meant to fit together, as if inviting a symbolic return to their state of oneness. In 1 Corinthians 11:11 we see that "neither is the man without the woman, neither the woman without the man, in the Lord." In God's great and eternal wisdom, these two puzzle pieces, man and woman, are to come together, drawing from each other what is needed to create individual wholeness and marital oneness. Elder Merrill J. Bateman stated, "Men and women complement each other not only physically, but also emotionally and spiritually. . . . Men and women have different strengths and weaknesses, and marriage is a synergistic relationship in which spiritual growth is enhanced because of the differences."[3]

Our differences not only complement each other, like two halves making a whole, but also invite personal growth, like two halves striving to be two wholes. It is in the process of becoming "whole" that husband and wife become "one."

Few differences between man and woman are more significant than in the sexual relationship. President Spencer W. Kimball's assertion of sexual problems, or so called "incompatibility" over sexual differences, as one of the primary causes of divorce,[4] attests to the serious consequences of couples not understanding each other sexually. Sexual incompatibility is really just a lack of understanding, empathy, or acceptance of sexual differences between husband and wife. Seeking oneness amidst sexual differences requires cooperation, consideration, and communication—along with some trial and error.

Sexual incompatibility is really just a lack of understanding, empathy,
or acceptance of sexual differences between husband and wife.

Much of the personal growth and understanding needed by men to fulfill their wives sexually is challenging for them. Much of the understanding and growth women need to be fulfilled and to fulfill their husbands is challenging for them. With marriage, and by extension, sexuality and the power of creation, as *the very key*[5] to the Plan of Happiness, it should come as no surprise that marriage is divinely designed to stretch and strengthen both husband and wife.

During a strengthening marriage course, one wife enthusiastically expressed her gratitude and relief that her husband finally understood how she felt about sex. Together they had reviewed the list of sexual differences. They were able to ask each other, "Is that how you feel?" and identify where on the continuum they were. She exclaimed, "Sometimes I didn't even know how to explain how I felt about sex until I had this list to point to and say, 'Yeah, that's how I feel! Yeah, that's me!'"

She said she also finally understood why her husband behaved as he did. She was glad not only for herself, but also for her husband to learn that she wasn't a "sexually impaired" wife. She chuckled as she concluded that now, at least, her husband realized that other husbands probably struggled with similar issues.

Since we know that sex is of God and that the glory of God is intelligence,[6] it's clear that sexual knowledge is also of God. Knowledge leads to understanding and understanding can lead to empathy. Understanding how men and women feel and function sexually can lead to empathy for differences—resolving resentment born of ignorance. Understanding and empathy can lead to increased willingness to meet each other's needs and work together toward mutual fulfillment.

Differences need not be dividing lines. While men and women may approach sex differently, they both share the common desire of mutual sexual fulfillment. Rather than responding as players on opposing teams, knowledge and understanding can allow husband and wife to come together as partners on the same team, working toward meeting each other's needs. In *A Parent's Guide* we read:

> Both husbands and wives have physical, emotional, psychological, and spiritual needs associated with this sacred act. They will be able to complement each other in the marriage relationship if they give tender, considerate attention to these needs of their partner. . . .
>
> Couples will discover differences in the needs or desires each partner has for such a relationship, but when each strives to satisfy the needs of the other, these differences need not present a serious problem. Remember, this intimate relationship between husband and wife was established to bring joy to them. An effort to

reach this righteous objective will enable married couples to use their complementary natures to bring joy to this union.[7]

Generalizations can be dangerous. Any time you make gender generalizations, there are many for whom they will not hold true. Imagine the sexual differences discussed below placed at two ends of a sliding scale—with the stereotypical male characteristic on one side and the female characteristic on the other. With considerate communication, couples can discuss these differences and determine where each fits between the ends of the scale.

Stronger Sex Drive   Weaker Sex Drive

1. Stronger Sex Drive / Weaker Sex Drive

It is said that men have a stronger sex drive than women. This stereotype, though well accepted, is actually a myth, and sometimes even reversed. There is a growing awareness that some men have a lower sex drive than their spouse.

The important sexual difference is not that men have higher desire or that women have lower desire, but that their sexual desire is differently wired. Regarding this faulty generalization, BYU professor, Dr. Brent A. Barlow, stated:

> Some people cling to old stereotypes, mistakenly perceiving women as being less sexual than men. Not long ago I was invited to speak to a group of LDS married couples on the topic of sexuality in marriage. At the conclusion of my remarks one young wife asked, "Why is the sex drive so much stronger in men than in women?" I told the group I seriously questioned whether or not it was. For years it has been widely believed that men have the greater interest and drive towards sexual fulfillment. In addition, many women have been culturally conditioned to believe that their sexual inclinations are less than those of men—and if they are not, they should be or something is supposedly wrong. But recent research indicates that the capacity for sexual response in women is just as great, and in some cases even greater, than that of males.[8]

Certainly the male sex drive is more obvious, with the female sex drive less apparent. Women simply have a *different* sex drive. It's the concept of pressing "play" on the CD player (male sex drive), versus fine tuning and warming up a violin to be played in the symphony of the sexual response (female sex drive). The female sex drive is no less strong than the male. The lack of sexual knowledge, intimate communication, sufficient time and effort in lovemaking combined with unnecessary inhibitions, have led men *and* women to accept this inaccurate stereotype. Christian author and speaker, Joe Beam, offered insight, hope, and help to resolve differences between the male and female sex drive:

> We still encounter men who think their wives have little to no sex drive. We respond that if he believes that, it may be that one of three things is happening. The first would be beyond his immediate control: His wife may have physical problems or emotional hang-ups from her past. Professionals can help her remedy that. The other two possibilities would be directly related to him, not her. Either he doesn't understand how a woman's mind and body prepare for sex or he isn't a good enough lover to bring her to excitement. We can help *him* remedy that.[9]

Included in this generalization is the notion that men want sex all the time, while women don't. This may simply mean that women are unfulfilled sexually—including emotional and spiritual intimacy. Something that is not enjoyable is not likely to be desired very often. As couples seek to meet the wife's sexual needs, which include emotional and spiritual needs, they may be pleasantly surprised to see her sexual desire increase.

While the male sex drive is celebrated, the "good girl" is generally discouraged culturally from having a sex drive and a sexual identity. She doesn't know that she's supposed to be a sexually passionate being who enjoys her sexuality, nor does she know *how* to enjoy it. If she has not developed a conviction of the sanctity of sex, she has most likely learned to stifle her sexual identity until it is nearly indiscernible. This is a factor in the inaccurate notion that women have a weaker sex drive.

So that men (and women) will not place undue significance on the male sex drive, Elder Hugh B. Brown put the sex drive in perspective, "The sex instinct is not, as some have claimed, the strongest urge in life. When compared with the urge for food and for security, it is relatively weak. We would not, however, underestimate its power for good or ill."[10]

2. Fast and Furious Passion and Fireworks / Slow and Satisfying Romance and Loving

The sexual expectations and preferences of husband and wife can be significantly different. Most men prefer a "hot and heavy" approach while most women prefer warmth and tenderness. Men may want it fast and furious—full of fireworks. Women may want it slow and satisfying—filled with glowing embers. When preferences are not understood or honored neither feels sufficiently satisfied from their sexual experiences.

Nowhere are differing expectations more evident than on the honeymoon. The honeymoon is crucial because it provides the foundation for healthy sexual relations and continued improvement, or it sours the experience for many moons to come. Many women have shared their honeymoon "horror" stories where expectations between husband and wife clashed, resulting in a negative sexual foundation for their marriage.

Amanda had romantic visions of her honeymoon where soft and slow lovemaking filled their days. She was completely unprepared emotionally and physically for the instant passion expressed by her anxious husband. In his rush to satisfy himself, being unaware of his wife's delicate needs and expectations, she felt fearful, used, and angry. Instead of a positive bonding experience it had been a rude awakening, setting the stage for her sexual disinterest throughout their marriage.

Understanding each other's sexual expectations is an important part of developing a satisfying sexual relationship. Ignorance is not bliss: it can be destructive. There is room for both spouses' sexual desires to be fulfilled. Both husband and wife need to understand and accept each other's physiology and psychology to attain complete sexual fulfillment.

3. Ready to Go / Need Time to Warm up

Most men are physically ready to go at a moment's notice. They are quick to warm up and quick to cool down, while most women are slow to warm up and slow to cool down. An unaware husband may assume his sweetheart is as turned on as he is. But she needs time to relax and warm up. This may be foreign to a man who engages in sex *to relax*, whereas a woman must first *be relaxed*. It has been said, "Sex cures headaches." For men that may be true. But if a woman is not sufficiently prepared and aroused, sex can *create* headaches.

Men quickly and easily switch gears from one activity or role to another. Women need time to transition from one role to another. Dr. James Dobson, founder of *Focus on the Family,* referred to the "difficulties a woman may experience in playing the three unique roles expected of her; she must be a wife, mistress, and mother. A loving wife who is diligently maintaining her home and caring for the needs of her family is unlikely to feel like a seductive mistress who tempts her husband into the bedroom."[11]

4. Sexual Desire Is Primarily Physical / Sexual Desire Is Primarily Emotional

God created men with strong sexual desires as a binding tie in families. This strong desire is primarily physiological. Christian minister Dr. Gary Chapman stated, "The desire for sexual intercourse is stimulated by the buildup of sperm cells and seminal fluid in the seminal vesicles. When the seminal vesicles are full, there is a physical push for release. Thus, the male's desire for sexual intercourse has a physical root."[12]

For women sex is more emotional; they want the feeling of intimacy and love. Dr. Chapman stated, "For the female, sexual desire is rooted in her emotions, not her physiology. There is nothing physically that builds up and pushes her to have intercourse. Her desire is emotionally based. If she feels loved and admired and appreciated by her husband, then she has a desire to be physically intimate with him. But without the emotional closeness she may have little physical desire."[13]

While men may not particularly like the emotional nature of their wife's sexual desire, they should at least understand it, and learn to work with it if they want to access it. A woman is significantly more likely to be negatively affected by external factors than her husband. A messy house, an argument or mental and emotional stressors might be overlooked or easily put aside by a man, while his wife may find it difficult to turn her attention and effort to awakening her sexual desire. Being attentive to his wife's most pressing needs and learning what makes her feel loved is key to reaching her emotionally and unlocking her sexual desire.

For a wife to feel loved and admired often requires a lot of communication. "Sometimes even before she can appreciate romantic gestures, a woman needs to communicate and feel heard."[14] Tender communication, as foreplay for women, may be likened to the response men get from seeing their wives naked.

While physical and emotional foreplay is important for both husband and wife, it is especially necessary for wives. Joe Beam stated, "For women, sex tends to be a broader experience. Not only are there pleasurable and exhilarating physical sensations, there are also pleasurable and deeply fulfilling emotional sensations. . . . One reason for foreplay—in addition to giving the woman's body time to prepare itself—is that it allows her to emotionally become more aroused. Therefore, foreplay should slowly and deliberately concentrate on acts that arouse emotions. Things like kissing, touching, romantic words, and the like."[15]

Though women desire the emotional component of sexual intimacy, they also have a less-acknowledged need for the physical experience of orgasm. When a woman receives only emotional fulfillment from lovemaking, such as warmth and closeness, without orgasm, it can lead her to lose her sexual desire and become lukewarm, even cold, to the sexual experience. When a man receives only physical fulfillment, without emotional fulfillment, he begins to feel emptiness within the sexual experience as well. Communication can help diminish the feeling of emptiness for men as they share in personal ways.

To believe that men and women only want sex for their separate reasons is to ignore the physical and emotional needs that *both* husbands and wives have. It's not that men have no *emotional* needs sexually, but that they have been conditioned to let their *physical* needs dominate. Likewise, it's not that women have no *physical* needs sexually, but that they have been conditioned to let their *emotional* needs dominate.

With men's primary desires being physical, and women's primary desires being emotional, it is conceivable that women can endure a sexless marriage more easily than men. We can also see why men tend to let relationship problems continue unaddressed as long as their sexual needs are being satisfied. If, however, each would invest greater time and effort into the parts of marriage important to the other, greater harmony, love and intimacy would result.

5. Stimulated by the Body Before the Person / Stimulated by the Person Before the Body

In keeping with the understanding that men are physically driven, we can understand how a man can be turned on sexually by an attractive person (her body) without knowing, or necessarily even liking, that person. Dr. Dobson stated, "Men are not very discriminating in regard to the person living within an exciting body. A man can walk down a street and be stimulated by a scantily clad female who shimmies past him, even though he knows nothing about her personality or values or mental capabilities. He is attracted by her body itself. . . . [Thus,] there is some validity to the complaint by women that they have been used as 'sex objects' by men."[16]

In contrast, women are attracted to the person before the body. Women need to feel warmth and an ongoing emotional connection for lovemaking to be satisfying. Dr. Dobson explained, "[Women's] desire is usually focused on a *particular* individual whom they respect or admire. A woman is stimulated by the romantic aura which surrounds her man, and by his character and personality. . . . Unless a woman feels a certain closeness to her husband at a particular time—unless she believes he respects her as a person—she may be unable to enjoy a sexual encounter with him."[17]

A woman may be appalled that her husband can be interested in sexual relations when they've had unkind words and tension between them all day. "It is confusing to her when he wants sex and they are not even talking or he has ignored her for days. To her, it seems as if he doesn't care if they have much of a relationship."[18] Dr. Dobson said, "The fact that he and his wife have had no tender moments in the entire evening does not inhibit his sexual desire significantly. He sees her on her way to bed in her clingy nightgown and that is enough to throw his switch."[19]

Understanding man's physical nature can also help women understand the vulnerability to temptation that is created when sexual relations are withheld or inhibited unnecessarily. Dr. Dobson elaborated, "When sexual response is blocked, males experience an *accumulating* physiological pressure which demands release . . . as maximum level is reached [in the seminal vesicles] hormonal influences sensitize the man to all sexual stimuli. Whereas a particular woman would be of little interest to him when he is satisfied, he may be eroticized just to be in her presence when he is in a state of deprivation."[20]

God designed sexual fulfillment in marriage as a safeguard to sin. This does not mean women are to "give in" and perform their "wifely duty" to protect their husbands from committing adultery. What it does mean is that husbands and wives have a responsibility to make any necessary adjustments to see that each others' needs are satisfied.

To overcome differences and show love to their husbands, women can accept and respect men's physical need for sexual expression and can initiate a physical display of love. To show love, men can accept and respect the emotional needs of their wives and do that which makes their wives feel connected, loved, and cherished. Christian medical doctor Ed Wheat and his wife, Gaye, gave couples wise counsel on the importance of the whole relationship when they stated:

Because your sexual relationship will tend to reflect your emotional relationship, it is important to realize that every meaningful, fully enjoyable sex act really begins with a loving, attentive attitude hours or even days before. Husband, you should be aware that your wife views the sex act as part of her total relationship with you, even though you, like other men, may think of it separately. When both partners assume the responsibility for giving of their total selves—physically, emotionally, and spiritually—sexual interaction becomes a dynamic way of fully expressing love for each other. *It is your daily behavior toward each other* that will measure the extent and depth of the pleasure you find in making love sexually.[21]

6. Need *Sex* to Feel Love / Need *Love* to Desire Sex

Men generally need to have their sexual needs met before they have a desire to provide the emotional love and intimacy their wife wants. But women need to have their emotional needs met before they have a desire to provide the sexual love and intimacy their husbands want. The vicious cycle created by his unmet physical needs and her unmet emotional needs must be broken.

Intimacy Needs Cycle

Physical Needs/Emotional Needs

Men   **Women**

Need love to desire sex
and give sex

Need sex to feel love
and give love

Women want to want sex, but they need to feel loved and emotionally connected before their sexual feelings can flow. Dr. John Gray, author of the well-known book *Men Are From Mars, Women Are From Venus*, stated, "When her emotional needs are met . . . her sexual needs become more important."[22] He went on to say, "By receiving the caring, nurturing, and sensuous support her female side craves, she begins to consciously feel her sexual yearnings. It is as though she doesn't even know she wants this stimulation until she gets it."[23]

As a man understands and strives to meet his wife's emotional needs for closeness, connection, and communication, he can open the door to her hidden reservoirs of sexuality. Not only can she awaken her sexual self and find greater joy in sexual intimacy, but it can heal her and make her whole as she experiences greater expression of her whole self.

When women are asked what makes their husbands feel loved, many underestimate the importance of the sexual relationship. Every person has a different love language, but, for most men, sexual expression is right up there at the top of their list. If a wife wants to show love to her husband, she should consider initiating and engaging in sexual relations. Marriage therapist Michele Weiner Davis shared a touching story of one couple who grasped the importance of sexual love in their relationship:

> Their marriage of 15 years was not on the verge of divorce . . . but it had grown distant. I asked about their sex life. . . . He said, "There really only is a two-hour window of opportunity on Friday nights between 10 and 12 when she is receptive. Otherwise, I don't even approach her, ever. . . . " She admitted that Friday night was the only time she felt relaxed enough to desire sex. And then she added, "And when, at other times, I don't feel like having sex, I never do. . . . "
>
> I then turned to Joe and asked, "What has that been like for you over the past fifteen years?" Joe hesitated because he had really never shared his feelings honestly with Mary. Slowly he spoke, "Every time I reached out for you and you said, 'No,' I feel unwanted, unloved. I wonder if you're still attracted to me. I question whether you think I'm a good lover or not. I wonder whether I turn you off. I worry whether you've fallen out of love with me. I feel hurt and distant from you. Your rejection leaves me feeling lonely."

As Joe shared his feelings with Mary, I couldn't help but notice that Mary's eyes were welling up with tears. After a long few moments of silence, Mary grabbed Joe's hand and spoke in a soft, low voice, "Joe, in all the years we've been married, I have never, ever thought about what it would be like to be you when I say 'No'. All I ever think about is me, whether I'm in the mood or not. I never wonder what it's like for you when I turn you down." And then their eyes met and she said, "I am so, so sorry." Joe cried, Mary cried and I must admit, I cried too.[24]

In his book *Mars and Venus in the Bedroom,* Dr. Gray taught a profound concept. He explained that during lovemaking men receive a unique opportunity *to feel* and connect with their emotions. The implications are significant:

> For thousands of years, men adapted to their primary job as protector and provider by shutting down their sensitivities, emotions, and feelings. Getting the job done was more important than taking the time to explore feelings. . . . For many men, other than hitting their finger with a hammer or watching a football game, sex is one of the only ways they can feel! . . . When a man is aroused, he rediscovers the love hidden in his heart. Through sex, a man can feel, and through feelings, he can come back to his soul again. . . . A woman's sexual responsiveness is the most powerful way he can hear that he is loved.[25]

It is not that men need sex just for physiological reasons, but also to restore their emotional wholeness. In women, it is generally her *sexual* self that is shut down, but in men it is often the *emotional* self. Wholeness is drawn from both husband and wife as they strive for mutual sexual fulfillment, demonstrating God's "high and holy" purposes for the sexual relationship in marriage. Dr. Gray shared his own experience of how sexual relations can open the heart of a man to the emotions of life:

> When the man touches the softness of a woman's bare breast . . . he begins to feel his own inner link to experiencing pleasure and love. Through touching her soft femininity, he can connect with his own softness and yet remain hard, focused, and masculine. . . . Many times after having great sex with my wife, I realize that I had forgotten how beautiful the trees are in our neighborhood. I go outside and breathe in the fresh air and feel alive again. . . . In a sense, great sex helps me to stop and smell the flowers.[26]

A wife can help her husband reconnect to his reservoir of emotions and feelings. Passionate sexual relations freely, lovingly, and genuinely given have great power to open a husband's heart and enable him to develop greater wholeness. Dr. Gray explained how men unconsciously long for wholeness:

> The more a man in his daily life is disconnected from his feelings, the more he will crave sexual stimulation and release. The intense pleasure of release at every stage of the sexual unfolding allows him to connect momentarily with his feelings and open his heart. . . .
>
> Although he may not be aware of it, his persistent sexual longing is really his soul seeking wholeness.[27]

7. Sex as a Reaction / Sex as a Decision

For men sexual desire and arousal can occur instantly as a *reaction* to sexual stimuli. Women must consciously *choose* to engage in sexual relations. Sexual desire may not occur *until after* a woman mentally agrees to engage sexually and becomes aroused. Joe Beam stated:

> Until women decide they want to be involved in sexual activity, their bodies typically don't prepare for sex. . . . Sex starts in their intellects and emotions before making its way to specific parts of their bodies. . . .
>
> When a woman decides she wants sexual fulfillment, her body reacts at a much slower rate than her husband's.[28]

Men who understand the sexual functioning of their wives will be aware of her need for mental and emotional preparation. A man who has invested genuine time and effort to do what his wife needs to feel close emotionally will be more warmly received when she is faced with the opportunity to engage in sexual relations. A man must understand that many times his wife will agree to proceed, but if the emotional closeness is not there, he may get her body, but he won't get her heart and mind. It's like the husband who makes advances on his sleepy wife. She mumbles, "Do what you want, just don't wake me up."

As women overcome inhibitions and negative sexual conditioning, it will become easier to choose to "Go for it!" in the anticipation that sexual desire will follow. Women can take charge of their thoughts when they may not feel like making love. They can accept sexual advances anyway—telling themselves to enjoy the experience, allowing the feelings to follow.

8. Stimulated Visually / Stimulated Mentally and Through Touch

It is well documented that men are visually stimulated. It is less understood that women must be stimulated mentally and through touch. Men want to see and enjoy their wives' bodies. Women want to have romantic thoughts and be touched in loving ways.

Women who are sexually inhibited may cause frustration for their husbands. Dr. Dobson described the difficulty this sexual difference causes many couples:

Men are primarily excited by *visual* stimulation. They are turned on by feminine nudity or peek-a-boo glimpses of semi-nudity. . . . Women, by contrast, are much less visually oriented than men. Sure, they are interested in attractive masculine bodies, but the physiological mechanism of sex is not triggered typically by what they see; [women] are stimulated primarily by the sense of touch. Thus, we encounter the first source of disagreement in the bedroom: he wants her to appear unclothed in a lighted room, and she wants him to caress her in the dark.[29]

Women cannot simply look at their husband's bodies and be turned on. Women must be turned on mentally and physically. At the same time women need to learn to overcome any reservations or inhibitions they may have, so that they can freely share their bodies with their husbands. Men need to provide an environment where their wives feel loved and cherished, so that their wives can focus on pleasurable thoughts. This emotional intimacy partnered with physical stimulation provides the climate that is needed for sexual climax.

9. Direct Stimulation / Indirect Stimulation

In addition to visual stimulation, men want their sexual stimulation to be more direct, with little beating around the bush. Dr. Gray described men as follows, "Directly touching his penis dramatically increases his pleasure. . . . A woman needs to remember that direct stimulation provides maximum pleasure for a man."[30]

Women warm up and are aroused more slowly. They want indirect, even teasing types of touches to slowly escalate their sexual energy. Women love to have their man dilly dally around until they are breathlessly longing for him to get to the good stuff. Dr. Gray described women's stimulation needs as follows, "She loves it when a man takes time to get to the point and circles around for a while. . . . Instead of being directly stimulated in her most sensitive places, as a man likes, a woman wants to be teased or gradually led to the place where she is longing to be touched."[31]

10. Excited Quickly / Excited Slowly

The obviousness of this sexual difference between men and women has resulted in humorous acknowledgment. Joe Beam shared the discussion from one of his seminars:

When I ask audiences in the *Love, Sex & Marriage* seminars how long it takes a man to be ready for sex, several women around the room instantly snap their fingers. While they exaggerate just a little, it is generally true that men can be prepared for sexual activity very quickly. Put the right stimuli before them, and their bodies rapidly make themselves ready for sex.

When I then ask the audiences how long it takes a woman to be ready for sex, we hear a chorus of witticisms that are almost always the same in every city.

"Four hours!"

"Three days!"

"I don't know; we've only been married twenty years!"[32]

For men who are quickly aroused "quickies" can be satisfying; but women who are slowly aroused need "longies." A husband can reach a climax before a wife has even gotten her mind off the evening meal. Dr. Gray shared a secret for men, "When I interview women about what they want most from a man, again and again they tell me they want a lover with a slow hand."[33]

Men and women are significantly different when it comes to time required for sexual fulfillment. Dr. Gray explained this difference:

> Basically, a man needs about two or three minutes of stimulation to have an orgasm. It is generally a very simple process. . . .
>
> If a woman is to have an orgasm, she generally needs about ten times that amount of time. . . .
>
> When a woman gets the time she needs, she can feel confident that she will get the fulfillment she is looking for. When a man understands that it is not so much what he does but how long he takes to do it that makes the difference, his confidence is also increased.[34]

In the beginning, especially if the wife has never had an orgasm, she may require an hour or more of sexual stimulation to reach orgasm. Patience is needed as both husband and wife learn the intimate intricacies of her sexual ecstasy.

Christian minister, Tim LaHaye, and his wife, Beverly, confirmed the importance of *time* for women's fulfillment:

> Most men don't seem to realize that a woman usually prefers a long, slow burn to the instant explosion. Because a man is an instant igniter, he often makes the terrible mistake of trying to adapt his wife to himself rather than to satisfy her needs. It is a wise husband who adjusts his style to his wife's emotional pattern by beginning early in the evening to show love and affectionate tenderness, then gradually building his wife to a strong desire for lovemaking. When properly prepared, a woman's entire body becomes sensitive to his touch, and he can develop great personal enjoyment by watching her respond to his tender caressing.[35]

It can be challenging for men to control their desires in order to take the time needed for their wives to be fulfilled. Joe Beam confessed, "We men are much too quick to blame our wives for our lack of sexual fulfillment when the problem is often the masculine approach to sex. We think too much about the immediate and the intense feelings of climax. Women don't. . . . They must be loved slowly."[36]

To find mutual sexual fulfillment, a husband must learn to take his time as he moves slowly through each movement, co-creating sexual melodies in the symphony of the sexual response. He must learn to control his desire and delay his climax in order to provide the slow crescendo of sexual stimulation his wife needs to reach her symphonic climax.

If distractions occur before she is sufficiently aroused, such as a child crying or sensitive spots being touched by calloused hands, a woman's pleasure train can be easily delayed or derailed. Dr. Dobson indicated, "Women are more easily distracted than men; they are more affected by the surroundings and noises and smells than are their husbands. The possibility of being heard by the kids bothers women more, and they are more dependent on variety in manner and circumstances."[37]

Because men are quickly aroused, circumstances and distractions don't bother them. But since women are more slowly aroused, distractions can be death to building sexual desire. Avoid potential distractions by locking the bedroom door, turning off the ringer on the phone, shaving or clipping fingernails—or do anything else that's needed to prevent interruptions in her escalating pleasure. Women must do their best to mentally focus on their pleasurable sensations even if distractions occur.

Debunking the myth of women having weaker sex drives, Joe Beam explained how the time required for female sexual fulfillment has affected our beliefs of men and women. He said:

> This slower preparation for sexual intercourse [in women] is what makes some men think their wives have weaker sex drives. But it means nothing of the kind. While it may take her longer to become ready, she may actually crave more sexual activity during their encounter than he can provide—especially if he is focused on his own pleasure. She also may need these sexual encounters more often than he. The reason a husband may not know this is that his wife may hesitate to tell him. Why? There could be many reasons, not the least of which could be that his too rapid lovemaking technique may be frustrating for her. . . .
>
> Men, don't let yourself be deluded into thinking your wife doesn't need sex as much as you just because she approaches it differently. As a matter of fact, you may discover that she wants and needs it more than you do once you learn to become a better lover.[38]

There remains a common dilemma for women regarding the time involved for love-making. Women's work is never done. There are always dishes, laundry, kids' home-work, or tomorrow's lunches requiring time and attention. Knowing that fulfilling lovemaking takes time can be a turn-off for women who already feel consumed by their responsibilities. Women can agree to "quickies" just to get it over with, or they can ask for help, or let some things slide, which can free them for more enjoyable love-making. If a wife will make sex a higher priority her husband is likely to make helping her a higher priority as well.

However, as men come to understand the importance of equally sharing in family and household responsibilities as a factor in their wives' sexual desire, they should not expect immediate payoff. It's the ongoing sharing of household responsibilities that has erotic potential—not a single occurrence of doing the dinner dishes. If a wife's emo-tional bank account has been overdrawn for some time, a single deposit is not likely to put her account in the black.

It's the ongoing sharing of household responsibilities that has erotic potential—not a single occurrence of doing the dinner dishes.

11. Pleasure as a Release / Pleasure from Gradual Buildup

How men and women experience sexual pleasure is often at polar ends of the pleasure scale. Dr. Gray explained:

> A man experiences pleasure primarily as a *release* of sexual tension. A woman expe-riences sex in an opposite way. For her, the great joys of sex correspond to a gradual *buildup* of tension. . . .
>
> When he becomes aroused, he automatically seeks release. . . . In a sense, he is trying to empty out while she is seeking to be filled up. . . . He seeks to *end* his excitement, while a woman seeks to *extend* her excitement to feel more deeply her inner longing.
>
> She relishes his ability to slowly build up her desire to be touched in her most sensitive zones. As one layer at a time is stripped away, she longs for the deeper lay-ers of her sensual soul to be revealed.[39]

Joe Beam referred to the Bible where Solomon and his wife exhibited their knowledge of the art of lovemaking. King Solomon understood his wife's sexual needs, "[Solomon] also knew that women build to a sexual crescendo slowly, so he took his time to execute what we today call 'foreplay.'"[40]

12. Constant Sexual Desire—Orgasm Is Predictable / Variable Sexual Desire—Orgasm Is Unpredictable

A man's sexual desire is fairly constant with relatively few ups and downs. Elder Boyd K. Packer addressed the importance of a strong male sex drive:

> This creative power carries with it strong desires and urges. . . . It was necessary that this power of creation have at least two dimensions: one, it must be strong; and two, it must be more or less constant. This power must be strong, for most men by nature seek adventure. Except for the compelling persuasion of these feelings, men would be reluctant to accept the responsibility of sustaining a home and a family. This power must be constant, too, for it becomes a binding tie in family life.[41]

Once a man is aroused in lovemaking there is nearly always release through orgasm. Ejaculation is fairly predictable. Women, however, may become aroused, but for various reasons may not be able to experience the climax of orgasm. A woman's sexual desire significantly varies depending on situation, circumstance, and mood. Sometimes she may be satisfied with a brief encounter. Other times she may want or need more. It is difficult to pinpoint what accounts for the variable sexual interest and response in women. Factors such as hormonal shifts, emotional states, relationship dynamics as well as day-to-day stresses may account for some of the unpredictability.

Infrequent female orgasm is certainly a factor in low sexual desire although of possibly greater impact is the sexual frustration it creates, leading to feelings of failure as a wife and a woman. Because orgasm can seem like a hit-or-miss endeavor for women, time, effort, and knowledge must be carefully and consistently applied. Couples must learn not only what is needed to foster her conscious choice to engage in sexual relations, but they must also strive to increase the frequency of her orgasm to the point that she feels fulfilled with their sexual relationship.

Dr. Brinley, in his book *Toward A Celestial Marriage*, provided suggestions for both husband and wife as they seek cooperation for their sexual differences. "In general men probably have a greater sexual 'drive' or interest (since orgasm is more predictable for them). . . . The husband will need to exercise self-control, restraint, and charity in being sensitive to his companion's needs, desires, and interests. On the other hand, a wife may want to make herself more available for sexual relations, or initiate intimacy more frequently with her husband, because she understands that to him love and sex are so closely related."[42]

13. Limited to One Orgasm / Capable of Multiple Orgasms

It is interesting to note that whereas men seem to be "more" or "faster" in most areas of sexual response, it is the woman who was created with the greater ultimate capacity for sexual pleasure. This is a significant heavenly indicator hinting at the hidden sexual potential of women. What would be the purpose of women having the potential for multiple orgasms if it was not to be used? Dr. Barlow confirmed the greater sexual capacity of women:

> It actually was a finding of William H. Masters and Virginia E. Johnson, who reported in *Human Sexual Response* (Boston: Little, Brown and Company, 1966) that we have underestimated and in many ways misunderstood female sexuality up until the recent past. . . .
>
> The capacity of women to respond to sexual stimuli is great in that they have the capacity to respond with several orgasms within just a few minutes. Men, however, can experience only one orgasm at a time with a varying refractory period (time between orgasms).[43]

14. Penis as Sexual Center / Clitoris as Sexual Center

Most people are well aware that the penis is the sexual center for men. What may be less known is that the clitoris is the sexual center for women. It cannot be overemphasized that the sole purpose of the clitoris is to provide sexual pleasure. The clitoris requires sufficient stimulation in a manner that is arousing to the wife. Couples must learn what kind of touch, how much pressure and how much stimulation is necessary for arousal to fill her body and soul.

While the penis is easy to find, the clitoris is smaller and somewhat concealed beneath a little hood-like mound of skin. It is located above the urethral opening at the top of the woman's vulva where the inner lips of the labia minora come together at a tip.

The penis and clitoris both need direct stimulation for sexual arousal and orgasm.

The lack of clitoral stimulation for women may be a primary cause of falling short of orgasm. Dr. Gray stated, "Men, imagine having sex without having your penis stimulated. It would certainly not be very much fun. In a similar way, for a woman to enjoy great sex, stimulation of the clitoris . . . is necessary . . . to have an orgasm."[44]

15. Sexual Peak in the Morning / Sexual Peak in the Evening

If women wonder why men seem interested in waking them early in the morning for a little fun, they may appreciate knowing that men's testosterone generally peaks at that time. Michele Weiner Davis, in her book *The Sex-Starved Marriage,* stated, "Studies show that in many men, testosterone surges in the early morning, around 7 or 8 A.M. . . . [Women's] testosterone spikes too. It may be later in the evening, in the middle of her menstrual cycle, or closer to the end of the month."[45]

This sexual difference can cause frustration and pain for both husbands and wives. A husband may feel deeply hurt and rejected by his wife's ongoing refusal of his sexual desires until he ultimately seeks to shut down his feelings and sexual needs to avoid the pain. A wife may feel put upon and frustrated by her husband's inattention to her early-morning pressures to get the kids up and off to school.

16. Lovemaking Ends with Orgasm / Lovemaking Ends with Afterglow

Men who are aware that women are aroused slowly, *and* that they also return to their non-aroused state slowly, will readily understand the importance of continuing tender caressing and embracing during the slow afterglow. Men may prefer to roll over and fall into a deep and satisfied sleep, but understanding the differing nature of his wife, he will wisely remain attentive and loving during the sexual resolution stage. Just as men are quickly and easily aroused, they are also quickly and easily returned to their non-aroused state. Of the afterglow, Joe Beam said:

> For men, lovemaking tends to be over with orgasm. We prepare quickly, have short-lived plateaus (if we aren't concentrating on our spouses), and find ourselves disinterested in sex after orgasm almost as quickly as we were ready for sex in the first place. Our sexual cycle is much faster than our wives'. For women, lovemak-

ing isn't over with their orgasm; it's only over when they've completed afterglow. Remember, for a woman, sex is as much emotional as sensual.[46]

17. Need to Control Sexual Energy / Need to Awaken and Free Sexual Energy

The area where men most need to focus their time, attention and energy is in controlling or mastering their sexual energy—to bridle their passions.[47] Women's greatest challenge is to fully awaken their God-given sexual potential—allowing their passions to flow freely. These two opposing challenges have the potential to create an eternal unity and oneness in marriage.

Women have culturally been designated the "keepers of virtue." They have contained and controlled their sexuality so well for so long they have nearly shut it out of existence. Many are barely able to go through the motions for their husband's sake. The constraints of the Good Girl Syndrome have taken a mighty toll on the sexual fulfillment of both husband and wife.

Women need men to be slow and controlled, so that they can be freed to let go and let their fires burn. It's almost as if to feel safe in the sexual experience, a woman must know someone is in control of the fire at all times. A woman instinctively senses when her husband loses his control, thereby arresting her passion and reassigning her to "control duty." As he masters his energy and is grounded, she can "let go" of her passion and fly. The more aroused and passionate the husband wants his wife to be, the more he must learn to master his sexual energy.

18. Simple Sexual Fulfillment / Complex Sexual Fulfillment

It should be fairly obvious that sexual fulfillment for men is rather simple, whereas sexual fulfillment for women is quite complex. According to Dr. Gray, "A woman's sexual fulfillment is much more complex than a man's. She requires a man with a skillful touch, lots of time, and a loving attitude."[48] Describing men, Dr. Barlow stated, "Men are often quite similar in their sexual responses. What stimulates one man will often stimulate others. And what stimulates a man on one occasion will usually stimulate him on another. Women, however, are more idiosyncratic or individualistic in their response to sexual stimuli. What stimulates one woman may not necessarily stimulate another woman. And what stimulates a woman on one occasion may not necessarily stimulate her on another."[49]

After seeing this list of sexual differences between men and women, it is no surprise that "sexual compatibility" is challenging to attain. I hope the knowledge shared here will erase ignorance, increase understanding and empathy, and provide a lighted path out of the darkness of sexual frustration and dissatisfaction. Mutual sexual fulfillment may not be quick nor easy, but it is possible, and it is worth it.

As two differently created puzzle pieces, husbands and wives can come together in cooperation and consideration as they strive for mutual sexual fulfillment and God-ordained oneness in marriage. Even with their differences, God invites husband and wife to seek completion, wholeness, and eternal oneness with each other.

Chapter 5—"Home" Work

- Develop greater understanding and empathy for your sexual differences by reading and discussing this chapter with your spouse. Decide how you can adjust to meet each other's needs as you strive for mutual sexual fulfillment.

NOTES

Chapter 5—Creating Understanding and Empathy for Sexual Differences

[1]Genesis 1:26–27; 2:18, 21–23.
[2]Genesis 2:23.
[3]Bateman, *Eternal Marriage*, 65.
[4]*See* Kimball, *Teachings of Spencer W. Kimball*, 312.
[5]*See* Packer, "Why Stay Morally Clean," *Ensign*, Jul. 1972, 111–12 (emphasis added).
[6]*See* Doctrine & Covenants 93:36.
[7]*Parent's Guide*, 47.
[8]Barlow, "They Twain Shall Be One," *Ensign*, Sep. 1986, 51.
[9]Beam, *Becoming One*, 130.
[10]Brown, *You and Your Marriage*, 73–74.
[11]Dobson, *What Wives Wish Their Husbands Knew About Women*, 127.
[12]Chapman, *Five Love Languages*, 121.
[13]Chapman, *Five Love Languages*, 121.
[14]Gray, *Mars and Venus in the Bedroom*, 191.
[15]Beam, *Becoming One*, 159.
[16]Dobson, *What Wives Wish*, 115.
[17]Dobson, *What Wives Wish*, 116.

[18]Gray, *Mars and Venus*, 18.

[19]Dobson, *What Wives Wish*, 116.

[20]Dobson, *What Wives Wish*, 118.

[21]Wheat and Wheat, *Intended for Pleasure*, 81.

[22]Gray, *Mars and Venus*, 18.

[23]Gray, *Mars and Venus*, 33.

[24]Weiner Davis, *Divorce Busting Newsletter*, 2003.

[25]Gray, *Mars and Venus*, 17–18.

[26]Gray, *Mars and Venus*, 28.

[27]Gray, *Mars and Venus*, 28–29.

[28]Beam, *Becoming One*, 139–40.

[29]Dobson, *What Wives Wish*, 114–15.

[30]Gray, *Mars and Venus*, 37.

[31]Gray, *Mars and Venus*, 35–36.

[32]Beam, *Becoming One*, 139.

[33]Gray, *Mars and Venus*, 37.

[34]Gray, *Mars and Venus*, 63–64.

[35]LaHaye and LaHaye, *Act of Marriage*, 338.

[36]Beam, *Becoming One*, 159.

[37]Dobson, *What Wives Wish*, 126.

[38]Beam, *Becoming One*, 140–41.

[39]Gray, *Mars and Venus*, 27–28.

[40]Beam, *Becoming One*, 159. *See also* Song of Solomon.

[41]Packer, "Why Stay Morally Clean," *Ensign*, Jul 1972, 111–12.

[42]Brinley, *Toward a Celestial Marriage*, 139–40.

[43]Barlow, *Just for Newlyweds*, 48.

[44]Gray, *Mars and Venus*, 42.

[45]Weiner Davis, *Sex-Starved Marriage*, 147.

[46]Beam, *Becoming One*, 163–64.

[47]*See* Alma 38:12.

[48]Gray, *Mars and Venus*, 72.

[49]Barlow, *Just for Newlyweds*, 48.

CHAPTER VIEW

Sexual Intimacy as a Stewardship in Marriage

1. Pray for Sexual Help

2. Schedule Time for Sexual Intimacy and Learning

3. Get Educated Sexually—Couple Sex Education

4. Discuss Sex Openly and Honestly

Why We Don't Talk about Sex

How to Talk about Sex

What to Talk about

Remember Variety Adds Vitality

Strive for Sexual Fulfillment for Both Spouses

Chapter 6—"Home" Work

Chapter 6

SEXUAL STEWARDSHIP — FINDING
SEXUAL FULFILLMENT IN MARRIAGE

I have this huge problem. I have no desire whatsoever to make love to [my husband]. . . .

I have tried very hard to . . . find out more about the why's, but have not come up with anything significant. I really want to have that closeness with my husband. . . .

I believe that sex is a very important part of marriage. I sometimes think that it is spiritual food in a way. I think that my [increased desire] to make love would improve and strengthen our marriage.[1]

Sexual Intimacy as a Stewardship in Marriage

The Family: A Proclamation to the World states, "Husband and wife have a *solemn responsibility* to love and care for each other. . . ."[2] This solemn responsibility is defined as a stewardship, sacred trust, a charge or guardianship. This stewardship is entrusted to us by God, not only for us to maintain, but also to improve. This requires our time and effort. Both husband and wife are stewards, caretakers, guardians and keepers of the marriage. Each is accountable to God for its well-being and success.

Designated by God and reserved specifically for marriage, sexual relations are an important part of the sacred stewardship of marriage. Couples are to improve intimacy and overcome barriers to sexual enjoyment. BYU professor Dr. Brent Barlow referred to sexual relations in marriage as a "sexual guardianship." He indicated how couples share the responsibility for guarding, tending and improving, or strengthening, the sexual relationship within the marital stewardship:

> When we see sexuality as a vital part of marital harmony and happiness, it becomes more than something we simply give or receive. I like to think of it as something a husband and wife can share. It might be called a sexual guardianship.
>
> In the parable of the talents, Jesus taught that we should improve on whatever has been entrusted to our care. (See Matthew 25:14-30.) And in marriage we are often given joint guardianships [or stewardships], such as children, fidelity, and the day-to-day maintenance of family members.[3]

Both husband and wife will likely face some struggles as they seek to improve upon their sexual stewardship and find sexual fulfillment. New and unwelcome information and emotions may emerge as couples work through these challenges. It will require courage, faith, love, persistence and patience to find the marital treasure of sexual fulfillment.

Improving sexual relations in marriage is an individual, yet jointly shared, expedition full of discovery and adventure. Some marital treasures may be discovered within; other treasures will be discovered together from without—such as sexual knowledge and techniques. As couples grow in knowledge about themselves and their spouses, treasures of marital intimacy and oneness will emerge.

Often we know *what* is wrong or *what* needs to change in our marriage but don't know *how* to change. The following suggestions can help couples flourish in their sexual stewardship in marriage.

1. Pray for Sexual Help

Does the Lord care about the sexual relationship in your marriage? You bet He does! Not only does He care, but He is the only one who can and will lead you along your personal journey of discovery. Seeking God's divine guidance can lead you to the people, information and resources you specifically need to overcome your challenges. He stands at the door, waiting for you to open it—wanting to bless you.[4]

No problem is beyond God's ability. "Many problems that arise in a family require wisdom and resources that are beyond our own abilities to provide. Few problems, however, are beyond solution if we seek divine help."[5] Praying for God's help, both individually and as a couple, should be your first priority.

I remember when my husband and I first began seriously praying for help with our sexual frustrations. We were a little uncomfortable at first as sex seemed an inappropriate topic for prayer, but we learned that God *did* care about our sexual happiness in marriage. Our convictions that sexual relations were truly ordained of God—intended for the benefit and blessing of both husband and wife—helped us realize that our request for help was righteous. God guided us to find the solutions we needed.

The Lord knows what you need before you even ask so you won't be surprising or embarrassing Him by your requests.[6] Your prayers for sexual fulfillment are not unreasonable or inappropriate. God will bless you with that which you righteously seek. Christian author and speaker Joe Beam gave wise counsel regarding prayer over sexual problems, "Pray for God to solve the problem. Ask Him to give each of you a clear understanding of the other. Ask Him to get each of you past whatever memories, misconceptions, misunderstandings, or hang-ups are causing problems. Ask Him to give you a wonderful, totally uninhibited sex life within the parameters of His boundaries. Ask Him, believing that He will answer."[7]

You may also need to pray for courage, faith, love, patience and persistence as you embark on your journey to fulfill your sexual stewardship. Christian author Tim LaHaye and his wife Beverly advocate the idea of sexual enjoyment as a rightful gift of God that couples can ask for. They stated, "I am convinced that God never intended any Christian couple to spend a lifetime in the sexual wilderness of orgasmic malfunction. He has placed within every woman the sexual capabilities He meant for her to enjoy. . . . If it isn't a pleasurable experience, He has something better in store for you, so pray about it and expect Him to direct you to an adequate solution."[8]

God stands waiting to grant your righteous desires and to show you the way to sexual fulfillment. It's as if He beckons to you to ask Him, so that he may pour out joy upon your marriage, "Hitherto have ye asked nothing [of sexual fulfillment in marriage] in my name: ask, and ye shall receive, that your joy may be full."[9]

2. Schedule Time for Sexual Intimacy and Learning

Everyone is busy. "I just don't have time" is a common assertion. But, what is important to you, you make time for. Priority time and energy is needed to expand knowledge, learn about each other, and have fulfilling sexual encounters. One of the best ways to make time for something is to schedule it. If you *schedule* time for improving your sexual relationship, the concept of "time tithing" may come into play. Time tithing is putting first things first, then surprisingly having time enough left over for whatever else needs to be done.

Imagine a wide-mouthed jar. You have some large rocks (representing the most important things you have to do), some smaller rocks, lots of gravel and lots of sand (representing the least important things to do). If you put the large rocks in first, then the smaller rocks, then the less-important gravel and finally the sand, you can fill up the spaces in between the rocks, allowing everything to fit (except maybe some of the least-important items). However, if you pour the gravel and sand in first, because it may be easier or take less time or effort, there will not be room enough for the more important rocks. Scheduling what matters most, and holding that time sacred, puts the big rocks *first* in your life.

Whatever time is scheduled for sexual learning and intimacy needs to be priority time—not leftover time. That means time must be given when energy and interest are still high. Dr. James Dobson agreed, "If sex is important in a marriage, and we all know that it is, then some time should be reserved for its expression. The day's working activities should end early in the evening, permitting a husband and wife to retire before exhausting themselves on endless chores and responsibilities. Remember this: *whatever* is put at the bottom of your priority list will probably be done inadequately. For too many [couples], sex languishes in last place."[10]

Applying time tithing to your sexual relationship can be done in many ways. One example might be scheduling Sunday evenings, after the kids are in bed, for reading and discussing this and other helpful books and doing the "Home" work assignments. That same evening, or another night, might end with a "quickie" as a thank-you or offering of love. Another night, maybe a weekend night, might be reserved as a special date night, a night of romance, especially for the wife to receive all the warm-up, time and emotional connection needed for an unrushed, no-pressure, fulfilling sexual experience.

Regularly scheduling an hour or more for relaxed, no-rush lovemaking assures that sufficient time be available for female sexual fulfillment. With renewed determination and effort, sex need no longer languish in last place.

If you have been unfulfilled and sexually neglected for some time, you may be hesitant about having to spend more time building physical intimacy. You may only want nonsexual touching and talking while you build up some hope and trust that sexual fulfillment awaits you. Talking and nonsexual touching is a wonderful way for you to rebuild hope that sexual fulfillment awaits. With new hope that improved sexual relations are possible commit the necessary time to seek solutions and the sexual fulfillment you both desire and deserve.

3. Get Educated Sexually—Couple Sex Education

With complete, correct and reverent sex education being rarely provided within families, many come into marriage with little or no understanding of how to create a satisfying sexual relationship. How well prepared were you for sexual fulfillment in marriage? Sexual knowledge is an important aspect of strengthening the sexual relationship. Sexual ignorance is not bliss.

Sexual ignorance is not bliss.

Elder Hugh B. Brown attributed many divorces to a lack of sexual knowledge. He stated "Ignorance and blundering on the part of newlyweds account in large measure for the fact that [many] marriages end in divorce."[11] He identified not only ignorance but also incorrect information as culprits in destroying marriages, "Many marriages have been wrecked on the dangerous rocks of ignorant and debased sex behavior, both before and after marriage. Gross ignorance on the part of newlyweds on the subject of the proper place and functioning of sex results in much unhappiness and many broken homes."[12]

People spend years studying to become proficient in their professions, but rarely do couples invest sufficient time to study the sanctifying aspects of sexual intimacy and fulfillment in marriage. Knowledge alone can be an energizing force, empowering you to improve your life. As you obtain and mentally process new information about intimacy in marriage, your soul can grasp the pieces it needs and begin to incorporate them into your knowledge bank and into your life. As couples, our stewardship is to have sufficient knowledge and wisdom to be able to govern ourselves sexually. This is a serious endeavor. Even though you may ask God for help, He will not wave a magic wand that will produce immediate sexual knowledge and satisfaction for you and your spouse.

What do you need to know to be sufficiently educated sexually? Important sexual knowledge includes: (1) the human sexual response, the mechanics and techniques; (2) knowledge about your body and its sexual functioning; (3) knowledge about your spouse's body and its sexual functioning; and (4) knowledge of general sexual differences between men and women to promote understanding and empathy for each other's needs.

How might you get educated? Where can you turn for answers? The following are some possibilities:

1. Ask God. The Lord is your best sex therapist. He created sex, He created your bodies, and He knows you personally. Through prayer and study of His words regarding marital intimacy, you can gain divine light and truth regarding your body and this important aspect of marriage. (Review Chapter 2 for God's word regarding the sanctity of sexual relations in marriage.) God will provide specific guidance and knowledge as you seek His counsel.

2. Read books. Reading Chapters 3 and 4, and the books referenced therein, can help you learn about the body's sexual functioning and response. Other books referenced throughout this book can also be valuable resources for sexual learning. Schedule a few minutes before bed for pillow talk time to read and discuss such material.

3. Learn from each other. Once you understand some basics of the sexual response and of the human body, the most important learning must come from each other. You will learn best about the specific sexual functioning and preferences of your spouse from your spouse. And he will learn best from you. Study, openly discuss, and experiment with what you learn.

4. Counsel with friends or family. If your spouse does not object and you do not share what would be considered too personal, trusted friends and family may provide helpful counsel and insights regarding successful sexual relations in marriage.

5. Seek Christian information. There are many good Christian literature and information sources online that may be helpful. (See the Appendix for a list of resources.)

6. Seek professional marital counseling. If your questions and concerns seem to be based in emotional or psychological issues, good professional counselors with training in marital and/or sex therapy can provide valuable guidance and assistance. One of the main purposes of a counselor is to teach. Professional help can speed up the processes of learning, healing and overcoming sexual barriers. Be sure you seek divine guidance in finding the right counselor. God will guide you to those who will help you best.

7. Seek medical help. If your problems seem to be physical in nature, seek the advice of medical professionals until you find acceptable solutions. You may need to find someone who has had special training in sexual functioning.

8. Seek ecclesiastical counsel. If your concerns are moral in nature, you might consider counseling with your bishop or church leaders. They can provide inspired counsel and direction. Keep in mind that while they are knowledgeable about moral issues, they rarely have sexual therapy training.

4. Discuss Sex Openly and Honestly

One of the biggest handicaps to improving sexual relations in marriage is the discomfort, embarrassment, hesitancy, and even inability of couples to discuss sex openly, honestly and frankly. Tim and Beverly LaHaye, as well as other professionals, are dismayed by this marital barrier to sexual happiness. The LaHayes stated, "I have been appalled to learn that even well-educated people find it difficult to discuss their love lives frankly. . . . They have never been able to communicate with one another on the subject."[13] Dr. Brent Barlow concurred, "Partners who [freely] discuss finances, discipline, recreational activities, and so forth, often feel uncomfortable discussing this intimate subject. And they sometimes assume that their intimate relationship should just 'naturally' work out and that to discuss it means something has gone wrong. This is simply not true."[14]

Dr. Dobson, disturbed by the lack of sexual communication in marriage, gave the following counsel:

> Though it seems impossible, an inhibited husband and wife can make love several times a week for a period of years without ever verbalizing their feelings or frustrations on this important aspect of their lives. When this happens, the effect is like taking a hot coke bottle and shaking it until the contents are ready to explode. Remember this psychological law: any anxiety-producing thought or condition which cannot be expressed is almost certain to generate inner pressure and stress. The more unspeakable the subject, the greater the pressurization. And . . . anxious silence leads to the destruction of sexual desire.[15]

Both men and women can have difficulty broaching the subject of sex. Women might assume their husbands will be more knowledgeable and open on the subject. This may not be true, according to the LaHayes who explain:

> Most Christian women go into marriage relatively uninformed about sex and often retain the naive idea that their husbands know it all and will teach them. Rarely has she anticipated the fact that discussion of their intimate relations is difficult for most men. In fact, it is frequently the most difficult subject with which a couple has to cope. Consequently those who are most in need of the free-flowing expression of ideas on the subject practice it the least.[16]

Why We Don't Talk about Sex

It may be helpful to understand why sex is such a difficult topic of conversation. Below are some of the reasons for the hesitancy to discuss sexual aspects of marriage:[17]

1. We are embarrassed. Many people may find sex too embarrassing to discuss. Some are even mortified by the thought. This can stem from unintentional negative conditioning. Remember Adam and Eve were commanded to become one flesh and were not ashamed.[18]

2. We think it's too personal. Sexual specifics that might be embarrassing to your spouse should not be shared outside of the marriage. Certain intimacies should remain between husband and wife, but general knowledge and sharing of ideas and suggestions can be discussed—and need to be discussed—for the sake of those who may be wandering in the marital desert.

3. We think it's too sacred. Sex *is* sacred, but the sacredness of sexual relations in marriage can lead some to believe that sex should not be discussed at all. When "sacred" becomes "secret," or unspeakable, sacredness may have been misconstrued.

4. We feel ashamed or fearful. If we do not accept or are ashamed of our sexual nature, we may try to hide it from ourselves and others. If there is unresolved sexual sin, sexual abuse, or other negative sexual experiences in our past, there can be great reluctance to discuss this topic. Ecclesiastical or professional help may be needed.

5. We have no example to follow. If children are not taught about sex by their parents, or if they believe their parents would never discuss sex with each other, they will not learn that sex is an appropriate topic for discussion. Sadly, silence on sexual matters is often perpetuated through generations. An example of positive, respectful discussion of sexual matters is needed to break this cycle.

6. We believe that spouses should read minds. While sexual feelings may be automatic, sexual fulfillment—particularly for the wife—is not. A husband will not automatically know what turns his wife on nor what she needs to feel fulfilled. Michele Weiner Davis stated:

> We have this crazy notion that our spouses are just supposed to know what pleases us. We shouldn't have to talk about having good sex; it should just happen. But good sex doesn't just happen. Since no two people are alike, no single formula works for everybody. What one person finds arousing and exciting is a pure turn-off to another. If you want your spouse to know how you feel and what you enjoy, you have to tell him or her. Leave mind reading to the soothsayers.[19]

It's almost ludicrous to assume that our spouse will know exactly what turns us on. How will your spouse know what you like if you don't or won't tell them? The following story of a husband who assumes his wife should have mind-reading capabilities provides a lesson for both husbands and wives:

> An engineer married to a schoolteacher for ten years reported, "After all this time my wife still doesn't know what turns me on." When I asked, "Have you ever told her?" he replied, "No, I find it embarrassing to talk about sex. Besides, I think she should know." He was surprised when I responded, "How should she? You're different. You feel and react differently than a woman, and you possess an entirely different reproductive apparatus. Who did you think was going to tell her?"[20]

7. We don't know what turns us on. If sex or sexual parts of the body are incorrectly believed to be bad or evil, the Good Girl may not have any idea how her body works or what arouses her sexually. Michele Weiner Davis suggested this as another barrier to sexual communication:

> Another reason you might not talk about what turns you on is that you don't really know yourself. Your body is as much a mystery to you as it is to your spouse. If you don't know what gives you pleasure, what makes you feel aroused, what triggers an orgasm, it's time to go back to school. You have to study your body. You need to know what feels good and what leaves you feeling cold. You can't teach your spouse what works for you if you are clueless.[21]

8. We don't want to hurt our spouse's feelings. Let's say you do know what you would like sexually, but you're afraid to correct your spouse. Guiding, teaching and sharing sexual information and desires can be done without offending. If you keep your sexual needs and desires a secret you will potentially do much more damage to your marriage and family than if you are open and honest in a gentle way.

9. We don't want to be considered selfish. There is a stigma implicit to selfishness. If we ask for what we want and need, we feel selfish. Instead of asking, we just hope our spouse will figure it out someday, so we won't have to feel that we are selfishly seeking our own sexual satisfaction. Women may have a particularly difficult time asking for what they want and need sexually. However, they must learn to ask, rather than wait around hoping their spouse will figure it out. A healthy focus on the "self" is needed in lovemaking for a woman to achieve sexual fulfillment.

Sheryl struggled with these conflicting feelings. Though her feelings may be a symptom of deeper issues, the example she shared represents the bind many women feel:

> I remember feeling the need to be touched and held, but could not bring myself to ask for a hug. I didn't want to bother my husband. I somehow wished he would just know what I needed and offer it—magically reading my mind. By not asking for the hug, I felt abandoned, lonely and angry, while my husband had no idea what was going on within me.
>
> At other times I have asked for something I've needed emotionally or sexually, but have felt guilty for asking. I believed I was being selfish or that I was bothering my husband with something he might not really want to do. Sometimes I feel guilty for having needs at all.

The ability and willingness to openly discuss sexual issues in your marriage can lead to sexual understanding and fulfillment. If couples can boldly and bravely talk about their sexual relationship and the emotions that attend it, they will probably be able to talk about anything. Opening the door to sexual discussion can open the door to emotional and spiritual intimacy as well. If either husband or wife will initiate conversations regarding sex, they will be doing their marriage a great service.

Much good can come from a willingness to openly discuss sexual matters and feelings. Jenny called me the day after a blowout between herself and her husband. He said he couldn't take it anymore. He was unsatisfied sexually and very unhappy. She knew things had to change, but she didn't know how to initiate that change. I gave her a few of the chapters of this book and then I prayed for them.

Weeks later I asked her how they were doing. With a big smile on her face, she said things were much better. I asked what had helped. She said, "After our phone call I knelt down and told Heavenly Father I really wanted to fix this. I wanted my husband to feel loved, and I wanted to feel sexual desire again. I read everything you gave me, then we talked about it that night. I shared everything I was feeling about sex. Just opening up that floodgate so we could talk about sex has made all the difference."

An experience of another couple who have been married over 30 years shows the importance of asking for what you want, or asking your spouse what he or she wants sexually. Lynn wrote:

> The other night we were in the beginning process of making love when I stopped and said, "Wait, I'm supposed to ask what you really like." My husband was embarrassed about the question but he went ahead and told me. My response was, "You're kidding me?! That's easy for me to do. I never knew. I'd much rather do that than other things I thought you liked. All these years. . . . It's so sad we didn't know."

Further heartbreak can be avoided through open and honest sharing. Elder Brown stated, "If they who contemplate this most glorifying and intimate of all human relationships would seek to qualify for its responsibilities, . . . if they would frankly discuss the delicate and sanctifying aspects of harmonious sex life which are involved in marriage; . . . much sorrow, heartbreak, and tragedy could be avoided."[22]

For another couple, the turning point in their marriage came when Mandy told her husband she hated sex, and always had. After six years of having a "good attitude" about sex, Mandy couldn't fake it any longer. Through all these years she had acted like she enjoyed it, but she had been lying—to herself and to her husband. Tears flowed as she told her husband the truth. Mandy felt like an object: a pleasure provider for her husband. Sex was a service she supplied—a chore and her wifely duty. What a blow this was to her surprised husband! But her willingness to be open and honest stopped the downward spiral and freed them to begin to find solutions.

Dr. Dobson has identified the danger when sex is a forbidden subject in marriage and encourages couples to open the door to sexual discussion. He stated:

> When conversation is prohibited on the subject of sex, the act of intercourse takes on the atmosphere of a "performance"—each partner feeling that he is being critically evaluated by the other. To remove these communicative barriers, [either spouse can] take the lead in releasing the safety valve. . . . That is done by [verbalizing] feelings, . . . fears, . . . aspirations. They should talk about the manners and techniques which stimulate—and those which don't. They should face their problems as mature adults, . . . calmly and confidently. There is something magical to be found in such soothing conversation; tensions and anxieties are reduced when they find verbal expression.[23]

How to Talk about Sex

How to actually speak about such a delicate, yet potentially volatile, subject may be a matter of concern for couples. As touchy issues arise, it may be helpful to use the couple's communication tool taught in Chapter 10 of this book. This tool allows both husband and wife the opportunity to be fully heard, validated and understood in a safe and effective way. "Pick a time when you both feel ready to talk. Don't do it when either of you is tired, in a bad mood, or angry at each other or when there are distractions. Make sure you have enough privacy so you don't feel squeamish or nervous about being interrupted or overheard. A safe, comfortable environment is very important."[24]

One of the best ways to talk about sex is to read and discuss helpful books together, allowing the conversation to flow casually. The recommended reading list in the back of this book, as well as books referenced throughout, can provide a rich reservoir of resources.

While it can be helpful to guide and encourage particular touches or caresses during lovemaking, this may not be the best time to initiate a lengthy conversation on sexual dos and don'ts. As Dr. John Gray pointed out, "It is just not romantic to ask a woman what she wants while you are having sex. It is best done either after sex or at another time when you are not immediately planning to have sex."[25]

What to Talk About

In addition to subjects encountered while reading this and other helpful books, here are some suggestions for topics of discussion:[26]

- Discuss what kinds of touch and caresses turn you on—what feels good?

- Discuss what turns you off—what doesn't feel good? What makes you uncomfortable or isn't pleasurable?

- Discuss how you can improve your sexual encounters.

- Negotiate differences in sexual interests and preferences.

- Share preconceived expectations and fantasies.

- Discuss what and how you were taught about sex.

- Share your vulnerabilities, fears, memories and inhibitions.

Remember Variety Adds Vitality

Even after couples learn to have great sexual relations, an ongoing effort will be necessary to keep vitality in the relationship. Variety renews vitality, and keeps the fires of passion burning throughout our lives. A little playfulness and creativity in appropriate ways can add vitality to your sexual relationship. Don't let lovemaking become predictable or routine—predictability can squelch sensuality. Use as many senses as you can—sight, touch, taste, smell, and sound. Vary the stimuli that your senses receive to keep lovemaking fresh and new. Here are a few ideas to get your creative juices flowing:

- Add music (or new music) to your sexual encounters. Create your own special collection of bedroom music.

- Wear lingerie. Regularly add new apparel to your intimate collection to keep things new and exciting.

- Reserve special silky bedding just for lovemaking.

- Try a new time of day. Surprise yourself and your husband by telling him to come home for lunch, or wake him after he's gone to sleep at night. You may not only be adding variety to your sex life, but also fulfilling his fantasies at the same time!

- Try new locations. Sex doesn't have to always be in the bedroom. Spread a blanket on the bedroom closet floor. Try the office (make sure you lock the door!). Shower or take a Jacuzzi bath together. Schedule regular overnight getaways.

- Use colored light bulbs in your bedroom lamp for a sensual ambience.

- Make love with more light or less light than usual.

- Change the routine—if you usually begin clothed, begin unclothed instead; if you usually begin naked, try undressing each other first.

- Try different positions.

- Change your hairstyle. Put your hair up or let your hair down.

- Use different scented candles. Keep a supply of delicious candles on hand.

- Wear perfume or cologne. Try different ones.

- Stretch yourself to "gift" your spouse with one of his or her sexual fantasies. You may be surprised at your spouse's overflowing willingness to "gift" you with your heart's desires in return.

A little playfulness and creativity in appropriate ways can add vitality to your sexual relationship. Don't let lovemaking become predictable or routine—predictability can squelch sensuality.

What else can you think of that would be fun and exciting? Ways of adding variety and vitality to lovemaking could be another topic of discussion during pillow talk time. There is much fun, pleasure and variety within God's realm of sexual relations in marriage. Seek His guidance and He will show you the way.

Strive for Sexual Fulfillment for Both Spouses

In the introduction to this book, four dangers of sexual dissatisfaction were identified. They were: (1) divorce; (2) emotional and physical ailments; (3) marital emptiness and mediocrity or parallel marriage; and (4) vulnerability to temptation. It is your sexual stewardship in marriage to learn about and then do all you can to create sexual fulfillment for yourself and your spouse to reduce the dangers to your marriage. By so doing, greater love, passion and aliveness can define your marital relationship.

Vulnerability to temptation can cause dangerous concerns for both husband and wife. Joe Beam noted his concern regarding this vulnerability:

> Sex in marriage is wonderful! But like all blessings, there can be an accompanying curse: When husbands and wives don't find sexual fulfillment in marriage, they will find themselves increasingly susceptible to sexual sin. To avoid that temptation, they have the duty before God to sexually fulfill their mates. That means that wives are to fulfill the sexual needs of their husbands and that husbands are to fulfill the sexual needs of their wives. . . .
>
> Each has needs and each has a "heavenly contract" allowing him or her to expect . . . that those sexual needs be met.[27]

The scriptures support the need for sexual fulfillment in marriage as a means of reducing temptation. In Corinthians we read about the sacred obligation couples have to fulfill each other:

> Nevertheless, to avoid fornication, let every man have his own wife, and let every woman have her own husband. Let the husband render unto the wife due benevolence: and likewise also the wife unto the husband. The wife hath not power of her own body, but the husband: and likewise also the husband hath not power of his own body, but the wife. Defraud ye not one the other, except it be with consent for a time, that ye may give yourselves to fasting and prayer; and come together again, that Satan tempt you not for your incontinency.[28]

Joe Beam continued his counsel to couples to seek sexual fulfillment for both husband and wife, "Make every effort to keep your sex life healthy. Never forget God's warning in 1 Corinthians 7 about Satan's attack. . . . Remove that avenue of attack from Satan's forces by keeping your mate thoroughly sexually satisfied."[29]

Solutions have been presented in this chapter for gaining knowledge and understanding of each other sexually. The opportunity to enjoy sex and feel completely fulfilled is available to all couples. Make it your goal to become the best possible lover you can be, not only for your spouse, but for yourself.

Regularly set small goals as steppingstones to improving your sexual relationship. Seek professional help when needed. Increasing sexual fulfillment not only removes susceptibility to sexual temptation, but also creates greater happiness, joy and oneness in your marriage. No matter your age or the current state of your sexual relationship, improvement is always possible.

Chapter 6—"Home" Work

- Pray for sexual help.

- Schedule time for sexual intimacy and learning.

- Get educated sexually.

- Discuss sex openly and honestly.

- Ask for what you want and need.

- Keep lovemaking fresh and new by being creative and adding variety.

- Strive for sexual fulfillment for both spouses.

NOTES

Chapter 6—Sexual Stewardship—Finding Sexual Fulfillment in Marriage

[1]Nay, "Depend Upon the Lord" online article (emphasis added).
[2]"The Family: A Proclamation to the World," *Ensign*, Nov. 1995, 102 (emphasis added).
[3]Barlow, "They Twain Shall Be One," *Ensign*, Sep. 1986, 52.
[4]*See* Revelation 3:20.
[5]Flinders, "Learning to Teach as Jesus Taught," *Ensign*, Sep. 1974, 65.
[6]*See* Matthew 6:8.
[7]Beam, *Becoming One*, 170.
[8]LaHaye and LaHaye, *Act of Marriage*, 147.
[9]John 16:24.
[10]Dobson, *What Wives Wish Their Husbands Knew About Marriage*, 128.
[11]Brown, *You and Your Marriage*, 75.
[12]Brown, *You and Your Marriage*, 73.
[13]LaHaye and LaHaye, *Act of Marriage*, 130.
[14]Barlow, "They Twain Shall Be One," *Ensign*, Sep. 1986, 51.
[15]Dobson, *What Wives Wish*, 125.
[16]LaHaye and LaHaye, *Act of Marriage*, 130.
[17]*See* Weiner Davis, *Sex-Starved Marriage*, 185–86.
[18]*See* Genesis 2:24–25.
[19]Weiner Davis, *Sex-Starved Marriage*, 185–86.
[20]LaHaye and LaHaye, *Act of Marriage*, 130–31.
[21]Weiner Davis, *Sex-Starved Marriage*, 186.
[22]Brown, *You and Your Marriage*, 21–22.
[23]Dobson, *What Wives Wish*, 125–26.
[24]Weiner Davis, *Sex-Starved Marriage*, 186.
[25]Gray, *Mars and Venus in the Bedroom*, 53.
[26]*See* Weiner Davis, *Sex-Starved Marriage*, 187.
[27]Beam, *Becoming One*, 136–37.
[28]1 Corinthians 7:2–5.
[29]Beam, *Becoming One*, 173.

CHAPTER VIEW

Sacred Work of the Soul

Identify and Share Sexual Beliefs, Memories,
   Experiences, and Inhibitions

Overcome Inhibitions and Negative Beliefs
   • *What Are Inhibitions?*
   • *Taming Toxic Thoughts*

Identify and Share Sexual Desires, Expectations,
   and Fantasies

Learn the Art of Auditory Arousal

What's Okay and What Isn't?
   • *Distinguishing Between Godly and Sinful Behavior*

Dealing with Sexual Differences

Chapter 7—"Home" Work

Chapter 7

OVERCOMING BARRIERS TO SEXUAL FULFILLMENT IN MARRIAGE

"You asked us to explore our deeper feelings about sex," Susan wrote. "I've had a hard time doing that. What I found wasn't pretty, and certainly wasn't positive. I first tried to write my feelings with my regular hand, then felt I wasn't getting to the heart of it. When I used my left hand to write, I seemed to get below the surface to the underlying stuff. I was able to get out of my head and into my heart. Here's what I found out about myself:

"I don't like sex. Only bad girls like sex. I'm a good girl. I don't like sex because I don't want to be bad. Bad girls are just sex objects for men. Only people who can't control themselves like sex. Sex is something bad people do. I'm afraid of sex. Why can't men control themselves?

"Sex is bad. Sex is dirty. Sex is evil. I could never like sex. I could never enjoy it because it's wrong."

Sacred Work of the Soul

When you open your heart and honestly explore the inner self, you tap into a whole new level of understanding and personal growth. These honest expressions of the heart from one woman (above), represent some unpleasant, yet sacred, work of the soul. It is part of the stewardship of marriage to uncover sexual barriers you may not have even known existed.

Stephen R. Covey once said that to touch the soul of a human being is to walk on holy ground. In this chapter you are invited to recognize that sexual ignorance is a barrier to sexual fulfillment and to explore the holy ground of the soul where the source of sexual inhibitions may be found. It's an adventure—much like an archeological dig. It may not always be pleasant, but if you are willing to embark on the expedition, the treasure you will ultimately find will be worth the effort.

Elder James E. Faust provided evidence of the need for inner self healing in the First Presidency Message in the February 2003 *Ensign* entitled "Strengthening the Inner Self." Throughout the article he shined a light into the relatively unknown and intangible world of the inner self. He said:

> [We are] to strive continually to improve inward weaknesses and not merely the outward appearances. . . . The healing that we all so often need is the healing of our souls and spirits. . . . If we are to further strengthen the inner person, the inner self must be purged and cleansed of transgression [others' or our own]. . . . As we undertake to strengthen the inner soul, we move beyond concern for things that we can hold and possess.[1]

Identify and Share Sexual Beliefs, Memories, Experiences, and Inhibitions

The negative conditioning, distorted teachings or lack of teaching identified in the "Good Girl Syndrome" may be the great underlying, unacknowledged and underestimated source of barriers to sexual fulfillment in otherwise healthy marriages. Many people have dark realities in their past, because of the imperfect world in which we live. However, to many the inner self is a foreign territory and talk of neuro-emotional issues is a foreign language that they resist. Negative thoughts and experiences often are shut out, locked away or ignored.

It takes courage, time and effort to overcome negative and unproductive beliefs and emotions through awareness, acceptance, and attention.

These blocked feelings don't disappear magically. It takes courage, time and effort to overcome negative and unproductive beliefs and emotions through awareness, acceptance, and attention. Once you have acknowledged your thoughts and beliefs regarding sex, the next step is to identify any underlying, negative associations you have with sex by writing them down. Make a list including all your thoughts, beliefs, memories, experiences and inhibitions related to sex. Schedule some distraction-free time. Begin with prayer to ask Heavenly Father to help you uncover what is needed to help you heal. Write everything you can think of to finish the following phrases:

- "I remember . . ." (List all your sex-related memories, personal experiences and attending feelings, e.g., your first kiss, positive or negative; your first sexual experiences or honeymoon experiences, positive or negative; memories from movies or conversations with friends; the first time you saw someone naked, e.g., accidentally seeing a parent when undressing or viewing pornographic literature.)

- "I think sex is . . ." (List all your honest thoughts about sex.)

- "I don't like . . . ;" "I hate . . ." (List all your dislikes or inhibitions regarding sex.)

- "I feel . . ." (List all feelings associated with sex.)

- "Sex . . ." (List anything else that comes to mind.)

In Chapter 12 you'll learn more about the healing power of touch. For now, let me suggest that you consider gently caressing your hands or face providing nurturing, safety and support during this process. If significant negative experiences and emotions come to mind, seek professional help in addressing those issues. Even if you have relatively mild negative sexual beliefs and/or experiences, a therapist can provide invaluable help to support and assist you in the healing process.

If you find your statements are coming from your head or intellect, rather than from your heart, you may need to write using your left (or nondominant) hand. Your nondominant hand can help to provide direct access to your subconscious mind without the interfering filter of the intellect and cultural conditioning.

After you make your list, you may or may not feel ready to share this sacred and sensitive information with your spouse. If you can, and your spouse has also made a list, give your lists to each other to read, or read the lists together, discussing as you go. Be gentle and patient with each other. Avoid any criticism or contempt.

It often happens that as we begin to clean out a closet or a cupboard, we temporarily make a bigger mess. So it is with exploring our inner, sex-related issues, but, with patience and persistence, great healing, openness and connection can ultimately take place.

These intimate revelations will provide insight into struggles you've had that have hampered your ability to be intimate in the way God intends. Looking into your heart releases the good and the bad into the light where awareness, acceptance and attention can be given. This is sacred work of the soul.

Overcome Inhibitions and Negative Beliefs

From the exercise above, you may have discovered some of the inhibitions preventing you from achieving the sexual fulfillment you deserve. Now that you are *aware* of your negative sexual associations, this section will address *how to remove* the inappropriate inhibitions allowing you to *relax*, *let go* and *mentally engage* in the sexual experience. These are necessary components of sexual fulfillment.

In the original marital bedroom in the Garden of Eden there was no shame, no embarrassment and no discomfort regarding nakedness. This understanding can also apply to married sexuality.[2] Many married couples today experience problems regarding the free sharing of their bodies within the ordained sexual relationship. Christian authors Tim and Beverly LaHaye shared one example of an inhibition:

Although modesty is an admirable virtue in a woman, it is out of place in the bedroom with her husband. The Bible teaches that Adam and Eve in their unfallen state were "naked, and felt no shame" (Gen. 2:25). . . . It may take time for a chaste woman to shake off the inhibitions of her premarriage days and learn to be open with her husband—but it is absolutely essential.[3]

What Are Inhibitions? Inhibitions might be thoughts or feelings characterized as frustrations, hang-ups, shame, guilt, reservations, problems or stumbling blocks that keep you from relaxing, letting go and experiencing enjoyment and ecstasy in your sexual relationship. Overcoming inhibitions does not mean that you must engage in whatever sexual behavior your spouse might desire, but instead it means a willingness to become comfortable enough with one's own body and the sexual experience that meaningful fulfillment is possible for both husband and wife.

Thoughts and feelings are so closely linked in the body and mind that inhibitions can simply be toxic thoughts that have been allowed to roam free—wreaking emotional havoc wherever they go. The following are some potentially dangerous inhibitions or toxic thoughts associated with sex:

- General fear of sex
- Fear, dislike or disgust with sexual body parts
- Inability to relax during sex
- Fear of the opposite sex
- Discomfort being naked and seen by spouse
- Dislike or even claustrophobic feelings during kissing or intercourse
- Fear of failure to achieve orgasm
- Embarrassment with any form of sex play
- Frustration regarding the time and effort required to produce female orgasm
- Inability or unwillingness to initiate, actively participate in, or enjoy sex

The sexual stewardship in marriage is to fully experience sexual pleasure as well as to meet each other's sexual needs. For many this will include overcoming inhibitions; the time and effort invested are worth it to attain mutual fulfillment in your marriage. Christian author Joe Beam stated:

Make it your unalterable goal to fulfill each other. If your mate wants something that you find uncomfortable, displeasing, or otherwise unpleasant, you should ask yourself if what he or she wants is within the parameters of God. If your spouse desires it and God didn't condemn it, the only barrier to your spouse's fulfillment is you. . . .

If you . . . are dealing with an emotional barrier, you should seek the remedy to that as well. If a person just finds something distasteful or if he or she carries scars from previous encounters, there is help available.[4]

Taming Toxic Thoughts. All things begin with a thought. Let's say as lovemaking begins you find yourself thinking, "I hate sex." Thoughts are like instructions to the brain. The thought, "I hate sex," tells yourself to hate it. It's pretty unlikely you will enjoy something you've just told yourself to hate. You can stop the negative thought cycle by becoming aware of your thoughts, challenging them, and replacing them with positive and productive beliefs such as, "I enjoy sex with my husband." This can also change the emotions surrounding those events.

Deeper than thoughts are core beliefs. We need to change the negative core beliefs about sex if we are to root out the source of the problem. The process of replacing negative thoughts and beliefs with positive ones takes time and effort. Because we are so familiar with the negative, positive thoughts may seem fake and unnatural. With repetition the new, positive programming can become natural and familiar.

There is a powerful technique called the Emotional Freedom Technique (EFT) addressed in the resources appendix that is not only effective in helping you overcome negative thoughts and inhibitions, but it can also be used to install positive thoughts and beliefs. Reprogramming negative thoughts with positive thoughts helps neutralize them and prevents them from recurring. It's like deleting old, ineffective programs on your computer's hard drive, and installing new programs to replace the old.

One idea may be to create a list of positive statements about sex that you can read to yourself on a regular basis, with the intent to reprogram yourself. You could also record those statements on tape to replay frequently. You might include on your recording the many affirming statements of Church leaders and from the scriptures provided in Chapter 2 on the sanctity of sex.

Identify and Share Sexual Desires, Expectations, and Fantasies

Before one is married, he or she has hopes and dreams of what the honeymoon will be like. Unfortunately, couples rarely share this information with each other and instead create disappointment and dashed dreams with the very first sexual experience. First impressions can be lasting. Lack of sex education, in addition to not knowing each other's expectations, can provide a poor foundation for sexual fulfillment in marriage. If you are not yet married, you might consider sharing your thoughts regarding sex with your fiancé as you travel to the honeymoon retreat. If you are already married, you can still share your sexual expectations and fantasies, significantly increasing the possibility that they might yet be fulfilled.

To begin, write a detailed description of your "dream honeymoon" or ideal sexual encounter. You might include sexual fantasies. Putting them on paper can help clarify what you really like, so you can teach your spouse how to fulfill your needs. Remember, there is no requirement to act upon these fantasies. The purpose of this writing is to create knowledge and understanding of each other's expectations and desires. This can help lead you to shared sexual fulfillment. Though neither spouse might ever totally fulfill the other's fantasies, it can be helpful to at least understand what those fantasies are.

Many scriptures identify the forbidden territory of fantasies involving someone other than the spouse by letting lust linger in the mind. If this happens, the Spirit is withdrawn and adultery is committed within the heart.[5] The wise husband and wife keep their sexual thoughts and fantasies focused on their own spouse, thus allowing shared fantasies to excite and enliven the physical relationship without leading into Satan's territory of sin.

Dr. John Gray provided a twist on sharing sexual desires. He suggested writing a "sex letter" to your spouse, and provided a few examples in his book *Mars and Venus in the Bedroom.* He stated, "Another secret for bringing back sexual feelings is to write a sex letter to your partner. . . . Imagine a romantic scene acting out your sexual feelings with your partner. In a letter to your partner, describe what you want to do and then describe the scene and your feelings as if it is really happening."[6] It is important to ensure the privacy of such communication between husband and wife. But sharing thoughts and feelings with one another can enable an enlightened understanding of a spouse's perspective on the sexual experience.

In addition to your description of the ideal sexual experience, it may be helpful to contemplate what turns you on, and compile a list. If you don't know what turns you on, you need to determine what does. It's not fair to expect your spouse to figure out what you like if you aren't sure yourself.

If you have no idea where to begin, start by keeping a private sexual learning journal or notebook and jot down what you learn and what you like or don't like about lovemaking. Figure out how your body works and what your preferences are. This assignment may be likened to doing an intimate study on the sexual functioning of your own body. This notebook can help you be more attentive to pleasurable sensations during lovemaking and to be more actively involved in seeking your own sexual satisfaction. Share these insights with your spouse. Take a minute some time after lovemaking to record some of your thoughts and feelings. Putting thoughts into words on paper can make you aware of sexual pleasures you hadn't noticed before.

Keeping such a journal about sexual intimacy also allows you to see your progress— which can provide encouragement throughout the journey. At one discouraging point in my journey, it seemed we were making very little progress. However, as I looked back over the issues and inhibitions I once had, I was fortified to move forward as I saw how much I had overcome. Your journal can also help you discover areas and issues that still need some work. Again, take care to protect the privacy of such information as you record it, but be open to the positive feedback that can come as you are honest and open with yourself.

Think about what is sexually arousing to you or that contributes to any part of the sexual experience. Examples might include specific ways your husband touches you. It might include things he says during lovemaking. It may include personal hygiene or other sexual preparation. It might include locations, time of day, apparel that makes you feel particularly sexy, and situations or circumstances that contribute to the intimate atmosphere. To help you begin this list of what turns you on, you might complete the following phrases:

- "I enjoy sex when . . ."

- "I love it when you . . ."

- "It turns me on when . . ."

- "I go crazy when you . . ."

- "I find myself letting go when . . ."

Once you have compiled the list of what turns you on, share this intimate information with your spouse. This provides an opportunity for your spouse to do the same. Share in a quiet, uninterrupted setting. Maybe schedule a special date night. Be sure to communicate with the purpose of providing insight, instead of criticism or judgment.

Books on the topic of sexual intimacy may provide helpful ideas for increasing sexual arousal, but the best sexual insights will come from within yourself and from your spouse. Husband and wife learn best as they explore together and teach each other what is personally sexually fulfilling.

Learn the Art of Auditory Arousal

Auditory expressions of sexual emotions can unlock arousal during lovemaking. This requires honesty, trust and tender vulnerability between husband and wife. Whether it is the feelings shared and the associated emotional connection, or some kind of physiological sexual trigger in the auditory system, verbal sexual expression can heighten sexual pleasure and even unlock the door to sexual ecstasy. One couple found great sexual benefit from verbal expressions. Their marriage counselor, Dr. Barbara De Angelis, shared their experience:

> The first major change both Lisa and Greg made was to express much more of how they were feeling *during* lovemaking. . . . Lisa began asking for what she wanted from Greg instead of hoping he'd figure it out himself. Greg worked on telling Lisa more of what he was feeling inside while they made love, rather than just thinking about how wonderful it was. At first, they were embarrassed to be so open and vulnerable. But they soon noticed that their feelings of intimacy and trust for each other deepened. The more Lisa asked for what she wanted, the more she received it, and the happier she felt. The more Greg expressed his love for Lisa along with feeling his own pleasure, the more turned on Lisa got, and the more pleasure Greg felt.[7]

Joe Beam counseled husbands about auditory arousal as a means of lovemaking in marriage. He shared the example of King Solomon from the Bible:

> One thing he [Solomon] did was *talk* to her—telling her what he was doing or going to do. He understood her love of poetic language. Talk to your wife as you begin making love to her; caress her with words throughout the entire lovemaking experience. Of course, you shouldn't say things that will turn her off; rather, use the poetic language that will "light her fire"—whatever that means for her. Some women like it more primal and some more aesthetic. Solomon also understood

her desire to share not only her body but her emotions. He made love to her with every part of his body, including his vocal cords.[8]

Kisses and caresses may be a turn on, but so can verbal sexual strokes, especially for women. Though men can also be aroused with words, women may have special auditory systems that make verbal expressions of love particularly pleasurable. Tim LaHaye stated:

> Rarely does one hear a man say, "Her voice excites me," whereas it is common to hear a woman exclaim, "His voice turns me on!" That auditory mechanism can be likened to the thermostat on the wall of your home. Entering the house at night, you can turn her thermostat up by speaking reassuring, loving, approving, or endearing words. You can likewise turn her thermostat down through disapproval, condemnation, or insults.[9]

Auditory arousal is also one way couples stay connected emotionally during lovemaking. Sheila shared an experience she had where verbal expressions made her feel close and cherished by her husband, providing erotic fuel to her escalating fire. As her arousal began to build, her husband began to voice some of his sexual feelings and observations of her in a way that was very romantic and sexy. She quickly progressed to the heights of orgasm and became convinced of the power of his verbal expressions as the key that unlocked the door to her ecstasy.

Sheila felt that when her husband spoke *to* her and *of* her, the verbal expressions kept her focused "in the moment." When he did not include arousing words of adoration during lovemaking, she felt disconnected from him, and her arousal waned. She also began to feel self-conscious during lovemaking—a sure inhibitor of a building intimate fire.

Verbal expressions need not be limited to the husband. The wife can also communicate her sexual feelings, increasing her arousal and emotional connection. Her expressions of pleasure and sensation can facilitate a shift in focus from her daily cares and concerns to the wonderful world of arousal. Thoughts of the day and tomorrow's "to do" list fade as women surrender to their sexual sensations.

Stretching yourself to open up verbally with your sexual thoughts and feelings can cause the sensual surrender that is needed for complete sexual fulfillment. It may be new and awkward to be so open and vulnerable, either asking for your husband's verbal expressions or outwardly sharing your own, but it can be worth the effort.

Victoria found that as she expressed her pleasure and sexual desires, it not only increased her own arousal, but also gave loving encouragement and guidance to her husband. During lovemaking she would say "I love it when you . . ." every time her husband would do something she liked. She also said it when she thought of some-thing she wanted her husband to say or do, as if to suggest it to him. Their lovemak-ing was filled with "I love it when you . . ." and she found herself more easily moving into the state of arousal and orgasm.

Couples can engage in auditory arousal by expressing more of how they're feeling during lovemaking. Focus on expressing what you like in an affirming way to avoid discouraging your partner. Use "I . . ." statements when expressing what you don't like in order to be considerate of your spouse's feelings. To apply the art of auditory arousal to your lovemaking, it may be helpful to create a list of words, phrases or statements that turn you on. The following phrases may help prompt you:

- "I love it when you look at me like that."
- "I love it when you touch me there."
- "I love it when you . . ."
- "You are so . . ."
- "It turns me on when you . . ."
- "It turns me on when you tell me . . ."

As you awaken more fully to your sexual senses and to your sexual self, add to your intimate treasury of verbal expressions and specific sexual guidance during lovemaking. This information can unlock the door to exquisite sexual enjoyment and be a priceless gift, not only to your spouse, but also to yourself.

Couples who speak to each other with care and warmth during lovemaking should also ask one another how each feels regarding such expressions. A spouse may uninten-tionally say something or use a word or phrase that dampens the other's sexual feelings or responsiveness. Share what you like with your spouse and learn to speak words that soothe and excite rather than words that offend, insult or diminish your spouse's desires.

What's Okay and What Isn't?

A discussion of sexual desires and fantasies inevitably invites the question of what's okay and what isn't. The LDS Church has stated in *The Family: A Proclamation to the World*, "We further declare that God has commanded that the sacred powers of procreation are to be employed only between man and woman, lawfully wedded as husband and wife."[10]

Church leaders provide much direction about what *is*, and *is not*, appropriate *outside* of marriage. However, they are careful not to suggest what *is* and *is not* appropriate *within* the marital relationship. Within marriage, sexual intimacy is approved and ordained of God. The marriage bed is a haven of privacy between husband and wife, in which they are meant to freely and openly learn, communicate and understand the unique and powerful blessings of sexual expression and interaction. Following the guidance of the Spirit, couples can work through their personal boundaries within the private space of marriage.

The sexual learning and experience of a husband and wife are meant to occur within an atmosphere of love, respect, trust and growth, *without* fear, anxiousness, guilt or shame. Both husband and wife should feel free to share their thoughts, feelings and their bodies. Couples should become comfortable with, and learn how their bodies respond sexually. Within this divine context, husband and wife can express their sexual responsiveness as a vital part of the marital experience.

In October 1982 the First Presidency of The Church of Jesus Christ of Latter-day Saints sent a letter to the priesthood leadership reminding them that it was inappropriate to delve into personal matters involving intimate relations between husband and wife. At a priesthood session of General Conference, President Gordon B. Hinckley stated the following when referring to intimate relations in marriage, "When the bishop interviews you for your temple recommend, he is not likely to get into these delicate and sensitive and personal things. You must judge within your heart whether you are guilty of any practice that is unholy, impure, or in any way evil before the Lord."[11] Again, in January 2003, during a worldwide Priesthood Leadership Training broadcast, Church leaders restated this position, reminding priesthood leaders to refrain from inquiring into the intimate relations of married persons.

When asked a specific sex-related question one bishop gave the following excellent response that may apply to any question regarding intimate matters between husband and wife. He said, "I will never ask you how much money you make or how you arrived at how much tithing you should pay; I will only ask you if you live up to your covenant to pay a full tithe and let you and the Lord work out the details." The gospel of Jesus Christ provides general principles, such as love, kindness, respect and forgiveness, by which to conduct ourselves within marriage, rather than specific practices. Couples should not feel the need for ecclesiastical permission to seek their particular path to sexual fulfillment. They should instead counsel with the Lord.[12]

Some couples wish for a laundry list of do's and don'ts for the intimate relationship

in marriage. Couples have many questions regarding oral sex, birth control or appropriate attire during lovemaking. This section, "What's Okay and What Isn't," should
be applied to any specific questions you may have regarding the intimate sexual relationship in marriage.

The Prophet Joseph Smith stated, "[We] teach the people correct principles and
they govern themselves."[13] Elder Boyd K. Packer confirmed the importance of principles over practices, particularly regarding the sacred powers of procreation. He stated,
"The gospel tells us when and with whom these sacred powers may be safely experienced. As with all things, the scriptures do not contain page after page of detailed
commandments covering every possible application of the law of life. Rather they
speak in general terms, leaving us free to apply the principles of the gospel to meet the
infinite variety of life."[14]

Couples may have heard that "behind bedroom doors anything goes." President
Spencer W. Kimball refuted that statement when he said, "There are some people who
have said that behind the bedroom doors anything goes. That is not true and the Lord
would not condone it."[15] Just because a couple is married doesn't authorize any and all
sexual behavior.

Some examples of unrighteous behavior include adultery and erotica, using sex
coercively or as manipulation, demanding any offensive or degrading behaviors (even
if it's only offensive to one spouse), or any physically abusive behaviors. It is likely that
past church counsel that has been given regarding specific sexual behaviors has come
due to the demands one spouse has put upon the other, making one feel exploited and
demeaned. Behaviors engaged in mutually, that enhance the relationship, and that are
in keeping with the Spirit of the relationship, may be considered appropriate.

Couples may have heard that if they have concerns or are uncomfortable with certain sexual behaviors, those behaviors ought to be discontinued. Without understanding the existence and significance of negative sexual conditioning, this counsel could
be interpreted as a license for those who dislike sex to end sexual relations altogether.

Couples may have heard the terms "unnatural, unholy and impure" to describe
inappropriate behavior in the sexual relationship. However, misunderstanding a couple's sexual differences can make this counsel license for some to inappropriately dis-
continue sex. It can also cause unnecessary concerns, due to the unspecific nature of
the words, among those already inhibited sexually.

Terms such as unnatural, unholy and impure can be broadly defined or interpreted
depending on one's knowledge, experience and perceptions of right and wrong. A

Christian mother, Susannah Wesley, provided a valuable yardstick to her son, John Wesley, that may help couples determine what is appropriate in marriage, "Whatever weakens your reason, impairs the tenderness of your conscience, obscures your sense of God, or takes off your relish for spiritual things, whatever increases the authority of the body over the mind, that thing is sin to you, however innocent it may seem in itself."[16] This counsel allows for the "infinite variety of life" as stated by Elder Packer, but also clearly identifies personal sin.

In the wisdom of God, He does not make an official decree or commandment for every little thing. The Lord has counseled, "It is not meet that I should command in all things; for he that is compelled in all things, the same is a slothful and not a wise servant."[17] If we are compelled one way or the other in all things, we do not develop wisdom, confidence or spiritual self-reliance.

The Lord has told us that the power is in us to do good, and to choose righteously being "agents unto [our]selves."[18] God has given us the gift of the Holy Ghost and trusts us to make correct choices. We must develop our spiritual senses, learn to have greater faith and trust the inspiration we receive.

One reason the Church may have taken a stance to refrain from addressing specific sexual questions and practices may be the Lord's desire to keep sexual responsibility and stewardship between husband and wife. Following the admonition to "teach correct principles" and let them "govern themselves" encourages husband and wife to seek the Lord *directly* rather than going through the bishop, the stake president or the general authorities.

King Benjamin, in the Book of Mormon, taught, "I cannot tell you all the things whereby ye may commit sin; for there are divers ways and means, even so many that I cannot number them."[19] It would be very difficult for anyone to create a specific list of "thou shalt nots" for the marital bedroom. Instead, the Lord has given a spiritual gift to all, "The Spirit of Christ is given to every man, that he may know good from evil . . . wherefore ye may know with a perfect knowledge [what] is of God."[20]

Imagine the Pandora's box that would be opened if the Church commented on specific sexual behaviors! This would set a precedent of needing a "letter from the Brethren" on every imaginable sexual question. Where would it end? Imagine the bishop—who is an accountant, a plumber or a financial planner—being given the responsibility to answer every sexual question he may receive. The Church would have to come up with a "Sexual Intimacy Handbook of Instruction" for priesthood leaders. What an incredible burden that would be on the bishop. God has wisely given the responsibility for the sexual relationship to both husband and wife—complete with the word of God through scripture and personal revelation.

The strict and specific written laws and commandments or the "letter of the law" of the Law of Moses were replaced by "intent" or the "spirit of the law" requiring greater spiritual insight and a greater ability to hear and heed spiritual direction. Elder Faust indicated that "the intent of a person alone becomes part of the rightness or wrongness of human action"[21] and that this "refinement of the soul," relying on the intent of the heart and mind, also leaves us to rely on the "promptings of the Holy Spirit."[22]

The doctrines of God's law allow for couples to move to a higher level of spirituality, growing line upon line, in their own time. To remove the responsibility from husband and wife for understanding God's intent in the sexual relationship would weaken members of the Church spiritually, rather than strengthen them. In the area of sexual fulfillment in marriage, husband and wife can rise to a higher level of spiritual understanding as they draw nearer to each other and seek divine guidance to distinguish between godly behavior and sinful behavior.

As I've pondered the approach the Church has taken in refraining from commenting on sexual behavior within marriage, it occurred to me that it might be similar to why the Savior used symbols and parables to teach divine truths. Parables and symbols allow for people to learn what they are ready to understand. Parables depend upon the Spirit to teach what is right. Depending on the knowledge, experience and degree of spiritual growth of an individual, one person may understand a principle of the gospel differently than someone else.

Only within the intimate and private context of a husband-and-wife relationship can they determine what is most fitting for their individual personalities and circumstances. Inevitably, what is acceptable to one couple will not be acceptable to another, making it very difficult for any one-size-fits-all statements regarding marital sexuality.

Distinguishing Between Godly and Sinful Behavior in the Sexual Relationship in Marriage. The Good Girl Syndrome, manifest in varying degrees among women (and men), adds a significant dimension to the question of what's okay and what isn't. I have identified two measures that must be considered in order to determine whether something is "okay" or not. These two measures are (1) the degree to which one is worthy and in tune with spiritual guidance, and (2) the degree of negative conditioning internalized.

What's Okay and What Isn't?
Measures to Consider

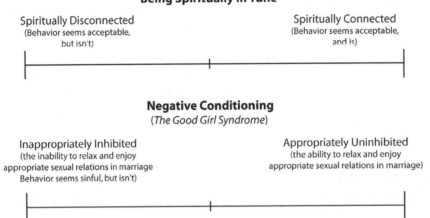

Being Spiritually In Tune

Spiritually Disconnected
(Behavior seems acceptable,
but isn't)

Spiritually Connected
(Behavior seems acceptable,
and is)

Negative Conditioning
(*The Good Girl Syndrome*)

Inappropriately Inhibited
(the inability to relax and enjoy
appropriate sexual relations in marriage
Behavior seems sinful, but isn't)

Appropriately Uninhibited
(the ability to relax and enjoy
appropriate sexual relations in marriage)

It's not enough to believe you are spiritually in tune with what's right and wrong, because negative conditioning and inhibitions can affect what you *perceive* as right and wrong. Following your instincts (or what you believe is the Spirit) may not be correct. Perception is made up of reality and illusion. The Good Girl Syndrome creates distortions and illusions about sexual relations. A behavior someone is uncomfortable with might not necessarily be "wrong," it may just be something they have some negative conditioning or inhibitions about. Conversely, being out of tune spiritually can make one think something is okay when it may not be.

Distinguishing between sexual inhibitions caused by negative conditioning, and inhibitions prompted by the Spirit of God, is no easy task. Couples must consider the possibility of negative sexual conditioning as well as how spiritually in tune they are when determining what's okay and what isn't.

*Couples must consider the possibility of negative sexual
conditioning as well as how spiritually in tune they are
when determining what's okay and what isn't.*

Let's take one example. A husband may want his wife to participate in a particular behavior, but she feels uncomfortable with it, and considers her feelings as a spiritual indication that the behavior is inappropriate. It is possible that the husband is out of tune spiritually and sees nothing wrong with the behavior that is not in keeping with God's design for sexual relations in marriage. It is also possible that the wife is unaware of her underlying negative conditioning that causes her to believe the behavior is sinful when it is not. As the husband grows spiritually, he may come to see that the behavior he previously desired was not appropriate. As the wife overcomes her inhibitions, the sexual activities she previously felt were sinful can now be seen as perfectly acceptable within the loving and intimate relationship of marriage.

If one spouse seems to have an overwhelming desire for a particular behavior to the point that it is causing difficulties in the relationship, then the desire for the sexual behavior may be out of balance. If the emotional climate and communication between the couple has become strained or hostile, then the spirit of the relationship has been offended. Don't let Satan's spirit of contention enter this or any other aspect of your marriage.

Though there may not be a clearly defined list of do's and don'ts, the Lord has not left couples alone on the important issues of intimacy in marriage. Couples can counsel with the Lord in all their doings—even in the area of sexual relations—and He will direct them for good.[23] The Lord knows every couple and is intimately aware of their lives and circumstances. He can lead each couple to the right counsel for them. He can direct them to certain books or information or put earthly "angels" in their path in the form of friends, family or professionals to guide them to light and truth.

The Lord expects husbands and wives to use wisdom to govern themselves, being in tune with the Spirit to determine what's okay and what isn't. We must be careful not to condemn or judge our spouse or others based upon our personal interpretation or perception of right and wrong.

The "Home" work assignments throughout this book provide practical application for recognizing and overcoming inappropriate inhibitions. Removing these unnecessary and unhealthy inhibitions can help clear the way for spiritual counsel to be received more faithfully on complex marital issues and questions. To determine how you can tell the difference between appropriate sexual relations and inappropriate behavior, or to know when neuro-emotional barriers are involved, consider the following suggestions:

1. Reread the statements and scriptures in Chapter 2 to have fresh in your mind God's approval of the sanctity of sexual relations in marriage.

2. Use the Couples Dialogue communication tool taught in Chapter 10 to fully discuss both your and your husband's perspectives on any issues of concern. It is particularly beneficial to use the Couples Dialogue if the discussion gets heated. When done with the right intent, the Couples Dialogue can provide a safe and effective way for both husband and wife to be fully heard and understood. The following questions may be helpful as you discuss any disputed sexual activity.

- Is either spouse demanding a particular behavior or does he / she seem obsessed with something?

- Does either spouse feel demeaned, degraded or objectified? Does the behavior maintain the dignity of both spouses?

- What is motivating the desire for the behavior? What is motivating the other spouse's response?

- Would God approve of the behavior?

- Once a resolution is reached, are both husband and wife willingly agreed to the action—neither feeling coerced, nor talked into it?

3. Seek divine help through prayer. Couples can pray to know what is acceptable to God in their relationship. They can be inspired to know if they are dealing with inappropriate inhibitions and what they need to do to overcome them. The Lord is the best resource to guide couples to distinguish between genuinely sinful behavior and inappropriate inhibitions caused by negative conditioning or past traumatic experiences.

Appropriate solutions to sexual concerns are most likely to be found as husband and wife counsel together, then allow the Lord to guide them in truth and light. As you seek divine assistance, the Lord can guide you to know when an activity is genuinely wrong and bless you with a lessening desire for it. God can change hearts.

Dealing with Sexual Differences

Although there are general sexual response patterns in men and women, the expression of sexual responsiveness varies widely among individuals. What is pleasurable to one woman (or man) may not be to another. Comfort level, personal boundaries, as well as type and style of stimulation preferred vary greatly. Feelings and preferences can change over the years as couples become more comfortable with each other, more knowledgeable sexually, and as they change physically and emotionally.

Over time different issues and challenges may arise, such as physical disability, periods of stress or illness and pregnancy, each affecting sexual response. Allowing for variety and adaptation in how couples interact sexually makes it possible for them to change as needed.

Determining appropriate behavior for the intimate marital relationship may be likened to determining appropriate behavior for keeping the Sabbath day holy. For some, there's no TV on the Sabbath; whereas others see nothing particularly wrong with it. For others, there is always a special family dinner with all the fixings; others may plan meals requiring minimal time and preparation. Everyone is different. Beyond what has been definitively stated by God such as, "thou shalt not commit adultery," God does not want us to spend our time and effort judging and condemning each other. The Lord allows each of us to learn and grow line upon line.[24]

Sharing personal boundaries and working through sexual differences is part of the stewardship in marriage. Dealing with sexual differences may not be much different than dealing with any other differences in marriage. One spouse may want a new car; the other thinks what they have is fine. You think it's his turn to do the dishes; he thinks it's your turn, because he just mowed the lawn. You may see a sexual issue in black and white or as wrong versus right, while he sees it in varying shades of gray. Whether your differences involve sexual relations or other aspects of marriage, you must be careful not to let differences become stumbling blocks.

Resolving differences requires understanding, respect and considerate communication. How your spouse feels about something is of primary importance. Those feelings are not to be dismissed, invalidated or violated. God wants husbands and wives to counsel together in a spirit of love to negotiate boundaries when differences arise. Remember, you're both on the same team. With God's help, couples can find solutions that both feel good about.

Chapter 7—"Home" Work

- *Identify and Share Sexual Beliefs, Memories, Experiences and Inhibitions.* Make a list including all your thoughts, beliefs, memories, experiences and inhibitions related to sex. You may need to use your non-dominant hand. Use the phrases on page 127 to prompt you. Share these insights with your spouse and/ or seek professional assistance.

- *Overcome Inhibitions and Negative Beliefs.* Learn the Emotional Freedom Technique (EFT) in the resources appendix. Use it to clear your negative beliefs and inhibitions. Create a list and/or recording of positive statements about sex. Read or listen to it regularly. Use EFT to reprogram your thinking to new, positive and productive beliefs.

- *Identify and Share Sexual Desires, Expectations and Fantasies.* Write a detailed description of your "dream honeymoon" or ideal sexual encounter, including sexual fantasies. Compile a list of what turns you on. Start keeping a sex journal or notebook to jot down what you learn and what you like or don't like during lovemaking. See page 132 for ideas and phrases to prompt you. Share this information with your spouse.

- *Learn the Art of Auditory Arousal.* Create a list of words, phrases or statements that turn you on. See page 135 for phrases to prompt you.

- *Resolve Sexual Differences.* Determine whether particular behaviors are sexual inhibitions, due to negative conditioning, or are simply ungodly behaviors. (1) Reread the statements and scriptures in Chapter 2. (2) Use the Couples Dialogue communication tool in Chapter 10 to discuss both of your perspectives and to discuss the questions on page 142 regarding any sexual behaviors in question. (3) Seek divine help through prayer.

NOTES

Chapter 7—Overcoming Barriers to Sexual Fulfillment in Marriage

[1]Faust, "Strengthening the Inner Self," *Ensign*, Feb. 2003, 4–6.
[2]*See* Genesis 2:25.
[3]LaHaye and LaHaye, *Act of Marriage*, 143.
[4]Beam, *Becoming One*, 170.
[5]*See* Doctrine & Covenants 42:23, 63:16; Matthew 5:28.
[6]Gray, *Mars and Venus in Bedroom*, 121.
[7]De Angelis, *How to Make Love All the Time*, 150–51.
[8]Beam, *Becoming One*, 160.
[9]LaHaye and LaHaye, *Act of Marriage*, 126.
[10]"The Family: A Proclamation to World," *Ensign*, Nov. 1995, 102.
[11]Hinckley, "Keeping the Temple Holy," *Ensign*, May 1990, 52.
[12]*See* Alma 37:37.
[13]Faust, "Weightier Matters of the Law: Judgment, Mercy, and Faith" *Ensign*, Nov. 1997, 54.
[14]Packer, *Eternal Marriage*, 143.
[15]Kimball, *Teachings of Spencer W. Kimball*, 312.
[16]Benson, *Teachings of Ezra Taft Benson*, 278.
[17]Doctrine & Covenants 58:26.
[18]Doctrine & Covenants 58:28.
[19]Mosiah 4:29.
[20]Moroni 7:16.
[21]Faust, "Surety of a Better Testament," *Ensign*, Sept. 2003, 3.
[22]Faust, "Surety of a Better Testament," *Ensign*, Sept. 2003, 6.
[23]*See* Alma 37:37.
[24]*See* 2 Nephi 28:30.

CHAPTER VIEW

Commanded To Be One

A Vision of ONEness

Three Dimensions of Intimacy
- *Emotional Intimacy*
- *Spiritual Intimacy*
- *Physical Intimacy*

Characteristics of Marital ONEness

Marriage Takes Three

Creating Your "Marriage Vision"

Chapter 8—"Home" Work

Chapter 8

ONENESS — THE ULTIMATE
PURPOSE OF MARRIAGE

Mindy felt she had finally found the missing marital secret. God's command, and His promise, that husbands and wives can and should "be one" inspired her.[1] To Mindy, the concept of three dimensions of intimacy, emotional, spiritual, and physical—each needing attention—enlightened her mind. She had known something was missing in her marriage, but had not been able to identify what it was. With an understanding of three dimensions of oneness, she now had a vision of how her marriage could be. She now believed there was hope and help for their struggling sexual relationship.

She and James felt close emotionally and spiritually, but physical intimacy was dissatisfying for both. Mindy's distaste for sexual relations had led her to discount its importance, especially since they had an otherwise good marriage. James and Mindy did their best to downplay the sexual aspect—attempting to keep it from damaging their otherwise great marriage, but she could see that the sexual dissatisfaction was beginning to permeate the emotional and spiritual dimensions of their marriage. She had hoped that if they just ignored it, maybe it would "go away." But the importance of physical intimacy could not be so easily dismissed by James. His bitterness, frustration and anger from repeated rejection festered, as Mindy either limited or ignored his need for sexual intimacy.

With a new understanding of oneness—the ultimate purpose of marriage—Mindy knew she had work to do. Now she had hope and a vision of how to stop the downward spiral of sexual dissatisfaction.

Commanded To Be One

God has given husbands and wives a sacred command with glorious blessings. He has commanded couples to be ONE. This all-encompassing command can be identified as an ultimate purpose of marriage. Elder Henry B. Eyring said:

> The Savior of the world, Jesus Christ, said of those who would be part of His Church: "Be one; and if ye are not one ye are not mine" (Doctrine & Covenants 38:27). And at the creation of man and woman, unity for them in marriage was not given as hope; it was a command! "Therefore shall a man leave his father and his mother, and shall cleave unto his wife: and they shall be one flesh" (Genesis 2:24). Our Heavenly Father wants our hearts to be knit together. That union in love is not simply an ideal. It is a necessity.[2]

Because we know that God gives no commandment that He does not also provide a way to accomplish,[3] a husband and wife *can* become one. President Spencer W. Kimball added his insights on the concept of oneness in marriage when he referred to God's creation of man—a *complete* man—as a husband *and* wife together as one. Quoting the book of Moses he said, "Let us make man (not a separate man, but a complete man, which is husband and wife) in our image, after our likeness; and it was so (Moses 2:26)."[4]

With the command to be one comes great blessings. Love, peace, joy, and communion with God are felt when husband and wife are united. President Joseph Smith stated, "Unity is power."[5] Unity in marriage is not optional. Elder Spencer J. Condie shared his conviction, "Unity—emotional and spiritual, as well as physical—is absolutely essential to a happy marriage, one in which the partners symbolically become one in all things."[6] Elder Condie also identified becoming one as a three-dimensional endeavor: physical, emotional, and spiritual.

A Vision of ONEness

The purpose of this chapter is to create a crystal-clear vision of complete oneness—including sexual oneness—which marriage can and should provide. The vision can provide power, potential, and divine purpose to your marriage. Vision is critical, for "where there is no vision, the people perish."[7] And where there *is* vision, marriages can thrive. Oneness might be thought of as two hearts with *one dream* or *vision* of where they want to go.

President Kimball helps us understand marital oneness, "There will come a great love and interdependence between you, for your love is a divine one. It is deep, inclusive, comprehensive. . . . The love of which the Lord speaks is not only physical attraction, but spiritual attraction [and emotional attraction] as well. It is faith and confidence in, and understanding of one another. It is a total partnership."[8] President Kimball identified many dimensions of love. He spoke of physical attraction, spiritual attraction, and he also identified many aspects of emotional attraction. These three dimensions create intimacy, love, and oneness in marriage.

Oneness defines the big picture, or vision of marriage, while intimacy defines the dimensions or specific forms of love that create oneness. Intimacy is defined as a close or confidential friendship; familiarity, fellowship, or closeness including sexual relations.[9] While the word *intimacy* is often thought of as sexual, that is only part of real and complete intimacy. Complete intimacy is sharing thoughts, feelings, and energies—both positive and negative—creating an emotional, spiritual, and physical connection. If we look closely at the word *intimacy* we can almost see the phrase, "in-to-me-see" suggesting that couples allow each other to see into their inner selves.

Three Dimensions of Intimacy

Elder Condie and President Kimball in the statements above identified the three dimensions of intimacy—physical, emotional, and spiritual. Alma 17:5 also identifies these dimensions of our being—body, mind, and spirit. The scriptures identify the spirit and the body as the soul of man.[10] The soul craves both physical intimacy (a function of the body) and emotional intimacy (a function of the mind). As three-dimensional beings, intimacy and oneness must also be three-dimensional[11] if we are to achieve a fulness of joy.

Three Dimensions of Intimacy

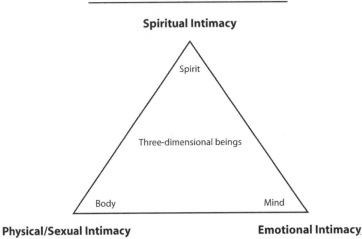

Emotional Intimacy. Emotional intimacy is a union of hearts. It is two hearts that are turned toward each other, longing to connect in meaningful ways. It is an open and honest sharing of thoughts, feelings, fears, and joys. Emotional intimacy represents acceptance, friendship, love, trust, and a feeling of warmth and connectedness. Connecting emotionally requires a willingness to be vulnerable and a profound sense of responsibility regarding each other's vulnerability.

Communication with compassion increases emotional intimacy exponentially. Listening, sharing, and discussing in such ways that both husband and wife feel heard, understood, and validated can make significant deposits into the marital emotional account. This sharing allows husband and wife to see and feel from the other's perspective. With the heart in the right place, you and your spouse can learn these critical communication skills, as taught in Chapter 10, and use them to bless your relationship.

Elaine's experience not only highlights the need for emotional intimacy, but also shows how applying these skills blessed her marriage. During a particularly dark and difficult time, date night was dedicated to a discussion of feelings and fears. Using valuable communication skills they had both learned, the heavy emotional burden Elaine felt was lifted week by week as she shared her struggles.

The closeness she and her husband created provided a light for her to look forward to each week. Through communication they created a lifeline for her to endure the darkness she felt. As her husband responded with understanding, empathy, and a desire to help, Elaine's heart filled with awe at the magnitude of the gift he had given her.

Emotional intimacy is a feeling of understanding and acceptance. To be known intimately and be accepted by another is a vulnerable, yet freeing, state of being. To share your innermost worries and weaknesses, and still be accepted by your spouse, can contribute enormously to emotional fulfillment and oneness.

Each dimension affects the others positively or negatively. The need to be loved, accepted, and understood drives the desire for emotional intimacy, and can be a powerful aphrodisiac, especially for women. Interestingly, these same needs in men often drive their desire for sexual intimacy. Feeling emotionally connected to your spouse provides warmth and security unmatched by any other earthly relationship, and can put light, love, and passion into your marriage. Being emotionally disconnected causes feelings of emptiness. Filling that void is necessary to avoid living disconnected, parallel lives.

Spiritual Intimacy. Spiritual intimacy is a union of spirits—connecting and sharing spiritual thoughts and feelings as husband and wife strive to come unto Christ. Because of the power of the Holy Spirit that can dwell within us and fill our hearts,[12] couples can enjoy spiritual intimacy and oneness with God by praying together, partaking of the sacrament weekly, repenting, renewing their covenants at the temple, or by fasting together for a common purpose. Spiritual intimacy strengthens marriages as couples invite the power of the Atonement into their lives.

Spiritual intimacy grows as husband and wife study the scriptures both together and individually, so that neither feels he or she is pulling all the weight spiritually or is being left behind. Couples can come to know God and His word more intimately as they read and discuss the scriptures, or lessons and principles taught at church meetings, then apply the teachings in their own lives. Spiritual intimacy can increase as couples consciously contribute to their spiritual knowledge and understanding.

Striving to become Christlike strengthens spiritual intimacy. Those who incorporate gospel teachings into their lives, striving to overcome imperfections and weaknesses, allow the gospel and God's personal tutoring to refine and purify their hearts. They rely on their spiritual reservoir as the refiner's fire of mortality cleanses their souls and converts them to God.

Spiritual intimacy is strengthened when husband and wife share similar spiritual goals. If husband and wife both strive to have an eye single to the glory of God, they will be filled with light.[13] These couples will desire to build the kingdom of God. They strive for eternal exaltation and long to return to their heavenly home. They show their love for God by attending the temple, not only to serve, but also to learn eternal truths and to be endowed with power that forms a spiritual core in their marriage.

Spiritual intimacy develops best when couples are equally yoked in the gospel. People are generally attracted to those they feel comfortable with and equal to. This equality facilitates similar marital growth. When couples are unequally yoked, spiritual intimacy can still grow, but it is hampered.

With an eye single to God, husband and wife can create Zion in their hearts and in their homes. The key is to shift the focus from spiritual "to do" lists and "going through the motions" to what they are becoming on the inside.

Couples striving for spiritual intimacy understand it is not so much what they *do* that matters, but what they *become*. Elder Dallin H. Oaks identified this critical element in his general conference talk, "The Challenge to Become." He stated:

> The Final Judgment is not just an evaluation of a sum total of good and evil acts—what we have done. It is an acknowledgment of the final effect of our acts and thoughts—what we have become. It is not enough for anyone just to go through the motions. The commandments, ordinances, and covenants of the gospel are not a list of deposits required to be made in some heavenly account. The gospel of Jesus Christ is a plan that shows us how to become what our Heavenly Father desires us to become.[14]

Spiritual intimacy is an essential component of complete oneness in marriage. Oneness might even be called "Zion." "The Lord called his people to ZION, because they were of one heart and one mind, and dwelt in righteousness."[15] With an eye single to God, husband and wife can create Zion in their hearts and in their homes. The key is to shift the focus from spiritual "to do" lists and "going through the motions" to what they are *becoming* on the inside. As Elder James E. Faust stated, "The basic program of the Church today is to strengthen the inner self."[16]

Physical Intimacy. Physical intimacy is a sharing or connecting of one's body. It includes not only sexual intimacy, but also touch and closeness, or nonsexual intimacy—commonly called affection. The physical energy or magnetism of two persons in physical contact with each other is a powerful force in marriage.

Both men and women need nonsexual intimacy (hugs, hand holding, hello and goodbye kisses) as well as sexual lovemaking. When couples understand the need for affection in marriage, it will not only be enjoyed for its own sake, but will do much to warm the heart for sexual encounters.

Sexual relations that serve both husband and wife represent the pinnacle of emotional and spiritual intimacy. Physical intimacy in marriage can be a transcendent experience—a consummation of the three dimensions of intimacy. Intimate relations not only unite husband and wife physically and emotionally but also draw them nearer to God as well.

With a firm conviction of the sanctity of sexual relations in marriage, we can accept the blending of physical intimacy with spiritual intimacy—including fun and pleasure. If this concept is difficult for you, re-read and ponder Chapter 2 to gain a firm conviction of the sanctity of sex as a commandment ordained of God. God has said, "All things unto me are spiritual, and not at any time have I given unto you a law which was temporal."[17]

We know from 1 Corinthians 6:16–17 that when we join our bodies together as husband and wife we also join our spirits with God. Elder Jeffrey R. Holland confirmed this concept when he said, "Physical intimacy is not only a symbolic union between a husband and a wife—the very uniting of their souls [body and spirit]—but it is also symbolic of a shared relationship between them and their Father in Heaven."[18] The symbolic nature of physical intimacy in marriage underscores its vast importance. In his book, *Becoming One: Emotionally, Spiritually, Sexually,* Christian author and speaker Joe Beam, stressed the significance of sexual relations in creating a sacred union within marriage:

> Sexual intimacy is important because an *essential* way that two humans become ONE is through the joining of their bodies. Since our bodies are part of who we are, and not just something we live in, the joining of two bodies in sexual intercourse is the joining of two beings. When we join our bodies in sexual union, we become, in essence, one person. . . .
>
> Not only do God-created body parts blend together perfectly in sexual intercourse to make one from two, but two people who lovingly and willingly join in this union become one in ways that transcend the physical.[19]

The first commandments given to Adam and Eve involved physical intimacy: "And God blessed them, and God said unto them, Be fruitful, and multiply, and replenish the earth;"[20] "Therefore shall a man leave his father and his mother, and shall cleave unto his wife: and they shall be one flesh."[21] Physical or sexual intimacy was commanded not only for procreation but also for them to become one and to bring about a fulness of joy.

A clear vision of the power and potential of oneness or complete intimacy—emotionally, spiritually, and physically—can become a personal vision for your marriage.

Take an inventory of your marriage. How "one" are you and your spouse in the areas of emotional, spiritual, and physical intimacy? Rate your marriage on a scale of 1 to 10 (1 being poor; 10 being excellent) in each of the three dimensions of intimacy. Invite your spouse to do the same. This exercise can help you see your areas of strength and the areas where you need to do some work. Recognize that no matter what the current state of your marriage is, intimacy can improve.

With such a lofty goal as complete intimacy and oneness, care must be taken to humbly and willingly strive to improve little by little to avoid feeling overwhelmed or discouraged. If, for example, you currently share spiritual intimacy at a level of six, work together to increase it to seven.

Characteristics of Marital ONEness

At times, I have caught glimpses of oneness in my own marriage. I hope you will catch glimpses in yours. The following examples, characteristic of couples striving for oneness, are idealistic and are meant only to define and inspire a day-to-day vision of marital oneness.

1. They are a unified team or partnership. These couples are united on all fronts. They cannot be divided and conquered. They work together. "Unity in marriage is an important foundation for rearing children successfully. If a husband and wife do not support each other, they greatly weaken their influence with their children."[22]

2. They are loyal and protective of each other. Couples that are striving to be unified stand up for one another. My three-year-old son was speaking disrespectfully to me one day when my husband came into the room. Wearing a grin, he said, "Don't you talk that way to Daddy's wife!" Later, wanting to show similar loyalty, when the kids were mauling their daddy, I said, "Hey you kids, be gentle with my husband!" Children learn quickly. When our little boys were playfully attacking me, our five-year-old daughter sternly stated, "You boys be gentle with Daddy's wife!"

The loyalty of a couple should extend outside the home. The husband or wife, striving to be one, does not betray confidences or belittle the other. One woman shared her frustration with attending a woman's group where it always seemed to spiral down into a husband-bashing session. She decided that as one half of a couple striving for unity, she would have no part of it.

3. They love each other the way each wants to be loved. Couples striving for oneness ask each other what makes them feel loved and then provide that love on a regular basis. They learn and speak each other's love language though it may require sacrifice and stretching. These couples don't mistakenly assume the other feels love the same way they do. They become experts at giving their spouse their special type of love. (See Chapter 10 for a discussion on learning to love in our spouse's love language.)

4. They are each other's greatest cheerleader and supporter. Unified couples are not only loyal to each other, but they praise and admire each other. They are each other's greatest supporter and most enthusiastic cheerleader. When the whole world seems to conspire against them, this couple can count on the love and support of each other, for they share each other's burdens and pray for each other.

5. They long to share and connect emotionally. Unified couples are each other's best friend. They share their lives. They make time, even schedule time for each other. They are not like roommates going about their individual days and individual lives, though they do have strong individual identities. They intersect. They share not only facts but feelings. They share not only joys but fears.

They look forward to daily phone calls, pillow talk and other moments to connect. Their first thought is of each other when they have news to share. Conversations revolve around more than money, children, and household responsibilities. They share and connect with their hearts.

6. They keep each other as their highest priority. Connected couples know that one day their children will be grown and it will be just the two of them. They nurture their most precious relationship daily, knowing they will continue into eternity as husband and wife. Careers, church callings, and children do not consume these couples. They understand that the most important unit is husband and wife and spend their time, effort and resources accordingly.

In D&C 42:22 we read, "Thou shalt love thy wife [husband] with all thy heart, and shalt cleave unto her [him] and none else." Referring to this scripture, President Kimball taught, "The words *none else* eliminate everyone and everything. The spouse then becomes preeminent in the life of the husband or wife, and neither social life nor occupational life nor political life nor any other interest nor person nor thing shall ever take precedence over the companion spouse."[23]

These couples rely on God to give personal guidance to help them know how to balance the many demands and responsibilities they have while still keeping first things first. Date night doesn't get ditched indiscriminately. Even when other demands temporarily dominate, these husbands and wives find ways to communicate their desire for each other.

7. They enjoy physical intimacy with each other. These couples understand that oneness is not only emotional and spiritual but physical as well. They enjoy and desire each other sexually, and find great pleasure and peace in pleasing each other. Physical intimacy to them is a time to reconnect, to renew and refresh the body, mind, and spirit.

8. They are committed to each other. Divorce is not an option. Small day-to-day grievances are resolved readily with repentance, forgiveness, humility, and kindness before they can escalate out of control. Physical, emotional, or spiritual crises and challenges may come their way, but these couples survive, by searching until they find solutions. They take a "united we stand" teamwork approach to their challenges. With the help of the Lord, they know they can make it through any crisis . . . somehow. They understand that part of the purpose of marriage is the stretching and sanctifying that occurs as they grow into oneness with each other and with God.

9. They are committed to God. They are equally yoked spiritually. They are both striving to come unto Christ and be perfected in him though neither is perfect. [24] They are working together on those things that matter most, and they are headed in the same direction. They set goals that move them closer to God and closer to their eternal exaltation.

Elder Holland and his wife, Patricia, come to mind as an example of unity and oneness in marriage. As a student, I fondly remember Elder Holland as president of Brigham Young University. I looked forward to their opening assemblies at the beginning of each semester, where they would stand together at the podium showing a bright example of what it meant to be a team. Their presentations were fondly referred to as the "Pat and Jeff" show.

Their tenderness and support of each other was apparent. His kindness and her courage were considerable. She wasn't thrilled with the prospect of public speaking, but she found the courage to support her husband in his position as president of BYU.

His tenderness toward her brings tears to my eyes, as I recall his loving encouragement and support of her. He was her greatest cheerleader. Though they exemplified oneness in many ways, they were not two halves creating a whole, but two wholes working towards divine oneness in marriage. Their son, Matt, confirmed my appraisal of them by this statement, "Mom and Dad are both very strong individuals. However, my mother gives her full, unreserved allegiance to my father's priesthood leadership, and my father constantly turns to my mother for counsel and insight."[25]

Our best example of oneness is God the Father and our Savior, Jesus Christ. They are one in purpose. They are of one heart and one mind.[26] But becoming one doesn't mean you become the same. You each have your own personality, your own interests and hobbies, your own strengths and weaknesses. Each of you is not the other *half* but the other *whole* in the relationship.

Oneness doesn't mean you lose something,
but that you become something so much more.

Oneness doesn't mean you lose something, but that you become something so much more. Consider this inspired poem by Kahlil Gibran that was recited by the temple sealer at a wedding I attended in the Seattle Washington LDS Temple:

ON MARRIAGE

You were born together, and together you shall be forevermore.
You shall be together when the white wings of death scatter your days.
Ay, you shall be together even in the silent memory of God.
But let there be spaces in your togetherness,
And let the winds of the heavens dance between you.
Love one another, but make not a bond of love:
Let it rather be a moving sea between the shores of your souls.
Fill each other's cup but drink not from one cup.
Give one another of your bread but eat not from the same loaf.
Sing and dance together and be joyous, but let each one of you be alone,
Even as the strings of the lute are alone though they quiver with the same music.
Give your hearts, but not into each other's keeping.
For only the hand of Life can contain your hearts.
And stand together yet not too near together:
For the pillars of the temple stand apart,
And the oak tree and the cypress grow not in each other's shadow.[27]

Husband and wife are each to be strong and sure individually. But united they stand even stronger. The synergistic power of marital oneness provides incredible potential in marriage. Where husband and wife have unity of feeling and purpose, the environment of the relationship allows them to learn and grow, aligning themselves with their divine spirit selves. Thus, they can fill the measure of their creation and fulfill their earthly missions.

Marriage Takes Three

God is the indispensable element in achieving this vision of oneness in our own marriage. God has the power to create ONEness in our marriages where we cannot do it alone. Elder Eyring taught that unity is possible *because* of the gospel of Jesus Christ and the influence of the Spirit. He said, "The gospel of Jesus Christ can allow hearts to be made one. . . . Through obedience to those ordinances and covenants, their natures would be changed. The Savior's Atonement . . . makes it possible for us to be sanctified. We can then live in unity, as we must to have peace in this life and to dwell with the Father and His Son in eternity."[28]

It is through coming unto Christ, living the gospel and applying
the Atonement in our lives that our hearts and our natures are changed.

It is through coming unto Christ, living the gospel and applying the Atonement in our lives that our hearts and our natures are changed. Atonement means "at-one-with." As we become one (or become whole) through Christ, we can become one with our spouse and God as He has commanded. The Savior helps us achieve wholeness and oneness through His Atonement, which can create miracles in marriage. With Christ we can give our best and He will give the rest—for marriage truly does take three:

MARRIAGE TAKES THREE

I once thought marriage took
Just two to make a go,
But now I am convinced
It takes the Lord also.
And not one marriage fails
Where Christ is asked to enter,
As lovers come together
With Jesus at the center.
But marriage seldom thrives
And homes are incomplete
Until He's welcomed there
To help avoid defeat.
In homes where Christ is first,

It's obvious to see,

Those unions really work,

For marriage still takes three.[29]

Oneness in marriage may be represented by the equation 1+1+1=1—husband, wife and God equal one.[30] In the diagram "Marriage Takes Three"[31] we see as husband and wife each draw nearer to God, they naturally draw nearer to each other until they become one at the point where they also become one with God.

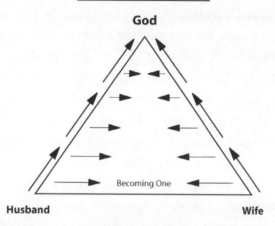

Marriage Takes Three

Complete oneness is God's vision for marriage. It is the ultimate purpose of marriage, for couples have been commanded to be one. Becoming one may not be easy, but it is worth it. Dr. Victor L. Brown, Jr. summed up the effort required with this statement:

> Complete trust and commitment are some of the roots of true intimacy. It is in a sustained, persistent effort in marriage that true intimacy of heart, mind, and body can be achieved, with all the problem-solvings and the complex inter-meshings which that implies. The fact that this is not easy, that it takes time, that it presupposes kindness, discipline, consideration, and a love based on commitment, are realities in the search for intimacy. The risks are inherent, but the rewards of success are tremendous.[32]

Complete oneness is what I imagine President Kimball had in mind when he made this inspiring statement, "Real lasting happiness is possible, and marriage can be more an exultant ecstasy than the human mind can conceive. This is within the reach of every couple, every person."[33] Oneness in marriage is a true principle, and it is possible.

Creating Your "Marriage Vision"

Having your own Marriage Vision provides a shining star to look up to of what your marriage can become. Once you have a vision of how you want your relationship to be it is easier to translate it into reality. For all things are created first in the mind. The mind is a powerful creator. When you put your mental energy and focus on something—positive or negative—it begins to emerge. Just as a focus on our spouse's weaknesses can magnify the weaknesses, so too can strengths be magnified. You are limited only by your ability to see and believe. Begin to see your spouse, as you want him to be, and believe that it can happen!

Borrowing an idea from Dr. Harville Hendrix, your assignment is to define a "Marriage Vision" for *your* marriage.[34] What does your ideal relationship with your spouse look like? List ten positive statements that describe the kind of marriage you want to have. If your spouse is willing, invite him or her to also list ten statements describing his / her ideal marriage vision. Here are some examples, "We are both working to be more like Christ"; "We both enjoy sexual intimacy in our relationship"; "We put each other first by scheduling regular pillow talk time and a weekly date night."

Once you have a vision of what is possible in marriage and can clearly see what you want, it is more likely you can create it. Remember there is magic in having big goals toward which you may strive. President Kimball quoted Daniel H. Burnham who said, "Make no little plans; they have no magic to stir men's [souls]."[35] With the help of the Lord, the grand vision and commandment of oneness in marriage is possible.

Chapter 8—"Home" Work

- *Identify How You're Doing.* Rate your marriage on a scale of 1 to 10 (1 being poor; 10 being excellent) in each of the three dimensions of intimacy—emotional, spiritual, and physical. Invite your spouse to do the same. What are your areas of strength? What areas need extra effort?

- *Create a Marriage Vision.* Begin to see your spouse, as you want him to be, and believe it can happen. List ten positive statements beginning with "We . . ." that describe the kind of marriage you want to have. Write these statements in the present tense. Invite your spouse to do the same. If you have both created vision statements, discuss them and combine them into one vision. Post your Marriage

Vision where you can both see it frequently and read it daily. Make a smaller copy to keep in your wallet or purse.

NOTES

Chapter 8—ONEness—The Ultimate Purpose of Marriage

[1] *See* Genesis 2:24.

[2] Eyring, "That We May Be One," *Ensign*, May 1998, 66.

[3] *See* 1 Nephi 3:7.

[4] Kimball, "Blessings and Responsibilities of Womanhood," *Ensign*, Mar. 1976, 70.

[5] Pinnock, "Blessings of Being Unified," *Ensign*, May 1987, 62.

[6] Condie, "Finding Marital Unity," *Ensign*, July 1986, 52.

[7] Proverbs 29:18.

[8] Kimball, "John and Mary," *New Era*, June 1975, 4.

[9] *Webster's Dictionary*, 288, 685.

[10] Doctrine & Covenants 88:15.

[11] *See* Beam, *Becoming One*, 41.

[12] *See* 1 Corinthians 3:16.

[13] *See* Doctrine & Covenants 88:67.

[14] Oaks, "The Challenge to Become," *Ensign*, Nov. 2000, 32.

[15] Moses 7:18.

[16] Faust, "Strengthening the Inner Self," *Ensign*, Feb. 2003, 3.

[17] Doctrine & Covenants 29:34.

[18] Holland, "Personal Purity," *Ensign*, Nov. 1998, 77.

[19] Beam, *Becoming One*, 32.

[20] Genesis 1:28.

[21] Genesis 2:24.

[22] *Family Home Evening Resource Book*, 239.

[23] Kimball, *Marriage and Family Relations*, 11–12.

[24] *See* Moroni 10:32.

[25] Grampa Bill's G.A. [General Authority] Pages, online.

[26] *See* Moses 7:18.

[27] Gibran, *The Prophet*, 15–16.

[28] Eyring, "That We May Be One," *Ensign*, May 1998, 66.

[29] Used by permission, Perry Tanksley, Dear Cards Company.

[30] *See Marriage and Family Relations*, 9.

[31] *See* Beam, *Becoming One*, 18.

[32] Brown, *Human Intimacy*, inside flap.

[33] Kimball, "Oneness in Marriage," *Ensign*, Oct. 2002, 40.

[34] Hendrix, *Getting The Love You Want*, 105.

[35] Kimball, "Gospel Vision of the Arts," *Ensign*, Jul. 1977, 3.

CHAPTER VIEW

The Need for Intimacy and ONEness

How Intimacy Is Created

- *Communication*
- *Time*
- *Action*
- *Heart*

Intimacy Diversions

- *Reprioritizing*
- *Removing*
- *Healing*

Intimacy Drains

Don't Settle for Less Than Complete Intimacy

Chapter 9—"Home" Work

Chapter 9

THE SEARCH FOR
INTIMACY AND ONENESS

Mark had worked late every night for the past few weeks, and had even more work to do when he got home. Uninterrupted quality time together had been nonexistent for weeks. Alisa missed their moments of togetherness where they could catch up with each other. Though she was busy all day caring for the children, she was beginning to feel disconnected, empty, and lonely. Family responsibilities plus his extra workload consumed their time.

One evening Mark popped his head into the room to say goodbye before dashing to a meeting. Alisa expressed how she was feeling. Though sympathetic, he had to rush to get to his meeting. When he returned he hugged Alisa, and she whispered, "I've missed you." The emptiness dissolved as they talked and touched—catching up on each other's lives.

The Need for Intimacy and ONEness

The very existence of mankind is rooted in the desire to be intimately connected and loved by another. This is the way God created mankind with a divine drive for companionship and connection.[1] Man was never meant to be a hermit. The desire for intimacy and oneness is a powerful force behind much of our thoughts and behavior. Dr. Victor L. Brown, in his book *Human Intimacy,* shared his belief, "[It is a] bedrock reality that at every stage of our life we seek intimacy as urgently as we seek food and drink. We seek our parents' love. We seek friendship. We seek emotional unity in marriage along with physical fulfillment."[2]

Our need for emotional, physical and spiritual intimacy compels us to fulfill God's command that man and woman "be one."[3] Marriage was divinely designed to drive us to seek companionship, closeness, and intimate connection to meet our needs for intimacy and love. We may not realize it, but this longing drives us to become one not only with our spouse, but also with God. President Harold B. Lee stated, "The divine impulse within every true man and woman that impels companionship with the opposite sex is intended by our Maker as a holy impulse for a holy purpose."[4]

It is the lack of intimacy that may be "the source of that restless, unhappy feeling that so many of us have come to live with."[5] At some point there comes an awakening, where weaknesses, cravings, or addictions demand our attention. We long for something more. We long to be better. We hunger to become whole and recover our divine self.

Marital difficulties and strivings for oneness between husband and wife have the holy purpose of awakening, stretching, and purifying the soul. Elder James E. Faust stated, "There is a divine purpose in the adversities we encounter every day. They prepare, they purge, they purify, and thus they bless."[6] The demands of intimate marital oneness invite struggles and soul-searching intended to "stir our divine potential . . . and satisfy basic human yearnings for intimacy, expression, and acceptance."[7]

When misguided, the yearning for companionship and intimacy can have devastating consequences leading into substitute fulfillment often followed by sin. The lack of intimacy in marriage can leave a hole in the heart that longs to be filled. Dr. Brown suggests that the weakened state of inner emptiness caused by incomplete intimacy creates fertile ground for Satan to deceive. He writes, "This universal human need is so powerful that we are vulnerable to deception. Loneliness brings a desperation that makes us willing to see almost anyone as desirable, almost any situation as endurable, *if* it holds out the promise of intimacy."[8]

When we do not have true and complete intimacy in marriage, inappropriate involvements, diversions, and distractions keep us from the exquisite potential of oneness in marriage. In his years of counseling as a Christian minister, Joe Beam encountered many heartbreaking occurrences of the longing for love and intimacy run amok. The following is one of the examples he shared.

Sam was a churchgoing, pillar-in-the-community businessman and father. He had been married for twenty years, but over time his relationship with his wife had drifted until they were living separate lives. Strip bars were not a part of his lifestyle, but on a particular night when he was feeling very empty and alone he walked into a world that had never existed for him before. He was looking for something; he just wasn't sure what it was.

After an eventful night and a drinking binge, he found himself at an all-night cafe with a stripper half his age. They talked of hopes and dreams and fears. In his empty state, he felt they had hit it off at some deeper level. He felt understood and longed for what he now felt. Within a week he had left his home and moved in with this young erotic dancer.

It wasn't long before he was filled with guilt, and awakened to the realization that he couldn't stand to spend another night with his new "soul mate." He surprised himself to realize he missed his wife. This broken man with shoulders down and head hung low found himself standing before Joe Beam, hoping he could somehow fix what he had done.

After the grief-stricken man recounted these events, there was a long pause. Joe Beam knew what was coming next, because he had heard it so many times before. He not only anticipated the question, but he knew the answer:

> "Why?" he begged. "Why would I do a thing like that? It's so foreign to everything that I believe, everything that I am. Can you tell me why I'm doing what I'm doing?"
>
> I paused just for a moment as an involuntary sigh escaped, then replied gently, "Sam, more of us have struggled with that question than you can ever know. I think I know exactly what is driving you—the same thing that drives so many people to misguided actions. It's the search for *intimacy*.
>
> "You crave a warm, intimate, close relationship with another human being, and

you were trying desperately to find something, someone, who promised to give it to you. Even though you didn't know what to call it, you knew that you wanted someone to share your very self with—your hopes, your dreams, your fears. That's what you thought you'd found in your stripper.

"But somehow, you've managed to discover what so many haven't yet figured out: *Sex and intimacy aren't the same thing.* That's why you told the stripper to leave. You longed for intimacy, but all you got was sex. . . . "

He interrupted my soliloquy by beginning to cry. Not the gentle, quiet weeping of tender moments. No, it was the bitter, angry expression of grief that accompanies a crushing discovery.[9]

It is not only men who can slip into serious sin. Women, too, become vulnerable when their intimacy needs are unmet, and the appearance of fulfillment is enticing them elsewhere. Not all misguided attempts to fill one's emptiness lead to serious sin. Some people may simply reach for a piece of pie, work a little later on an important project at work or fill their lives with "busyness" to avoid the pain of loneliness and emptiness. The lack of love and complete intimacy can also be a factor in depression or suicide. The realization that emptiness is an instigator of counterfeit intimacy, depression or sin has profound implications for the longings in our lives.

The realization that a lack of intimacy can cause increased vulnerability to temptation is a heavy burden, especially for those who struggle with intimacy in marriage. Fears and frustrations are compounded when couples don't know what to do about it.

A marriage where needs are met is within the reach of every couple. "No matter what your marriage is like right now, no matter how you feel about your spouse today . . . new feelings of love and intimacy [can grow] where none exist or enrich the loving relationship you may already have."[10] Joe Beam continued by expressing his universal confidence in the ability of couples to create the marriage of their dreams, "Our experience with thousands of couples makes us extremely confident of this: With God's help you can make your marriage all it should be and all you crave it to be—no matter what it's like now."[11]

As couples come together to fill each other's individual intimacy needs, empty hearts can heal. Marital vulnerabilities of all kinds can be removed. Marriages can come alive and thrive. President Boyd K. Packer promised, "In marriage all of the worthy yearnings of the human soul, all that is physical and emotional and spiritual, can be fulfilled."[12]

How Intimacy Is Created

While couples long to have intimacy in their marriages, they don't always know how to go about creating it. It may be helpful to understand specifically how intimacy is created. Though I will share some of his highlights, I highly recommend the book *Becoming One: Emotionally, Spiritually, Sexually* by Joe Beam, Christian author, speaker and founder of the *Family Dynamics Institute*. This book provides an excellent understanding of marital intimacy and its three dimensions. From his book we find a simple analogy for creating intimacy:

> Intimacy is like electricity in that it is produced by indirect means. It is a by-product of other elements. Send enough water with enough pressure through turbines, and you get electricity. In a similar way, if you combine enough of the right *elements* with the right *intensity,* you get intimacy. Unfortunately the opposite is also true: Divert the river and electricity stops. Similarly if the elements that create intimacy for one's spouse are diverted to something or someone else, the process of developing intimacy with the spouse will come to a halt.[13]

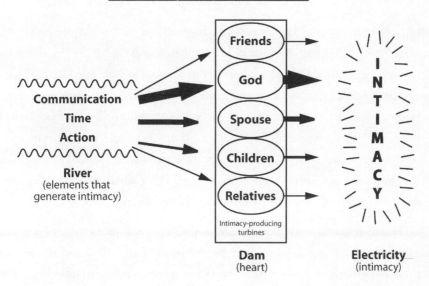

The Correct Flow of Intimacy

From the diagram above we can see that the critical elements of intimacy are communication, time, and action.[14] The state of the heart provides the environment and affects how well intimacy can be created. Let's define each one:

Communication. Communication is needed to share facts and feelings. Like a window into another's soul, communication allows couples to come to intimately know each other—their likes, dislikes, thoughts, dreams, and fears. Communicating allows couples to see and understand each other emotionally, spiritually, and sexually. Both verbal and nonverbal communication play an important role in building intimacy. "For intimacy to grow, two people have to know each other on more than a superficial level. Communication that develops intimacy isn't just sharing ideas or thoughts but interacting on a deeper level. Communication is a verbal (and sometimes written) intercourse, a sharing of your life—what you've done, what you're doing, and how you feel."[15]

Time. To communicate and create intimacy requires time. One of the ways we show love is by making time for each other. Think about the number of hours in a week you spend together as a couple. This might include daily phone calls, pillow talk, and dates. Most things of value take time. Intimacy is built by spending time together. "We tend to develop the greatest levels of intimacy with those people with whom we spend time—quality time in generous quantities. It takes time to communicate on intimate levels. It takes time to fulfill the sexual and emotional needs of another person."[16]

Action. Love is an action. "Let us not love in word, neither in tongue only; but in deed and in truth."[17] Actions often speak louder than words. What do you do to show your love for your spouse? Do those behaviors make your spouse feel loved? We must be sure we do specific behaviors that our spouse wants and needs—not just what we think they want or what we want to give—in order for him or her to feel loved. Joe Beam stated, "While sharing leads to the opening of one's heart so that intimacy can grow, it is the intentional effort to fulfill a person's sexual and emotional [and spiritual] needs that gives intimacy solid roots in that heart. Only when a person *acts* can we know what he or she really is and whether he or she speaks truthfully."[18]

Heart. Though communication, time, and action are essential elements for creating intimacy, there's something missing. It is our hearts. The openness and intent of the heart creates the environment in which the elements of intimacy function. One man attending a course on strengthening marriage identified the need for this fourth element by suggesting that a couple can communicate, make time for each other, and even serve each other and still have a "parallel marriage." Parallel marriage can be defined as a couple sharing a home, but not their hearts.

*Communication, time, and action are
essential elements for creating intimacy.*

At the time of his comment, I didn't fully appreciate the truth he had shared. But as I pondered how intimacy is created, I realized his observation was insightful. If the heart is not in it, the feeling that accompanies our communication, time, and actions will be hollow. Intimacy cannot grow there. Not only does our heart need to be open and softened for intimacy to grow, there must be something there to give.

An empty heart is like an empty bucket that has developed holes from excessive giving, unrelenting stresses, long-term unmet needs or past emotional hurts. We may try to fill our bucket, but until the holes are repaired and the bucket is refilled, we may find it difficult to love from the heart. Instead, we go through the motions, keep up appearances and "do"—simply out of duty.

Husband and wife each enter marriage with varying capacities to love and vary-ing needs for love. If either or both husband and wife become empty, action must be taken to restore wholeness. Many can benefit from professional counselors who can help them repair the holes in their heart and teach them how to restore their inner self to wholeness. Elder Marlin K. Jensen described the need for personal reserves of the heart when he said, "The greater our own personal substance is and the deeper our own mental, emotional, and spiritual reserves are, the greater will be our capacity to nurture and love others, especially our companion."[19]

The Lord wants hearts to be healed and whole. He wants us to be able to love our spouses and give from an abundance of the heart. He has promised He can make us one by *changing* the empty heart and *healing* the heart of stone, "And I will give [you] one heart, and I will put a new spirit within you; and I will take the stony heart out of [your] flesh, and will give [you] an heart of flesh."[20]

With so many demands on our time and energy, it is the state of our heart that will determine our priorities. The "Correct Flow of Intimacy" diagram, above, identifies the correct priorities for our relationships. God comes first; spouse is second; children are third; and friends and relatives are fourth. Putting God first is not synonymous with putting a church calling first, though it can be. Spiritual discretion is required.

Understanding how the elements of intimacy—communication, time, and action—function and are affected by the heart (or environment)—are important as we discuss becoming one emotionally, spiritually, and physically in the following chapters. But before we can build emotional, spiritual, and physical oneness, we must look at the barriers to intimacy and remove them, so that intimacy can flow freely. Barriers to intimacy can be described as diversions or drains. As we discuss these barriers we will see how the state of our heart affects the degree of dominance intimacy diversions and drains have over us.

The Diverted Flow of Intimacy

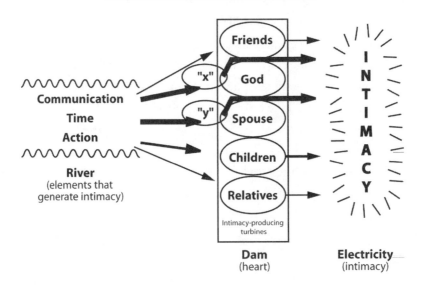

Intimacy Diversions

In the above diagram we see how communication, time, action, and the heart in the right place can create intimacy when they flow freely to our spouse.[21] When something else gets in front of our spouse, consuming our time, communication and actions, intimacy is diverted. Diversions might also be referred to as "self-medicating behaviors," "coping strategies," "self-defeating behaviors," "addictions," or "exits" (ways we "check out" or "shut down"). Diversions deflect our time, energy, and attention away from creating greater emotional, physical, and spiritual intimacy with our spouse. We create diversions to soothe, compensate, avoid, or deaden our pain or fear that our intimacy needs won't be met.

Diversions can create a vicious cycle that sabotages us from getting the very intimacy and oneness we crave and need in order to heal and be whole. They are generally one of three things: (1) a thing—like money, a hobby, or the television; (2) a person—like our boss, over-attention to our children, or an extramarital affair; and (3) an unfulfilled emotional need—usually for something intangible like love, understanding, acceptance, or belonging.[22] Unfulfilled emotional needs are often the underlying motivation for the first two types of diversions.

The diversion behavior itself may not necessarily be bad, but too often good things crowd out the essential. Elder Richard G. Scott said, "All too often the wrong things take highest priority. . . . Satan has a powerful tool to use against good people. It is distraction. He would have good people fill life with 'good things' so there is no room for the essential ones."[23]

Though a diversion can be almost anything that has gotten out of balance, or is given too high a priority, some examples of common diversions may be helpful to identify those you might be using to *avoid* intimacy or to *compensate* for the lack of it:

- Alcohol use
- Anger
- Blaming
- Busyness
- Criticizing
- Drug abuse
- Eating disorders— anorexia, bulimia
- Excessive exercise, reading, sleeping, or television
- Excessive involvement with sports—watching football, playing golf, etc.
- Extramarital affairs
- Gossiping
- Hobbies—fishing, scrapbooking, gardening
- Nagging
- Overeating
- Overspending
- Over-attention to children
- Perfectionism
- Pornography
- Procrastination
- Religiosity or self-righteousness
- Sexual abuse
- Working too much

In the diagram "The Diverted Flow of Intimacy" we see that "x" and "y" are getting in the way of the flow of the elements of intimacy. What are the "x" and "y" in your life? What do you do to distance yourself? What do you do to avoid intimacy or to compensate for the lack of it? What does your spouse do to avoid connecting with you?

You may already know in your heart what is diverting your attention away from your spouse. Maybe your diversion is the computer and the Internet. Maybe it's an ailing parent. Maybe it's sports or scrapbooking. Maybe it's exercise or food. Let's say "x" and "y" in your life are a church calling and your children. They are both good things and important, but if they are consuming all your time, communication, and effort—keeping you from creating intimacy and oneness with your spouse—then they are out of balance and have become intimacy diversions.

Another common diversion is using food to self-medicate. Chocolate can solve anything, right? A feeling of uneasiness, anxiety, or sadness may come up. Instead of identifying what the feelings are really about we head for the fridge or grab the nearest bag of M&Ms. Keeping a notebook handy can help us stop and begin to identify the unconscious processes. We can ask ourselves what's going on inside, and write until we uncover it.

We can learn to ask for and get what we need, instead of diverting the true need to a substitute or counterfeit. While we may experience a temporary "high" from food or other self-medicating behaviors, there is usually a downside, and it never really satisfies.

While couples often focus on the surface issues or symptoms, such as overspending or a pornography addiction, a more effective approach is to look to the root of the problem. Diversions are often manifestations of deeper hurts needing healing, rather than mere "behaviors" needing to be changed, managed, or controlled.

Professional therapist Dr. Harville Hendrix, shared his frustration with surface-oriented approaches to solving marital problems. As a new therapist his initial approach was to help couples negotiate a contract to reduce their negative behaviors. This was standard problem-oriented, contractual marriage counseling. While couples better learned about each other and developed improved communication skills, few seemed able to overcome their struggles. Instead of arguing about the initial problem that brought them into therapy, they were now arguing about who had violated their behavioral contracts first.[24]

It was several years before Dr. Hendrix discovered that in order to be effective, surface issues such as money problems, role expectations, or sexual problems should not be the focus. Underneath these problems were unresolved needs often stemming from childhood. Communication skills and behavioral contracts were not going to address these deeper issues. Fundamental causes had to be examined. With this knowledge, he began to work with couples more intensively, and more effectively—searching beneath surface problems for foundational issues.[25]

Intimacy diversions can be eliminated by (1) reprioritizing, (2) removing them, or (3) through inner healing.

Reprioritizing has us put first things first—making God and spouse our highest priorities. This assures they will receive priority time and attention rather than letting lesser important endeavors consume our resources. President Ezra Taft Benson said, "When we put God first, all other things fall into their proper place or drop out of our lives. Our love of the Lord will govern the claims for our affection, the demands on our time, the interests we pursue, and the order of our priorities."[26]

Removing. Sometimes intimacy diversions must be removed all together. We may believe we can continue as PTA president, or keep a questionable relationship going and still build intimacy with our spouse, but we are only kidding ourselves. Removing the diversion may be the one thing we yet lack in attaining the sweet intimate relationship we are meant to have in our marriage.

In the parable of the rich young man, he wanted to know what he yet lacked in devotion to God.[27] Joe Beam compared this parable to intimacy diversions in marriage. He stated:

> Some diversions cannot be repaired by *reprioritization;* they must be *removed* altogether. That's apparently why Jesus told the young man that he had to give all his wealth away. To keep it and pretend to love God wouldn't do. Sometimes that's how it is in our marriages too. Sometimes it's impossible to funnel *any* of our energy into a diversion and still have the intimacy God wants us to have with our spouses.
>
> Make sure you don't fool yourself into thinking reprioritization is all you need if the real solution lies only in removal.[28]

Healing. The first two types of diversions: a thing (such as a hobby), or a person (such as a friend) can be given adjusted priority or can be expelled from your life. The third type of diversion, unmet emotional needs, must be satisfied and healed. Healing underlying emotional emptiness, such as a lack of self-love or acceptance, or healing other psychological wounds is often required before intimacy diversions can be rendered impotent.

Emptiness and emotional scars often manifest themselves as selfishness, indicating a need for healing of the heart. Selfishness occurs when one doesn't trust that their deepest needs will be met. Without awareness, they determine that they must meet their own needs as if in self-survival mode. They are simply doing whatever they can to try to satisfy their emotional, spiritual, and physical needs. Like a homeless child who steals to feed himself, we too commit behaviors that seem selfish or sinful on the surface, but are simply symptoms of emptiness.

The more empty one is, the more ingrained, extreme, immoral, or dangerous the diversion or self-medicating behavior can be. Diversions can become addictions weakening one's ability to choose wisely and wreaking havoc in their personal lives. President Packer stated, "Addiction has the capacity to disconnect the human will and nullify moral agency. It can rob one of the power to decide."[29]

President Kimball identified selfishness as the all-encompassing cause of marital problems and divorce. He stated, "Every divorce is the result of selfishness on the part of one or the other or both parties."[30] This is true. But with new understanding, we can see selfish or sinful behaviors in ourselves and others as symptoms of deeper hurts. This is how the Savior saw sin. "Jesus saw sin as wrong but also was able to see sin as springing from deep and unmet needs on the part of the sinner."[31]

President Kimball encouraged deeper exploration into the heart to better understand shortcomings. He said, "We need to be able to look deep enough into the lives of others [and ourselves] to see the basic causes for their failures and shortcomings."[32] This new perspective allows us to have empathy for those who "sin differently" than we do, and moves us toward healing and wholeness as we better address each other's real intimacy needs.

We *are* accountable for our actions, and have a responsibility to do what is needed to stop our negative behaviors. However, people can change more easily in an environment of compassion than in one of criticism and condemnation. We can be more like the Savior who looked with compassion upon personal weakness. He "healeth the broken in heart, and bindeth up their wounds."[33] We can revolutionize the way we see intimacy diversions in ourselves, our spouses and others by seeing selfishness in this new more compassionate light. The next time you are tempted to label your spouse as selfish, consider the possibility of emotional emptiness instead.

Pray for help to know what's hindering intimacy in your marriage and what you can do about it. God will help you identify and overcome what is keeping you from complete oneness with your spouse, for "God knoweth your hearts."[34]

Intimacy Drains

In addition to intimacy diversions, our conduct can also be described as intimacy drains.[35] Intimacy drains are any behaviors you do *or fail to do* that cause your spouse to lose positive feelings of love and affection toward you. Joe Beam described the difference between diversions and drains:

> Diversions keep a person's communication, time, and action from being *directed* to the right "turbine" in his or her heart. Drains work differently. They keep the intimacy generated by the "turbine" from being *felt* by the person it's intended for. This occurs when a person does the right things but those right actions are negated by wrong actions. . . .
>
> For example, if a husband spends great quantities of time communicating with his wife in an open and meaningful way but also shames her in public by ridiculing her or explodes in tantrums toward her, he negates all his positive efforts by his negative behavior. The negative behavior in a sense "drains" the effect of intimacy-producing elements.[36]

Intimacy Drains

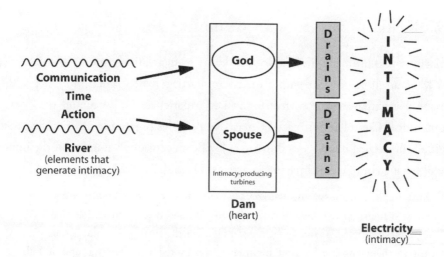

I love what Elder Henry B. Eyring said about showing love, "What matters in what the giver does is what the receiver feels."[37] One way of removing intimacy drains from your marriage is to learn your spouse's "Love Language" and do those specific things that make him or her feel loved. It is a powerful tool that we will discuss in Chapter 10.

A particular behavior could be an intimacy diversion, or it could be a drain—depending on the situation. For example, busyness could be a *diversion* or a way to avoid intimacy by always being preoccupied instead of spending time with your spouse. Busyness could also be a *drain* if it makes your husband feel unimportant or as if he is a low priority in your life. Other examples of drains that soak up positive feelings are forgetting birthdays and anniversaries, harboring anger or bitterness toward your spouse, or self-righteousness that can sour attempts at loving behavior.

To make the concept of diversions and drains real in your life, list two or three behaviors that keep you from giving your time, communication, action, and your heart to your spouse. Ask your spouse to make his own list of his diversions and drains. If you can, share your lists with each other. If you want your spouse to be honest, do not get defensive or angry. Honesty is critical for creating intimacy. If you cannot safely or calmly share your intimacy diversions and drains, wait until you learn the communication skills in Chapter 10 to provide a safer environment for open and honest discussion. If you can go further, ask your spouse what diversions and drains *he* sees in you. This can be invaluable insight if you are able to receive it.

Don't Settle for Less Than Complete Intimacy

Marriages where intimacy diversions and drains seem relatively mild are still at risk. Don't let yourself be content with a mediocre marriage when much more is possible. Marriage doesn't have to be perfect for you to experience the peace and the oneness God intended. Complete intimacy in marriage provides protection against the potential pitfalls of parallel marriage and divorce. Joe Beam cautioned couples on the importance of having complete intimacy in marriage. He said:

> Don't think that everything will be okay and that you should just accept and endure a marriage without intimacy. Incomplete marriages—marriages that have not achieved ONEness—may seem acceptable on the surface, but the people who exist in them continually find themselves confronted with temptations or failings that wouldn't exist—or at least wouldn't have the same level of power—if ONEness existed in their marriages. Their susceptibilities to these pitfalls aren't because of some inward evil or lack of moral fiber, though they may end up committing moral evil. Their struggles with sexual temptations or unacceptable emotional involvements or excessive striving for success, fame, and recognition or a host of other character weaknesses come as an indirect result of their unfulfilled need for complete intimacy.[38]

Husbands' and wives' needs for intimacy must be filled. Complete intimacy is a key to peace and joy. Joe Beam concluded:

> *Intimacy* is the key. We seek it from the moment we are conscious that we are alive and continue until the moment we have our last conscious thought on this planet. Only when we live in an intimate relationship with another person *and* an intimate relationship with God do we have the very treasure we live our lives to find.
>
> God made us that way.[39]

Couples must commit to themselves, their spouse and to God to open the floodgates for intimacy to flow. This can be done by reprioritizing, removing or healing intimacy barriers in marriage. With God's help couples can determine what they individually need to do to begin to create more complete intimacy and oneness with each other.

Marriage is a vulnerable venture. It requires faith. When we have a testimony of God's command for husband and wife to "be one"—emotionally, physically and spiritually—then we can exert the necessary effort and make the crucial changes in our lives to experience God's divine design of marriage. With the following words, Dr. Brown encouraged couples to strive for complete intimacy and oneness, "Intimacy is one of the highest ideals of the human heart and, as such, deserves the most exceptional efforts."[40] Unlike any other relationship, marriage can provide the most wonderful and exquisite human experience where true happiness, wholeness, and oneness are possible.

As couples learn to love and fulfill each other's intimacy needs, their own capacity to give and receive love grows. Hearts and relationships can be healed, as couples reach inside themselves to the spirit divine within. With a sacred stewardship for each other, couples can follow the Savior's example to be each other's keeper, to "learn the healer's art" and to "show a gentle heart" to one another who are wounded and weary.[41] In marriage, husbands and wives can begin the cycle of loving and healing each other into wholeness. It is in our search for intimacy and oneness in marriage that we become whole and become one—fulfilling all the longings of the heart and soul.

It is in our search for intimacy and oneness in marriage that we become whole and become one—fulfilling all the longings of the heart and soul.

❧

Chapter 9—"Home" Work

- Pray to identify your intimacy diversions and drains. Ask God to help you remove them, heal them, or help get you past them.

- List two or three behaviors that keep you from giving your time, communication, action, and your heart to your spouse. What are you doing to avoid intimacy or closeness with your spouse? What are you doing to compensate for intimacy that is lacking? What are you doing that is negating your positive attempts to show love toward your spouse?

- If your spouse is willing, ask them to make their own list of diversions and drains. If you can, share your lists with each other. If you can go even further, ask your spouse what diversions and drains they see in you.

NOTES

Chapter 9—The Search for Intimacy and ONEness

[1] *See* Genesis 2:18.

[2] Brown, *Human Intimacy,* xiv.

[3] *See* John 17:21.

[4] Lee, *Teachings of Presidents,* 112.

[5] Beam, *Becoming One,* 2.

[6] Faust, "Refiner's Fire," *Ensign,* May 1979, 59.

[7] Brinley, *Toward a Celestial Marriage,* 109.

[8] Brown, *Human Intimacy,* xiv.

[9] Beam, *Becoming One,* 8–10.

[10] Beam, *Becoming One,* 2.

[11] Beam, *Becoming One,* 24.

[12] Packer, "Marriage," *Ensign,* May 1981, 15.

[13] Beam, *Becoming One,* 55.

[14] *See* Beam, *Becoming One,* 57.

[15] Beam, *Becoming One,* 56.

[16] Beam, *Becoming One,* 56.

[17] 1 John 3:18, JST.

[18] Beam, *Becoming One,* 56.

[19] Jensen, "Union of Love," *Ensign,* Oct. 1994, 48.

[20] Ezekiel 11:19.

[21] *See* Beam, *Becoming One,* 59.

[22] *See* Beam, *Becoming One,* 63.

[23] Scott, "First Things First," *Ensign,* May 2001, 7.

[24] *See* Hendrix, *Getting the Love You Want,* 103.

[25] *See* Hendrix, *Getting the Love You Want,* 104.

[26]Benson, "The Great Commandment," *Ensign*, May 1988, 4.

[27]*See* Mark 10:21–24.

[28]Beam, *Becoming One,* 68.

[29]Packer, "Revelation in a Changing World," *Ensign*, Nov. 1989, 14.

[30]Kimball, *Marriage and Divorce*, 19.

[31]Kimball, "Jesus: The Perfect Leader," *Ensign*, Aug. 1979, 5.

[32]Kimball, "Jesus: The Perfect Leader," *Ensign*, Aug. 1979, 5.

[33]Psalms 147:3.

[34]Luke 16:15.

[35]*See* Beam, *Becoming One,* 69.

[36]Beam, *Becoming One,* 68.

[37]Eyring, *Gifts of Love*, 3.

[38]Beam, *Becoming One,* 21–22.

[39]Beam, *Becoming One* 11.

[40]Brown, *Human Intimacy*, 1.

[41]*See Hymns,* 220.

CHAPTER VIEW

Becoming One Emotionally

Knowing, Loving, and Accepting Your Self

Forgiving and Accepting Your Spouse

Nurturing Love and Friendship in Marriage
1. *Asking for What You Want and Need*
2. *Learning to Love in the Right Love Language*
3. *Continuing Courtship—Date Night*
4. *Communicating—Sharing Facts and Feelings*
5. *Using Communication Skills—Learning and Using the Couples Dialogue*
6. *Creating Marriage Traditions*

Chapter 10—"Home" Work

Chapter 10

BECOMING ONE—EMOTIONAL INTIMACY

Conversation warmed Ann's heart. She found herself feeling drawn to Gary physically when they talked, listened, and shared feelings. She was amazed that connecting emotionally stirred sexual desire within her.

Jenny was turned off by the emotional intimacy her husband offered because it seemed to have strings attached. Her husband only spent time talking and listening to her, or helping with the children and household responsibilities, when he wanted something in return—sex. To her, he was not listening out of a genuine love and concern for her, but from a desire to do what he thought was needed to get what he wanted. Emotional intimacy became a turn off for her.

Becoming One Emotionally

Becoming one emotionally represents having a relationship of profound trust, feeling wholly accepted, respected, and admired in the eyes of your spouse. It is a mutual sharing of each other's innermost selves—a disclosure of the heart and soul. Emotional intimacy requires faith in each other, as couples openly, honestly, and vulnerably reveal their truest self. Where there's emotional intimacy, there's a feeling of coming home. Emotional intimacy is closeness, warmth, and connectedness. Becoming one emotionally requires communication, time, effort, and having one's heart in the right place.

We crave emotional intimacy, yet often avoid it for fear of being rejected, ridiculed, or judged. Opening the door to emotional oneness requires learning to know, love, and accept ourselves so that we can willingly offer our authentic self without reservation or fear. In order for our spouse to do the same, we must also learn to forgive them regularly and accept them unconditionally. Acceptance frees the self and spouse to grow toward their divinity and to love from an abundance of the heart, paving the way for greater intimacy, as love and friendship in marriage is nurtured.

Knowing, Loving, and Accepting Yourself

God's second commandment requires us to love our neighbors (our spouse) *as ourselves.*[1] (1) To love oneself requires us to know and accept who we are; (2) As we come to know and accept who we are, we become one or whole within ourselves; (3) It is then we can become *one* with another person. Elder D. Todd Christofferson described the need for personal, inner oneness when he said, "Becoming at one within ourselves prepares us for the greater blessing of becoming one with [our spouse,] God and Christ."[2]

Loving and accepting ourselves is an important step in being able to love our spouse and become one with them. Loving and accepting ourselves frees us mentally and emotionally to make necessary changes in our lives. Our capacity to love is related to our personal well-being—our mental, emotional, and spiritual reserves or the "wholeness" of our heart. We can increase our ability and capacity to love by increasing love and acceptance for ourselves. If we do not develop sufficient love for ourselves, our life focus is on *getting* love instead of *giving* love. Christian author and speaker, Joe Beam, stated:

> Love yourself if you want to learn to love others. If you don't love yourself as [God] wants you to, the need for that self-love will become the diversion that interferes with intimacy with others. Your desire for love will loom so large it will overpower any effort you make to give love.
>
> But how do we put this self-acceptance into practice? We do it by accepting the truth about ourselves.[3]

To accept the truth about ourselves requires accepting that we make mistakes, and that it's okay. It requires that we acknowledge and accept our weaknesses and imperfections, knowing we are still loved and valuable. If we can't be honest and real with ourselves, it will be difficult to form any kind of honest, emotional connection with others.

Most importantly, we must accept—not just in our head, but in our heart—that we are children of a Heavenly Father who loves us. We can sing the song, "I Am A Child of God"[4] until we are blue in the face, but if we don't really believe it, then it will have no power in our lives. God loves us as we are. We don't have to DO anything to be loved. We just are!

Because of how we may have been scolded, punished, or rejected in the past, we may be conditioned to believe we are not as loveable when we make mistakes. We have learned to hide, shut down, or hate the "unaccepted" parts of ourselves in order to receive love. In our strivings for perfection we forget to have patience with ourselves and accept where we are in our progression. Heavenly Father sees our hearts. He loves us each unconditionally and looks for opportunities to love, not condemn. Through Jesus Christ He extends the power of the Atonement to purify us with His love, acceptance, and mercy.

In a world of images and appearances, we often fall prey to putting on a happy face when we don't want anyone to see our "real" self. When that becomes the norm, over time we forget who our "real" self is. To become whole again we must learn to love and accept all parts of ourselves—the positives and negatives. We must be ready and willing to honestly examine our hearts—looking into the deepest and darkest corners—to grant acceptance to the sides of ourselves we feel the need to hide. To do this is no simple task. It is an archaeological dig and excavation of the soul.

As we accept that it's okay to be imperfect, to make mistakes, to have weaknesses and failings, then we can let our real selves into the light. Judgment from others becomes less threatening. In an honest environment our authentic self is free to be.

As we come to know, accept, and be honest with ourselves, we provide safety and the opportunity for others to do the same. Honest self-acceptance can help heal the holes in our hearts and free us to give greater love.

It's hard to love yourself if you don't know who you really are. Begin to get to know who you are on the inside and what you think and feel. The following are some helpful guides to begin this exploration:

- Engage in open and honest, written conversations with yourself. Keep a notebook handy and record your thoughts and feelings regularly. This writing is not for posterity, but for you to learn about yourself. Free-flowing writing can be very therapeutic and instructive about your inner self.

- Write with your nondominant hand to provide more direct access to your inner self.

- Spend time in prayer and solitude. Breathe deeply to relax the body and mind.

- Do the exercises throughout this book to help you discover your positive and negative beliefs.

- Engage in the Couples Dialogue communication process that will be taught in this chapter. This can also help you learn more about yourself through the "mirror" your spouse provides.

More specifically, to awaken to and accept the realities of the self, list at least five things you dislike about yourself. For each item, say aloud, *"I deeply and completely love and accept myself even though I . . . ."* You must also accept your God-given gifts, talents and strengths. Make a list of all the things you like about yourself. For each item say aloud, *"I deeply and completely love and accept myself because I . . . "* The repetition of this statement for each positive thought is a gift of love and acceptance to the self.-Continue to do these two exercises until you begin to see and feel the divine being that you are.

Pray for God to help you feel His unconditional love and acceptance, and free you to discover the divine within. He will help you feel the same unconditional love for yourself He already feels for you. Comparisons to "Patty Perfect" and "Molly Mormon" will diminish as we choose substance over appearance, honesty over hypocrisy. As hearts begin to heal of hidden holes and emptiness through self-acceptance we can then give greater warmth, genuine love, and acceptance to our spouse and others.

Forgiving and Accepting Your Spouse

Couples make mistakes every day. Both husband and wife need each other's forgiveness on a regular basis to keep the gates of love open. Forgiveness is not so much a personal gift to your spouse as a willingness to turn the offense over to God. Forgiveness is a gift of acceptance that acknowledges weaknesses and imperfections in our spouse while exhibiting faith in the divinity within him. The need for forgiveness and acceptance in marriage is great.

Forgiveness is not so much a personal gift to your spouse
as a willingness to turn the offense over to God.

One of the keys to building emotional intimacy is for couples to be able to open their hearts to each other—freely and honestly sharing facts *and* feelings. If either spouse feels unaccepted, unforgiven for past mistakes, or believes they will be rejected or criticized for things they say, they may simply choose to remain silent. Joe Beam identified this dilemma between husband and wife:

> Some don't talk to their mates because they cannot accept themselves as they are. . . . Others don't because they feel their spouses reject them when they do try to share what they've done, are doing, or plan to do. Since their spouses can't accept facts, they don't even consider that their mates would accept how they *feel*. They quit talking openly and honestly because they fear the recriminations of the conversations. . . . They'd rather say nothing at all than feel the rejection of the person they're married to.[5]

Many women who long to have their husbands talk to them and share their deepest feelings have unknowingly hindered emotional intimacy. When wives respond defensively, unkindly or negatively to honest thoughts and opinions, or follow by shutting down, leaving, or brow-beating their spouse, they in essence take advantage of their husband's vulnerability. Such behavior teaches them to resist communicating or to lie. Intimate communication requires us to be willing to hear the positive and the negative—the honest thoughts, opinions, and feelings of our spouse. Thanks to the Couples Dialogue (to be taught later in this chapter) couples can learn to communicate their true thoughts and feelings in a safe and honest way.

Accepting ourselves and our spouse has a marvelous side effect: it frees us to change.

William James wisely stated, "When I accept myself as I am, I change. When I accept others as they are, they change."[6] Acceptance is the key to unlock our divine potential, freeing us from personal prisons we have created to protect ourselves and our vulnerability. The power to significantly change our whole marriage is great. Even one spouse can choose to unconditionally love and accept themselves and/or the other spouse, thus creating a sizable shift in the dynamics of the relationship.

To give the gift of acceptance to your spouse, compile a list of *their* strengths and weaknesses. For positive characteristics repeat the statement, *"I deeply and completely love and accept my spouse because . . ."* For negative characteristics repeat, *"I deeply and completely love and accept my spouse even though . . ."* If there is built-up resentment or bitterness over past errors, seek God's grace to grant the gift of forgiveness. Put the full power of the Atonement into practice by wiping the slate clean for your spouse each week as you partake of the sacrament and repent of your own sins.

Nurturing Love and Friendship in Marriage

Once couples learn to accept their true selves and each other, the door for mutual emotional nurturing is opened. The need for emotional nourishment in marriage is often ignored in our busy lives. In many marriages neglect may be a greater problem than sin. President Spencer W. Kimball taught the importance of marital nourishment:

> Love is like a flower, and, like the body, it needs constant feeding. The mortal body would soon be emaciated and die if there were not frequent feedings. The tender flower would wither and die without food and water. And so love, also, cannot be expected to last forever unless it is continually fed with portions of love, the manifestation of esteem and admiration, the expressions of gratitude, and the consideration of unselfishness.[7]

Distant or disconnected relationships occur when intimate emotional nourishment is lacking. "You do your thing and I'll do mine" is the sad state of many marriages. Without proper time and attention, many marriages whither . . . or die. These marriages can be reconnected and come alive again when extra care and attention are given.

When couples lack emotional intimacy, they often find themselves in what is called a "parallel marriage." Dr. Charles B. Beckert, LDS marriage and family therapist, described parallel marriage as a "devitalized relationship," a "malnourished marriage" like parallel lines lying in the same plane but never intersecting.[8] He shared the increasingly common experience of Megan and Matt who found themselves unhappy in marriage:

Megan and Matt sat tentatively on two of the upholstered chairs in my office. They had moved the chairs close enough to hold hands tenderly as the conversation began. Their surprise, and perhaps embarrassment, at finding themselves in marriage counseling seemed evident not only from the subdued manner in which they spoke but also in the way they looked at each other.

Theirs had been almost a storybook wedding. Matt was a returned missionary, and Megan was the faithful sweetheart who waited. They had maintained their worthiness during their engagement and enjoyed the blessing of a temple sealing on their wedding day 11 years earlier. What had gone wrong?

They had done all they had been taught to do growing up. . . . Yet here they were, disappointed in the current state of their relationship and sitting in front of a stranger trying to figure out what had happened to their dreams.

Matt and Megan, and others like them, describe their relationship as confusing and contradictory. They don't fight and quarrel, don't criticize and demean, don't ignore one another. They sincerely love each other and care about one another's welfare. Yet they are bored and dissatisfied with the relationship.[9]

Neglecting emotional nourishment leads many into parallel marriages, where neither husband nor wife is truly happy or satisfied—creating dangerous conditions where they become vulnerable to temptation. President Kimball warned against the lack of nourishment in marriage, "There are many people who do not find divorce attorneys and who do not end their marriages, but who have permitted their marriage to grow stale and weak and cheap. There are spouses who . . . are in the low state of mere joint occupancy of the home."[10] Couples must dedicate the necessary time and effort to make marriage beautiful again.

There are many ways to nurture love and friendship in marriage. Marriage books are filled with suggestions. But every couple has different needs for love and intimacy. Every individual *feels* loved differently. The best marital suggestions center around each other's specific wants and needs rather than imposing a blanket of marital nourishment, which may or may not satisfy. One husband understood the need to give his wife her own special brand of love. He would often ask her, "What is one thing I can do right now to make you love me even more?" This care and concern for her individual needs filled her with admiration and provided emotional intimacy in substantive ways.

I have chosen to focus on six effective ways couples can increase emotional intimacy in their marriage. These are:

1. *Asking for what you want and need;*

2. *Learning to love in each other's love language;*

3. *Continuing courtship with regular dating;*

4. *Sharing more facts and feelings;*

5. *Learning and using the Couples Dialogue communication skill; and*

6. *Creating your own "marriage traditions."*

1. Asking for What You Want and Need

Husbands and wives are often reluctant to ask for what they need. Some believe if their spouse really loved them they would just know what they needed. But neither husbands nor wives read minds. Though it may be difficult to ask for the love you need, you must learn to communicate your needs openly, specifically and directly. This is much more effective than hinting or hoping your spouse will figure it out.

Regularly paying attention to each other's needs and asking for what you need can be a great gift in a marriage relationship. Dr. John Gray shared the following experience between him and his wife, which illustrates the importance of asking for the love we need:

> I remember when Bonnie first asked for a hug. It made such a difference in our relationship. Instead of resenting me for not offering hugs, she would simply ask.
>
> It was such a gift of love to me. She began to understand that the way to love me best was to help me be successful in loving her. . . .
>
> I still remember the first day she asked for a hug. I was standing in my closet, and she was making different sounds of exhaustion. She said, "Ooohhh, what a day."
>
> Then she took a deep breath and made a long sigh on the exhale. In her language, she was asking for a hug. What I heard was a tired person and wrongly assumed that she probably wanted to be left alone.
>
> Instead of resenting me for not noticing or responding to her request, she took the big step to ask for what she wanted, even though to her it seemed obvious.
>
> She said, "John, would you give me a hug?"
>
> My response was immediate. I said, "Of course." I went straight over to her and gave her a big hug.
>
> She let out another big sigh in my arms and then thanked me for the hug. I said, "Any time."
>
> She chuckled and smiled. I said, "What?"
>
> She said, "You have no idea how hard it was to ask for a hug."
>
> I said, "Really? Why should it be hard? I am always willing to give you a hug, if you want one."

She said, "I know, but it feels so humiliating to have to ask. I feel like I am begging for love. I want to feel like you want to give me a hug as much as I want one. I have this romantic picture that you will notice that I need a hug, then automatically offer one."

I said, "Oh . . . well, from now on I will definitely try to notice and offer to give you hugs. And I really thank you for asking. If I forget to notice in the future, I hope you will keep asking."[11]

2. Learning to Love in the Right Love Language

Each person has very individual needs for love. Only your spouse can tell you what *he* most needs to feel loved. Only *you* can tell him what *you* most need. Husbands and wives fill each other's love buckets as they fine-tune their loving by learning *exactly* what makes the other feel loved. Many couples do not really know what makes the other feel loved. But this can be easily remedied. Learning and applying this simple, but profound principle makes our efforts to love more effectively received in a meaningful way. We all love our spouses in the best way we know how, but once we know better, we can do better!

If you were to express love to your husband in German, but he only understood English, your attempts at loving him would misfire. If your husband insisted on expressing love to you in Portuguese, and you only understood English, no matter how sincere his efforts, his loving words would be fruitless. Love must be expressed in the specific love language your spouse understands and feels.

We often talk about the Golden Rule, "Do unto others as you would have them do unto you."[12] Maybe the higher law of the Golden Rule is, "Do unto others as *they* would have you do unto them." Behaviors have their own meaning to each person emotionally. Giving your husband flowers (because *you* like to receive flowers) may have little meaning to him. Too often we give to others what *we'd* like to receive instead of giving what the other really wants and needs. Not understanding how our spouse feels loved can not only neutralize our efforts but also cause serious problems over time. Of course, each spouse can be grateful for the intent, but why not make our efforts more effective by learning to love in the right way in the first place?

Christian author and speaker, Dr. Gary Chapman, has written a wonderful book that should be required reading for all couples entitled *The Five Love Languages*. In it he describes the universal need we all have to feel loved (the search for intimacy and oneness). He uses the analogy of an inner "love tank" longing to be filled. He profoundly changes the rules of the "game of love" by proposing that we must learn the particular "love language" or specific kind of love our spouse wants and needs in order to be successful in loving them. He encourages couples with this admonition, "WARNING: Understanding the five love languages and learning to speak the primary love language of your spouse may radically affect his or her behavior. People behave differently when their emotional love tanks are full."[13]

While many people feel loved in various ways, Dr. Chapman suggests everyone has a primary love language. He identifies the five love languages as: (1) words of affirmation, (2) quality time, (3) receiving gifts, (4) acts of service, and (5) physical touch. They are described below:

Words of Affirmation. Words of affirmation include receiving notes, cards, or phone calls where verbal and nonverbal expressions of appreciation, love, and encouragement are given. This love language includes compliments and being asked nicely to do something, rather than being told or commanded.

Quality Time. Those with a primary love language of quality time want to spend time together receiving undivided attention. They want to do things together. They want to share thoughts, feelings, and experiences or just be together.

Receiving Gifts. Some spouses feel love most by receiving gifts, which indicate time and thought on their behalf. These tangible gifts may be a flower, a note, a candy bar, or money to redecorate the house or buy a new car. There are also intangible gifts of self that can provide profound expressions of love. Gifts to the children can also count as gifts of love.

Acts of Service. For the "acts of service" spouse any service, such as doing housework, making dinner, doing laundry, changing diapers, or washing the car, picking up dry cleaning and reading to the children can all be expressions of love.

Physical Touch. Touch is a biological need from the time we are born. Touch is both sexual and nonsexual. Physical touch can convey love by holding hands, a kiss, a pat on the back, hugs or snuggling on the couch, as well as by sexual relations.

Spouses should identify their love language and share it with one another, though individuals often feel love from more than one category. Dr. Chapman suggested the following questions to determine what makes you feel loved[14]:

1. *What does your spouse do, say or fail to do that hurts you most deeply?* (The opposite of this is probably your love language.)

2. *What have you most often requested of your spouse? What is your most frequent ongoing complaint?* (Your requests are most likely what would make you most feel loved.)

3. *What do you regularly do or say to express love to your spouse?* (Chances are you're doing for him what you wish he would do for you.)

While it can be valuable to know the primary and secondary love language, it is even more beneficial to know the specific behaviors that are most important to you or your spouse. Rather than a general laundry list of ways to increase emotional intimacy in marriage, it is best to get a specific list from your spouse to be sure your efforts at love are the most meaningful and effective.

Both husband and wife should make a list of ten things that most make them feel loved and cared about. Be specific, positive (what you want, instead of what you *don't* want), and descriptive using quantifiable language (how much of what you want, and when you want it). Be as specific as you can be to make it as easy as possible for your spouse to be successful at loving you.

Some examples might be "I feel loved when . . . *you kiss me and tell me you love me each time you leave the house*" or ". . . *the house is clean and the kids are in bed when I get home from my evening meeting.*" Complete the following phrase, "I feel cared about / loved when . . ." then share your lists with each other. You might also consider making a list of the things you do for them that make *you* feel good, and see how many of them have similar meaning to your spouse. You might be amazed to realize how many things you do for each other that don't have the intended intimate impact.

Many couples may find that what their spouse needs *most* requires some stretching. Marriage is meant to stir our divine potential. If your spouse needs physical touch to feel loved, but that is hard for you to give, remember his needs will draw from you your wholeness increasing your ability to become one. It may be equally difficult for him to open up and share feelings, which you may need to feel loved. Love is not always easy. Sometimes love is doing what you don't want to do or don't like to do knowing there is purpose and growth. Love is not just a feeling. Love is an action. Love is a choice. When an action doesn't come naturally it is an even greater gift of love.

I remember how much I hated having my husband touching me when we would fall asleep. It took a long time, but I pushed myself to learn to be comfortable with touch because I knew it made him feel loved. Now I can easily fall asleep wrapped in his arms. I have developed a part of my being that had once been shut down.

If you and/or your spouse's emotional bank accounts are overdrawn, a simple and powerful solution to reverse the downward spiral is to learn each other's love language and begin making deposits. You might ask your husband what you could do to make him feel more loved. You will not only learn his love language, but you will also be filling his needs for love in the most meaningful way. You may be surprised to find how willing and able he is to meet your needs for love as you meet his.

Emotional love can be reborn. It may take time to get emotional accounts out of the red, but it is worth the effort. Even one spouse can drastically change a marriage by making personalized love deposits regularly. Commit to do at least one thing every day that makes your spouse feel loved.

3. Continuing Courtship—Date Night

Before marriage, dating was a separate world where we put our best self forward and left our stresses at home. Within marriage dating provides a respite from our daily cares as love and friendship is renewed. Continuing courtship can help satisfy the need for constant nourishment in marriage, and can be fitted to meet the individual needs of the couple. Regular dates provide opportunities to give each other quality time and our undivided attention. Dates provide talk time, touch time, and maybe even treat time! Courting nurtures love *and* friendship, an important dimension of marriage. Elder Marlin K. Jensen observed:

> Friendship is . . . a vital and wonderful part of courtship and marriage. A relationship between a man and a woman that begins with friendship and then ripens into romance and eventually marriage will usually become an enduring, eternal friendship. Nothing is more inspiring in today's world of easily dissolved marriages than to observe a husband and wife quietly appreciating and enjoying each other's friendship year in and year out as they experience together the blessings and trials of mortality.[15]

Love says, "I love you," but friendship says, "I like you." Marriage needs both love and friendship. Friendships are built by getting to know each other, spending time together, and being there for each other. Regular dates help couples communicate love and friendship, making marriage and each other a priority.

I remember as a young wife with very young children hearing a woman bear her testimony of the importance of date night, and suggest we make it a priority. I remember thinking, "Yeah, sure. If we didn't have young children who made it so hard to leave, or we didn't have to pay a babysitter." But as life got busier, I began to feel the emotional connection slipping between my husband and myself. I realized the importance of date night as I recognized how easy it would be to slowly drift apart until one day I woke up and found my husband had become a stranger.

My husband and I began to schedule Friday night for date night to be sure we had time together each week. Dedicating a night to each other significantly increased our emotional intimacy and connection. I have since gained my own testimony of the importance of date night. Couples need regular opportunities to get away, change roles from parent to spouse, and create positive memories as a couple.

In The Church of Jesus Christ of Latter-day Saints, Monday night is reserved for Family Home Evening. I'd love to see the day when Friday or Saturday night becomes as sacred for date night or "marriage night" as Monday is for "family night." Elder L. Tom Perry taught, "The most important meeting of the week is sacrament meeting, and the second most important is date night."[16] When I corresponded with him to confirm this quote he added, "I do believe it is very important that you put first on your calendar, after sacrament meeting, time together as husband and wife."[17]

I'd love to see the day when Friday or Saturday night becomes as sacred for date night or "marriage night" as Monday is for "family night."

Elder Joe J. Christensen also encouraged couples to make time together a priority. He said, "Keep your courtship alive. Make time to do things together—just the two of you. As important as it is to be with the children as a family, you need regular weekly time alone together. Scheduling it will let your children know that you feel that your marriage is so important that you need to nurture it. That takes commitment, planning, and scheduling."[18]

Date night is something husband and wife can look forward to each week. It can be a respite from the daily cares of life, and a time to rekindle the spark in your relationship. Dating need not be an expensive undertaking. Sometimes all you might be able to afford is the babysitter. Other dates can be had at home after kids are in bed. Husband and wife may want to each make a list of their ten favorite date ideas then use an idea from each list, alternating weeks. It's the time spent together and attention given each other that counts, not the activity itself.

In marriage there are many different dimensions that need nurturing.[19] The more areas your relationship includes, the more fulfilled you will feel. What works well for some couples is to schedule their weekly dates to include their most important activities—one week for attending the temple together; another week for just talking or using the Couples Dialogue, then one week for his choice and one week for her choice.

Below are a few ideas under each dimension to get you spending more time alone together. They can be simple or simply magical. These ideas can put a spark in your marriage and inspire your own creative or inexpensive ideas:

Physical

- Exercise together—go jogging, bike riding, play racquetball, etc.
- Take a dance class or golf class together.
- Share a quiet evening treating each other to a good hand, foot, or back massage, with no strings attached.

Sexual

- Read and discuss this book.
- Take a bath or shower together.
- Have intimate time together.

Recreational

- Invite some couples over and have a game night.
- Do crossword puzzles, put a puzzle together or play a favorite game like Checkers, Othello, or Scrabble.
- Play computer games or surf the internet together.
- Visit the Hallmark store and see who can find the funniest or best cards.
- In the summer make dinner or a picnic, and eat it in a tent you set up in your backyard.
- Pop popcorn then watch a video together at home after the kids are in bed.
- Attend a high school (basketball, football, baseball, etc.) game together. Rekindle those memories.
- Test drive your dream car. (But be careful . . . this could be hazardous to your finances!)

- If you can't think of anything else you'd like to do . . . you can go out to dinner and/or to a movie.

Educational

- Choose a new recipe and make it together.
- Take a community education course on marriage, parenting, or family history research.
- Take up a new sport or hobby together.
- Attend local exhibits such as a home show, car show, boat show, arts and crafts show, or food show.

Intellectual

- Choose a news story to read and discuss.
- Spend time at the library.
- Read a biography together.

Emotional

- Go where you can be alone to just talk, listen, and support each other as you share what's going on in your lives and discuss important issues. Practice using the Couples Dialogue.
- Update your lists of what makes you feel loved.
- Get the book *365 Questions for Couples* and ask each other some of the questions.

Spiritual

- Attend the temple together and linger to discuss any insights or questions that come to mind.
- Read and discuss an *Ensign* article or a Sunday lesson at the park, the mall, in a big hotel lobby, or your home after the kids are in bed.
- Start a scripture study program for the two of you.

4. Communicating—Sharing Facts and Feelings

Communication is a powerful contributor to intimacy in marriage. Couples can increase their emotional connection by sharing experiences, facts, and feelings from their daily lives. This can be done verbally with phone calls, pillow talk time, and date night. Nonverbal communication can also build intimacy through cards, notes, letters and e-mails. Communication can be freer and more effective at times when it is non-verbal.

As couples connect emotionally through communication, they will also be able to more easily give the gift of acceptance. Joe Beam taught the power of sharing simple facts to increase intimacy. He stated:

> For many couples, intimacy would increase if they simply started sharing facts that are completely nonthreatening. For example, if a couple set aside twenty to thirty minutes every day to talk about their days—who they saw, what they ate for lunch, and the like—they could actually increase intimacy. The very acts of spending time together and communicating (two of the keys to intimacy) feed the intimacy turbine. . . .
>
> Sadly, many couples hardly talk at all. He wants to forget work when he gets home. She's had a horrible day and would rather forget that it ever happened. They each talk to the kids—if they talk at all—and communicate with each other only in short, essential statements. For these couples, the turbine has gone dry. It isn't producing any intimacy because *nothing* is feeding it. . . .
>
> If you want to start increasing intimacy in your marriage, start talking more than you do now.[20]

When husbands and wives feel accepted by each other and have a method for sharing non-intimate feelings safely, they are more likely to share the deeper parts of their hearts. Beyond facts, sharing feelings can significantly increase intimacy. Elder Spencer J. Condie stated, "The honest sharing of one's emotions, needs, thoughts, and beliefs is an important dimension in becoming one in marriage. . . . Husbands and wives often feel ill at ease in sharing their true feelings about various matters for fear of hurting their mate's feelings or becoming embroiled in attacks and counterattacks."[21]

Couples should strive to share feelings more frequently by paying attention to their emotions and sharing at least one feeling with their spouse every day. For heart-to-heart talks couples need to remember that just as physical intimacy requires foreplay, so does intimate communication. There is a special power associated with emotion. Sharing and listening are therapeutic in marriage. What you can feel, you can heal. It's not just *talk therapy* that is needed, but *feeling therapy.*

To assist couples with creating more intimacy in marriage, Dr. Michael J. Beck and Stanis Marusak Beck created a great little pocket book entitled, *365 Questions for Couples.* While I consider some of the questions to be improper, it is otherwise a great resource for increasing intimate communication. Couples can carry this book with them and ask each other interesting questions to prompt the sharing of facts and feelings from each other's lives. The introduction to the book states, "The most basic question can probe the deepest facet of one's psyche. Simple inquiries can provide boundless insight into someone's emotions and feelings. The problem is, the questions just aren't asked. When was the last time you shared a dream, a memory, or a feeling with your partner? If it has been a while, it's time to get started."[22]

The Becks continue in the introduction by expressing the difficulty of and the need for more sharing within marriage. They encourage couples to simply ask more questions:

> In our busy world, emotional connections are buried under the pressures of daily life, closing lines of communication within families. . . . All of our questions will bring you closer to understanding the person with whom you share your time. People often remark that the best part of a relationship is the beginning, when a mutual interest is shared, and couples learn eagerly about each other's past. Our book will guide you back to that state, an at-home therapy session which will provide all participants with a link back to their relationship's roots.[23]

The book is divided into the following categories of questions: Our Relationship, Relationships with Others, Emotions and Dreams, Goals and Fantasies, Life Experiences and Beliefs, Memories, and Sex. The following are sample questions from the book:

- "Tell me what you found attractive about me when we first met. How has this evolved or changed since we first met?"[24]

- "Would you like a relationship that is similar to your parent's relationship, or one which is drastically different?"[25]

- "What makes you feel secure and safe?"[26]

- "What is a talent that you wish you possessed?"[27]

- "What is your worst personality flaw? What sparks it?"[28]

- "Tell me about the best birthday you ever had"[29]

- "What do you remember about your first date? Where did you go, and why did you pick this person?"[30]

5. Using Communication Skills— Learning and Using The Couples Dialogue

Making time to talk is an important part of building intimacy. Elder Christensen suggests that we schedule it regularly.[31] Elder Russell M. Nelson gave couples encouragement to make talk time a priority, "Husbands and wives, learn to listen, and listen to learn from one another. . . . Taking time to talk is essential to keep lines of communication intact. If marriage is a prime relationship in life, it deserves prime time! Yet less important appointments are often given priority, leaving only leftover moments for listening to precious partners."[32]

One of the missing puzzle pieces for creating deeper intimacy in all dimensions of marriage is the ability to safely and effectively communicate about tender feelings and important issues, so that each person feels fully heard, validated, and understood. Everyone talks about talking, but nobody quite explains how to do it effectively. The Couples Dialogue communication tool is the most effective process for couples to stop reactively communicating. The Couples Dialogue allows couples to be fully heard and understood, and helps create a self-transcending experience of profound empathy for the experience and perspective of another.

Listening empathically can help others find their own solutions. While talking may not always solve a specific problem, the process of consciously listening, with the intent to understand, validating the other's point of view, and experiencing the emotions of another's reality provides healing not only to the sender, but also to the receiver.

Dr. Harville Hendrix, creator of *Imago Relationship Therapy*, designed the Couples Dialogue or Intentional Dialogue process. This communication tool may not be needed for all verbal interactions, but it can be especially effective when you want to be listened to, fully heard and understood. It can be helpful in discussing a topic you think might be "touchy," or when you are upset or excited about something and want to talk about it. The Couples Dialogue process contains three parts: mirroring, validating, and empathizing.

Mirroring is *accurately* reflecting back the content of the message your spouse wants to send. Mirroring correctly indicates a willingness to defer your own thoughts and feelings, or interpretation of the message, to see from your spouse's point of view.

Validating is confirming that what your spouse is saying "makes sense," or that you can see their point of view and accept its validity from their perspective. You don't necessarily have to agree to validate. When you validate your spouse, you temporarily suspend your point of view, allowing your spouse's subjective perspective to take priority and have its own reality, logic, and validity.

Empathizing is the process of reflecting, imagining, or participating in the feelings of your spouse. Empathy allows couples to transcend their separateness for a moment, and meet in the emotions of the event or situation being discussed. The empathic experience has profound healing power. Empathy is the natural outgrowth of charity, the pure love of Christ. Learning and using the Couples Dialogue is one of the ways we can develop greater compassion and Christlike love for our spouse. It is the intent of the heart that affects whether a communication tool builds intimacy or becomes merely a weapon.

Couples can use the following *Couples Dialogue Process* during their discussions to learn the skill until they become proficient.

Couples Dialogue Process (Intentional Dialogue)[33]

SENDER	RECEIVER
1. The one who wants to send a message can take the initiative by saying, *"I would like to dialogue about something. Is now okay?"*	*1.* It is the Receiver's job to grant a Couples Dialogue as soon as possible. *"I'm available now."* If not available, set a time, so that the sender knows when s / he will be heard.
2. Begin to send your message about a topic you wish to discuss. (Use "I . . ." statements.)	*2.* MIRROR:. *"So . . ."* (Paraphrase the sender's message.) When there is a natural pause in the conversation, you can say one of two things: ACCURACY CHECK: *"Did I get it? Did I hear you accurately?"* ENCOURAGEMENT: *"Is there anything more you'd like to say about that?"*
3. Continue sending (or resending) message until Receiver gets it all (and correctly) on a particular issue. Keep it simple.	*3.* When the Sender has finished sending and the Receiver has mirrored it all accurately, the Receiver *summarizes* all of the Sender's message to check for accuracy with this lead-in: *"Let me see if I got all of that . . . ."*
4. Listen to the summary and give confirmation of accuracy.	*4.* VALIDATE: Receiver states the logic of the Sender's point of view by saying *"You make sense, because . . ."* or *"I can understand that . . ."* until the Sender feels validated. If you cannot validate say *"Help me understand that better"* until you can validate their point of view.

SENDER *continued*	**RECEIVER** *continued*
5. Listen to validation. Acknowledge when you feel validated.	**5.** **EMPATHIZE**: Receiver now tries to imagine how it might feel to be the Sender. A lead-in phrase might be: *"I can imagine you might be feeling . . ."* or *"I imagine you might have felt . . ."* or *"I can see you are feeling . . ."* (if feelings are obvious). Feelings are stated in *one* word (e.g., angry, confused, sad, upset, etc.). If your statement entails more than one word it is probably a thought. "You feel that you don't want to go with me"—this is a thought. "You feel sad"—this is a feeling. Check if you got the feelings accurate by saying: *"Is that what you are feeling?"* or *"Did I get it right?"*
6. Listen. If Receiver did not get the correct feelings or all the feelings, share them again.	**6.** If the Sender shares with you other feelings, mirror back what is said: *"So . . ."* (Paraphrase the sender's message.)
7. Once all three parts are completed (**MIRRORING**, **VALIDATING**, and **EMPATHIZING**) and you feel fully heard, validated and understood, switch roles.	**7.** When the Sender acknowledges completion, Receiver becomes the Sender to respond *on this issue*. *"I would like to respond now."* This allows for an interactive process, not a long airing session for one person.

The Couples Dialogue is a powerful method that stops the hopelessness and ineffectiveness of the communication merry-go-round. Understanding and healing can occur simply from the process, in addition to finding suitable solutions to problems. The Couples Dialogue is the gourmet home-cooked meal of communication.

During a difficult time, my husband and I dedicated most of our dates to the Couples Dialogue process because I so desperately needed the emotional closeness it provided. These dates became my lifeline as the emotional intimacy between us filled my empty bucket. Our emotional intimacy grew exponentially. This wasn't my husband's first choice for a date, but his generous gift of time and love was a great blessing.

Though not intended to arouse sexual desire, the Couples Dialogue, as well as other intimate communication, can make couples feel closer to each other emotionally and sexually. BYU professor, Dr. Lynn Scoresby commented that the only true aphrodisiac is prolonged conversation, which literally puts husband and wife "in sync with each other and prepares them for more intimate interaction."[34] When there are no strings attached the emotional connection of intimate communication can be a powerful aphrodisiac.

6. Creating Marriage Traditions

Many families have fun traditions in their home to strengthen family relationships and build loving bonds. Couples can create continuing opportunities for strengthening their marriage relationship and increasing intimacy and oneness by creating "Marriage Traditions." Marital traditions send the message that marriage is a priority. Marriage traditions ensure ongoing opportunities to nurture your intimate connection.

While we speak of the family as the central unit of the gospel, it is actually the marriage relationship that is the principle building block of eternity. It is husband and wife who will "come up in glory and dominion" together.[35] The marriage relationship deserves a sufficient supply of ongoing time, effort, and attention best ensured by making marriage traditions. The following are a few ideas to inspire your own traditions:

- Establish nightly routines of couple prayer and expressions of love.

- Schedule weekly dates.

- Make regular opportunities to use the Couples Dialogue communication process.

- Have regular pillow talk time.

- Update your Love Language lists on Valentine's Day.

- Read and discuss each other's Patriarchal Blessings on birthdays to remember your divine potential and purposes.

- Have your wedding rings cleaned and polished for your anniversary.

- Celebrate your wedding anniversary by going to the temple to do sealings.

- Watch your wedding video or look through your wedding albums on your anniversary.

- Plan an annual weekend getaway to celebrate your anniversary.

Becoming one emotionally is an important dimension of building complete intimacy and oneness in marriage. Learning to love in your spouse's love language, continuing to court through regular dating, increasing effective intimate communication by sharing facts and feelings, as well as using the Couples Dialogue can significantly increase emotional fulfillment and intimacy in marriage. Choosing loving behaviors that are important to each other, then making them marriage traditions, can ensure ongoing opportunities for closeness and emotional connection between husband and wife.

Chapter 10—"Home" Work

- Get to know yourself better through writing your thoughts and feelings regularly, spending time in prayer and solitude, and by using the Couples Dialogue.

- Learn to accept yourself. List at least five things you *dislike* about yourself. For each item, say aloud, *"I deeply and completely love and accept myself even though I . . . "* Make a list of the things you *like* about yourself. For each item say aloud, *"I deeply and completely love and accept myself because I . . ."*

- Pray for God to help you feel His unconditional love and acceptance, and to free you to discover the divinity of who you really are.

- To give the gift of acceptance to your spouse, compile a list of their strengths and weaknesses. For their positive characteristics repeat the statement, *"I deeply and completely love and accept my spouse because . . ."* For their negative characteristics repeat, *"I deeply and completely love and accept my spouse even though . . ."* Each week wipe the slate clean for your spouse as you repent of your own sins during the sacrament.

- Ask for the love you want and need by communicating your needs openly, specifically, and directly.

- Make a list of ten specific, positive, and quantifiable things that make you feel loved and cared about. Have your spouse do the same. Share your lists with each other. Commit to do at least one thing every day that makes your spouse feel loved.

- Schedule a regular date night. Each of you compile a list of your ten favorite date ideas, then use them on alternating weeks.

- Share more facts and feelings with each other. Pay more attention to your daily emotions and share at least one feeling with your spouse every day.

- Use the book *365 Questions for Couples* to learn more about each other and to build intimacy.

- Learn the Couples Dialogue process and use it on a regular basis.

- Ensure ongoing opportunities for closeness and emotional connection by creating your own "marriage traditions."

NOTES

Chapter 10 — "Becoming One — Emotional Intimacy"

[1] *See* Matthew 22:39.

[2] Christofferson, "That They May Be One," *Ensign*, Nov. 2002, 72.

[3] Beam, *Becoming One*, 90–91.

[4] *See Hymns*, 301

[5] Beam, *Becoming One*, 117–18.

[6] Beam, *Becoming One*, 97.

[7] Kimball, "Oneness in Marriage," *Ensign*, Oct. 2002, 43–44.

[8] Beckert, "Pitfalls of Parallel Marriage," *Ensign*, Mar. 2000, 22.

[9] Beckert, "Pitfalls," *Ensign*, Mar. 2000, 22.

[10] Kimball, *Marriage and Divorce*, 22.

[11] Gray, *Mars and Venus in the Bedroom*, 184–85.

[12] *See* Matthew 7:12 or 3 Nephi 14:12.

[13] Chapman, *Five Love Languages*, 24.

[14] Chapman, *Five Love Languages*, 124–25.

[15] Jensen, "Friendship: A Gospel Principle," *Ensign*, May 1999, 64.

[16] Perry, CES Employees Meeting.

[17] Perry, personal correspondence, March 20, 2001.

[18] Christensen, "Marriage and the Great Plan of Happiness," *Ensign*, May 1995, 65.

[19] De Angelis, *How to Make Love All the Time*, 140.

[20] Beam, *Becoming One*, 106.

[21] Condie, "Finding Marital Unity through the Scriptures," *Ensign*, July 1986, 54.

[22] Beck and Beck, *365 Questions for Couples*, xiii–xiv.

[23] Beck and Beck, *365 Questions*, xvi–xvii.

[24] Beck and Beck, *365 Questions*, 9.

[25] Beck and Beck, *365 Questions*, 28.

[26] Beck and Beck, *365 Questions*, 57.

[27] Beck and Beck, *365 Questions*, 74.

[28] Beck and Beck, *365 Questions*, 98.

[29] Beck and Beck, *365 Questions*, 134.

[30] Beck and Beck, *365 Questions*, 162.

[31] Christensen, "Marriage," *Ensign*, May 1995, 65.

[32] Nelson, "Listen to Learn," *Ensign*, May 1991, 22.

[33] *See* Hendrix, *Getting the Love You Want: A Couples Workshop Manual*, 1997, 23–24; and Hendrix, *Getting the Love You Want: A Guide for Couples Home Video Workshop Manual*, 1993, 78. *See also* Appendix III for more information.

[34] Barlow, *Just for Newlyweds*, 50.

[35] McConkie, "Celestial Marriage," *New Era*, June 1978, 12.

CHAPTER VIEW

Righteousness, Spiritual Intimacy, and ONEness

Identifying and Removing Barriers to Spiritual ONEness

Improving Spiritual Intimacy as a Couple

1. *Read and Discuss Patriarchal Blessings*

2. *Increase Faith and Obedience*

3. *Pray Together Daily*

4. *Study and Discuss Scriptures*

5. *Repent and Forgive Each Other Regularly*

6. *Reverence the Sabbath*

7. *Fast Together with Common Purpose*

8. *Attend Church Services and Discuss What You Learn*

9. *Have Weekly Family Home Evenings*

10. *Keep a Balance as You Serve in Church Callings*

11. *Serve, Worship, and Learn in the Temple*

12. *Strive to Have God's Pure Love*

Chapter 11—"Home" Work

Chapter 11

BECOMING ONE—SPIRITUAL INTIMACY

Righteousness, Spiritual Intimacy, and ONEness

Taking on the "luster of Christ" leads husbands and wives to spiritual ONEness as they come unto Christ, and become purified and perfected in Him.[1] Couples striving together for spiritual intimacy share personal and spiritual thoughts, experiences, and emotions. They strive to be united in their love and faith in God.

To become *one* in marriage requires more than just husband and wife alone. It also requires God. In many marriages God is the missing element. Spiritual intimacy and marital oneness require righteousness, which is a love of God, a desire to be like Him, and a willingness to keep His commandments. Righteousness is the surest way to happiness. Following the Savior's example and adhering to gospel principles brings happiness both in marriage and in life. President Spencer W. Kimball taught, "To be really happy in marriage, there must be a continued faithful observance of the commandments of the Lord. No one . . . was ever sublimely happy unless he was righteous."[2]

Righteousness is the surest way to happiness.

In marriage, it is the gospel of Jesus Christ that provides the true key to happiness. It is loving, serving, and seeking the Lord together that permits the Spirit to create a level of happiness in marriage that is otherwise unattainable. President Kimball taught:

> If two people love the Lord more than their own lives and then love each other more than their own lives, working together in total harmony with the gospel program as their basic structure, they are sure to have this great happiness. When a husband and wife go together frequently to the holy temple, kneel in prayer together in their home with their family, go hand in hand to their religious meetings, keep their lives wholly chaste, mentally and physically, so that their whole thoughts and desires and love are all centered in one being, their companion, and both are working together for the upbuilding of the kingdom of God, then happiness is at its pinnacle.[3]

Righteousness or coming unto Christ not only increases happiness in marriage, it also increases love and mutual respect. Righteousness increases our *ability* and *capacity* to love. The more we love God, the more we will love our spouse. In the "Marriage Takes Three" triangle in Chapter 8 we can see that as husband and wife draw nearer to God (or move up their side of the triangle) they naturally draw nearer to each other. Elder Orson Pratt taught:

> The more righteous a people become the more they are qualified for loving others and rendering them happy. A wicked man can have but little love for his wife; while a righteous man, being filled with the love of God, is sure to manifest this heavenly attribute in every thought and feeling of his heart, and in every word and deed. Love, joy, and innocence will radiate from his very countenance, and be expressed in every look. This will beget confidence in the wife of his bosom, and she will love him in return; for love begets love; happiness imparts happiness; and these heaven born emotions will continue to increase more and more, until they are perfected and glorified in all the fulness of eternal love itself.[4]

It is through personal righteousness and the Spirit within us that husband and wife can become one. For the gift of the Holy Ghost "increases, enlarges, expands and purifies all the natural passions and affections; and adapts them, by the gift of wisdom, to their lawful use. It inspires, develops, cultivates and matures all the fine-toned sympathies, joys, tastes, kindred feelings, and affections of our nature. It inspires virtue, kindness, goodness, tenderness, gentleness, and charity."[5]

The gift of the Holy Ghost does so much to bless our lives. It can prompt husbands and wives to do things that increase intimacy and oneness. John and Kimberly Bytheway shared a wonderful example of this:

> One time, driving home from Idaho, John did something brilliant. It had been a long day, and we were anxious to get home. In the rush of everything, I had felt a little neglected. It was already dark, and we had a four-hour drive ahead of us. As we passed through Idaho Falls, John had a prompting. . . . He thought to himself, "Pull the car over and give your wife a hug." At this point, John asked [himself], "What for?" But the prompting returned. So, although we were in a hurry, John pulled the car over, pulled me close, and gave me a hug. No words were spoken, and he didn't look at his watch and ask, "I wonder how long I have to hug her for it to count," he just held me close for probably half a minute. Then, without a word, he sat back, restarted the car, and resumed the journey. A few miles down the road, I said, "You have no idea how much I needed that." John later told me he wanted to reach up and high-five whoever put that thought in his head.[6]

Righteousness has everything to do with romance. Striving to follow the Savior's example and the Holy Spirit provides the foundation upon which marriage education can be applied to bring greater blessings. Elder Jeffrey R. Holland taught couples to find the surest path to love and happiness by being disciples of Christ. He said, "You want capability, safety, and security . . . in married life and eternity? Be a true disciple of Jesus. Be a genuine, committed, word-and-deed Latter-day Saint. Believe that your faith has *everything* to do with your romance, because it does. . . . Jesus Christ, the Light of the World, is the only lamp by which you can successfully see the path of love and happiness for you *and* for your sweetheart."[7]

Merely going through the motions of righteousness in marriage is insufficient for happiness. Righteousness is not simply being *active* in church, it is being *alive* in Christ.[8] It's not just our actions, but also our hearts and our minds that matter. Truman Madsen identified this important difference when he said, "One supreme compliment to a member of the church is, 'He is active.' But so are falling rocks and billiard balls. The word the Lord uses, and the question derived from it is, 'Are you a lively member? Are you alive [in Christ]?'"[9]

Couples can go through the motions of spirituality and righteousness, but without sharing thoughts and feelings associated with righteous behaviors, spiritual intimacy may still be lacking between husband and wife. Elder Spencer J. Condie described one couple who *did* all the right things, but couldn't *share* their hearts. They ". . . prayed together, studied the scriptures together, held family home evening and attended church together, indicating a strong degree of spiritual intimacy. But when it came to sharing personal feelings, they didn't seem to be very adept."[10] Building spiritual intimacy is an extension of sharing emotional intimacy.

As couples strive for marital oneness by embarking upon a multi-dimensional recovery of their emotional, sexual, and spiritual wholeness, they recover the sacred within themselves and within their relationship. Elder James E. Faust identified the rarely explored recovery individuals and couples need, "God can not only help us find a sublime and everlasting joy and contentment, but He will change us so that we can become heirs of the kingdom of God. This is really the recovery of the sacred within us."[11]

Spiritual intimacy is not only personal righteousness and a disclosure of spiritual thoughts, emotions, and experiences, it is also joining our spirits through our bodies. We can gain understanding of the interconnectedness of physical and spiritual intimacy from 1 Corinthians 6:16-17, 19-20, "What? know ye not that he which is joined to [another] is one body? for two, saith he, shall be one flesh. But he that is joined unto the Lord is one spirit. . . . What? know ye not that your body is the temple of the Holy Ghost which is in you, . . . therefore glorify God in your body, and in your spirit."

In these scriptures we learn that as husband and wife become one physically, they become one spiritually. When their bodies, which house their spirits, join in sexual relations, so, too, do their spirits. The interconnectedness of the three dimensions of intimacy is profound. Joining our bodies in the sacred sacrament of sexual union is one of the ultimate ways we join spiritually.

Identifying and Removing Barriers to Spiritual ONEness

To develop greater spiritual intimacy in marriage, couples must identify their intimacy barriers and strive to remove them. Christian author and speaker, Joe Beam, realizing the importance of spiritual intimacy in creating complete oneness in marriage, sought to find answers. "We quickly discovered that understanding the significance of spiritual intimacy and knowing how to grow it in a marriage are *not* the same thing. In order to teach couples how to become ONE spiritually, we had to discover why so many spouses fail in this particular area of marital life."[12]

Being Unequally Yoked Spiritually. One barrier may occur when couples are of different faiths or have differing levels of commitment to and love for God. It can be more challenging, though not impossible, to seek God together when differing beliefs are significant. Couples are wisely counseled to marry one to whom they can be equally yoked spiritually, making it easier to fulfill the scriptural command to "be one"[13] and to "fulfil ye my joy, that ye be likeminded, having the same love, being of one accord, of one mind."[14]

Elder Condie warned of the difficult challenge of marital unity and happiness when couples are not connected spiritually, "When couples are not like-minded about the things that matter most in life, it is extremely difficult to achieve marital happiness, 'for intelligence cleaveth unto intelligence.' (Doctrine & Covenants 88:40)."[15] President Harold B. Lee taught the great importance of eternal marriage and of selecting a companion with whom you could work and progress eternally side-by-side:

> Marriage is a partnership. . . . At the marriage altar you are pledged to each other from that day to pull the load together in double harness. . . . "Be ye not unequally yoked" (II Cor. 6:14.). . . .
>
> But even more important than that you be "yoked equally" in physical matters, is that you be yoked equally in spiritual matters.[16]

Individuals are most often attracted to those of general like-mindedness, though they may differ to some degree. After marriage, individuals may change. One spouse may continue to grow spiritually while the other remains stagnant. Or one spouse may decide on his or her own to develop spiritually where neither previously had much interest. Through the apostle Paul the Lord emphasized the majesty of the marriage covenant, while encouraging couples to preserve their marriage even in the face of spiritual differences. Paul taught the hope-filled doctrine of the unbelieving spouse being sanctified by the other:

> If any brother hath a wife that believeth not, and she be pleased to dwell with him, let him not put her away. And the woman which hath an husband that believeth not, and if he be pleased to dwell with her, let her not leave him. For the unbelieving husband is sanctified by the wife, and the unbelieving wife is sanctified by the husband: else were your children unclean; but now are they holy. . . . For what

knowest thou, O wife, whether thou shalt save thy husband? or how knowest thou, O man, whether thou shalt save thy wife? But as God hath distributed to every man, as the Lord hath called every one, so let him walk.[17]

The *unbelieving* spouse can be sanctified and blessed by a *believing* yet humble and merciful spouse. Righteousness must not slip into *self-righteousness* where the other's faults become the focus. True spirituality leads to Christlike compassion, not self-righteousness and condemnation. The prophet Joseph Smith taught, "It is the doctrine of the devil to retard the human mind, and hinder our progress, by filling us with self-righteousness. The nearer we get to our Heavenly Father, the more we are disposed to look with compassion on perishing souls; we feel that we want to take them upon our shoulders, and cast their sins behind our backs. . . . If you would have God have mercy on you, have mercy on one another."[18]

Couples with differing beliefs, behaviors, or levels of spiritual commitment can still improve spiritual intimacy in their marriage. They can find common ground and work together to make God a bigger part of their lives. It is with love, kindness, and patience that spiritual intimacy grows. Remember the prophet Joseph Smith's words, "Nothing is so much calculated to lead people to forsake sin as to take them by the hand, and watch over them with tenderness. When persons manifest the least kindness and love to me, O what power it has over my mind, while the opposite course has a tendency to harrow up all the harsh feelings and depress the human mind."[19]

Many couples may appear equally yoked spiritually, although they are not. Joe Beam identified this problem and suggested a plan of action to bring couples together spiritually:

> The vast majority of situations we encounter involve a godly woman married to a man—often a godly man—who won't pray with her, study the Bible with her, or teach their children the ways of God. Whether the problem lies with the husband, the wife, or both, the path to spiritual ONEness is the same: (1) the couple must analyze why spiritual intimacy between them doesn't exist, (2) they must remove spiritual barriers, and (3) they must make a plan to bring both of them to spiritual intimacy.[20]

In searching for answers, Joe Beam found three other reasons for the lack of spiritual intimacy in marriage: "*spiritual lethargy, misplaced priorities*, and *fear of openness*."[21]

Spiritual Lethargy. Couples may see the value of developing spiritual intimacy, but may not have the energy, interest, or knowledge to make it happen. They just don't seem to have time for anything else in their already hectic schedules. Intimacy diversions may be the culprit. One spouse may think watching television should be replaced with meaningful spiritual interaction, while the other may see this activity as essential to unwind from a busy or stressful day. Husbands and wives, fathers and mothers have a responsibility to grow spiritually and to teach their children the Word of God. Countering spiritual lethargy requires a desire to make time for things of God.

Misplaced Priorities. People make time for whatever is most important to them. To make their marriage last, couples must put each other first. God has counseled us to put first things first, and to set our homes and lives in order.[22]

In June 1965 President David O. McKay spoke to the members of the new building committee of the LDS Church regarding priorities. Fred A. Baker, a member of that committee, recounted President McKay's warning that their new assignment would stretch them to the limits of their time and effort. He told them not to sacrifice the most important things for the least important. He then assured them that some day they would have a personal interview with the Savior. He told them the order in which Jesus Christ would ask for an accounting of their earthly responsibilities:

- *First,* the Savior will request an accountability report about your relationship with your spouse;

- *Second,* He will want a report about your relationship with each of your children;

- *Third,* He will want to know what you have personally done with the talents you were given in the premortal existence;

- *Fourth,* He will not be interested in what assignments you have had in the Church, but how you served and fulfilled your stewardships;

- *Fifth,* He will have little interest in how you earned your living, but if you were honest in all your dealings;

- *Sixth,* He will ask for an accounting of what you have done to contribute in a positive manner to your community, state, country and the world.[23]

Misplaced priorities involving worthy activities can be even more insidious than blatantly destructive activities. In an attempt to fulfill the need to feel valued and important, good and worthy activities such as community or church service are sometimes given precedence over the needs within the family. As Joe Beam said, "If you neglect your family for some good work—even a godly work—you, too, seek the wrong goal. You cannot honestly justify your neglect of your own family by claiming that God called you to minister to others. He never told anyone to abandon the greatest responsibility of all—the one to our own spouses and children—to do good for someone else. You minister first to your own, then to others."[24] Finding the delicate balance requires the guidance of the Spirit.

As we put God first, spouse second, children third, church callings fourth, and our contribution to society through careers and community service fifth, we put first things first, gain better eternal perspective, and align our lives with the highest priorities. The key is often scheduling. President Ezra Taft Benson said, "When we put God first, all other things fall into their proper place or drop out of our lives."[25]

Actively putting Godly priorities in your planner protects against Satan's diversions and distractions. Turn off the TV, cancel one activity or project, then schedule time for building spiritual intimacy with those that matter most.

Fear of Openness. The third barrier to spiritual intimacy is fear of openness. This is related to the need for forgiveness and acceptance of ourself and our spouse. Couples must feel safe to be open and vulnerable, sharing their spiritually intimate insights, emotions, and experiences with each other. Letting our spouse in on our intimate relationship with God means letting him or her see our struggles, our shame, our sins, and our feelings of unworthiness. This honesty and vulnerability may be scary but is essential to break down the barriers that keep us at arms' length. Joe Beam shared how these fears can be significant barriers to spiritual intimacy and oneness:

> Perhaps the greatest reason that one person won't study or pray with another is because he or she fears being open and vulnerable in the presence of the other . . . .
>
> When prayer is a pouring out of our lives and hearts to God, we sometimes have to speak of things that we don't want others to hear. We confess to God the failings and faults with which we struggle. We beg Him for things we can't accomplish ourselves. We tell Him not only what we've done but how we feel about what we've done. Sometimes we even tell Him what we *want* to do, begging Him to prevent us from doing it.
>
> No spouse could pray like that before the other if he or she isn't already living an honest life.[26]

Improving Spiritual Intimacy as a Couple

Once barriers are identified and removed, efforts to increase the spiritual connection between husband, wife, and God can be more effective. Though individuality and personal differences remain, as couples grow together spiritually, they synergistically become even stronger as one. Just because a couple is striving to become *one* doesn't mean they are striving to become the *same*. While couples often have an idea *what* they should do, suggestions on *how to do it* can be helpful. Choose just one of the following ways to strengthen your relationship spiritually:

1. Read and Discuss Patriarchal Blessings. Each of us has a "divine nature and destiny."[27] As divine spirit beings, each of us is endowed with talents, gifts and blessings to help us fulfill our earthly missions. Patriarchal blessings can provide vision and inspiration.

Seeing ourself and our spouse as God does can inspire us to use our capacities to fulfill our eternal purposes. Where we once saw ourselves as a mere caterpillar, we can instead believe God's vision of a butterfly. During personally difficult times, I have frequently relied on a vision of myself and my husband building God's kingdom by serving missions together in the future. When you know who you *really* are and what you're here for, Satan loses power to tempt you and thwart your earthly mission.

When you know who you really *are and what you're here for,*
Satan loses power to tempt you and thwart your earthly mission.

Having an eternal perspective of each other provides a positive atmosphere in marriage and a strong foundation upon which to build spiritual intimacy. Periodically read and discuss your patriarchal blessings to keep one another's divine potential at the forefront of your minds.

With desire, prayer, pondering, and quiet reflection, study your patriarchal blessing and find out who you really are. Your spark of divinity is waiting to ignite. For even greater insight into your divine self make three columns on a page and put the pieces of your blessing into the following categories: (1) Who am I? (2) What are my promises, gifts, and blessings; and (3) What counsel and warnings have been given to me? Encourage your spouse to do the same, then share with each other.

WHO AM I?	MY PROMISES, GIFTS AND BLESSINGS	COUNSEL AND WARNINGS TO ME
• He sent you forth with great hope for you. • You will always be an obedient daughter to your Heavenly Father.	• Before you left His bosom, He endowed you with certain strengths to forge ahead and be successful. • You will be able to comprehend the unfolding of the ways of the Lord in these latter days.	• Live in a way that you'll be able to put temptation behind you. • You are encouraged to be mindful of others.

To lift marriage to a higher plane, President Gordon B. Hinckley suggested seeing our spouse as an important part of God's eternal purposes:

> Companionship in marriage is prone to become commonplace and even dull. I know of no more certain way to keep it on a lofty and inspiring plane than for a man occasionally to reflect upon the fact that the helpmeet who stands at his side is a daughter of God, engaged with Him in the great creative process of bringing to pass His eternal purposes. I know of no more effective way for a woman to keep ever radiant the love for her husband than for her to look for and emphasize the godly qualities that are a part of every son of our Father and that can be evoked when there is respect and admiration and encouragement.[28]

2. Increase Faith and Obedience. Faith is an anchor to the souls of men.[29] Faith is confidence and trust in God. Faith is not knowing *what* the future holds but knowing *who* holds the future. Faith requires mental discipline to maintain a belief through time and adversity. Faith is doing your best, then trusting God to do the rest. Faith is the foundation upon which all righteousness is built. As you pray for greater faith, God will help you.

A simple formula for increasing faith is to increase obedience to God. Elder Robert D. Hales taught, "Obedience to the laws and ordinances of the gospel is essential to obtain faith in the Lord Jesus Christ."[30] Imagine every act of obedience to God as spiritual fuel to increase your faith. Every time you pray, heed spiritual promptings, go to church, fulfill your callings, or pay tithing you are blessed with faith for your obedience. It's a wonderful cycle that builds upon itself. As you are obedient you gain more faith. As you gain more faith it is easier to be more obedient.

Cycle of Faith and Obedience

Faith

Obedience

3. Pray Together Daily. While prayer together is often the first thing to go when couples encounter marital troubles, it *can be* the first thing to heal and restore love in marriage. When couples feel loved and accepted by each other, couple prayer can open a sacred window into each other's soul. Some couples like to take turns praying. Others discuss what they would like to have included in the prayer just prior to praying. Others kneel in prayer both voicing alternating "paragraphs" until all the yearnings of the heart have been heard.

Jason shared a marital tradition he and his wife treasured. Each night they knelt together at their bedside to pray. Before prayer they read a verse of scripture or a statement from President Hinckley's little book of daily devotions entitled *Stand a Little Taller.* They discussed the verse, then took turns praying, thanking the Lord for each other. Afterward they exchanged verbal expressions of love and a kiss. He told me it symbolized a renewing of their marriage covenants as they knelt before the Lord in prayer. What a wonderful reminder couple prayer can be as it builds spiritual strength and increases sweetness in marriage. President Hinckley counseled:

> I know of no single practice that will have a more salutary effect upon your lives than the practice of kneeling together as you begin and close each day. Somehow the little storms that seem to afflict every marriage are dissipated when, kneeling before the Lord, you thank him for one another, in the presence of one another, and then together invoke his blessings upon your lives, your home, your loved ones, and your dreams.
>
> God then will be your partner, and your daily conversations with him will bring

peace into your hearts and a joy into your lives that can come from no other source. Your companionship will sweeten through the years; your love will strengthen.[31]

4. Study and Discuss Scriptures. Meaningful scripture study opens a direct conduit of light and truth from God. The scriptures teach about God and how to be more like Him. There are many wonderful ways couples can study, discuss, and learn from the scriptures. Some couples read together every morning or night. Some couples read and discuss general conference articles together on Sunday. What has worked especially well for my husband and me is for us to have our personal scripture study during the week, then come together on Sundays to share what we have learned.

The personal scripture study system I have discovered and developed has been a blessing to me and has revolutionized my scripture study. I didn't want to just go through the motions of scriptures study to "get it done." I wanted to learn something. I wanted to be inspired and enlightened every time. Of all the approaches I've used over the years for studying the scriptures, this system has been an open conduit of light and truth. Some of the elements may be familiar to you, while others may be new. A brief overview of this system follows:

1. *Prepare* — Get a notebook and pencil. Reading alone has only a 10 percent retention rate, but if you read and do, or write it down, retention can increase up to 90 percent.[32]

2. *Pray* — Pray for the Lord to guide you in your study. Seek the Spirit to inspire you with light and truth.

3. *Choose* — Choose one scripture (or passage of scripture) to study rather than a whole chapter.

4. *Liken to Yourself* — Write the scripture in your notebook, changing the words to have the verse speak directly to you or about you personally, then read it aloud.

5. *Personalize* — Write your own personal commentary on what you think or feel about this scripture. What thoughts does it generate?

6. *Ask Questions* — What questions come to mind about this scripture and its teachings? Write down your questions and the answers that will come.

7. *Ponder* — Take a minute to ponder or think about what you're studying. Do any thoughts, impressions or promptings come to mind? Be sure to write them down. It is not so much what you read in the scriptures but what the Spirit teaches that

transforms your life. Personal revelation can illuminate your heart and mind as you invite the influence of the Spirit into your scripture study session.

8. *Apply and Take Action* — What are you going to do with or about this new insight? How will you apply it in your life? Be a doer of the word, and not a "reader" only.[33]

With a notebook filled with personal scriptural commentaries, come together as husband and wife and discuss your insights. It's an incredible experience and your spiritual intimacy will be strengthened. When we read the scriptures and don't get anything out of it, it weakens our resolve to study the scriptures again next time. With this scripture study system, I am edified every time I study. There is truly a divine return on my investment of time and effort. I become the recipient of the light and truth that is there for the taking.

In case you need a reminder of the great blessings and promises to those who will study the scriptures regularly, the following is the testimony of President Marion G. Romney:

> I feel certain that if, in our homes, parents will read from the Book of Mormon prayerfully and regularly, both by themselves and with their children, the spirit of that great book will come to permeate our homes and all who dwell therein. The spirit of reverence will increase; mutual respect and consideration for each other will grow. The spirit of contention will depart. Parents will counsel their children in greater love and wisdom. Children will be more responsive and submissive to the counsel of their parents. Righteousness will increase. Faith, hope, and charity—the pure love of Christ—will abound in our homes and lives, bringing in their wake peace, joy, and happiness.[34]

5. Repent and Forgive Each Other Regularly.

We all make mistakes—regularly! We all have weaknesses and imperfections. As we repent and offer the gift of forgiveness to our spouse, daily marital disturbances can be washed away through the blood of the Atonement. Regular repentance and forgiveness keeps molehills in our marriage from becoming mountains. Repentance removes barriers to spiritual intimacy and spiritual progress while strengthening faith. During the sacrament we humble ourselves and repent of our sins. As we wipe our own slate clean each week, we can also forgive our spouse for their sins and imperfections and grant them a clean slate, too.

Forgiveness is the process of turning our heartache's over to God and letting Him take care of them. Some experiences are harder to forgive than others. Pray for the spirit of forgiveness, ready your heart, then warmly receive it when it comes. Elder H. Burke Peterson taught, "Forgiveness of others for wrongs—imaginary or real—often does more for the forgiver than for the forgiven."[35]

6. Reverence the Sabbath. One of the best ways to reverence God and increase spiritual intimacy in marriage is to honor the Sabbath and keep it sacred. Observing the Sabbath can strengthen a marriage as well as a family. The Sabbath day provides couples such opportunities as attending church services together, praying, studying the scriptures, the *Ensign,* or Sunday lessons, writing in journals or doing family history work. Elder Marlin K. Jensen shared his experience from the early years of his marriage when he and his wife dedicated themselves to honoring the Sabbath and using their time to strengthen their marriage:

> [My wife and I] rarely met in all our individual comings and goings, and our relationship with each other was suffering noticeably. Even Sundays were burdensome as we tried to fulfill our Church callings and catch up on studies and school preparation. Finally, we sat down one evening and decided that if our marriage was a very important part of our lives, we had better start acting like it. We agreed to completely honor the Sabbath by refraining from all work, including our studies, and to devote ourselves to building a stronger marriage. We experienced an immediate surge in our feelings toward each other and noticeable improvement in other areas, including my grades and Kathy's teaching.[36]

7. Fast Together with Common Purpose. Fasting strengthens the spirit, and draws us closer to the Lord. Spiritual strength is manifest by increased personal power over bodily appetites and passions. Fasting also humbles the soul.[37] Seeking special blessings and striving to learn God's will in our lives is an important part of fasting. Husband and wife can kneel together before the fast to discuss and share what they are fasting for, then combine their faith for added power. Kneel together to close your fast, strengthening your spirits and renewing your spiritual resolve.

8. Attend Church Services and Discuss What You Learn. Sacrament and other Sunday meetings regularly provide doctrinal and spiritual nourishment. That nourishment is enhanced when husbands and wives make time in their Sabbath day schedule to share what they learned, and then determine ways to apply or take action on the insights. Couples can also grow in love as they sit together at meetings, physically touching in some way, such as holding hands.

Couples can gain doctrinal enlightenment and build spiritual intimacy as they discuss what was taught at church, examine comments that were made, and review or preview Sunday lessons. This spiritual and intellectual learning increases their like-mindedness. Having husbands and wives study from the same Priesthood / Relief Society manual was inspired as a way to increase spirituality in the home.

9. Have Weekly Family Home Evenings. Fathers and mothers have a divine responsibility to teach their children light and truth. Weekly family home evenings allow husband and wife to exercise and share this stewardship while strengthening their family spiritually. The primary purposes of family home evening are "to build family unity and teach gospel principles."[38] The power of true doctrine must be firmly rooted in ourselves and in our children to combat Satan's army. Satan has so many opportunities to spread his lies and distortions that couples and parents must take full advantage of their weekly opportunity to reinforce righteousness with revealed truth.

10. Keep a Balance as You Serve in Church Callings. Putting God first sometimes means putting your church responsibilities first, but other times it means putting your spouse or children first. Putting God first should never mean that your family is relegated to receiving your leftover time and energy. Only the Lord knows which need is most important at any given time. He will guide you as you seek direction from Him.

Keeping first things first requires reordering and removing some things from your life. It will require a healthy degree of delegating and wise budgeting of time and energy. Preemptively scheduling time for spouse and children will assure them priority time and prevent other responsibilities from consuming your life. Vigilant attentiveness to the proper balance will be needed as you serve in church callings while putting the needs of your spouse and children first.

President Lee wisely counseled couples to remember the importance of the work we do within the home and taught that serving God would never require sacrificing spouse or family:

> Remember always that the most important work we will ever do will be within the walls of our own homes.
>
> Anyone who has a testimony of the gospel of Jesus Christ is willing to give his all to the kingdom, but in the process of that kind of dedicated service, it is important that we do not ignore what Jesus called "the things of most worth. . . ." God will never ask any man to sacrifice his family in order to carry out his other duties in the kingdom.[39]

11. Serve, Worship, and Learn in the Temple. Marriage is an eternal partnership where husband and wife are sealed together in the holy temple of God as eternal best friends. Returning to the temple often to serve, worship, and learn renews our covenants with God and each other. In this day of Satan's power and influence, couples cannot afford to underestimate the power and protection of temple covenants and temple service.

Through temple attendance, lives, marriages, and families are blessed beyond measure, for the temple is a place of learning, revelation, power, peace and comfort. President Hinckley stated, "If we are a temple-going people, we will be a better people, we will be better fathers and husbands, we will be better wives and mothers. I know your lives are busy. I know you have much to do. But I make you a promise that if you go to the house of the Lord, you will be blessed, life will be better for you."[40]

In a letter from The First Presidency of the Church, members were "encouraged to replace some leisure activities with temple service."[41] When couples are scheduling their weekly dates, attending the temple together should be first on their list—where possible.

To prepare their hearts and minds, couples might pray together before entering the temple, asking the Lord to open their minds to greater understanding and insight. During the session couples can pay close attention to any insights or promptings they may receive or questions they are pondering. They can plan to spend time in the celestial room quietly sharing and discussing their thoughts and feelings. Growing together in light and truth while in the temple of the Lord is a wonderful way to increase spiritual intimacy and oneness in marriage.

In 3 Nephi 17:3 the Lord provided a formula for temple worship. When Jesus visited and taught the Nephites He perceived they could not understand all His words. He suggested they go home and ponder what they had been taught. He told them to ask Heavenly Father to help them understand, and to help prepare their minds, so that when they returned they could better understand His teachings.

We too can go to our homes, ponder what we learn in the temple, and ask for spiritual enlightenment as we seek to better understand the teachings of the temple. As we hunger for greater light and truth we prepare our hearts and minds to receive greater light and truth. When we go again to the temple, we will find greater spiritual knowledge and strength.

12. Strive to Have God's Pure Love. "Charity is the pure love of Christ."[42] It is the highest, noblest, strongest kind of love we can offer. It is the kind of love Christ has for each of us, and the love He asks us to have for each other.[43] We must have charity, for without it we are nothing. Having charity isn't easy. It requires a softened heart. It must come from within. Charity requires that we give and serve from the heart, not simply go through the motions to "do our duty." We must be changed from within.

As couples strive to develop this ultimate spiritually intimate kind of love, they are blessed with peace, joy, and power to overcome all things for charity suffereth long, is kind, envieth not, and is not puffed up. Charity seeketh not her own, is not easily provoked, thinketh no evil, and rejoiceth not in iniquity but rejoiceth in the truth, beareth all things, believeth all things, hopeth all things, endureth all things and never faileth. Cleave and bind your heart unto charity. It is the greatest of all.[44]

This is not an insurmountable feat. Choose just one element of charity and work toward it. Pray unto Heavenly Father with all the energy of your heart that you might be filled with this love, which God bestows upon all who are true followers of His Son, Jesus Christ. We may have this hope: that we may be purified, even as He is pure. We can become the sons and daughters of God. And when He shall appear, we shall be like Him.[45]

Striving to improve spiritual intimacy can open up a divine depth and dimension in marriage. As you read this book and pursue marital oneness, you may find that one spouse might especially like the information in the chapters on *sexual* intimacy, but may be more reluctant regarding the *emotional* and *spiritual* intimacy material. The other spouse may be excited about the *emotional* and *spiritual* intimacy suggestions, but not so thrilled about the *sexual* intimacy information. This dilemma identifies an important purpose in marriage. The differences between husband and wife encourage them to grow in the specific areas in which they may be weak. This helps couples develop personal wholeness and completeness, which allows them to become one with one another and with God.

Chapter 11—"Home" Work

- Strive for greater spiritual intimacy in marriage through personal righteousness and more frequent sharing of spiritual thoughts, emotions, and experiences.

- Identify barriers to spiritual intimacy between you and your spouse, and strive to remove them.

- Make time for your spiritual priorities by scheduling regular dates to the temple, weekly family home evening, couple and family prayer, couple and family scripture study, and time to discuss insights from church meetings.

- Overcome any fear of openness by seeking forgiveness and confessing to God and/or spouse any sin or shame you are holding onto that is creating an intimacy barrier.

- Frequently read and discuss each other's patriarchal blessings. Divide your blessing into three categories: "Who Am I?"; "My Promises, Gifts and Blessings"; and "Counsel and Warnings to Me."

- Pray for greater faith. Be more obedient to strengthen your faith.

- Pray together daily.

- Study and discuss the scriptures regularly.

- Repent and forgive each other regularly.

- Develop a greater spirit of reverence in your home by observing the Sabbath as a sacred day, and spending time strengthening your marriage spiritually.

- Fast together with common purpose.

- Attend church meetings and discuss what you learn.

- Have weekly family home evenings to build marital and family unity, and to learn the principles and doctrines of the gospel.

- Keep a balance as you serve in your church callings, assuring that your highest priorities receive sufficient time and attention.

- Serve, worship, and learn in the temple often. Pray before going to the temple, and spend time there discussing your insights.

- Pray to be filled with God's love.

NOTES

Chapter 11—Becoming One—Spiritual Intimacy

[1] *See* Moroni 10:32.

[2] Kimball, *Marriage and Divorce*, 23.

[3] Kimball, *Marriage and Divorce*, 24.

[4] Condie, "Finding Marital Unity through the Scriptures," *Ensign*, July 1986, 55.

[5] Perry, "That Spirit Which Leadeth to Do Good," *Ensign*, May 1997, 70.

[6] Bytheway, *What We Wish We'd Known*, 37–38.

[7] Holland, "How Do I Love Thee?" BYU devotional address, 15 Feb. 2000. *See also Marriage and Family Relations Instructor's Manual*, 2000, 28.

[8]*See* 2 Nephi 25:25.

[9]Madsen, *Highest In Us*, 26.

[10]Condie, "Finding Marital Unity," *Ensign*, July 1986, 53.

[11]Faust, "Heirs to the Kingdom of God," *Ensign,* May 1995, 63.

[12]Beam, *Becoming One*, 180.

[13]John 17:11, 21–22.

[14]Philippians 2:2.

[15]Condie, "Finding Marital Unity," *Ensign*, July 1986, 54.

[16]Lee, *Teachings of Presidents*, 109.

[17]1 Corinthians 7:12–17.

[18]Madsen, "Tolerance, the Beginning of Christlike Love," *Ensign*, Oct. 1983, 29.

[19]Hales, "Strengthening Families: Our Sacred Duty," *Ensign*, May 1999, 34.

[20]Beam, *Becoming One*, 180–81.

[21]Beam, *Becoming One*, 181.

[22]*See* Doctrine & Covenants 93:43, 50.

[23]Personal Interview with Fred A. Baker, March 8, 2004.

[24]Beam, *Becoming One*, 191–92. *See also* 1 Timothy 5:8

[25]Benson, "The Great Commandment," *Ensign*, May 1988, 4.

[26]Beam, *Becoming One*, 192–93.

[27]"The Family: A Proclamation to the World," *Ensign*, Nov. 1995, 102.

[28]Hinckley, "Except the Lord Build the House," *Ensign,* June 1971, 71–72.

[29]*See* Ether 12:4.

[30]Hales, "Aaronic Priesthood: Return with Honor," *Ensign,* May 1990, 39.

[31]Hinckley, "Except the Lord," *Ensign,* June 1971, 72.

[32]Boyd, "Impact of Instructional Method on Retention," 1992.

[33]*See* James 1:22.

[34]Benson, "Book of Mormon: Keystone of Our Religion," *Ensign,* Nov. 1986, 7.

[35]Peterson, "Removing the Poison of an Unforgiving Spirit," *Ensign,* Nov. 1983, 60.

[36]Jensen, "Union of Love & Understanding," *Ensign,* Oct. 1994, 47.

[37]*See* Psalms 35:13.

[38]*Family Home Evening*, v.

[39]Lee, "A Sure Trumpet Sound," *Ensign,* Feb. 1974, 77.

[40]Hinckley, "Excerpts from Recent Addresses," *Ensign,* July 1997, 73.

[41]"News of the Church," *Ensign,* June 2003, 76.

[42]Moroni 7:47.

[43]*See* 2 Nephi 26:30.

[44]*See* Moroni 7:45–46.

[44]*See* Moroni 7:48.

CHAPTER VIEW

Touch is a Biological Need

The Healing Power of Touch

Touch Deprivation

Becoming One Physically

Nonsexual Physical Intimacy

Sexual Physical Intimacy

- *Developing Your Sexual Identity*
- *Body Image Acceptance*
- *Nurturing Touch*
- *Intimate Learning*

Starting Over Sexually—Awakening Sexual Senses

Sensate Focus Purposes

Sensate Focus Exercises

- *Week 1—Nonsexual Touching*
- *Week 2—Spooning*
- *Week 3—Blissful Caress*
- *Week 4—Touching and Caressing Avoiding Genitals*
- *Week 5—Kissing*
- *Week 6—Touching and Caressing Including Genitals*
- *Week 7—Orgasm and Intercourse*

Chapter 12—"Home" Work

Chapter 12

BECOMING ONE—PHYSICAL INTIMACY

Touch Is a Biological Need

From the moment of birth until we draw our last breath, we need the emotional, physical, and spiritual nourishment of touch. We never outgrow the *need* for tactile nourishment though we are often unaware of it and even deny it. Few things are more comforting than a hug or a loving hand over ours when we are hurt, scared, lonely, or tired. Touch is the universal language of love. It can communicate love, compassion, comfort, and understanding more powerfully than words. Touch in its many forms connects two persons emotionally and physically. It has been stated, "Touch is the satisfying feeling of skin-to-skin contact. Touch can be soothing, healing, caring, affectionate, comforting, or reassuring. It may take the form of stroking, patting, massaging, caressing, cuddling, hugging, or holding. It may vary from a brief brush to the massive tactile stimulation of sexual intercourse."[1]

Biologically, we need touch to survive. Universally, touch represents love. Loving touch is essential for emotional and physical health not only in children but also as adults and within marriage. Studies done on children in orphanages and on newborn babies regarding the effects of touch have shown physical, emotional, mental, and behavioral differences based on how much a child is lovingly held and touched. Some babies may even wither and die if they do not experience enough loving touch.[2] It is such a strong biological need that some children will take negative touch over no touch at all. They may subconsciously resort to provoking spankings or other physical punishment just to receive touch from someone.

Touch provides benefits to us biologically, psychologically, and socially. It helps develop our sense of self and builds self-esteem. It creates a sense of safety and security,[3] and has the power to comfort, reassure, and even heal emotional emptiness. The warmth, caring, and support of a simple hug is a tactile delight. When touch is shared as God intended in marriage, the massive physical nourishment of sexual touch and orgasm can flood the mind, body, and spirit with fulfillment. Touch can truly be one of the ultimate desserts of life.

In our culture where loving touch is minimized while purely sexual touch is highly promoted, the longing a person feels for loving touch often gets confused with a desire for sexual touch. Dr. Phyllis K. Davis has speculated that premarital sexual behavior is often an unconscious attempt to obtain love and tenderness through touch. Her theory was confirmed by the seniors in her interpersonal communications classes. She recounts:

> The first time I said to my group of seniors . . . that I believed that much of what went on in the back seats of cars, or motels or wherever, was not so much a need for sex as a need to be held—to be touched, to be affirmed in a most fundamental way, to reach outside their own bodies to find gentleness, tenderness, and understanding—I expected either embarrassed silence or denials, at least from the boys. I got neither. They agreed. They already knew. . . . When asked for reasons [for having sex], few [girls] spoke of overwhelming sexual urges. They talked about wanting to be loved, wanting to be held, wanting to be wanted, and the only way to get the boys to oblige them was to oblige the boys.[4]

The Healing Power of Touch

Touch has the power to heal by transferring vital energy between human beings. When two people touch they, in effect, plug themselves into an outlet of physical and emotional energy and nourishment. The implications for nonsexual touch are great. But within marriage sexual touch may be even more profound and powerful as a means of healing lonely or troubled hearts.

We instinctively understand the need for touch to heal hurts. Parents hold, hug, and kiss their children when knees are scraped or tears are streaming down. My youngest son always wants me to rub his tummy when he is sick. Without awareness we "transfer our healthy energies to loved ones in physical or emotional distress"[5] by hugging, holding, and caressing.

I remember being very sick one day at college. A dear friend stopped in to check on me. She brought physical food, but it was the emotional and psychological nourishment she gave that I needed most. With a sincere desire to help, she asked if there was anything she could do. Through tears I asked if she would hold my hand. It was as if I could feel her strength and vitality flowing into me.

Touch alleviates pain by providing pleasurable tactile sensations that block pain impulses to the brain.[6] The following are some additional ways touch has the power to heal:

- Hugging, stroking, or holding hands helps put our mind at ease. It helps to relax the body, which in turn induces the body to respond. Touch also reduces stress while stimulating the spirit or will to live.[7]

- Touch induces a positive emotional state, aiding the body in its healing process. It reduces the fear, frustration, and sense of helplessness often generated through illness.[8]

- Medical professionals who deal with traumatic injuries believe touch can function as a major antidepressant by increasing the production of endorphins.[9]

- Cradling, like a mother holding her child, can internally assist in healing someone who originally had poor expressions of love from parents.[10]

- While memories are stored in the brain, the older, deeper, more intense and more difficult-to-find memories seem to be stored in the body. These are called *body memories* or *tissue memories*, because they are accessed by touch rather than by conscious thought. Loving touch has the power to access and release these memories.[11]

The greatest healer of all, Jesus Christ, healed many through the power of physical touch. Though faith was required to be healed, the Lord did not simply *look at them, speak to them,* or *point to them* to heal them. *He touched them.* The following brief scriptural moments illustrate but a few instances of the Savior's touch communicating love and compassion as He healed physical *and* emotional wounds:

- "And he touched her hand, and the fever left her."[12]

- "A woman, which was diseased with an issue of blood twelve years, came behind him, and touched the hem of his garment. . . . And the woman was made whole from that hour."[13]

- "And as many as touched were made perfectly whole."[14]

- "Jesus came and touched them, and said, Arise, and be not afraid."[15]

- "Jesus had compassion on them, and touched their eyes: and immediately their eyes received sight."[16]

- "And the whole multitude sought to touch him: for there went virtue out of him, and healed them all."[17]

Touch Deprivation

Just as we need the physical nourishment of food, we need the tactile nourishment of touch. Few are lucky enough to receive a sufficient supply to meet their basic needs for love, comfort, and reassurance. American culture often seems touch–inhibited, depriving us of the tactile nourishment we need for well-being. For example, Dr. Davis has noted, "Compared to many [other cultures], Americans are cold fish, though we certainly don't think of ourselves that way. U.S. friends in a coffee shop tend to touch each other an average of only twice an hour—but French friends touch 110 times, and Puerto Rican friends, 180 times."[18] Rather than the expressions of caring, supportive touch that is evident in many other cultures, many subsist on minimal physical contact or the shallow, insufficient diet of sexual touch without love or commitment that is glamorized in society.

Most touch deprivation goes unnoticed or misdiagnosed since few understand or are aware of the critical need for touch. Dr. Harvey L. Gochros explained the seriousness of this need:

Touching is a basic . . . instinct. Nature seems to have designed it that way. We crave the emotional nutrition that comes from touch, just like an essential vitamin. . . . The truth is, we can't live without it. We develop a form of emotional scurvy, although we call it by different terms: depression, stress, anxiety, aggression, and midlife crisis . . . . Lack of touch is just as detrimental to our health as a lack of vitamin C and just as easy to remedy.[19]

A deficit in loving touch has been related to a condition where some children experience "failure to thrive." Deprived of caring touch from others, they fail to reach their full potential and their development is challenged. Remember the classic LDS film adapted by Carol Lynn Pearson, "The Cipher in the Snow"? (It originally came from a well-known Reader's Digest article.) It is the story of a shy and lonely boy who one snowy day stepped off the bus and died for no apparent reason. Upon closer inspection of his barren life, it was found that he was treated as a person of no importance, a non-entity in the world. The lack of love, attention, belonging, warmth, and touch slowly atrophied this young boy's spirit and his will to live.

Nancy once told me how she craved for someone—anyone—to touch her. She lived alone and worked two jobs and had few opportunities for social contact. Her touch deprivation was so great she would purposefully brush up against passersby just to receive some of the tactile nourishment she was starving for. To her, the biological and emotional need for touch sometimes felt like tangible pangs of hunger.

Gail vividly remembered a time when she must have been starved for touch because of the powerful effect one touch had on her. She said, "I was at the doctor's office. I was undressed, but was wearing a gown. During the course of the medical examination the doctor's hand rested on my shoulder while he examined my neck. The feeling was so intense my heart jumped. I audibly sighed—almost a moan. It was not a sexual feeling. It was just like that first swallow when you are very thirsty. I did not want him to stop. Of course he did, but I relived that moment over and over, amazed at the profound effect such a simple touch had on me."

Dr. Davis further identified the symptoms of touch deprivation and the lengths to which we will go to satisfy our unrecognized need for touch:

Behavioral scientists have given this deprivation of touch the term *skin hunger.* . . . Some people confuse skin hunger with restlessness, sexual desire, loneliness, or stomach hunger. We go to great lengths to satisfy our skin hunger without ever realizing what it is that we need. We attempt to satisfy it with food, with drugs, with entertainment; by burying ourselves in work, in talk, in activities, or with promiscuity. Yet it remains, this desire for the most basic form of communication [and love]—touching.[20]

The description that Dr. Davis shares of skin hunger closely resembles intimacy diversions in marriage addressed earlier in this book (see Chapter 9). Being unaware of the significant physical and emotional need for touch may account at times for people searching for love in all the wrong places. Serious touch deprivation causes some to become touch avoidant—withdrawing from the very thing they need most. Some cannot even stand to see others touching due to the emotional upset it causes them.

Why are we so touch deprived? There are many fears and inhibitions limiting loving touch. A reluctance to touch can be caused by a fear of rejection. The pain of rejection leads some to believe it is better not to need it at all, thus denying such a need exists. Another fear is that touch will be misinterpreted as sexual when it is merely meant to be loving. Sexual harassment concerns have all but extinguished touch among adults, especially employers and employees, or teachers and students. Same-gender touch carries additional stigmas and fears, especially for men.

Parents may also contribute to touch deprivation by consciously or unconsciously withholding love and touch. The lack of loving touch and affection gets passed down from generation to generation. "Non-touchers" often marry "touchers," causing misunderstanding and a clash in their relationship. Parents may also contribute to touch deprivation by punishing various forms of touch, sending a clear message that touch is unacceptable, dangerous or sexual. How many times in a day does a parent say, "Don't touch that," "Don't touch your sister," or "Just don't touch anything!"

Parental touch usually diminishes over time while a child's *need* for it doesn't. In our western culture touch between a parent and child tends to taper off for boys around age 5 - 6, when they are expected to be "big boys" now. For girls, touch continues longer than for their brothers, but tends to end when breast development begins (especially touch from fathers).[21] From such young ages, children are basically deprived of that essential "Vitamin T." The need for touch doesn't go away. Instead it is merely suppressed, manifesting itself in other ways that never satisfy.

If family members and individuals in society would hug and touch more in positive, caring ways, unmet emotional needs for touch leading to premarital sexual activity among youth might be reduced. Dr. Davis provided additional insight into the underlying touch deprivation factor among adolescents, stating, "Gradually, during adolescence, the major need to touch and be touched, suppressed and depressed for many years, becomes not only an impersonal search for sensory fulfillment, but also a symbolic search for love—for intimacy, security, acceptance, comfort, and reassurance. With the important avenues for touch fulfillment through parental contact and friends usually blocked off, adolescents learn to seek fulfillment through sexual exploration."[22]

*Understanding the importance of loving physical touch, as a need
similar to the need for water, air and shelter, can provide motivation
for all to be more free and frequent with loving touch.*

Understanding the importance of loving physical touch, as a need similar to the need for water, air and shelter, can provide motivation for all to be more free and frequent with loving touch. The need for this kind of touch can be satisfied not only by *receiving* hugs and other loving touches, but also by *giving* touch to others. One therapist suggested that as children we heal our emotional hurts and reduce touch deficits by *receiving* loving touch, but after age 12 we can also heal by *giving* loving touch.

Becoming One Physically

The universal need for touch and the existence of touch deprivation have important implications for marriage. Caring physical touch must become a bigger part of loving behavior between husband and wife, not only to fulfill basic needs, but also to increase intimacy and oneness.

Nonsexual Physical Intimacy

Physical intimacy in marriage is touch, closeness, and the electromagnetic energy of two living beings in physical and sexual contact with each other. Physical intimacy often implies only sexual contact, but should not be so limited. Nonsexual touch and affection *can* and *should* account for a larger portion of the physical intimacy and love shared between husband and wife.

Because of the prevalence of a "touch is sexual" mindset, it is difficult for some husbands and wives to disconnect touch from sex and enjoy nonsexual affection as a pleasure in itself. Because of the explosive nature of sexual intercourse, the simpler pleasures of nonsexual touch have a hard time competing. Dr. Phyllis Davis shared an unfortunate example of this, "You can usually tell when people have started having intercourse—they stop touching! They perform only ritual or perfunctory touching. Women definitely feel the loss, and many men will admit to the same feeling. . . . When two people consummate their relationship sexually, the loving touching soon stops, but intercourse can in no way meet all or even most of our loving touch needs."[23]

Couples find something is missing in their marriage relationship when they rarely engage in the pure, unadulterated pleasure of loving physical touch—holding hands, affectionate cuddling, stroking a partner's hair or arm, and holding each other. Nonsexual touch is something both husband and wife need to rethink, relearn, and reintroduce into their repertoire of loving behavior in marriage. Unfortunately, both husbands and wives have too often become accustomed to thinking that touch is primarily something that leads to sex. This need not be the case.

We can relearn that touch can be a simple manifestation of love without necessarily having sexual intent. However, to change this pattern it must be addressed openly with a proactive plan to reintroduce loving touch *with no strings attached!* One wife complained, "I enjoy cuddling. He never wants to cuddle or 'make out.' Sometimes all I want is a little affection, and I definitely resent that the slightest show of affection has to lead to sex. Why can't affection just be shown for affection's sake?"[24]

It's a common complaint among married couples that one spouse seems incapable or unwilling to touch in ways that are simply affectionate without becoming sexually aroused. Lucile Johnson, popular LDS author, speaker, and marriage counselor, participated in conducting a study among 1000 women. They were asked what is the one thing they would like to have added to their marriage to enhance their relationship. Sixty-eight percent of the women responded almost identically—they wanted their husbands to touch them, hold them, and embrace them with no strings attached.[25]

Many couples believe if arousal occurs it has to go all the way. But with practice and patience couples can learn to enjoy nonsexual touch (whether arousal occurs or not) without continuing on to the sex act. And what they often learn is that as the quality and frequency of nonsexual touch increases in their relationship, the feelings of affection and sexual attraction between them tend to improve as well.

If affection is always associated with the expectation of sex, some spouses may choose to avoid affection altogether. However, touchless marriages create resentment and increase the touch deprivation many already feel. The following real-life examples of the lack of nonsexual touch in marriage illustrate the unnecessary frustration many wives feel:

> Jane avoided even nonsexual affection like the plague. It turned her off. She was concerned about the example she was setting for her children who could see she didn't like being hugged or kissed. Sometimes she wanted "a little drink of water" in the form of loving touch, but had learned that she would get a downpour instead. She would rather go thirsty than endure the downpour.
>
> She couldn't even think of asking for a hug or other shows of affection for fear her husband would get other ideas. She wished she could just enjoy affectionate touch with her husband, but had learned from experience that it wouldn't end there.

> Lynn loved to hug and cuddle with her husband, but felt bad every time because she felt like she was leading him on when she didn't want it to lead to anything else. She hated having strings attached to affection. She also hated feeling guilty if she didn't let it go all the way. She felt it was her fault he got turned on, which made her mad about his "easily-turned-on" nature. Because of the heavy dose of guilt she experienced when she didn't want to let touch lead to something else, she felt trapped, unable to enjoy affection as an end in itself.

It isn't just men who need to do something about restoring nonsexual affectionate touch to marriage. Women can and must express their need for this kind of touch and expect it to happen. Dr. Davis discussed the possibilities of women changing the cultural attitude regarding nonsexual touch:

> Some women contribute to the problem because they discourage any form of touching when they don't feel in the mood for sex. They believe, or know from experience, that if they make any kind of contact, their partners will assume it will lead to sex. The irony here is that such women merely encourage their [husbands] to associate touch with intercourse. This reinforces the problem, rather than helping their partner to accept and recognize the need for nonsexual touching.[26]

Couples can help each other *get affection* without having to *give sex* by proactively scheduling time for touch. They might schedule one night a week, for instance, for cuddling, touching, massaging, and talking ONLY! When the expectations are set up front, it is easier for both to relax and enjoy. Some couples may want to alternate sexual encounters with nonsexual encounters to meet each other's needs. This may work especially well when one or the other feels his or her needs for physical or sexual touch have been neglected. Both husband and wife need to express their feelings and adapt to each other's needs. It is unfair for one spouse to constantly expect that affectionate touch will result in sexual intimacy, but it is also unfair for one spouse to consistently avoid sexual intimacy when loving touch is given or shared.

Couples may also decide to spend a few minutes each night snuggling as they fall asleep. Many women discover that, over time, as their needs for nonsexual touch begin to be filled, they are more sexually attracted to their husbands. But remember, nonsexual touch must be given with NO STRINGS ATTACHED!

One woman, Jackie, was creative at finding a way to teach her husband to enjoy touch without it leading anywhere. She would undress, get into bed and say to her husband, "No sex tonight. You just get to enjoy me." This method also provided a wonderful way for her to get more comfortable with sexual touch without the expectation of intercourse.

The challenge for some spouses may be that they feel they don't get enough sex as it is, so to have to endure "cuddling" when they want "more" seems like some form of torture. If one spouse can understand and fulfill the other's *emotional* need for *nonsexual* touch, it is more likely that their spouse will come to understand and fulfill their *physical* need for *sexual* touch.

Along the way the spouse with the lower libido may happily find their desire for sexual touch increasing. And as one spouse stretches, if necessary, to meet the other's need for affection, they may also be surprised to find their own need for nonsexual touch increases. Nonsexual touch provides benefits and communicates love in ways that are different from sexual touch. While it is generally women who want more *nonsexual* touch and men who want more *sexual* touch, Dr. Davis provided insight into men's need for sex, and how it connects to their biological need for touch:

> When men want sex frequently or act as though they do, they may not always realize that they really need affection—to be held and touched. Men also need the feelings of acceptance, comfort, reassurance, and approval that can come from being lovingly touched. They know how to ask for sex and have been taught that it is quite acceptable to do so. They don't always know how to ask for nonsexual affection and touching.
>
> Most men, if willing, can learn to truly enjoy holding, caressing, stroking, hugging, and lots of tender communication. I believe they yearn for this, though it may be unconscious in many cases. They would reap many benefits if they would

learn to enjoy this kind of intimate communication. Their needs for touch, however submerged, would be met. . . . Most relationship and marriage problems could be cured if those involved would reach out and touch each other.[27]

Sexual Physical Intimacy

Sexual touch is the celebrated dimension of physical intimacy in marriage. Sexual intimacy is a combination of physical touch as well as emotional and spiritual intimacy. However, without an emphasis on the emotional benefits, touch may become simply a sexual *trigger* or *technique,* causing couples to miss out on its greater purposes. Touch is best given as an expression of love rather than merely a means toward a sexual goal.

Touch must become a form of loving communication rather than a service, a trigger, or a technique. Couples touch each other in the right places to get aroused, then touch some more to have an orgasm.[28] Without the emotional dimension of touch, however, lovemaking becomes consensual genital manipulation for the purpose of gratification rather than an expression of love. Touching, with the intent of connecting emotionally as well as sexually, can bridge the separateness between two people—counteracting loneliness and creating an intimate oneness.

One husband discovered his wife was having an affair. He couldn't understand why, since she was getting plenty of sexual attention at home. She told him, "But that is all I'm getting. No love, no touching, no talking—just plain sex."[29] Touching, *with the intent of communicating love*, constitutes the main difference between "making love" and "having sex." Making love is a full-bodied, emotional, spiritual and physical experience where lives are rejuvenated. It has been beautifully described as "an act of regeneration and healing whereby each spouse is validated anew."[30]

Marriage is incomplete without fulfillment of the emotional, spiritual, and physical needs of both husband and wife. Wise couples pay careful attention to these aspects of love to ensure all of their needs are being met, because *sex alone isn't enough*.

Marriage is a commitment to meet each other's needs. Meeting nonsexual and sexual intimacy needs within marriage may require husband and wife to stretch beyond their comfort zones. One spouse may need to learn to give love more fully in the form of affection and nonsexual touch. The other may need to learn to more fully give their whole self—mind, body, and spirit—to the sexual experience. The stretching of the soul to create sexual satisfaction for both husband and wife may be part of the "sanctifying" intended in the sexual relationship of marriage.

Understanding the universal need for touch and its power to nurture, heal, and provide pleasure provides a grander vision of nonsexual and sexual intimacy in marriage. Touch has the power to transform marriage from the mundane to an exalted plane, where full sexual fulfillment is experienced regularly and with great passion. Sexual and nonsexual intimacy soothes emotions, rejuvenates the spirit and conveys commitment to love one another.

The following are some additional insights, especially for women, to unlock sensual pleasure, as they learn to experience the physical and emotional delights God intended in marriage.

Developing Your Sexual Identity. Having a healthy sense of sexual identity refers to an individual's understanding of the divine purposes of sexuality. It is accepting oneself as a sexual being, and being comfortable with one's own body, and the existence of sexual feelings. Being a sexual person and enjoying sexuality is nothing to be ashamed of.

Developing a healthy sexual identity is not a major emphasis in a young woman's life. In fact, with the existence of what I have called the Good Girl Syndrome and the extensive, though unintended, negative conditioning regarding sex and the body that many have received, it is difficult for many women (and some men) to have a healthy sense of their sexuality. The good girl has generally been influenced to downplay, deny or be ashamed of her sexuality, rather than acknowledge it, accept it and be comfortable with it. But, like our first parents in the Garden of Eden, we should not be ashamed of our God-given sexuality and its righteous function within marriage.[31] God never intended sexuality to be ignored or excluded from life, but to be accepted with gratitude and reverence for its divine place and purposes.

The spouse with a higher libido, or sex drive, may feel dizzy with love at times and experience desire as fireworks, while the lower-desire spouse may experience desire as flickering sparks—leading them to believe they are less sexual, when that may not be true. Women have such a different system of sexual arousal and desire they may mistakenly believe they just aren't sexual beings. They may think, "Gee, I'm not like a man who thinks about sex all the time, and who is easily turned on. So, I guess I'm just not a sexual person."

One spouse may have sexual thoughts and feelings that are so subtle and fleeting that they often go unnoticed. The other spouse may have such an abundance of sexual thoughts and feelings that they are ever on guard to keep them in check.

A noted marriage therapist, Michele Weiner Davis, has stated, "If you give yourself half a chance to discover the rumblings of sexual desire rather than wait for the big bang, you may surprise yourself. You might discover that when you listen harder to your mind and body, the signals have been there all along. The reception just hasn't been very good up until now, but you can fix that."[32]

By paying more attention to even fleeting and flickering sexual sparks, one can develop a healthy sexual identity and appreciation for one's sexuality. He or she can relish appropriate sexual thoughts, feelings, and desires (keeping them directed toward their spouse) by welcoming them rather than shunning them. Women can cherish, celebrate, and bask in the feelings—no matter how fleeting—and chalk them up as proof of their divine sexual identity as a daughter of God.

For men, sex begins primarily in the body. For women, it begins primarily in the mind. What a woman thinks and feels about sex and her sexuality, as well as her mental ability to focus on pleasurable sensations during lovemaking, are keys to an uninhibited sexual response.

Men and women were divinely designed as sexual beings from the very beginning. Sexuality, in its true light, is a characteristic of every child of God. This understanding must merge with a firm belief in the sanctity of sexual relations within marriage. Men and women can and should seek to develop a healthy sexual identity, a godly gratitude for their sexuality and a righteous willingness to allow their sexuality to blossom within marriage.

Body Image Acceptance. An acceptance of the divinity of sexuality requires acceptance of the body as a gift from God, complete with its flaws and imperfections. According to Dr. Michael Farnworth, professor at BYU Idaho, "Your sexuality is the relationship that you have with your own body. How you feel about it. Your femininity. . . . Your affection. Your acceptance. It is not about the other person . . . it is about you."[33]

You must be comfortable with your own body before you can intimately share it with your spouse. Your feelings about your body have to do with the memories, experiences, beliefs, and conditioning you've had throughout your life. If you have difficulty in being comfortable with your own body, it is appropriate to ask yourself what has contributed to this difficulty. Have you had experiences that have made you feel embarrassed about your body as a whole or parts of your body? Have you been mistreated in any way that has contributed to your feelings about your body? Identifying such influences on your feelings can help you begin thinking of ways to address negative feelings in a more positive way.

To develop acceptance of your sexuality and your body, complete with its flaws and imperfections, focus on the parts of your body you are most uncomfortable with. What if you had to go without that body part? Each part of the body is given to us by God for a purpose. A hand can touch, caress and bless. The eye can gaze and communicate love. The most private parts of the body can assist in creating life or giving nourishment. In God's design, each part of the body is noble and a gift that we have been given to enjoy. And in that design, each of us has also been given the opportunity in marriage to share our bodies in giving and receiving pleasure through sexual love. Not only is a physical body necessary in mortality, but each part of the physical body has a necessary and important role. Does understanding that truth change your feelings about any part of your body? For some, it may be necessary to overcome negative thoughts and inhibitions about the sexual parts of the body. The suggestions for overcoming inhibitions, discussed in Chapter 7, may be helpful.

Some therapists also prescribe standing unclothed before a full-length mirror, affirming every part of the body from head to toe—perfect or not, sexual or not—by saying, "I love and accept my . . . (part of the body)." This simple assignment is repeated until a sense of acceptance and respect for every part of the body is felt. Though this may seem unconventional, simply thinking about the idea can give you a sense of how you feel about your body. If you feel resistance to this thought, or any suggested exercise that is not immoral in any way, you may have encountered an emotional, mental, or psychological block that needs to be addressed.

Nurturing Touch. Loving touch can also be given to oneself to heal the touch deprivation or skin hunger many people feel. Rather than resenting or longing for the touch we didn't receive as children or do not receive from our spouse, we can provide some of our own nurturing touch any time, anywhere. Nurturing touch is not sexual in nature. It may be done by stroking the face, arms, or fingers, or by holding your own hand with the intent to reassure and comfort. It can communicate love and acceptance of the self. We can be more gentle with ourselves through tender loving touch.

Nurturing touch contributes to the fulfillment of our tactile needs, helps us become more comfortable with our bodies, and increases our attention and sensitivity to physical sensations in general. This increased awareness can also heighten sexual pleasure within the intimate relationship of marriage.

Intimate Learning. Understanding the intricacies of the body and the intimate interactions of husband and wife are vital to fully enjoying the gift of sexual intimacy in marriage. Intimate learning might include reading books about the human sexual response and other aspects of lovemaking, or exploring the body to learn what makes each other intimately satisfied. Many people are unaware of some of the delicate and complex aspects of intimate relations, and are not even sure it's appropriate to learn about such things. Such was the case with Amanda who shared the following:

> I have struggled my whole married life of 25 years with what you call the Good Girl Syndrome. I was raised that you just don't think about or read about this subject. So when I got married I think I was the most naive person in the world. For 12 years I didn't even know what an orgasm was until a friend explained it to me.

Because of the external nature of male genitals, men are generally more familiar with their bodies and how they function. Many women, however, are less aware of their sexual parts, especially the clitoris, and may not have ever even seen that part of their body. One woman explained that the only time she had ever used a mirror to see her genitals was more than 20 years ago, the first time she had used a tampon.

One of the primary reasons we come to earth is to gain a body. God expects us to learn about this great gift, and to discover how to experience the incredible pleasure and joy afforded husband and wife. Women particularly have a responsibility to learn about and understand the functioning of their own bodies, as well as their husband's. This is part of the sacred marital stewardship to give and receive sexual expressions of love, in order to create a mutually fulfilling intimate relationship. Intimate learning is an antidote for merely doing what comes naturally, because profoundly meaningful sex is truly a learned behavior.

If a woman is unfamiliar with her own anatomy and sexual functioning, or has not yet been able to experience an orgasm, she may need to reassure herself of God's permission to learn about her body and its functioning. Initiating such learning may be embarrassing or uncomfortable for some women. Where there is strong resistance, there is likely to be negative mental conditioning and unnecessary inhibitions regarding sexual learning.

Some women may need to remind themselves of the sanctity of sexual relations in marriage in order to overcome any feelings of shame, guilt, or embarrassment they may associate with learning about the body and their God-given sexuality. Also, by seeking God's guidance, women can know what is acceptable to God regarding the intimate needs of their relationship. With sexual frustrations as a primary cause of divorce, couples have a responsibility to go to the Lord for help, when needed, so that they can create the intimate oneness He intended.

Intimate learning about sex and the body—male and female—can provide a significant step forward toward unlocking sexual inhibition by facing any fears and negativity that may exist. Proactively learning about something that may seem forbidden can help one find the courage necessary to look under the bed to see there is no monster. Intimate learning can be therapeutic psychologically, and also provide important and necessary insights.

While relationship issues are often a cause of sexual dysfunction, it may also be that too few women have sufficient sexual understanding of their bodies and their functioning to attain intimate fulfillment. Sexual ignorance in marriage is not bliss. For many women the intimate learning that they are missing is an understanding of their sexual anatomy—particularly the functioning of the clitoris and vagina. Women need to know the purpose of these body parts, where they are located, and what kind of stimulation is most arousing to them.

Ideally, young brides-to-be are lovingly given specific information and counsel from their mothers immediately prior to marriage. If that does not occur, or if a woman has not yet been able to experience orgasm after some time within marriage, she may need to gain additional understanding about her body through some form of intimate learning.

Drs. Lamb and Brinley suggest that the reason women do not experience orgasm is most often because of a lack of clitoral stimulation.[34] Understanding the importance of the clitoris, and knowing what kind and quantity of touch she needs are critical to sexual fulfillment. Both husband and wife should actively participate in learning what is sexually arousing to the wife, and see that each other's needs are met. Women who willingly learn to give and receive pleasure within lovemaking are engaged in a sacred, marriage-building pursuit as husband and wife come to truly "know" each other.

Understanding the Differences Between Appropriate Sexual Touching, Masturbation, and Intimate Learning. The concept of intimate learning often invites misunderstanding of the differences between appropriate sexual touching within marriage, inappropriate masturbation, and intimate learning. One woman expressed concern that any manual stimulation of each other's genitals during lovemaking seemed inappropriate—wrongly assuming that all needed stimulation would automatically occur during intercourse.

While sexual touching or "petting" *outside* of marriage is inappropriate, *within* marriage it is a wonderfully right and proper part of lovemaking. Sexual stimulation involves touching the sexual parts of each other's body to arouse sexual emotions. This shift in thinking from wrong (outside of marriage) to right (within marriage) is a difficult transition for some to make. Couples need to understand that sexual touching is indeed vital to happiness and fulfillment within the intimate relationship of marriage.

Masturbation (or solo self-pleasuring) is touching one's own body for self-pleasuring outside the husband/wife relationship. It is an impulsive means of self-medicating or self-satisfying, and can send an unfortunate message to the spouse that he or she is not good enough in bed. Masturbation can become an ongoing habit or addiction, and is an act of lust for personal pleasure and gratification. Masturbation causes distortions regarding genuine love and sexuality, and results in a "loss of confidence," "lessened control of sexual impulses" and "loss of the Spirit."[35] It weakens or replaces the marriage relationship, since individuals seek their sexual satisfaction alone instead of the more difficult work of building the intimate relationship together with their spouse.

Intimate learning, whether it be reading about sex or exploring each other's bodies, is a conscious choice to improve expressions of love, and build the intimate relationship between husband and wife. It requires effort and personal growth. It shows a healthy understanding of the divinity of the body—expressed as a desire to learn how to please each other within the marriage relationship. When following the guidance of the Spirit, intimate learning can have the wonderful result of helping couples achieve the mutual intimate fulfillment in marriage that God intended.

Couple Learning. The intent of intimate learning is to provide couples with their own private garden of love where peace, emotional safety, and intimate passion can be present. This sacred and appropriate environment within the marital relationship allows husband and wife to discover and develop their sexuality, share intimate desires, and come to know each other. I hear from many husbands who want to know what they can do to help their wives experience greater enjoyment and passion in lovemaking. Intimate learning provides an opportunity for women especially to identify what they like and share that with their husbands. The Sensate Focus exercises in this chapter can help husbands and wives both experience the intimate learning that will provide a solid foundation for their sexual relationship.

As couples learn and grow together intimately, they must feel free to learn how to express their love, and to seek each other's sexual enjoyment. If the focus is on fear of doing something wrong, rather than on learning and growing together, the intimate relationship will be stymied. This contributes to the high rate of divorce, as well as the marital dissatisfaction that has become so prevalent in marriages. Intimate learning, as determined by husband and wife under the guidance of the Spirit, must be understood as an appropriate and legitimate sanctuary where intimate exploration, enjoyment and fulfillment can flourish.

It is necessary to understand that the sexual response in both men and women is facilitated by familiarity with and sufficient stimulation of the sexual organs. The art of mutually fulfilling lovemaking takes time and intimate attention to one's spouse, as well as to one's own sexual responses. Together husband and wife can experiment and determine what works best for them.

Remember, the primary sexual challenge for most women is to awaken and free their sexuality, whereas for most men, their main challenge is to contain and channel their sexuality. An understanding of this and other sexual differences can help them determine their own path of intimate learning toward mutual fulfillment.

Starting Over Sexually—Awakening Sexual Senses

Therapists often recommend a system of graduated exercises called Sensate Focus as a means of "sensual awakening" to improve sexual functioning in marriage. LDS professionals, Drs. Lamb and Brinley, identify the "expectation-free" Sensate Focus techniques as helpful for increasing sexual arousal and overcoming orgasmic problems.[36]

Sensate Focus Purposes

Sensate Focus can bless *any* couple with a fresh, new, re-sensitized approach to lovemaking. It's not just for those who are having sexual difficulties. The many marital benefits of these sensual exercises are explained in the following descriptions of the purposes of Sensate Focus:

- *To develop and build up positive, pleasurable associations, memories and experiences with touch and sexuality.* Sensate Focus helps couples build intimate trust and become more comfortable with touch. With the graduated sensual involvement of the exercises, women especially are better prepared mentally and emotionally to let go and allow pleasurable sensations to flow. This helps to build up positive sexual associations in the brain to generate an uninhibited sexual response. Dr. Wheat stated, "Your goal will be to build up memories of pleasurable sexual feelings. When those are combined with some new experiences and a realization of your husband's loving desire to give you sexual pleasure, this will increase the number of signals to the brain, which can build up to an uninhibited sexual response."[37]

- *To awaken and increase sensuality and awareness of positive and pleasurable sensations in the body.* When a part of our being is ignored or not used to its fullest potential, it atrophies, creating emptiness or dysfunction in that part of the self. These exercises can restore wholeness to the soul and open the door to our fullest sexual potential.

- *To get to "know" or acclimate husband and wife to each other's bodies and sexual desires.* The scriptures do not refer to intimate marital relations as "sex." Instead the terms "know" or "knew" are used to designate the sacred intimate union of husband and wife.[38] As intended by God, the very act of sexual relations is a deeply intimate knowing of each other.

- *To learn from each other where, how and what touch is most pleasurable and stimulating.* The Sensate Focus exercises provide an excellent opportunity for couples to show each other what to do by placing their spouse's hand where, when, and how they want to be touched, reducing the need for words, which sometime get in the way sexually.

- *To learn to enjoy giving and receiving the tactile pleasure of sexual intimacy (stroking and being stroked) for its own sake without the psychological pressure and expectation to proceed to climax.* Sexual and nonsexual touch produces pleasure that is often missed in the rush to orgasm and intercourse. Dr. Phyllis Davis suggests, "Stroking the skin, exploring the texture, and investigating the contours of bone and muscles can be an end in itself and can convince the person being touched that he or she is loved, valued, and cherished as more than just a sexual partner."[39]

- *To help couples learn to be more conscious, attentive, and fully present in their lovemaking.* Conscious lovemaking, where the physical and emotional are integrated, is how couples can become one. Intentionally reconnecting emotions to the physical experience of lovemaking breaks the routine of simply going through the motions and helps eliminate boredom in the bedroom.

- *To help men develop greater control over their sexual energy.* The Sensate Focus exercises provide a perfect opportunity for men to bridle all their passions,[40] exemplifying self-mastery or the ability to govern and direct that power for good.

- *To provide an opportunity for couples to "clear the slate" and start over sexually.* Sometimes it's easier to start from scratch than to try to fix everything that's broken. Starting over can erase negative patterns and habits that have developed in the sexual relationship, and create new more positive patterns.

Sensate Focus Exercises

Amanda's honeymoon had been an unpleasant experience to say the least. She felt rushed, used, and unprepared emotionally and mentally for her husband's anxious advances. After learning of the Sensate Focus exercises, she wished she had known about them before her honeymoon. She called them "The Perfect Honeymoon Plan." She felt it would have made for a much smoother transition, a more pleasant experience, and would have provided a positive foundation for their sexual relationship rather than the "rude awakening" she experienced.

With the help of this book, newlyweds will now be much better prepared for a positive honeymoon experience. For those who are willing, the Sensate Focus exercises could be modified to meet both the husband's and wife's needs and provide an ideal sexual transition on the honeymoon or in the early part of marriage. With the Sensate Focus exercises in mind, couples could discuss and create their own plan for the honeymoon to avoid a rude awakening, providing positive and pleasurable sexual memories from the beginning.

When I first learned of Sensate Focus, I knew it would be helpful in our marriage, but for over a year I kept finding excuses as to why we couldn't get started. I had not yet overcome my negative beliefs and inhibitions, so the Sensate Focus exercises filled me with fear and nervousness, bringing all my inhibitions to the surface. This can be viewed as a positive or a negative depending on your determination to overcome barriers and improve your sexual relationship.

If your resistance to do this program is great or if you feel significant discomfort, it may be helpful to go back and review Chapters 2 and 7. The "Home" work assignments in these chapters help to develop a healthy foundation of belief in the sanctity of sexual relations, as well as help remove unnecessary sexual inhibitions. For many couples a review of Chapters 2 and 7 will help provide the necessary conditions to embark upon the sensual adventure of the Sensate Focus exercises.

Because some Sensate Focus exercises[41] can be either inappropriate or are "too much, too soon," I have compiled a unique combination of techniques. These self-help techniques are particularly valuable as something couples can do in the privacy of their own relationship, especially since most couples do not have access to good sex therapists. (Sadly, many couples in need would not go to see them even if one was available.)

The system used here is a great way to put a spark into any marriage and can be repeated as often as desired. Going through the exercises or adapting them to meet your needs may be a great anniversary tradition to keep your relationship fresh, alive, and pleasurable.

Discuss with your spouse when you will start this seven-week exercise. You'll need to plan for three opportunities each week. It will increase your success if you schedule these occasions. As you proceed, realize it will require some stretching, patience, and possibly even courage from both of you.

No orgasm or intercourse is allowed until specified in the seventh week. Some couples may think it impossible to go that long without sex. It can be done. Hopefully it is evident that the benefits listed above outweigh the sacrifices. Some couples may not feel a need for this exercise, but I would encourage them to consider doing the exercises anyway for the extra dimension, depth, and revitalization that can occur in an already healthy sexual relationship.

Psychologically, freedom of expression is critical to a relaxed environment in which couples can feel free to appropriately explore, experiment, and express what is mutually pleasurable within the sanctity of their relationship. Couples should remember the sexual relationship in marriage is like their own private sanctuary. God has ordained marriage and sexuality as good. If couples have any questions or concerns, they may want to review the section in Chapter 7 on "What's Okay and What Isn't."

Couples may want to use special silk bedding, soft music, or candles to provide a comfortable, inviting and relaxing environment. During the exercises each spouse will take a turn being the "giver" or the "receiver." The giver will touch their spouse for 15– 45 minutes in the specified manner. Always start with the lower-desire spouse being the receiver first. The one *receiving* the touch always determines when the touching session will end; then they will switch roles. To avoid mental distractions and keep the focus on bodily sensations and pleasure, the receiver should focus on their breathing.

Week 1—Nonsexual Touching. Week one is simple. With clothes on, the receiver will choose how they want to be touched nonsexually for 15–45 minutes.

The next receiver then chooses how *they* want to be touched nonsexually. This non-sexual touch may include cuddling on the couch, lying together on the bed with arms around each other, giving a back, hand or foot massage, or sitting on your spouse's lap while your hair is being stroked. The emotional intimacy of this exercise lays the foundation for future fireworks. Do this exercise three times this week.

Week 2—Spooning. Week two is a wonderful opportunity to experience the intimate nurturing position called "spooning." Both spouses undress and get into bed lying on their left sides. For 15–45 minutes the giver warmly envelops the other in a loving embrace. The receiver's back is snuggled right next to the giver's body, like two spoons lying together—one nestled within the other. It may be most comfortable for the giver to put his arm through / under her neck, so that she is not lying directly on his arm. Adjust your pillows so you are comfortable.

Refrain from talking, so that you can savor the sensations of touch, and bask in your closeness. Hands should not touch sexual areas. Pay attention to your breathing, bringing it into harmony until it is synchronized. When the receiver signals, switch positions. The new touch giver will move behind the other so they can still lie on their left sides while spooning.

Week 3—Blissful Caress. This week will begin to awaken sexual senses providing three more blissful, tactile experiences. Husband and wife will undress together in the light, with the first receiver lying on the bed. You may want to consider using a portable heater if it's cold, since you will be undressed without covers.

For 15–45 minutes the giver will caress the receiver with the most tender, yet electrifying caress you can imagine. As the giver, imagine your hand drawing sexual energy to the surface of the skin everywhere you touch. You will barely touch the body as your hand slowly glides over her skin from head to toe—including sexual areas. Like a soft breeze blowing across the body, the giver should caress both the back and front of the body with his open hand. As the giver's hand slides along the body, it will feel almost as if tiny soft kisses are being placed wherever it touches.

The intent of the blissful caress is to awaken sexual sensations from the depths of the soul rather than to simply arouse sexually. This caress sensitizes the body and helps awaken the sexual responses. The giver should make every caress a conscious movement, being attentive to the awakening energy in his or her spouse. As the receiver closes her eyes and concentrates on savoring every sensation, she may begin to feel sexual stirrings. The whole body should feel electrified with energy, like electricity being brought to the surface just below the touch of the hand. When the receiver signals, the couple will switch roles.

Week 4—Touching and Caressing Avoiding Genitals. Week four begins direct and definitive sensual pleasuring using the hands and lips to caress, stroke, and kiss the entire body, avoiding breasts and genitals of both husband and wife. Avoiding sexual areas allows the rest of the body to catch up sensually. Where sexual areas usually receive all the attention, the rest of the body will now have a chance to become erogenous, as if learning how to be sexually sensitized.

Again, for three sessions this week the couple will undress in the light, and the receiver will lie down on the bed. She will close her eyes and relax, focusing on her breathing, savoring each touch and caress. The receiver can add to her arousal by expressing her pleasure with auditory expressions such as, "I love it when you . . ." or "I love it when you do that," or even just a blissful "Mmmm!" This teaches or reinforces what is pleasurable in a positive way.

The giver will try to caress every part of the body, except breasts and genitals, noticing the textures and sensitivities of the body. If any touch or caress becomes irritating, the receiver can communicate by moving the giver's hand. Remember it is up to the receiver to teach what touch feels good to them. When the receiver signals, they will switch.

Awakening to tactile pleasure may create a profound sense of aliveness. One woman stated, "I feel like I'm coming out from under an anesthetic. I didn't realize how numb I'd been until I started the exercises."[42]

As husband and wife become re-sensitized to the pleasures of touch, without it leading to sex, a door opens to more frequent touching and closeness. One couple enthusiastically shared their discovery of how their relationship outside the bedroom had changed, "We have a small kitchen, and we used to be forever dodging each other in it. . . . But after we got into the exercises, we just let ourselves bump into each other. Friendly bumps and brushes. Even a few snuggles. I don't know what's going on, but I like it."[43]

Week 5—Kissing. Many couples have lost the art of kissing. Before marriage, kissing is a savored experience. After marriage many couples virtually abandon sensual, lip-to-lip kissing not only because additional sexual pleasures are now available, but for other more intimate reasons. Noted sex therapist, Dagmar O'Connor said, "In its own way, kissing is far more intimate than sexual intercourse. When we kiss, we cannot depersonalize the experience the way we can if we are merely [joining our sexual organs]."[44]

This week, the couple will again undress together. The couple may choose who would like to be the giver first. The husband will sit supported by pillows against the wall or headboard with his legs criss-crossed. The wife will sit on his crossed legs with her legs around his back. The couple will sit silently for a moment facing each other, connecting and communicating only with the light in each other's eyes.

The giver will then initiate kissing, licking, nibbling or touching the lips, face, neck and ears—being as creative as possible in providing pleasure. The giver should go slowly and concentrate on his own sensations—brushing his lips against hers, or tracing his tongue around her lips. Couples should keep the focus on sensations in the face and neck by avoiding any other sexual contact.

The receiver is to simply relax and relish every kiss. The receiver is not to kiss back, but passively *receive* the kisses and caresses. At first it may be easier to keep one's eyes closed, but as comfort increases couples may find the increased emotional intimacy of eye contact a desirable addition. The receiver can communicate nonverbally by pulling away if anything becomes unpleasant. The receiver is to learn new pleasurable sensations, as well as to teach the giver what is pleasurable to them. These sessions will be only 5–15 minutes. The receiver will decide when to switch.

On the third kissing session of this week, husband and wife will both respond to each other's kisses and caresses. Both can give and receive in this shared sensual experience intended to restore the art of sensual kissing to lovemaking.

Week 6—Touching and Caressing Including Genitals. Week six is similar to week four, but with genitals and breasts now being included. Orgasm and intercourse are still prohibited. Couples will again undress in the light. On the *first session,* the giver will spend at least 15 minutes on the nonsexual areas until the receiver signals that they can move to the breasts and genitals. The giver will touch, caress, and stroke the receiver's entire body.

Intentional touch, which characterizes an attitude of attentiveness, is necessary for these exercises. Love is conveyed in a more powerful way, and pleasure is increased with watchful care of each caress and response instead of with a bored or disinterested attitude.

The receiver should close their eyes and relax, focusing on their breathing, as they continue to savor each touch and caress. This step gives both husband and wife the opportunity to learn to *linger in arousal,* riding the waves of pleasure as they rise and fall throughout lovemaking. To increase her arousal and passion, the wife may want to do Kegel exercises (contractions of the vaginal muscles) during her receiving session, since these mimic orgasmic contractions. The wife must learn to relax and focus her mind on the pleasurable sensations so that she can let go sexually. A willingness to openly and freely communicate sexual pleasure through verbal expression also helps her focus on the sensations and significantly increases her sexual arousal.

Dr. Lindsay R. Curtis taught the following regarding the best kinds of sensual touch in lovemaking. He said, "Caresses must be gentle, never harsh, brusk, or forced. If they are light, fleeting and *teasing* in nature they serve to arouse the imagination to a much greater degree. When a caress is too prolonged or too persistent, it runs the risk of becoming boring. Even worse it may become irritating or annoying. The lips, the breasts (especially the nipples) and the clitoris are the principal erotic areas, and skillful stimulation of these usually provoke a crescendic desire for [orgasm and] intercourse."[45]

On the *second session,* the receiver will take a more active part. After at least 15 minutes of touch of nonsexual areas, the receiver will move her hand over her partner's to guide him as he stimulates her. This is valuable intimate knowledge for a spouse, as they learn how to give you what you want, when you want it.

It is especially important for women to teach their husbands exactly how they like their breasts to be touched. Women often go through life allowing their husbands to touch them in ways that aren't particularly pleasing, instead of teaching them what is pleasurable. A husband's pleasure is always increased by his wife's genuine pleasure and passion. If any touch or caress becomes unpleasant the receiver can move the giver's hand. When the receiver signals, switch roles.

On the *third session,* give each other a guided tour of your body. This may produce some discomfort or even nervousness or shyness, since many have learned to feel shame and embarrassment about their bodies. The purpose is to see and learn about each other's sexual organs and functioning, as well as learn of other sexual hot spots. Decide who wants to go first then, using a mirror if necessary, show and share your sex organs in a teaching manner. Identify your sexual parts and how you like to be touched. Also share the other parts of your body that are your favorite erogenous areas and how you like them to be touched.

Week 7—Orgasm and Intercourse. While couples may now touch back when moved to do so, and orgasm and intercourse are now permissible, couples should still go slowly since relaxation, especially for the wife, is key to full and uninhibited orgasm. With goal-oriented sex being the norm, couples should focus on communicating love as they bask in the sensations of pleasure, even as they proceed to orgasm and inter-course.

The first receiver should be the lower-desire spouse to make their wants and needs the priority. In general, efforts to fulfill the wife's orgasm should come first, since it's difficult for men to keep their sexual flame afire after ejaculation. Seeking to fulfill the wife first helps men gain greater self-control, as they develop greater mastery over their sexual energy. During this week's sessions, begin with (1) nonsexual touching, (2) a blissful caress of the whole body, (3) sensual kissing, and (4) gentle touching of sexual areas in preparation for full sexual arousal and orgasm. Try various positions to find what provides the most pleasure and the right clitoral stimulation.

According to Drs. Lamb and Brinley, orgasm for women is largely a learned response requiring patience, sensitivity, and communication in the relationship.[46] A relaxed environment free from emotional and psychological barriers is needed. The delicate nature of the female orgasm requires husband and wife to lovingly make a sig-nificant investment of time and effort.

If orgasm has been difficult or nonexistent for the wife, you will both need to be creative to find the right intensity, quality, pressure, and type of clitoral stimulation needed to reach orgasm. In the beginning, some women may even need an hour of direct stimulation. That can be quite a test of endurance. For learning purposes, and if needed after other efforts do not seem to work, some couples may want to consider using a vibrator.

A vibrator can provide a more consistent and enduring source of stimulation to help the wife reach climax. Once a woman experiences orgasm and knows what those intense sensations feel like, a couple can more easily work together to recreate an orgasm with only manual or penile stimulation. Because the vibrator produces an intensity of stimulation that is difficult to manually duplicate, it is wise to make stim-ulation with a vibrator a temporary learning solution. Couples should work together toward orgasm and complete sexual fulfillment without mechanical assistance during the intimate interplay of their lovemaking.

For more information about sexual therapy techniques couples may want to con-sider a book by Christian sex therapists, Dr. Clifford Penner and his wife Joyce Penner, entitled *Restoring the Pleasure: Complete Step-by-Step Programs to Help Couples Overcome the Most Common Sexual Barriers.*

One woman, Tami, was thrilled with her response to the Sensate Focus exercises. The phases each built upon the other, softening her heart and mind, while preparing her physically for full and uninhibited sexual ecstasy. She loved the spooning and felt like she was in heaven. She was amazed at the electrifying feelings created by the blissful body caress, as if she was awakening from a deep sleep. Kissing had practically made her sick to her stomach previously but now she enjoyed the full range and depth of intimacy that kissing provided. She could feel how much it increased the intensity of her arousal and pleasure during lovemaking. As she came to understand God's blessing upon the sexual relationship in marriage she was able to relax and let go—finally finding the sexual fulfillment she had been missing for so long.

Affection as well as sexual touch is vital to a healthy and happy marriage. The universal need for touch must be fulfilled with generous helpings of tactile nourishment. The additional issues of developing sexual identity, body image acceptance, nurturing touch and intimate learning can also be important to awakening and freeing mind, body, and spirit to the sexual ecstasy available between husband and wife. All couples can benefit from the Sensate Focus exercises as they gain a fresh new start sexually, and awaken or re-awaken sexual senses.

Chapter 12—"Home" Work

- Touch and hug more.

- Learn to express your need for touch with no strings attached, and expect it to happen. Schedule one night a week for nonsexual touch. Alternate sexual encounters with nonsexual encounters or just spend a few minutes each night snuggling as you fall asleep.

- Pay more attention to sexual thoughts and feelings toward your spouse during the day. Welcome and relish them as proof of your divine sexual identity.

- Stand before a full length mirror, unclothed, affirming every part of the body from head to toe—perfect or not, sexual or not—by saying, "I love and accept my . . . (part of the body)." Repeat until you feel a sense of acceptance and respect for every part of your body.

- Become comfortable nurturing yourself by holding your hand or by stroking your face, arms, or fingers.

- Give yourself permission to learn about your body. If you have not yet experienced orgasm, figure out how to create orgasm so that you can teach your husband.

- Decide with your spouse when you will do the seven-week Sensate Focus exercises. Enjoy!

NOTES

Chapter 12—Becoming One—Physical Intimacy

[1]Davis, *Power of Touch*, 19–20.

[2]Davis, *Power of Touch*, 37.

[3]Davis, *Power of Touch*, 28.

[4]Davis, *Power of Touch*, 73–74.

[5]Davis, *Power of Touch*, 143.

[6]Davis, *Power of Touch*, 153.

[7]Davis, *Power of Touch*, 153.

[8]Davis, *Power of Touch*, 153.

[9]Davis, *Power of Touch*, 152.

[10]Davis, *Power of Touch*, 152.

[11]Davis, *Power of Touch*, 144.

[12]Matthew 8:15.

[13]Matthew 9:20, 22.

[14]Matthew 14:36.

[15]Matthew 17:7.

[16]Matthew 20:34.

[17]Luke 6:19.

[18]Davis, *Power of Touch*, 80.

[19]Weiner Davis, *Sex-Starved Marriage,* 32.

[20]Davis, *Power of Touch*, 111–12.

[21]*See* Davis, *Power of Touch*, 67–68.

[22]Davis, *Power of Touch*, 71.

[23]Davis, *Power of Touch*, 123.

[24]Weiner Davis, *Sex-Starved Marriage,* 164.

[25]Johnson, *Language of Love*, 1999.

[26]Davis, *Power of Touch*, 129.

[27]Davis, *Power of Touch*, 135–36.

[28]*See* Davis, *Power of Touch*, 129–30.

[29]Davis, *Power of Touch*, 133.

[30]Lamb and Brinley, *Between Husband and Wife*, 20–21.

[31]*See* Genesis 2:25.

[32]Weiner Davis, *Sex-Starved Marriage,* 30.

[33]Farnworth, "Our Sexual Natures" slide 131.

[34]*See* Lamb and Brinley, *Between Husband and Wife*, 149.

[35]Barlow, *Worth Waiting For,* 49.

[36]*See* Lamb and Brinley, *Between Husband and Wife*, 88, 91.

[37]Wheat and Wheat, *Intended for Pleasure*, 112.

[38]*See* Moses 5:2, Moses 5:16, Moses 6:2, Genesis 4:1, Genesis 4:25.

[39]Davis, *Power of Touch*, 130.

[40]*See* Alma 38:12.

[41] *See* O'Connor, *How to Put the Love Back into Making Love*, 1989.

[42] O'Connor, "Take Six Steps to Better Sex," 142.

[43] O'Connor, "Take Six Steps," 142.

[44] O'Connor, "Take Six Steps," 142.

[45] Curtis, *And They Shall Be One Flesh*, 54 (emphasis added).

[46] *See* Lamb and Brinley, *Between Husband and Wife*, 90.

CHAPTER VIEW

Marriage as a Refiner's Fire
- *Three Dimensions of Wholeness*
- *The Marital Mirror*
- *Marital Stewardship*

Covenants
- *Contract versus Covenant Marriage*

Commitment
- *Divorce Is Not an Option*

Challenges
- *Building a Firm Foundation for Marital Growth and Development*
- *Common Challenges in Marriage*
- *The Missing Dimension of Personal Wholeness*

Overcoming Challenges Together

Overcoming Challenges Alone

It Only Takes One to Change a Marriage

Creating a Conscious Marriage

Chapter 13—"Home" Work

Chapter 13

MARITAL STEWARSHIP—COVENANTS, COMMITMENT, AND CHALLENGES

Marriage as a Refiner's Fire

A dangerous myth about marriage is that you'll get married, and *all will be well*. You will finally be happy. "And they lived happily ever after . . ." is how the fairy tale ends. The truth is *happily ever after* requires a lot of time, effort, sweat, and tears mixed in with the joy and love. Marriage can be blissful, but blissful moments are mixed in with a lot of hard work—the most difficult being soul-expanding personal growth. In designing marriage the Lord was very wise. He not only provides for the fulfillment of our deepest desires for intimate connection, but He also requires some of our greatest struggles and personal growth.

One of the divine purposes of marriage is purification of the *soul* through personal growth. The *soul* is comprised of a person's body (including the mind) and spirit.[1] Each requires our attention and effort to build physical, psychological, and spiritual health. These are the three dimensions of wholeness (see diagram below).

Marriage draws husbands and wives toward wholeness through
their complementary and sometimes conflicting natures. . . .
[It's a] quest for wholeness of body, mind, and spirit.

Wholeness is a concept foreign to many people. Rather than being whole or having strengths in all three dimensions, men and women may possess differing strengths. Men often have strengths in physical, logical, or quantitative areas, whereas women may have strengths in emotional, spiritual, or qualitative areas. Marriage draws husbands and wives toward wholeness through their complementary and sometimes conflicting natures. Parts of the self that have been dormant, lost, ignored, neglected, or are weak demand to be reawakened and developed. Marriage takes us on a quest for wholeness of body, mind, and spirit.

Three Dimensions of Wholeness

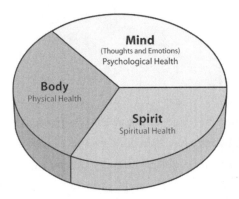

When you marry you enroll yourself in an intensive personal development course. Intimate relationships demand personal growth that is not always easy or comfortable. Carol Matthau has said, "I don't think marriages break up because of what you do to each other. They break up because of what you must become in order to stay in them."[2] Change is hard. People want to change the world but they don't want to change themselves, or they don't know how.

God has provided an opportunity for personal purification within marriage. He invites husbands and wives to cleave unto each other and become one.[3] If husband and wife will do what it takes to *become one* they will avoid or significantly diminish other life challenges especially those associated with parenting.

God invites husband and wife to come unto Him and be purified in Him.[4] Marriage provides a way for rough edges to be smoothed. If we allow it, marriage can provide the refiner's fire—producing sufficient heat and pressure for the "coal" to become a "diamond." Elder Boyd K. Packer referred to the power and potential of marriage to provide a "crucible"—the trial and the test capable of determining our eternal destiny.[5]

In marriage, problems or challenges are actually invitations for growth that can lead toward personal wholeness and marital oneness. These invitations keep coming until we humble ourselves sufficiently to allow the refiner's fire to teach and change us. Personal growth is accelerated when we humbly and willingly yield our hearts to God with the intent to learn and grow.

While there is much we can individually do to develop ourselves emotionally, spiritually, and physically, the committed intimate relationship of marriage provides opportunities for growth that may not be available any other way. Healing takes two. Husbands and wives provide healing and support to each other through the power of nonsexual and sexual touch. Couples gain insight and healing by mirroring, validating, and empathizing in the process of communication and dialogue. A third way couples heal is by stretching to meet each other's needs for love without expecting anything in return.

Husband and wife provide therapy in many ways to each other's heart and soul. If couples would develop valuable and necessary relationship skills, the need for marriage counselors could significantly diminish. Dr. Harville Hendrix said, "*Marriage itself is in essence therapy,* and your partner's needs chart your path to psychological and spiritual wholeness."[6]

The intimate nature of marriage provides a mirror reflecting our rough edges. Mortal foibles can't hide for long. The at-times seemingly incompatible natures of husband and wife reflect each other's weaknesses especially as they strive to become one. Husbands and wives crave the emotional, spiritual, and physical closeness and connectedness that only a spouse can provide. The paradox is that couples don't want each other to get *too* close, or provide too much honest reflection.

Being imperfect, we may not like what we see in the mirror our spouse provides. But the reflection of personal weaknesses is essential to bringing awareness to the areas in which we need to grow and in motivating us toward personal wholeness and eternal oneness. Few like to acknowledge their imperfections—much less work to overcome them. But we must grow and change if we are to meet each other's needs and become one.

Within the stewardship of marriage, one spouse's growth—their stretching to meet the other's needs—provides healing for the other. This adds purpose to our personal willingness to stretch and grow. As women stretch to meet their husband's sexual needs, for example, they awaken dormant parts of their being, increasing their wholeness, as well as providing healing for their husbands by meeting their needs. As men stretch to meet their wife's nonsexual and emotional needs, they also awaken or develop areas that may have been dormant, increasing their wholeness and providing healing for their wives.

As we develop deeper, more divine understanding of the eternal purposes of marriage, we come to realize it will take more effort and sacrifice than we were led to believe by the childhood fairy tales. With this new understanding, when challenges arise couples will not simply question their choice of marriage partners or believe they've fallen out of love, but instead will rely on their commitment to each other and to God to pull them through. Marriage may be divinely designed as one of God's greatest agents for personal growth. This may be why it is so central to God's Plan of Happiness. Some challenges require more than we feel we can give. These challenges compel us to "come unto Christ" and partner with Him to get us through.

From the parable of the talents we can learn that our stewardship in marriage is to improve upon what we are given.[7] It is our responsibility to accept the invitations we are given to learn and grow through the challenges we encounter. With God's help we can find answers to our questions and sustaining support through our struggles. The "exultant ecstasy" of peace, joy, pleasure, and mutual fulfillment of our deepest yearnings for intimacy is available to every couple who will allow the refiner's fire to transform their hearts and souls as they faithfully fulfill their marital stewardship to each other and to God.

Covenants

Many couples see marriage as a contract relationship that can be canceled at will. Other couples understand marriage not as a contract but as a covenant—a solemn promise between themselves and God. All marriages are a covenant with God because marriage was created and ordained by God. Elder Bruce C. Hafen explained the difference between contract and covenant marriages:

> When troubles come, the parties to a contractual marriage seek happiness by walking away. They marry to obtain benefits and will stay only as long as they're receiving what they bargained for. But when troubles come to a covenant marriage, the husband and wife work them through. They marry to give and to grow, bound by covenants to each other, to the community, and to God. Contract companions each give 50 percent; covenant companions each give 100 percent. Marriage is by nature a covenant, not just a private contract one may cancel at will.[8]

When people are unhappy in marriage or are in "marriage survival mode," they often believe that there are only two choices—either get divorced or endure an unhappy marriage. There is another way. Husbands and wives can commit to their individual personal growth and begin the mountainous climb toward true love and oneness. Unhappiness in marriage signals the need for personal growth so that two can become one.

When people are unhappy in marriage . . . they often believe that
there are only two choices—either get divorced or endure
an unhappy marriage. There is another way.

When we view our marriage as a covenant—a promise with God—we have greater power and allegiance to keep those promises. A full understanding of the covenant of marriage removes the mental option to cancel at will, providing instead determination to "love, honor and cherish," and to seek God's hand for help when the trials come. Those who enter holy wedlock with an understanding of and commitment to the covenant of marriage have power and protection like mortar holding them together through better or worse.

Members of The Church of Jesus Christ of Latter-day Saints have boundless blessings sealed upon them by entering into the new and everlasting covenant of marriage in a holy temple of God. The temple endowment provides a shield of power and protection against the adversary. It bestows greater power to overcome obstacles. Keeping temple covenants makes better husbands and wives, fathers and mothers.

The power and blessings of the temple are available to all couples who keep their covenants to each other and to God. Elder Henry B. Eyring promised, "The fruit of keeping covenants is the companionship of the Holy Ghost and an increase in the power to love. That happens because of the power of the Atonement of Jesus Christ to change our very natures."[9] Elder Hafen has added, "When we observe the covenants we make at the altar of sacrifice, we discover hidden reservoirs of strength."[10] And of the marriage covenant, Elder Packer concluded, "Eternal love, eternal marriage, eternal increase! This ideal, which is new to many, when thoughtfully considered, can keep a marriage strong and safe. No relationship has more potential to exalt a man and a woman than the marriage covenant. No obligation in society or in the Church supersedes it in importance."[11]

Through revelation from God we know that the new and everlasting covenant of marriage is the strait gate and narrow way that leads to eternal lives. Regarding Doctrine and Covenants 132:22 and 25, which outlines the blessings of celestial marriage, President Harold B. Lee said, "Marriage for time and for eternity is the strait gate and the narrow way."[12] Not only is it vital that couples prepare themselves to enter the holy temple and be sealed eternally by one with God's authority, but couples must also invite God into their marriage. God can make more of them and their marriage than they can. Inviting God into marriage provides the secret ingredient couples need to love, honor, and cherish each other throughout eternity.

Keeping temple covenants doesn't just mean having a temple recommend in hand: it requires daily, determined effort to love each other, and to obey the command to become one.[13] Being true to our marital covenants helps to keep the spark in our marriages and our hearts full of love.

Commitment

Marriage, as designed by God, is meant to be a permanent eternal relationship. Covenant marriage has no divorce clause. Understanding marriage as a promise between husband, wife, and God, makes commitment to God and each other the mortar to hold couples together through the storms of life. Couples need more than a "velcro marriage" that holds them together only until the pressure is on.

While there are some circumstances warranting divorce, an eternal perspective and commitment to the covenant of marriage creates a mental mindset that *divorce is not an option*. Couples instead opt for the strenuous effort to work through their challenges or endure them with faith. President Gordon B. Hinckley pleaded with couples, "Determine that there will never be anything that will come between you that will disrupt your marriage. Make it work. Resolve to make it work. There is far too much of divorce, wherein hearts are broken and sometimes lives are destroyed."[14] President Spencer W. Kimball also taught, "Divorce is not a cure for difficulty, but is merely an escape."[15]

With an understanding that marriage is meant to stir our divine potential and draw from us our wholeness, divorce merely trades one set of challenges for another. Seen in this light, divorce has too high a price. Personal growth will still be demanded of each spouse in a new marriage. It is better to choose the difficult path of personal purification and growth than to exit the marriage and start over again.

An internalized concept of the marriage covenant where divorce is not an option could revolutionize marriage and society. Culturally we've learned what divorce has to offer. So now we should work to end that pattern and get on track toward a better way. It's not that divorce is *never* warranted, but it has become so widely accepted that lives and families are regularly being destroyed over matters that can be resolved. President Kimball identified the *ready acceptance* of divorce as a significant evil. He stated, "Divorce itself does not constitute the entire evil, but the very acceptance of divorce as a cure is also a serious sin of this generation."[16]

The measurable and devastating effects of divorce—not only on the children involved, but also on the husband and wife—are costly. Satan is thrilled when couples stop seeking divine help and give in to divorce. Divorce has become so common that nearly every family is affected by it in some way. President Kimball believed that the cancer of divorce was one of the primary tools of Satan to tear down faith, frustrate lives as well as weaken and destroy marriages and families.[17]

While turning the tide on a high divorce rate would be wonderful, I am also concerned about those who stay married but are still unhappy. Many of these couples choose the road of parallel marriage rather than the mountainous climb of personal growth. Often it is a lack of knowledge of *how* to improve their relationship, or a lack of energy, that accounts for those who allow their marriage "to grow stale, weak and cheap."[18] God never intends couples to *just stay married*; He intends for them to *grow and flourish* together.

When divorce is not considered an option, it is easier to endure life's challenges and work them out by trusting God to help. One couple, committed to the covenant of marriage, inspired their posterity to hold marriage sacred by showing enduring love—for better or for worse. The following comes from a letter written by one of their daughters:

> When I was growing up, I used to wish my parents would divorce, and we would go live with my dad. My mother was a manic depressive schizophrenic, so she was not mentally capable of raising my brothers and sisters (six in all). . . . My father played both mother and father. He would go to work, come home, fix dinner, clean the house and then play with us. I never heard him complain about his life. She was extremely hard to live with and unrelenting because of her disease. She had very few good days (as we called them) but my father always treated her with love and respect. Everyone who knew our situation said he was a saint.
>
> I once asked my father why he didn't leave her because of all the pain she caused all of us. He expressed the following: that she, before her illness, was an amazing woman whom he loved dearly. When she was at her worst he thought very hard about leaving (this was about 1961), but decided he couldn't because we would all be put in foster care and no one would take care of her. He said he put his trust in God to help out on the bad days. It was truly for better or for worse. . . .
>
> My mother in the last few years of her life had mellowed more and had more better days than bad. They lived in an assisted living facility for the last two years of their lives. The nurses told us they had never seen a more loving couple than my parents. When the nurses woke them up each morning, they were cuddled together. My mother worried about my dad as much as he worried about her. They were married 55 years until they both passed away within two months of each other.
>
> My parents' example of love has spilled out to all of us children including the grandchildren. My five married brothers and sisters have not experienced divorce . . . and are in their marriages for better or worse. . . . When I think of my parents, I know they are holding hands in heaven. My mother is normal and the wife my dad always knew he had deep down he has now, and my father is his smiling self. I think now he is living the life he has always deserved with the woman he always loved. And she is living the life she's always wanted.[19]

Satan hopes our encounters with adversity will destroy our marriages. God hopes our encounters with adversity will draw us closer to each other and to Him. Sister Sheri L. Dew stated, "Lucifer is determined to devour marriages and families, because their demise threatens the salvation of all involved and the vitality of the Lord's kingdom itself."[20] Our understanding of the covenant nature of marriage and our commitment to work together to overcome our challenges can be the secret weapon securing our victory in the war Satan is waging against marriage and family.

The blessings of commitment to each other and to God throughout the storms of life are many. Safety, security, and peace amidst trials can truly make marriage a haven in a heartless world.

Challenges

It's been said that if you have a marriage, you have marriage problems. All marriages have unexpected trials, struggles, and setbacks. Marriage may be likened to a surprise grab bag. You never really know what you're going to get. You carefully and prayerfully choose your marriage partner, but it isn't until after some time in marriage that you are able to see inside your spouse, and inside yourself as you are reflected in them. Additionally, you may encounter some kind of "marital surprise" such as chronic disease, depression, overwhelming debt, dashed dreams of having children, or disrespectful behavior between husband and wife.

Marriage requires faith in God—trust that He will get you through whatever challenges you encounter. Elder Hafen taught, "Covenant marriage requires a total leap of faith: [couples] must keep their covenants without knowing what risks that may require of them."[21]

Under the best of conditions, marriage is the merging of two different personalities, personal habits, preferences, attitudes, beliefs, and family traditions. Marital adjustment is required. Conflict and tension generally occur due to external conditions. But the real struggles stem from internal attitudes, feelings, traits, and beliefs. It is not necessarily the finances, children, or in-laws that create marital challenges, but how we feel about and react toward them due to our negative core beliefs. Common causes of marital conflict are listed in box #3 of the diagram below.

Building a Firm Foundation for Marital Growth and Development

Marital Growth and Development is. . .

A day-to-day, dynamic and lifelong process required in all marriages.

Marital growth and development are required by external conditions

3. CHALLENGES
(External Conditions)

- Physical intimacy issues
- Finances
- Parenting and discipline
- Time and energy demands- careers, callings, and recreation
- Parents and in-laws
- Role expectations/ division of labor
- Tragedy and setbacks

How we react toward external conditions is determined by internal emotional factors

2. EMOTIONAL FOUNDATION
(Internal Factors)

- Self-esteem
- Maturity
- Emotional/Mental health
- Attitudes, thoughts, and beliefs
- Personality
- Training/upbringing
- Life experiences
- Communication and relationship skills
- Personal tastes, habits, and desires
- Personal weaknesses and imperfections
- Feelings - anger, fear, patience, etc.

Internal emotional factors are profoundly influenced by knowledge of and commitment to gospel principles

1. SPIRITUAL FOUNDATION
(Internal Factors)

- Faith
- Repentence
- Forgiveness
- Humility
- Testimony
- Pure love/charity
- Compassion
- Respect

An understanding of the roots of marital adjustment and growth in the diagram above can be helpful to see how important it is to develop personal wholeness in marriage.[22] The strongest and surest source of strength when the storms of life rage is our spiritual foundation and commitment to gospel principles. The second level of a sure foundation in marriage is our emotional, mental, or psychological well-being. Internal factors such as self-esteem, thoughts, core beliefs, feelings, and attitudes determine how we respond to external challenges. How we were raised and taught, for example, significantly affects how we handle conflicts and challenges. Challenges—which all couples encounter—are merely external conditions inviting internal growth toward spiritual and psychological wholeness.

In addition to spiritual commitment, our psychological well-being has everything to do with our ability to give and receive love. Elder Marlin K. Jensen taught, "The greater our own personal substance is and the deeper our own mental, emotional, and spiritual reserves are, the greater will be our capacity to nurture and love others, especially our companion."[23]

As members of The Church of Jesus Christ of Latter-day Saints, we are blessed with the Word of Wisdom to guide us in matters of physical health.[24] We understand how prayer, fasting, and feasting upon the words of Christ can feed us spiritually. We are fairly adept at understanding what's needed for physical and spiritual nourishment, but when it comes to understanding psychological factors (thoughts and emotions of the inner self), we are less proficient.

Though improving one dimension of health can affect the other areas, psychological health requires different approaches and different methods than physical and spiritual health. If we ignore, discount, or denigrate issues of the inner self, which affect our experience with external influences, we will be less able to learn and grow from life's challenges. Until we develop greater understanding and mastery of the mental and emotional self, we will be unsuccessful in our search for intimacy, happiness, and wholeness.

The Missing Dimension of Personal Wholeness

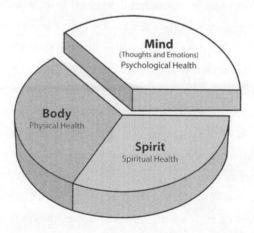

Psychological health may be the missing link in our quest for personal health and wholeness (see diagram above). Matters of the heart and mind (thoughts and emotions) often go unacknowledged and unaddressed. The Lord cares about our mental and emotional well-being. Jesus saw that our struggles and sins, in all their varieties, often stemmed from unmet emotional needs—matters of the heart.[25] Having our needs met for love, belonging, acceptance, and achievement nourishes the heart and mind.

Our thoughts also have a powerful effect on our emotions. Toxic thoughts can poison the soul. Learning how to harness the power of the mind by clearing negative barriers and reprogramming ourselves with positive mental and emotional images is vital to psychological well-being. Changing our thoughts can change our feelings, increasing the flow of positive healing energy throughout the body, mind, and spirit.

Mental and emotional health is a foreign territory into which few are willing to wander. We must become more skilled at nourishing the psychological self if we want to attain wholeness. As we gain understanding of the workings of both our thought processes and our emotions, we can reconnect the missing dimensions of our personal wholeness, and move closer to the peace and joy of marital oneness.

In an attempt to overcome marital struggles, many couples spend their time and effort addressing only the "presenting problem," such as sexual issues, finances, parenting issues, or role expectations (see diagram "Building a Firm Foundation. . . "). They rarely get to the underlying emotional and spiritual factors that need to be acknowledged and addressed. Couples can more meaningfully and permanently resolve their external challenges by focusing first on the dimension from which their problems originate. Often this will require strengthening their spiritual and emotional foundation.

When couples spend all their time and effort on an external problem, they often lack the energy to do the more important and more effective work on the inner or root problem. Unfortunately, when one spouse finally realizes the need to get some help, the other may have already checked out emotionally—leaving little to work with to save the marriage. This is why it is critical that couples not only nourish their marriage regularly, but also seek professional help as needed while problems are still manageable.

Any couple can improve their relationship with the help of an effective counselor. Since dealing with issues of the inner self (the spirit, heart, and mind) can require assistance, a professional therapist who works in such areas can be very helpful in teaching and assisting in the personal growth process. The answers to our most difficult challenges lie within ourselves. Your spirit, as well as the Spirit of God which resides within you, knows what you need to learn and what you need to do. Professionals can help you discover and understand the answers that are waiting inside you. Just as a medical doctor is helpful in addressing physical health, a professional counselor can be helpful in addressing psychological health and well-being. For help in finding a good counselor, see Appendix II "Seeking Professional Help" in the back of this book.

Overcoming Challenges Together

When couples accept and commit to their marriage covenant, they can develop an "us against the world" attitude. Dr. Wendy L. Watson encouraged husbands and wives to change their perspective from *me against him* to *us against it*.[26] This "us against the problem" approach makes the *problem* the enemy rather than our *spouse*. The attitude of overcoming challenges together encourages teamwork—with husband and wife on the same team. It's an attitude of "us against the pornography," "us against the depression," or "us against our financial problems" rather than "us against each other."

Seeing personal weaknesses as unmet needs of the heart, rather than as permanent flaws, allows couples to have an environment of compassion as they overcome their problems, while preserving and strengthening their family. Since all couples will experience problems, some suggestions as to how they might approach them can be beneficial:

1. Pray for Guidance. I've been continually amazed at the people, books, and information that have been put in my path when I have asked the Lord for direction. When the student is ready, the teacher appears. Assume the Lord knows how to resolve your struggles and expect him to show you the way. But be prepared to wait upon the Lord's divine timing, then get up off your knees and get to work, moving forward with whatever light you currently have.

2. Begin with a Positive End in Mind. Decide together what you ultimately want to create or how you want your relationship to be in a given area in which you are currently struggling. Having a vision of what you want provides mental energy and motivation to reach that ideal.

3. Obtain Wisdom and Knowledge. Knowledge alone has power. It not only *shows* a better way, but it also motivates action *toward* the better way. Many spouses are honestly doing the best they know how. This is why education is often the key. It's hard to do better if you don't know better. Read books, attend classes, and talk to others who have overcome similar problems or are successful in the area in which you are struggling.

Gain greater clarity and a deeper understanding of your struggles by writing down all your thoughts about your situation—as if you were explaining it to a friend or your Heavenly Father. Look for your contribution to the problem.

4. Take Action. With the Spirit as your guide, think of what *you* could do to better your situation. List all the ideas that come to mind. In marriage, as in most things, you get what you put into it. If you give mediocre effort, you'll have a mediocre marriage. If you give exceptional effort, you'll be more likely to have an exceptional marriage.

Sit down for a heart-to-heart talk about meeting each other's needs. Schedule a regular date night. Seek professional help. A counselor's primary job is to teach while helping *you* discover the answers you need. Good counselors are skilled at addressing and removing underlying causes, as well as the presenting problems. A counselor can significantly speed up your growth, leading to greater peace, happiness, and marital fulfillment, as you learn and apply their professional suggestions.

5. Keep Praying for Strength. Since it often takes a lot of time and effort to work through your challenges, pray continually for strength and sustenance. Elder Richard G. Scott has counseled, "Much like the mending of the body, the healing of some spiritual and emotional challenges takes time."[27]

If both husband and wife will focus their time and energy on developing themselves and overcoming their own weaknesses, then faultfinding will end and the presenting problems or challenges will be more easily and *permanently* resolved. Relationships grow sweeter and deeper with time as couples learn, grow, and overcome their challenges together. Couples show their commitment to each other, to God, and to the marriage covenant as they keep a united approach to their trials. The Lord doesn't usually remove the mountains in our lives, but He helps us to climb them by teaching, strengthening, and even carrying us. We are never alone in our struggles, nor are we unknown to the Lord. Heavenly Father is intimately aware of the challenges each of us is facing, as well as the individual growth we yet need.

(See Appendix I for an example of how couples can overcome pornography problems together.)

Overcoming Challenges Alone

I've often been asked what one can do if his or her spouse won't participate in improving their relationship. Even one spouse who is willing to make personal changes, and better meet the other's needs, can affect the whole relationship. When one spouse changes, the energy and dynamics of the relationship shift, inviting and influencing change in the other as well. Hearts soften and relationships improve.

The best ways to improve your marriage are to: (1) change your thinking to create a positive vision of your relationship; (2) turn your attention away from your spouse's problems onto your own weaknesses; (3) find ways to better meet your spouse's needs; and (4) pray for divine guidance.

1. Mentally Create the Relationship of Your Dreams. All things begin with a thought. The mind is a powerful creator, since thought is energy. If you can imagine a happy, fulfilling relationship with your spouse then you can create it. Instead of believing your spouse will never change, begin practicing the mental discipline of seeing your spouse and your relationship as you want them to be. If you can perceive your spouse positively, you will project positive energy onto him. He will respond to your expectations, whether positive or negative.

2. Focus on Your Own Weaknesses. We cannot change our spouses, but we can change our own thoughts and actions. Improving our individual responses to a situation will correspondingly improve the marital environment and dynamics of our relationship.

In describing President John Taylor, B. H. Roberts spoke of the focus of his life and of his efforts to fill his life with the best things—leaving little room for the wrong things. Brother Roberts said, "These things filled his soul, engrossed his attention and left but a small margin of time to him in which to [focus on the wrong things]."[28] This provides an excellent analogy for couples. If husband and wife will engage themselves in their own spiritual, emotional, mental, and physical development, there will be little time or energy left in which to find fault with each other.

We all have weaknesses and failings. When we focus on the faults of our spouse, we magnify them, not only in our own eyes, but also in the eyes of our spouse, causing damage to his or her self-esteem. One husband experienced an accusatory "dumping session" from his wife. He later explained how he had always done the best he knew how, but had felt so rotten and deficient as a husband after being dumped on that it took him a long time to heal from the experience and move forward toward emotional intimacy with his wife.

We cannot *directly* change our spouse, no matter how much we hope, plead, criticize, or nag. We may think ourselves helpful by pointing out our spouse's failings, but faultfinding is rarely helpful. Elder Joe J. Christensen stated, "Generally each of us is painfully aware of our weaknesses, and we don't need frequent reminders. Few people have ever changed for the better as a result of constant criticism or nagging. If we are not careful, some of what we offer as *constructive* criticism is actually *destructive*."[29]

Some of the negative patterns that contribute to divorce are: (1) not understanding that marital problems and difficulties are invitations for learning and personal growth; (2) the inability or unwillingness to see our part in the problem; and (3) the inability or unwillingness to change what we can personally change. Many couples instead focus on the other person's problems and weaknesses, "Well, he (or she) is the one that won't. . . ." The scriptures identified this problem and counseled that it is wise for couples to focus on overcoming their own faults instead. We read, "Why beholdest thou the mote that is in thy [spouse's] eye, but considerest not the beam that is in thine own eye? How wilt thou say to thy [spouse]: Let me pull the mote out of thine eye—and behold, a beam is in thine own eye? Thou hypocrite, first cast the beam out of thine own eye."[30]

President Spencer W. Kimball expressed his concern over couples spending their energy focusing on each other's faults rather than their own, and added this counsel:

> If each spouse submits to frequent self-analysis and measures his own imperfections . . . and . . . sets about to correct self in every deviation found by such analysis rather than to set about to correct the deviations in the other party, then transformation comes and happiness is the result. . . .
>
> For every friction, there is a cause; and whenever there is unhappiness, each should search self to find the cause or at least that portion of the cause which originated in that self.[31]

Faults in our spouse that bother us have related roots in our own weaknesses, which is why the marital mirror has brought them to our attention. Our spouse's problems do not occur in a vacuum. It takes the other spouse, as the reflecting mirror, to manifest complementary, even conflicting, areas.

President Nathan Eldon Tanner offered this wise counsel regarding the willingness to improve ourselves rather than focus on our spouse's weaknesses, "Let us remember . . . that the further out of line or out of tune we ourselves are, the more we are inclined to look for error or weaknesses in others and to try to rationalize and justify our own faults rather than to try to improve ourselves."[32]

3. Meet Your Spouse's Needs. Even one spouse can change a marriage by determining what needs are being unmet in the other, and making sincere efforts to meet those needs more fully. If you've already done the "Home" work on each other's Love Language and know what makes your spouse feel loved, you can commit to giving that personalized love everyday. Be prepared: what is most needed by your spouse will likely be difficult for you to give.

Selfishness in a spouse might actually be a state of emotional starvation. When nourished with the right kind of love, hearts soften and love can flow. Meeting your spouse's needs makes it more likely he or she will want to meet your needs in return. It may be difficult to choose to give love when you don't believe your spouse deserves such loving care or if you are feeling unloved and empty yourself. You may need to find ways to fulfill your own needs while you are striving to fulfill your spouse's.

Beware of self-righteousness and be attentive to your motives. Any time you give love with strings attached it can come across as manipulation rather than genuine love. Consider your extra effort as an eternal marital investment even if it is initially unnoticed or unappreciated. With a long-term view, the investment can pay big dividends.

4. Pray for God's Guidance and Strength. Pray for strength to give love and endure as long as it takes. Pray to know specifically what you can do. Pray to be able to give whatever is needed to improve your relationship. Express gratitude for what you want to experience in your relationship as if thanking Heavenly Father in advance, exhibiting your faith that He will bless you with your desires.

Creating a Conscious Marriage

Marriage is a psychological journey to wholeness. It leads us from *romantic love,* through the *power struggle, awakening* and *transformation,* upward to *real love* and *oneness.* Understanding this journey to wholeness helps couples see purpose to their wanderings in the darkness of the forest, and provides light to show the way out.

Dr. Harville Hendrix, founder of *Imago Relationship Therapy,* has helped thousands of couples understand why they have married whom they have married. He has helped them see past the power struggle into the purposes and potential of their relationships. He offers genuine insight into how the journey of marriage can go from romance to real love and oneness in marriage. The following diagram illustrates the five stages in the psychological journey of marriage:[33]

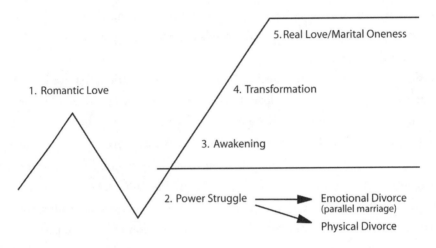

The Psychological Journey of Marriage

A Journey to Wholeness and Oneness

5. Real Love/Marital Oneness

1. Romantic Love

4. Transformation

3. Awakening

2. Power Struggle → Emotional Divorce (parallel marriage)

Physical Divorce

Stage 1 — Romantic Love. There is a reason you have married your spouse. Your spouse's psychological and spiritual makeup fit with yours in such a way as to create a sense of wholeness, as if you have "come home." Your spouse plays a vital role in developing your wholeness, and you play a vital role in developing your spouse's wholeness. Without realizing it, you are often attracted to a spouse who fills the "psychological gaps" inadvertently left by your parents or that exist in your personality.[34] This unconscious "image" acts as a blueprint for the kind of spouse you will fall in love with—one who can help you become whole.

When you find someone who meets your wholeness blueprint or unconscious match, a "chemical reaction occurs and love ignites. . . . We feel alive and whole, confident that we have met the person who will make everything all right."[35] Romantic love is designed to attract you to someone who can help you regain the lost or underdeveloped parts of the self and finally get your needs met. Understanding this can strengthen your commitment to your personal growth and encourage you to work through marital challenges instead of setting up a pattern for divorce.

This Romantic Love stage of courtship and on into marriage is often referred to as the honeymoon stage. It was never intended to last forever. It was designed to provide a delicious taste of the potential in marriage. The stage of Romantic Love functions like an anesthesia to blind you sufficiently to your spouse's weaknesses to lure you into marrying him or her, so that you can regain your inner wholeness. Romantic love brings two "incompatible" people together for the purpose of mutual growth.[36] These initial stirrings of love include romantic interest, sexual attraction, and a deepening sense of attachment to your spouse.

The psychological journey of marriage provides additional insight to the observations of President Kimball who spoke of the temporary and illusion-filled nature of romantic love. He addressed the need to get beyond the fantasy of marriage to the personal sacrifices requiring individual growth and development. He stated, "One comes to realize very soon after marriage that the spouse has weaknesses not previously revealed or discovered. The virtues that were constantly magnified during courtship now grow relatively smaller, and the weaknesses that seemed so small and insignificant during courtship now grow to sizeable proportions."[37]

Stage 2 — The Power Struggle. Once we are married, the anesthetic of romantic love begins to wear off. The Power Struggle begins when *conscious* expectations collide with *unconscious* expectations. You begin to see the painful reality that all your needs may not be met by this "perfect" spouse. At this point the dream of marital bliss temporarily dissipates, as couples grieve the death of the illusion of their romantic love. They go through the stages of grief: shock, denial, anger, bargaining, and despair.[38]

Some see the power struggle as an indicator that they've married the wrong person. But it is actually "a sure sign that we are with the right person for our maximum potential growth"[39] and well on our way to lasting love, personal wholeness, and eternal oneness. Both romantic love and the power struggle are meant to be temporary stages in the psychological journey of marriage.

Unfortunately, without understanding the divine purpose of the power struggle or having commitment to the marriage covenant, about half of married couples abort the personal growth process. They escape the power struggle by starting over again at step one, looking for another "perfect someone" to meet their needs. Too many of the remaining couples who stay married engage in an *emotional divorce,* creating a parallel marriage.[40] In a parallel marriage couples have many intimacy diversions and seek most of their happiness outside the relationship. Not enough couples push forward into the awakening, realizing significant time and heart-expanding effort are needed to climb to the mountaintop where the deeply fulfilling and intimately connected relationship of oneness is found.

Stage 3 — The Awakening. Once a couple, aware of the costs, commits to personal growth and healing, and determines to willingly endure to the end with each other, the awakening begins. The awakening provides the realization that you need to make some fundamental personal changes if you are to become whole in order to become one to experience the fulness of joy that awaits in marriage. As couples become better aware of the divine purposes and potential of marriage, they may be able to skip the power struggle altogether, immediately and fully committing to the awakening and transformations necessary to achieve true love.

The despair experienced toward the end of the power struggle is intended to invoke a humble surrender of our illusions, ending the "unconscious" marriage. The awakening fosters a new acceptance and reality of each other and an enlightened realization of marriage as the means for personal growth.

Once couples commit to personal growth and healing, a *conscious marriage* begins. "A conscious marriage is a marriage that fosters maximum psychological and spiritual growth; it's a marriage created by becoming conscious and cooperating with the fundamental drives of the unconscious mind: to be safe, to be healed, and to be whole."[41] In a conscious marriage, real love, safety and passion are the hallmarks. A conscious marriage consists of the following characteristics[42]:

- Couples realize the divine purposes of healing and personal growth that are necessary to achieve wholeness and oneness. They accept the difficulties inherent in creating a "celestial" marriage. They understand that commitment, discipline, and the courage to grow and change are required.

- Husband and wife are willing to acknowledge, accept, and embrace their own and each other's negative traits and feelings rather than projecting or dumping them onto each other. They accept a more accurate image of their spouse and marriage. They educate each other about their emotional wounds, strengths, and weaknesses.

- Husband and wife learn to accept each other's unique way of perceiving reality, by learning and using the Couples Dialogue process to communicate and explore each other's worlds. They are better able to get their needs met as they are fully heard, validated, and understood empathically.

- Couples become more intentional in their interactions. They keep the relationship's energy within the bounds of the relationship rather than emotionally exiting through intimacy diversions.

- Each other's needs and wishes become as important as our own. Husband and wife take responsibility for constructively communicating needs and desires.

- Couples begin to take an active interest in acquiring strengths and abilities they are lacking, rather than relying on their partners to make up for what they are missing. Where they once completed each other, they now desire to be whole themselves.

- Couples come to understand their inner search for emotional, spiritual, and physical intimacy. They strive for wholeness and oneness with each other and with God. As they successfully attain wholeness and oneness, they can begin to direct their excess energies outside the relationship to the betterment of society.

For more information on creating a conscious marriage, read *Getting the Love You Want: A Guide for Couples,* 1988, or *Keeping the Love You Find: A Personal Guide,* 1992, by Dr. Harville Hendrix.

Stage 4 — Transformation. Once a couple closes all psychological exits toward a parallel marriage and all physical exits toward divorce, the energy in the relationship can be channeled toward building the relationship rather than getting out. When divorce is no longer an option, couples can move beyond the power struggle into the awakening and transformation to create real love because of the security and safety now present within the relationship.

During this transformation stage new information and skills are gained line upon line, as difficult repairs and healing occur. Peeling away the layers of an onion aptly describes the transformation process. The awakening and transformation involves the purifying process of completely aligning ourself with our divine spirit self and our will with God's will. This is a heart-rending excavation of the soul that too few are willing to embark upon.

The "Home" work assignments throughout this book have been intended as transformational opportunities to develop the self and create an intimate and conscious marriage.

Stage 5 — Real Love/ONEness. Dr. Harville Hendrix has described the state of Real Love as a spiritual *experiencing* with "many moments of ecstatic highs, . . . an immense sense of well-being, a 'relaxed joyfulness' [and] . . . vibrant aliveness." He contends, "Real love lasts. It is built upon the rock of character change, which makes it possible to hold the experience and maintain it when the storms come."[43]

Real love may be natural to our divine self, but it is unnatural to the mortal self. Real love must be learned and earned. It does not occur automatically. Harville Hendrix teaches how the joys of romantic love can be enduring and transform into real love if we are willing to pay the price, "The euphoria of romantic love, the sense of wholeness, the feelings of connection and communion can become a constant in your relationship; such qualities are the prevailing tone of real love. But they are available only on the other side of the valley of conflict and fear."[44]

It is on the mountaintop of real love that husband and wife may find the oneness spoken of in the scriptures—where emotional, spiritual and physical intimacy are united. It is after the power struggle, awakening and transformation that husband and wife become one with God in thought, desire, and purpose, aligning their lives with God's will, fulfilling His command to *be one.*[45] Real love is charity, the pure unconditional love of Christ. The state of pure Christlike love is defined by an outpouring of gratitude, and a fulness of joy. In this state, couples not only become aligned with God's will, but also His pure love and energy, radiating Christ's love from within.

Creating complete oneness within marriage not only prepares couples for their eternal celestial relationship, but it also frees them to more fully fulfill their personal and joint missions in mortality. When all is well within yourself and your marriage, your mental and emotional resources are freed up to focus outside the self.

Oneness in marriage is an ever-evolving journey of learning, growing, and experiencing—not a destination. Even as couples become more conscious, more whole, and more one, they will still experience challenges. But, conscious couples have the commitment, the inner resources and have developed the skills to better handle life's challenges.

As couples ponder and practice the suggestions outlined in this book they can begin to experience the exultant ecstasy available in marriage. Glimpses of eternal oneness and momentary experiences of ecstasy provide vision and motivation to continue the climb. Peace, joy, pleasure, and mutual fulfillment of the deepest longings of the heart await those couples who are willing to pay the price. As we allow the refiner's fire to transform our heart and soul, we can attain personal wholeness and eternal oneness in marriage, faithfully fulfilling our marital stewardship to each other and to God.

Chapter 13—"Home" Work

- Commit to marriage as a covenant. Develop the mental mindset, "Divorce is not an option." Understand that marriage is a quest for growth and healing. Determine to work through whatever challenges come your way.

- Continually develop your spiritual and psychological (mental and emotional) foundation to better handle life's challenges.

- Work on the root of your problems, not just the "presenting problem."

- Strive to overcome challenges together: (1) pray for guidance; (2) begin with a positive end in mind; (3) obtain wisdom and knowledge; (4) take action; (5) pray continually for strength.

- Work to overcome challenges, alone if necessary: (1) mentally create the relationship of your dreams, (2) focus on your own weaknesses, (3) meet your spouse's needs, (4) pray for God's guidance and strength.

- Strive to move beyond the power struggle to create a conscious marriage filled with real love.

- Read and re-read this book, choosing one new thing each time to implement in your lives. Begin to experience the exultant ecstasy and oneness available in marriage.

NOTES

Chapter 13 — Marital Stewardship — Covenants, Commitment and Challenges

[1] *See* Doctrine & Covenants 88:15.

[2] Ban Breathnach, *Something More*, 117.

[3] *See* Genesis 2:24.

[4] *See* Moroni 10:32.

[5] Packer, "Marriage," *Ensign*, May 1981, 13.

[6] Hendrix, *Keeping the Love You Find*, 247 (emphasis in original).

[7] *See* Matthew 25:20.

[8] Hafen, "Covenant Marriage," *Ensign*, Nov. 1996, 26.

[9] Eyring, "Witnesses for God," *Ensign,* Nov. 1996, 32.

[10] Hafen, "Covenant Marriage," *Ensign*, Nov. 1996, 27.

[11] Packer, "Marriage," *Ensign*, May 1981, 15.

[12] Lee, *Teachings of Presidents*, 111.

[13] *See* Doctrine & Covenants 38:27.

[14] Hinckley, "Life's Obligations," *Ensign*, Feb. 1999, 2–3.

[15] Kimball, *Marriage and Divorce*, 8.

[16] Kimball, *Marriage and Divorce*, 12.

[17] *See* Kimball, *Marriage and Divorce*, 10.

[18] Kimball, Marriage and Divorce, 22.

[19] Schlessinger, 2001.

[20] Dew, "It is Not Good for Man or Woman to Be Alone," *Ensign,* Nov. 2001, 12.

[21] Hafen, "Covenant Marriage," *Ensign*, Nov. 1996, 26.

[22] *See Achieving a Celestial Marriage*, 56.

[23] Jensen, "A Union of Love and Understanding," *Ensign,* Oct. 1994, 48.

[24] *See* Doctrine & Covenants 89.

[25] *See* Kimball, "Jesus: The Perfect Leader," *Ensign*, Aug. 1979, 5.

[26] *See* Watson, *Purity and Passion*, 129.

[27] Scott, "Finding Joy in Life," *Ensign*, May 1996, 26.

[28] Taylor, *Teachings of Presidents of the Church*, 173.

[29] Christensen, "Marriage and the Great Plan of Happiness," *Ensign,* May 1995, 64 (emphasis in original).

[30] 3 Nephi 14:3–5.

[31] Kimball, *Marriage and Divorce*, 19.

[32] Davidson, *Our Latter-day Hymns*, 277.

[33] *See* Hendrix, *Getting the Love You Want*, 1988; and Hendrix, *Keeping the Love You Find*, 1992.

[34] *See* Hendrix, *Keeping the Love You Find*, 21.

[35] Hendrix, *Keeping the Love You Find*, 21.

[36] *See* Hendrix, *Keeping the Love You Find*, 230.

[37] Kimball, *Marriage and Divorce*, 12–13.

[38] *See* Hendrix, *Getting the Love You Want*, 1988, 81–82.

[39] Hendrix, *Keeping the Love You Find*, 231.

[40] *See* Hendrix, *Getting the Love You Want*, 1988, 82.

[41] Hendrix, *Getting the Love You Want*, 1988, 90.

[42]*See* Hendrix, *Getting the Love You Want*, 1988, 90–92; and Hendrix, *Keeping the Love You Find*, 1992, 245–47.
[43]Hendrix, *Keeping the Love You Find*, 294.
[44]Hendrix, *Keeping the Love You Find*, 293.
[45]*See* John 17:21 and Doctrine & Covenants 38:27.

CHAPTER VIEW

Chapter 14

PREPARING FUTURE GENERATIONS FOR SEXUAL FULFILLMENT IN MARRIAGE— PREPARING TO TEACH

Implementing the principles taught throughout this book will not only bless your own marriage, but can better prepare future generations for marital fulfillment. By preparing to teach your children you also get a fresh new education about sexuality. This bonus section includes guidance on preparing to teach children as well as what, when, and how to teach.

This chapter will help you better understand and prepare to have positive experiences teaching your children the sanctity of sexual relations in marriage. Chapter 15 gives an outline of the most important principles to teach. Chapter 16 gives insights on how and when to teach, and provides a sample discussion outline. You can study the principles in Chapter 15, then use the sample script as a format to prepare your own discussions—depending on the age, maturity, and gender of your children.

Parents' Responsibility to Teach Their Children

Parents have the opportunity to better prepare their children for lasting fulfillment in marriage by confidently teaching them the sacred and sanctifying nature of sex in marriage. As parents take advantage of their opportunities to teach, they legitimize the divinity of sexuality. Parents must not abdicate this solemn responsibility, leaving their children to be tossed to and fro by the wiles of the world.

Dr. A. Lynn Scoresby informally asked the students in his BYU child development classes "how many had parents who contributed at least half of their knowledge about physical development and human reproduction." Never did he have a class in which more than 20 percent of the students said they had parents who taught them to that extent. In one of his classes of 247 students, only 23 indicated they had learned more than half from their parents.[1] The question is, if parents aren't doing this teaching, then who is and what are our youth learning?

A loving home is the best place for children to learn. God has designated this sacred responsibility to parents saying, "I have commanded you to bring up your children in light and truth."[2] Like Adam and Eve, parents have the responsibility to make "*all* things known unto their sons and their daughters."[3]

This means that it is up to parents to provide for their children the vision of God's plan and purposes for the body and for sexuality. In addition to the sacredness of sexual intimacy within marriage, parents also need to teach children respect for the body and its functions. But before parents can expect their children to adhere to God's standards of sexual behavior, they must teach God's plan and principles. This way your children can understand why God asks them to remain sexually chaste until marriage.

As parents you have special wisdom and insight gained from time and experience, as well as immeasurable love for your children and understanding of them individually. No other person or organization is as invested in your children's well being and happiness as you are. "God expects parents . . . to teach their children about procreation and chastity and to prepare them for dating and marriage. This responsibility should not be left to schools, friends, playmates, or strangers. Heavenly Father wishes His children to understand how to use this great and holy power wisely and reverently."[4]

Parents must prepare themselves, then actively present God's perspective on the body and sexuality. Passive parenting will not persuade youth to stand strong for morality and chastity—especially if they don't even understand what they are and why they are important. Satan gains power over lives when the counsel to teach light and truth goes unheeded. God has warned, "You have not taught your children light and truth, according to the commandments; and that wicked one hath power, as yet, over you, and this is the cause of your affliction."[5] Parents be warned that Satan seeks to spread his dominion and darkness,[6] but that you have the advantage, for "they that be with us are more than they that be with them."[7] Satan has no power where light and truth dominate.

Secular sexual information can't be avoided, so the appropriate action is for you to actively counter the world's view, not with negativity and fear, but with true doctrine and a positive godly perspective. Because of the hold Satan has on people's hearts, our young people "cannot avoid hearing about sexuality. However, much of what they hear in the world promotes the abuse of the sacred power of procreation. Children—and especially teenagers—need accurate information and true doctrine about these subjects. Parents must help them gain strength to withstand the falsehoods taught in the world. They must teach children the Lord's plan for the use of the power of procreation."[8]

When you don't teach your children correct principles, you create a vacuum for others to fill. The void is filled by friends, movies, magazines and music, which rarely present God's perspective on the sacred power of procreation. Teach your children the sanctity of sex in marriage with its attendant joys and blessings. Help them to avoid the misuse of the sacred powers of procreation and to have a clear vision and understanding of their proper place and divine purposes.

Don't Delay. Sex education begins very early—even as parents respond to a baby's earliest physical needs. Children are sensitive to their parent's attitudes when taking care of their bodily needs such as changing diapers, potty training, or cleaning up bathroom accidents. If parents display disgust or scold their children, children may begin to associate negative feelings with certain body functions. Parents must be attentive to the early sexual education they may unknowingly provide. Portraying the idea that the body is a gift from God, and that *all* parts of the body are good and have necessary functions can help children develop a healthy love and respect for the body and build a positive sexual foundation.

Sex education continues as children display natural curiosity about their bodies. The attitude and atmosphere surrounding innocent questions contribute to the child's sex education. Such questions, when awkwardly avoided or incorrectly answered, can create potential problems. To a child, questions about sex are as natural as questions about anything else. When a child asks what measuring spoons are and what they are used for, parents patiently explain. But if a child asks if girls have penises, many parents blush, stammer, or react with dismay or disgust.

How you respond to a child's questioning, exploration of his / her body or innocent sex play sets the stage for the child's sexual attitudes. Children also learn whether it is safe or not to go to their parents when they have serious or sensitive questions. You should be first and foremost in teaching your children about sexuality. This helps to reduce negative effects and the need to "un-teach" incorrect information later on.

I learned this for myself one night when I asked my son if he knew what sex was. He said he didn't really know, but that he knew it was bad. I asked how he knew that. He told me the word came up in his 1st grade class and a little girl, who was also LDS, had said her mom told her it was bad. When I heard this, I knew we needed to get busy teaching correct principles before we had too much "un-teaching" to do. (What to teach will be addressed in the next chapter.) It's much easier to teach correct principles initially than to undo incorrect teaching later. Actively seek out opportunities to teach the sanctity of sexual relations. Establish a positive foundation and clear up any incorrect information that may have been encountered. Do not delay teaching these sacred truths.

Attitudes about sex, gender knowledge, and gender acceptance are contributing to your children's sex education nearly every day of their lives.

Sex education should not be a one-time event. As your children develop in maturity, additional information must be given. Be prepared to provide this education as they are ready for it. Be attentive to teaching opportunities in the early years. The sooner you become partners in your child's sex education, the better. Attitudes about sex, gender knowledge, and gender acceptance are contributing to your children's sex education nearly every day of their lives. Open the door for your children to receive positive principles regarding moral purity and sexual fulfillment after marriage.

Lighting the Way

A prophet of God has called upon parents to rise up and take the lead in teaching and showing the way for children and others to follow. He has sounded the clarion call for you to let your light shine that the world may see God's light through the mists of darkness. President Harold B. Lee stated, "I say to you Latter-day Saint mothers and fathers, if you will rise to the responsibility of teaching your children in the home . . . the day will soon be dawning when the whole world will come to our doors and will say, 'Show us your way that we may walk in your path.'"[9]

As you accept and act upon the opportunity to provide sacred instruction, you not only bestow needed vision and understanding to your children, you also light the way for other parents to follow. God's way is not readily known throughout the world. Many are kept from the truth simply "because they know not where to find it."[10] Many good parents hunger to know how to provide safe passage for their children through the teen years.

One mother told me about some boundaries she had set for her teenage daughter. Upon learning of these boundaries, the mother of one of her daughter's friend's called her with genuine interest to find out what she was doing and why. The friend's parents then changed their rules to match the rules this mother had set. This is an example of how one parent confidently let her light shine, lighting the way for others to follow.

Parental Preparation to Teach

It is a sacred duty to teach your children, and with preparation you can do so with confidence and conviction. Mothers and fathers must both partner in this sacred teaching, since each parent contributes insights and experience that the other does not have, presenting ideas in "differently effective" ways.

Parental Barriers

You may encounter barriers that threaten to keep you from fulfilling your divine calling to teach your children about sexual intimacy and marriage. A list of common barriers and helpful solutions follows.

Embarrassment. The world isn't embarrassed to parade its sexual perspective—bombarding youth with distorted images and attitudes. If you are too embarrassed or too unsure of yourself to teach your children, Satan gains free rein of their hearts and minds. We know that Satan uses any and all tools at his disposal. Embarrassment is a particularly effective tool he has found to keep parents from teaching their children eternal truths regarding the sanctity of sexuality.

Lack of Personal Conviction Regarding the Sanctity of Sex. Parents who were not taught adequately or correctly by their parents may yet be ignorant of God's divine plan and purpose for premarital sexual purity and sexual fulfillment after marriage. Parents cannot teach with conviction what they don't themselves understand or believe.

Lack of Knowledge. The thought of discussing sexual matters is intimidating for some parents who have no idea what to say or how to answer sexual questions. Preparation through study and learning can address and overcome this obstacle.

Fear. You may have personal fears about opening sexual discussions with your children. You might also fear that your children will be more likely to get into trouble sexually if you talk about sex with them. LDS counselor, Romel W. Mackelprang stated, "Although there is no evidence that accurate sexual knowledge promotes premature sexual activity, it is clear that the lack of knowledge leads to problems."[11] Dr. Mackelprang went on to say that teaching the subject of sexuality in the home actually improves the chances that youth will avoid serious sexual problems. LDS psychologist and author, Dr. Wayne Anderson, wrote:

> Some parents contend that sex education will lead to sexual experimentation and promiscuous activities. There is a good possibility that behavior of this nature will occur it parents simply impart information that they often call the "facts of life." However, if both father and mother see sex education for what it really is—a continuous process of acquiring information and learning how to build a wholesome and satisfying life, a process that goes on as long as one lives and breathes—[the children] will accept the fact that sex education is as much a part of life as eating and sleeping.[12]

Certainly parental wisdom and knowledge regarding what and how much a child can handle at a given age needs to be considered. But in general terms of teaching God's plan and purpose for sexuality and moral purity, light and truth provide power to avoid temptation. Christian author and speaker Joe Beam agreed. He said:

By telling . . . the truth about God's intent for sex in marriage, we [don't set them] up for temptation or sin or anything but a wonderful marriage. . . . Besides, we know that the forces of Satan work best in the dark, not in the light [see John 3:19-20]. It's the misguidance and misinformation that teens get from each other or provocative TV shows and movies that sets up temptation. The truth—the light—gives the power to overcome those temptations.[13]

What Parents Can Do to Prepare

The suggestions shared below can help parents prepare to teach their children light and truth regarding premarital moral purity and the sanctity of sexual fulfillment in marriage.

1. Invite the Spirit. We are promised in the scriptures that as we seek the Holy Ghost, it will tell us all things that we should do.[14] If parents will invite the Spirit to guide them as they prepare, study, and then teach, the preparation and the message will be more effective. In 2 Nephi 33:1 we learn that when we teach by the Spirit it will carry the message into the hearts of the hearers, having a greater impact on their lives. Teaching with the Spirit makes the power of light and truth available. Parents are not alone in this awesome and sacred responsibility, "If parents will seek the guidance of the Spirit in humble prayer, it will help them teach their children about this sacred power."[15] Teaching can be more powerful when prayer and fasting are part of the preparation.

2. Gain a Testimony of the Sanctity of Sex. Review Chapter 2 to refresh your mind of the divine nature of sexual relations and to gain a conviction of the sanctity of sexual relations in marriage.

3. Remove Negative Beliefs and Inhibitions. Many parents will be in the unfortunate position of having to overcome their own inhibitions and re-educate themselves with a positive perspective of sexuality before they can teach their children. Do your best to recognize and remove any embarrassment, shame, discomfort, or even disgust you may have associated with sexuality. If you dislike sex and think it's dirty or evil, your children will sense it. If you are embarrassed talking about it, they will feel it. Children need their parents to teach with confidence and conviction, and with a healthy attitude and reverence for sexuality. Whatever you believe about sex will be subtly communicated in your teachings. You might want to review Chapter 7 for suggestions on overcoming negative thoughts, feelings, and inhibitions.

4. Educate Yourself. You may not know what to say or where to begin a discussion on sexuality. Study and learn about sexual anatomy and functioning so that you can discuss this topic with greater confidence—removing paralysis regarding sexual teaching. Dr. Anderson suggests six general categories you may want to study:[16]

- Bodily organs and their functions
- Physical differences between boys and girls
- Origin of babies
- Intrauterine growth
- Birth process
- Father's role

As you read various materials suggested here you may want to make some notes, create questions, or compile an outline of what you want to teach and what you think your child is ready for. It may also be helpful to understand the natural stages of child development and sexual interest. This can alleviate concerns and allow you to respond appropriately toward particular behaviors. (Drs. Lindsay Curtis and Wayne Anderson provide developmental information on page 201 of their book *Living, Loving and Marrying.*)

Another approach is to use Linda and Richard Eyres' book *How to Talk to Your Child about Sex*, which provides parents with dialogues for different age groups. My husband and I were not yet aware of the Eyres' excellent book when we prepared to teach our first son, so we did the groundwork ourselves. This turned out to be a very important part of my own sex education and provided personal growth in ways I may not have otherwise experienced. In Chapter 16 I will provide a sample script or discussion outline of our first discussion with our son.

Sex education is more than just sexual facts. Eternal principles and the blessings of obedience are needed beyond explanation of the birds and the bees. These additional teachings are provided in Chapter 15.

5. Have Open and Healthy Discussions about Sex with Your Spouse.
One of the best ways to prepare to teach in a relaxed and confident manner is to be able to have intimate sexual discussions with your spouse. If you will discuss your sexual relationship, work to resolve differences, and teach each other your own sexual needs and desires, you will be more relaxed and better prepared to have meaningful discussions with your children.

6. Role Play Discussions. Practice the actual discussions you intend to have with your children. Practice saying the correct terms out loud. Practice asking the questions you've compiled as well as your responses. Practice speaking in front of a mirror, or go through the full discussion in a role-play with your spouse. Practicing will help you be more comfortable and confident in your teaching. Children are best served by hearing you speak of sacred and sensitive things with confidence and conviction.

Why Kids Indulge in Premarital Sexual Behavior

Knowledge of the underlying causes of sexual transgression can help you be more powerful in creating an environment for effective sexual teaching. Kids know they're not supposed to engage in premarital sexual activities. They know about the dangers of sexually transmitted diseases, unplanned pregnancy, and parental or church discipline. So why do they do it? Agency is part of the answer, but addressing the sources or contributing factors of sexual transgression, rather than the surface symptoms makes parental efforts much more effective.

Unmet Emotional Needs. When children feel unloved, unaccepted, or unimportant, they are more susceptible to sexual temptations. One psychiatrist noted that in all his years of treating adolescents who had been involved in sexual misconduct, he had never found one whose needs for love had been sufficiently met. It was his perception "that almost all sexual misconduct in adolescents [was] rooted in an empty emotional love tank."[17] The Savior also understood how unmet emotional needs could lead to sinful behavior. President Kimball said, "Jesus saw sin as wrong but also was able to see sin as springing from deep and unmet needs on the part of the sinner."[18]

Look for signs of emotional emptiness and begin to meet those needs, avoiding the need for them to be filled superficially by sexual sin. If children's needs for love, acceptance, and feeling valued and important are met within the home, they will be less likely to seek substitute love elsewhere.

*If children's needs for love, acceptance, and feeling valued
and important are met within the home, they will be
less likely to seek substitute love elsewhere.*

Rebellion. A contributing factor to sexual indulgence also related to unmet emotional needs is rebellion. Though teens may not realize what they are doing, when their emotional needs are not being met they seek to fill those needs in ways that will hurt their parents—who they see as neglecting their needs. Something insignificant to a parent could have dramatic consequences to a vulnerable child. Bishop J. Richard Clarke, former counselor in the presiding bishopric, shared the tragic story of a young man who felt unloved and rejected by his father, which lead him into serious sexual sins as an act of rebellion. These are the words of a young man who wrote to Bishop Clarke:

> At a very young age . . . I became convinced that my father didn't love me. It stemmed from an encounter when one evening I went to kiss him good night and he brushed me away. I'm sure he doesn't remember, and it had no significance to him, but I was devastated: my entire sense of security and my world crumbled into ashes as I stood there.
>
> Not knowing what else to do, I ran from this new stranger in a panic to my mother and whispered tones to her of my calamity, which she denied, but did not convince me. That night I watched my father as I stood in the shadows of my darkened bedroom. I swore to myself that I would close the door until he sought to open it. I would ignore him until he sought after me.
>
> He didn't notice. If he did, he never asked me what was wrong. Well, needless to say, through the next years I went through the motions and rebelled to get his attention, which I got in the form of anger. At any rate, I developed into a homosexual, a vitiating disease, and was soon entrenched in my prison. I didn't know myself. And I have felt for more years than I can remember that the Lord didn't love me either.[19]

Touch Deprivation. In Chapter 12 we discussed the powerful universal need for physical touch. Many children are touch deprived. One day I asked our son whether I was giving him enough hugs. He said I was doing okay, then added, "But sometimes when I don't get enough hugs, I feel lonely." Over time, as touch deficits increase, youth experience increased susceptibility to sexual temptation. In today's society, loving touch and sex have become so confused that adolescents often seek sexual fulfillment when they are simply in need of loving touch.

Telling a touch-deprived adolescent not to engage in sexual behavior may be like telling a hungry child not to eat the cookies sitting out on the table. Until we address the underlying hunger for physical touch, efforts to end immoral behavior will be ineffective.

Boredom and Unhealthy Habits. Particularly during preadolescent years, children may discover pleasurable feelings associated with parts of their bodies, and may engage in these activities out of boredom or because they have developed unhealthy habits. If children have too much time on their hands, or if parents are not sufficiently attentive, children may develop unhealthy habits of soothing themselves through sexual stimulation. Parents can help children develop healthy habits by channeling their energies into constructive activities.

Lack of Divine Understanding. Kids engage in inappropriate sexual behaviors when they don't have a strong enough understanding of why they should wait until marriage. This is where a testimony of God's plan and purposes of sexual relations in marriage comes into play. When youth have the power of light and truth behind them and a positive understanding of why they should wait and what the value or blessings are of waiting, they are able to find greater desire and strength to resist temptations.

Strengthening the Parent / Child Relationship for Sexual Discussions

In addition to the above steps to help you prepare for sexual discussions, there are substantive ways you can strengthen the personal foundation upon which children can best receive and carry the teachings into their hearts. If there is a strained relationship between you and your child, you may want to hold off teaching for a time as you work to restore the relationship.

1. Build Relationships. If children feel loved and accepted, they will be more likely to receive your teachings. They will be more likely to view special one-on-one talks about sex as special occasions, rather than as lectures or something to dread. If children can trust that you won't overreact or shame them, they will be more likely to come to you with their questions and concerns. Children must know you are open and willing to discuss this topic or they will go elsewhere for their information—and you may not like the information they find elsewhere.

Trust is often thought of as something the child must earn, but parents, too, must earn the trust of their children. Can your children trust you to teach them correctly? Can they trust you to respond calmly? Can children trust you to keep confidences and not casually discuss with others their concerns or problems? Work on building your own trustworthiness in the eyes of your child.

2. Give Loving Touch. There's a healing power in physical touch that communicates love and acceptance in a way nothing else can. Feed your child's need for loving touch with lots of hand holding, hugs, kisses, or a comforting hand on their shoulder. If you find it difficult to give loving touch to your children, try touching them gently as they sleep. Whisper words of love as the stillness of the night carries them into their hearts. As you provide more tactile nourishment to your children, their touch needs will be filled and susceptibility to sexual temptation will decrease.

3. Provide Positive Flooding. Flood your children with encouragement. This is not the same as praise. Encouragement is personal and specific whereas praise is more general. Positive flooding comes in the form of lots of "I love it when you . . ." or "I love it that you're . . ." as well as lots of "I love you!" Children need as much personal and positive encouragement as possible. Making eye contact with your child also helps the two of you to connect in meaningful ways.

4. Spend One-on-one Time. Scheduling regular one-on-one time not only prepares the relationship for more important discussions, but also sends the message: "You are important. You are worth my valuable time." Make a point to create special one-on-one time by taking a child with you as you do simple errands, such as grocery shopping or picking up dry cleaning. You can also schedule parent / child dates to go out for ice cream or to walk around the mall together. Just Dad and child or Mom and child occasions will create opportunities for casual conversation and prepare you both for the special discussions you will have about sexuality.

5. Hold Personal Parent Interviews. Personal parent interviews (PPIs) are another wonderful way to build relationships. If you begin when children are young—and make the experience enjoyable—children may even remind you to have monthly PPIs. You can start doing PPIs at any age and still be effective. We have found that a special PPI candy jar works wonders. We also keep a PPI binder with pages for us to record our visits. On our PPI pages we record name, date, monthly message, one-on-one activity for the month, personal goals, personal journal notes, and parent notes.

Each fast Sunday either Dad or Mom holds PPIs with each child, rotating every other month. We begin with a treat and prayer, then discuss the monthly message, plan our one-on-one activity, and discuss personal goals the child is working toward. We often ask some additional questions as well.

Questions are a great way to prompt discussions. Here are a few examples of questions we use: What do you like best about school? Is there anything or anyone that makes you sad or angry? How am I doing as your parent? Is there anything I could do better? Do you have any questions or concerns about anything? How do you like our babysitters? How do you like your Primary / Sunday School teachers?

Show your children that you care by asking probing and pertinent questions about their feelings and their problems. Children need your help and long for your guidance, attention, and active participation in their lives. Don't be afraid to ask questions, thinking your child will resent your prying. If parents are safe, trustworthy, and loving in their interactions, children will be more receptive to their parents' questions and teachings. One young woman stated that she wished her parents would ask her about her feelings and her problems more. Though she didn't always act appreciative of their efforts, she really did want her parents to take an active interest in her life.

6. Learn to Love in Your Child's Love Language. Chapter 10 provided information on learning to love in your spouse's love language. Each of your children also has an individual love language. To be most effective in loving and building a relationship with your child, you need to know exactly what makes him or her feel loved and cared about. This can be a topic for PPIs where you ask your child to tell you ten ways he or she feels loved. Commit yourself to doing those things on a regular basis, so that you can build up loving feelings in your child before having sensitive discussions. For more information on learning to love your children in a way they can best receive it, check out the books *The Five Love Languages of Children* and *The Five Love Languages of Teenagers* by Dr. Gary Chapman.

7. Use the Intentional Dialogue Communication Tool. Using the Intentional Dialogue (Couples Dialogue) from Chapter 10 in your discussions with your children is another great way to provide a safe and open forum for discussion. The mirroring, validating, and empathizing allow you and your child to be fully heard, validated, and understood even with difficult or heated subjects. The process of mirroring alone can keep emotions in check and ensure that understanding is occurring at every step of the conversation.

The Need for Positive Sex Education

Lack of knowledge, lack of understanding, and incorrect or negative beliefs can not only put children at risk in their youth, but can cause unnecessary problems within marriage. Dr. Brent Barlow, marriage counselor and BYU professor asked:

> Why does something so beautiful sometimes become a source of so many problems? Part of the difficulty stems from mistaken ideas. Some people still believe that sexual intimacy is a necessary evil by which we have children. These people get an inaccurate view from parents who were too embarrassed to discuss such matters with their children or who were so concerned that their children live the law of chastity that they taught only the negative consequences of the improper use of intimacy.[20]

It is fairly well established that *more* and *improved* sex education is needed to better prepare future generations for sexual fulfillment in marriage. Christian physician Dr. Ed Wheat stated, "Unfortunately most of us were not counseled in these matters before we married and so we stumbled through the first few years, at least, trying to find our way to happiness. As a family physician for almost four decades, I have observed that marriage with its tremendous significance often turns out to be the least-prepared-for event of life. Even as divorce takes on epidemic proportions, young couples continue to venture into marriage remarkably unprepared."[21]

Understanding the Good Girl Syndrome with its unintended negative conditioning by parents, church, and society, will help to confirm the need for a more positive approach to sex education. Positive teachings are a greater long-term deterrent to sexual deviance than threats of "hellfire and damnation." With positive teachings and greater understanding, reverence can replace recklessness among our youth. Biological facts and how-tos do not provide sufficient sexual education; what is needed is an attitude and an atmosphere surrounding all aspects of sexual matters so that learning is an ongoing process.

To avoid inappropriate guilt and negative conditioning, place the focus more on the blessings of premarital purity and the sanctity of post-marital sexual relations than on the consequences and warnings of immorality. Dr. Wheat stated, "We need to treasure and share with our children these positive values God Himself teaches in Scripture concerning the love / sex relationship, always placing sex in marriage in an entirely different light from sex outside of marriage. Sex apart from marriage is spelled out as obviously wrong. Sex in marriage is wonderfully right. Let us never forget it!"[22]

These sentiments are made very clear in the New Testament, which says, "Marriage is honorable in all and the bed undefiled."[23]

Since the various components of the Good Girl Syndrome are often the primary causes of the lack of sexual fulfillment in marriage, you may find it helpful to review them before beginning to teach your children. The main problems associated with the Good Girl Syndrome include:

- Underlying negative thoughts, beliefs, and feelings associated with sex and the body;

- Discomfort, embarrassment, or inability to appropriately discuss sexual matters;

- Negative moral training based on shame and fear, and warnings of the dangers and consequences of sex;

- The lack of complete and correct sex education—including the biological facts and specific techniques for finding fulfillment within marriage; and

- The belief that if one keeps all the commandments and remains chaste, everything sexual within marriage will turn out well.

The goals of teaching children and youth about sex should go beyond having our youth safely married in the temple; we need to help them learn what is needed to live "happily ever after." Not only do we need to teach premarital morality, but we also need to teach how to secure marital happiness and sexual fulfillment. Premarital chastity alone will not ensure sexual fulfillment in marriage. By opening our view to the post-marital ramifications of our teachings, parents and leaders can significantly improve their approach and attitude when teaching about sexuality.

Reverence, respect, and responsibility are crucial components of a positive sex education. Sexual information must emphasize the positive impact, or blessings of following God's counsel, rather than over-emphasizing the negative consequences of disobedience. If we focus on the negatives, we will get more negatives in return. Sex education must not convey an ominous feeling of lurking evil and impending doom. Instead, it should emphasize sexual relations in marriage as a potential for exquisite joy and a sacred ordinance saved for marriage. When we focus on the positive, we get more positive outcomes. A shift in focus from the premarital "don'ts" to the marital "do's" could change the dynamics of the whole discussion and transcend the sexual struggles many youth face.

Parents must teach God's plan and purposes of sexual intimacy in marriage before expecting children to understand why they should wait until after they are married to enjoy sexual intimacy. Love of God and a desire to keep His commandments are greater motivators than fear or punishment. Knowing God's plan and purpose for marriage can lead to a wholeness otherwise unattainable.

The message "Good Girls Do . . . but they wait until marriage" will be a welcome relief to the shame some feel, and will ease the difficult transition from the don'ts to the do's. Imagine how this shift in focus would change the whole tone of a Standards Night or a parent / child sex discussion. Dr. Mackelprang confirmed the need for a change in tone when he counseled us to emphasize "the joys and rewards of physical intimacy rather than focusing exclusively on the pitfalls of immorality."[24]

Knowing that the physical attraction placed within men and women is a glorious gift from God when used in its rightful time and place, can provide youth with a healthy sexual understanding and put them in a more positive and powerful position to resist temptation. Respect can replace recklessness as youth gain a more inspired understanding of God's promised power and the blessings that come from reverencing the body and sexuality. Parents can experience special parent / child bonding as they make the time and effort to teach a godly perspective regarding sexuality. Some resources are listed below that can help parents start preparing for their divine opportunity to teach their children the blessings of moral purity and sexual fulfillment in marriage.

Resources for Parents and Youth Leaders

Church Resources

- *A Parent's Guide,* 1985.
- *For the Strength of Youth: Fulfilling Our Duty to God* booklet, 2001.
- *Family Home Evening Resource Book,* "Teaching about Procreation and Chastity," 253–60, 1983.

Church Articles

- "Protecting Purity" by Brent L. Top, Bruce A. Chadwick and Matthew T. Evans, BYU Magazine, Summer 2003, Volume 57, Number 3, 47.

- "I Have a Question: 'Why is it important for us to teach our children in the home about physical intimacy in marriage,'" by Brent Barlow, BYU professor, *Ensign,* June 2000, 58.

- "Helping Youth Choose Sexual Purity," by Joy Saunders Lundberg, *Ensign,* Oct. 1991, 21.

- "Teaching Children about Physical Development," by A. Lynn Scoresby, *Ensign,* June 1988, 39.

- "Of Souls, Symbols, and Sacraments," BYU Devotional address, Jan. 12, 1988 (available at http://speeches.byu.edu/).

- "Talking with Your Children about Moral Purity," *Ensign,* Dec. 1986, 57.

- "Teaching Morality to Your Children," by Terrance D. Olson, *Ensign,* Mar. 1981, 14.

Books

- *How to Talk to Your Child about Sex: It's Best to Start Early, but It's Never Too Late: A Step-by-Step Guide for Every Age,* by Linda & Richard Eyre, 1998.

- *Living, Loving & Marrying: Thoughts for LDS Teens and Young Marrieds,* by Lindsay R. Curtis, M.D., and Wayne J. Anderson, Ph.D., 1968.

- *Growing Up: Gospel Answers about Maturation and Sex,* by Brad Wilcox, 2000.

- *Worth Waiting For,* by Brent Barlow, 1995.

- *On Guard!: Seven Safeguards to Protect Your Sexual Purity,* by Gary and Joy Lundberg

Chapter 14—"Home" Work

- Prepare to teach your children God's perspective on the body and sexuality through study, prayer and fasting.

- To effectively teach your children about sex and the body, strive to overcome the teaching barriers of embarrassment, lack of personal conviction of the sanctity of sex, lack of knowledge and fear.

- To prepare to teach:

  1. Invite the Spirit to guide as you study, prepare, and teach.

2. Gain your own testimony of the sanctity of sex.

3. Remove your negative beliefs and inhibitions.

4. Educate yourself more fully about human anatomy and sexual functioning by reviewing the resources listed earlier.

5. Have open and healthy discussions about sex with your spouse.

6. Role play and practice the discussions to become more comfortable and confident on the subject.

- Strengthen the foundation for sexual discussions:

  1. Build strong relationships with your children.

  2. Give more loving touch.

  3. Provide positive flooding.

  4. Spend one-on-one time.

  5. Hold personal parent interviews (PPIs).

  6. Learn to show love to your child in his or her love language regularly.

  7. Use the intentional dialogue communication tool with your children so that both parent and child will feel fully heard and understood.

- Pay attention to your children and their activities to see that boredom does not lead to unhealthy habits.

NOTES

Chapter 14—Preparing Future Generations for
Sexual Fulfillment in Marriage: Preparing to Teach

[1]Scoresby, "Teaching Children about Physical Development," *Ensign*, June 1988, 39.
[2]Doctrine & Covenants 93:40.
[3]Moses 5:12.
[4]*Family Home Evening Resource Book*, 253.
[5]Doctrine & Covenants 93:42.
[6]*See* Doctrine & Covenants 82:5.
[7]2 Kings 6:16.
[8]*Marriage and Family Relations, Instructor's Manual*, 70.
[9]Lee, *Teachings of Presidents of the Church*, 149. *See also* Micah 4:1–2.
[10]Doctrine & Covenants 123:12.

[11]Mackelprang, *Multiply and Replenish*, 51.

[12]Curtis and Anderson, *Living, Loving & Marrying*, 200.

[13]Beam, *Becoming One*, 134–35.

[14]*See* 2 Nephi 32:5.

[15]*Family Home Evening Resource Book*, 253.

[16]*See* Curtis and Anderson, *Living, Loving & Marrying*, 208–16.

[17]Chapman, *Five Love Languages*, 163.

[18]Kimball, "Jesus: The Perfect Leader," *Ensign*, Aug. 1979, 5.

[19]Clarke, "Ministering to Needs through LDS Social Services," *Ensign*, May 1977, 85.

[20]Barlow, "They Twain Shall Be One," *Ensign*, Sep. 1986, 50.

[21]Wheat and Wheat, *Intended for Pleasure*, 19.

[22]Wheat and Wheat, *Intended for Pleasure*, 18.

[23]Hebrews 13:4.

[24]Mackelprang, *Multiply and Replenish*, 50.

CHAPTER VIEW

Light and Truth Regarding the Sanctity of Sexual Relations

Gender Acceptance and Role Learning

The Body Is Good and Is a Gift from God

The Essentials of Procreation

Sex Can Be Controlled

God's Standards

Sexual Fulfillment Takes Time and Effort after Marriage

Blessings of Righteousness
1. *Companionship of the Holy Ghost*
2. *Peace and a Clear Conscience*
3. *Happiness*
4. *Confidence in Self and in God*
5. *Faith*
6. *Self-discipline*
7. *Proper Focus in Life*
8. *Self-respect*
9. *Trust*
10. *Firm Foundation for a Strong Marriage and Family*

Chapter 15—"Home" Work

Chapter 15

PREPARING FUTURE GENERATIONS FOR SEXUAL FULFILLMENT IN MARRIAGE— WHAT TO TEACH

Light and Truth Regarding the Sanctity of Sexual Relations

Children desire light and truth. When parents and leaders endow children with light and knowledge regarding God's plan, purposes, and standards for sexuality, they become "as wise as serpents [to Satan's craftiness]."[1] They become enlightened and endowed with power. They are armed with the sword of light and truth to cut through the mists of darkness that prevail in society. Youth given this power can uphold God's standards and stifle Satan's strategies, which lead them into sin.

Satan seeks to keep all from the light. Parents unwittingly play into his hands when they do not teach light and truth. God is "the light which shineth in darkness."[2] Teach youth the power of light, which is truth. Teach them to follow the light. "I am the way, the truth, and the life."[3] Teach them to "Pray always that [they] may come off conqueror; yea, that [they] may conquer Satan, and that [they] may escape the hands of the servants of Satan that do uphold his work."[4]

Elder Jeffrey R. Holland taught parents that youth are ready and willing to hear it straight. He said, "I love what President J. Reuben Clark said of our youth well over a half century ago. . . . '[They] are hungry for the things of the Spirit,' he said. 'They are eager to learn the Gospel, and they want it straight, undiluted. . . . You do not have to sneak up behind [them] and whisper religion in [their] ears; . . . you can bring these truths [out] openly.' Satan is certainly not subtle in his teachings; why should we be?"[5]

Society is saturated with sexual information—most of it negative, distorted, even corrupt. It is time for those with knowledge of God's light and truth to go on the offensive, teaching a healthy and holy understanding of sexuality. President Gordon B. Hinckley counseled parents to "teach their children the sanctity of sex, that the gift of creating life is sacred."[6] Parents and youth leaders must look beyond the "no's" of today to the "yes's" of tomorrow. Their teaching must be transformed from an almost exclusive emphasis on dire premarital warnings against sexual intimacy, to a hearty dose of after-marriage blessings. A positive emphasis on the blessings of sexual purity can give power to youth to get them past the difficult teen years, safely into the covenant of marriage.

Christian author and speaker Joe Beam expressed his frustration that many of the young couples he has counseled have been so poorly prepared for sexual intimacy in marriage. He and his wife determined to do differently with their daughters by teaching that sex is wonderful within marriage, "As we sat down with Joanna, I started with words I hope she remembers throughout her lifetime. 'Honey, the first thing you should know is that sex is good. It's the most wonderful way God gave a husband and wife to say, "I love you" to each other.'"[7]

Beam became weary of the many young women he saw who were so negatively conditioned regarding sexual intimacy in marriage. He knew they had an uphill battle to see sex as the God-given gift that it is:

> Young women [have been] taught for years, "Sex is bad. Sex is bad. Sex is bad . . ." and then later, "Oh, you're getting married tomorrow, then sex is good!" You can't undo a life of teaching in a couple of days, weeks, or months. We see too many young women, especially from Christian homes, who've been given such conflict-

ing information about sex from their parents and church that they enter marriage with conflicting emotions about the sexual union they're about to have with their husbands. They want to enjoy lovemaking but feel somehow that they're doing something wrong, something shameful. We've had to help so many young couples with this struggle that we purposed not to have that happen with our daughters.[8]

Sex as a Sacred Marital Ordinance. When Jeffrey R. Holland was president at Brigham Young University he gave an inspired discourse on human sexuality entitled "Of Souls, Symbols, and Sacraments." Defining sexual relations in marriage as a sacrament or sacred marital ordinance, he stated, "Sexual intimacy is not only a symbolic union between a man and a woman—the uniting of their very souls—but it is also symbolic of a union between mortals and deity. . . . Human intimacy is a sacrament, a very special kind of symbol."[9] He defined a sacrament as an act or ordinance that unites us with God and his limitless powers.[10] He went on to say, "Sexual union is also, in its own profound way, a very real sacrament of the highest order, a union not only of a man and a woman but very much the union of that man and woman with God."[11]

Youth of the noble birthright have the ability to understand sex as a "sacred ordinance" of marriage and reverence it as such. Youth can understand the sacred nature of a baby blessing, a baptism, partaking of the sacrament, or of a marriage sealing in the temple. Aligning marital intimacy with these sacred ordinances can have a subtle but powerful influence and provide the spiritual insight and understanding youth need to resist temptation. Reverence and respect can be instilled within the hearts and minds of youth as they are taught that sex is a symbolic sacred ordinance, reserved by God for marriage. This will also provide a much broader and stronger vision regarding the seriousness of toying with sexual intimacies outside of marriage.

Dr. Michael Farnworth, BYU-Idaho professor, supported this line of thought by stating, "Going on the assumption that the sexual procreative act is an ordinance, would any of us be so spiritually dead or immature as to mimic and make a mockery of a sacred ordinance?"[12] Youth who understand sexual relations as a sacramental union can more powerfully resist indulging in sexual intimacies outside of marriage. They can see through the lenses of light and truth that such sexual indulgences are the means of defiling, violating, and profaning something equally as sacred as the ordinance of baptism or the sacrament.

The vision of sexual union in marriage as a sacrament provides a grand and glorious foundation upon which to build a strong, satisfying, and sanctifying sexual relationship within marriage. A latter-day prophet of God, Joseph F. Smith, taught that sexual relations in marriage were not only for procreation, but also for the "development of the higher faculties and nobler traits of human nature."[13] He taught that sexual union, when participated in with the right intent, was "honorable and sanctifying" having the power to purify and to cleanse.

God's Purposes for Sex in Marriage. With correct and balanced teaching, the concept of sexual relations as a righteous means of enjoyment and pleasure in marriage need not be foreign to our youth. Physical intimacy in marriage is ordained of God and has holy purposes. Don't give children the impression that sex is somehow evil, dirty, sinful or something to be ashamed of. Teach your children that God created the sexual union of husband and wife for many purposes, such as: expressing love and passion; for companionship; for physical, emotional, and spiritual bonding and healing; and for mutual pleasure and joy.

Pleasure is generally taught and thought of as negative—something for which we must repent. This can make it difficult for some to grasp the concept of sexual pleasure as permissible or as a Godly purpose of sexual relations even after marriage. However, youth can be taught about the marital blessings of sexual intimacy not only for pro-creation, but also for pleasure and the other important purposes, thus preparing them more perfectly for sexual fulfillment in marriage.

Gender Acceptance and Role Learning

The Proclamation on the Family states, "All human beings—male and female—are created in the image of God. Each is a beloved spirit son or daughter of heavenly parents, and as such each has a divine nature and destiny. Gender is an essential characteristic of individual premortal, mortal, and eternal identity and purpose."[14] It is important that parents teach that there is a special reason for gender. The LDS Church counsels:

> It is in this early stage of life, as the roles of male and female are acquired, that the foundation of sexual health is laid or sexual distress begins. By age three most children should have firmly accepted their identity as male or female. When family unhappiness has led them to feel unaccepted, they may become confused about their self-esteem and their gender role. . . . Unkind parenting can plant seeds of self-doubt and even confusion about the gender role. These seeds can germinate into personal problems in the following years unless parents change and show increased affection and acceptance.[15]

The *Proclamation* continues with the statement, "Children are entitled . . . to be reared by a father *and* a mother." For healthy gender identity to develop, children need the influence, involvement and teachings of both the father and mother. Families were created with two different-gender parents on purpose. Mothers tend to teach feminine characteristics and perspectives. Fathers tend to teach masculine characteristics and perspectives. Both characteristics and perspectives are needed for a balanced life. Both parents provide silent teachings about eternal roles through their attitudes and behaviors. Together, parents can model and teach eternal traits that transcend gender, such as faith, charity, knowledge, patience, temperance, diligence, and love. If nurturing and teaching come from only one parent, the child's learning is unbalanced and will be missing critical perspectives. Single parents may find it useful to elicit the assistance of friends, family, and church members to help bridge any void.

The Body Is Good and Is a Gift from God

Our bodies were created in the image of God.[16] Our physical bodies are one of our greatest earthly gifts. Elder James E. Talmage taught, "We have been taught . . . to look upon these bodies of ours as gifts from God. We Latter-day Saints do not regard the body as something to be condemned, something to be abhorred. . . . We regard [the body] as the sign of our royal birthright. . . . We recognize . . . that those who kept not their first estate . . . were denied that inestimable blessing. . . . We believe that these bodies . . . may be made, in very truth, the temple of the Holy Ghost."[17]

Let us teach our youth that we are spirit children of our Heavenly Father and that the body was created as a temple in which our spirit dwells. President Spencer W. Kimball stated, "The human body is the sacred home of the spirit child of God."[18]

Our bodies are not only the home of *our* spirit, but also of *the Spirit of God,* which dwells within us after we are baptized and have received this gift. Our bodies are literally holy temples for God's Spirit as well as for our own. "Know ye not that ye are the temple of God, and that the Spirit of God dwelleth in you? . . . The temple of God is holy, which temple ye are."[19] Youth who fully understand that God's spirit resides within their bodies understand that they have a powerful and personal protector to help them resist the devil's deceptions.

Understanding the sacred purposes of the body as a temple for the spirit self can instill reverence for the body. We would never defile or misuse a house of the Lord, neither should we defile nor misuse our bodies for sexual pleasure outside of marriage.

There are many blessings the body provides us, such as providing a home and protection for our spirit. The body also provides the opportunity for husband and wife to express profound love for each other and to join with God in the sacred calling of creating children. God *blessed* husband and wife by creating sexual desire between them.[20] Focusing on the blessings of the body and its divine purposes in a spirit of honor and reverence can create a feeling of awe and respect for these God-given gifts.

Though some may believe the body and sex to be "carnal, sensual and devilish" due to Satan's deceptions, they are mistaken. Satan and his followers do not have bodies, so they deceive and attempt to get us to destroy ours. Because we chose God's plan in the premortal world, we were given the great gift of a physical body. Satan and his followers seek to destroy us by encouraging us to mistreat, misunderstand, and misuse our bodies. Though many in the world do not understand the blessings of the body and its divine nature, teach your children that because they know the truth, they have power to resist Satan's evil intentions.

Teach children to take special care to nourish and keep their body clean. Teach correct names for body parts and model their healthy acceptance. Teach children that *all* parts and *all* functions of the body are good and of God, and they will reverence and respect their body as a precious gift.

Children are not curious about things they already know about. Parents of young children must remember that exploration of the body is natural to a child. How parents respond to innocent exploration will affect a child's feelings about themselves, their bodies and their sexuality. Dr. Romel W. Mackelprang noted that some of the earliest negative conditioning about sex and the body (which contributes to the Good Girl Syndrome) comes from parents who react adversely, even punitively, to natural explorations of the body.[21] Keep emotions neutral as you instead distract and redirect their attentions. Teach acceptable behaviors rather than punish negative behaviors. This will satisfy your children's curiosity while eliminating the element of shame. Shame inflicted on children often continues as shame within the sexual relationship of marriage.

Though children under eight are incapable of sin, they still need direction to make good choices.[22] Teach children to respect and protect their bodies. Parents can do much to prevent self-stimulation and self-abuse by being actively attentive to the activities of their children. Keep bedroom doors open. Check on children frequently. Talk with them when you first notice behavior that concerns you and problems are small. Don't just tell them what not to do, but help them identify what they *can* do instead.

Teach children to respect others' bodies as well as their own. Teach them not to touch the sacred parts of their body carelessly nor to touch anyone else's. Help children avoid sexual abuse by teaching them that no one should touch the sacred parts of their body. We have been taught that "very young children should be given clear and simple information about the sacred nature of their bodies. This understanding helps them protect themselves from those who may try to take advantage of them."[23] Teach children to listen to their feelings if someone is making them uncomfortable. Teach them to say "NO!" and to get away quickly and immediately tell a parent or adult what has happened to make them uncomfortable. Do not dismiss a child's reports of inappropriate behavior.

The Essentials of Procreation

As suggested by Dr. Wayne Anderson, LDS psychologist, there are six general categories of information that need to be taught about procreation: (1) bodily organs and their functions; (2) physical differences between boys and girls; (3) the origin of babies; (4) intrauterine growth; (5) birth process and (6) the father's role.[24] Some good Christian books that may be particularly helpful in this area are:

- *The New Learning About Sex* Series by Concordia Publishers:
  Book 1—*Why Boys & Girls Are Different*—Ages 3-5, Carol Greene, 1998.
  Book 2—*Where Do Babies Come From?*—Ages 6-8, Ruth Hummel, 1998.
  Book 3—*How You Are Changing*—Ages 8-11, Jane Graver, 1998.
  Book 4—*Sex and the New You*—Ages 11-14, Richard Bimler, 1998.
  Book 5—*Love, Sex and God*—Ages 14 and up, Bill Ameiss, 1998.

- *Growing Up: Gospel Answers about Maturation and Sex* by Brad Wilcox, 2000, especially good for ages 10 -15.

- *How to Talk to Your Child about Sex: It's Best to Start Early, but It's Never Too Late: A Step-by-step Guide for Every Age* by Linda and Richard Eyre, 1998.

- *Living, Loving & Marrying: Thoughts for LDS Teens and Young Marrieds* by Lindsay R. Curtis, M.D. & Wayne J. Anderson, Ph.D., 1968.

- *Intended for Pleasure: Sex Technique and Sexual Fulfillment in Christian Marriage* by Ed Wheat, M.D. and Gaye Wheat, 1997.

- *The Act of Marriage: The Beauty of Sexual Love* by Tim & Beverly LaHaye, 1998.

Sex Can Be Controlled

Some youth, particularly young men, have come to believe that they simply cannot control themselves when it comes to indulging in sexual behavior. This is a lie. Sexual feelings and behavior *can* be controlled. Elder Holland stated:

> I have heard all my life that it is the young woman who has to assume the responsibility for controlling the limits of intimacy in courtship because a young man cannot. Seldom have I heard any point made about this subject that makes me want to throw up more than that. What kind of man is he, what priesthood or power or strength or self-control does this man have that lets him develop in society, grow to the age of mature accountability, perhaps even pursue a university education and prepare to affect the future of colleagues and kingdoms and the course of the world, but yet does not have the mental capacity or the moral will to say, "I will not do that thing"? No, this sorry drugstore psychology would have him say, "I just can't help myself. My glands have complete control over my life—my mind, my will, my entire future."[25]

The Lord has asked that we refrain from sexual relations outside of marriage. We know the Lord will ask nothing of us that we will not be able to do.[26] Youth must learn that they *can* control their appetites and passions. They need not be deceived. Dr. Terrance D. Olson, BYU professor, taught that "one of the false notions of our society is that we are victims of our appetites and passions. But the truth is that the body is controlled by the spirit which inhabits it."[27] As youth strengthen their spiritual will, they can learn to be master of their bodies.

. In *A Parent's Guide* we are taught, "From the time we are born, we each need to be physically and socially nurtured. The changes of puberty permit us to experience remarkably heightened pleasures of touch and arousal. But we have the agency to control the emotions and behaviors leading up to intentional sexual arousal. We can control when, where, how, and with whom we express our sexuality."[28]

A word of counsel to parents and youth leaders: if in our zeal to teach sexual abstinence we inadvertently extinguish or shut down righteous sexuality, youth may pay a price in unnecessary sexual inhibitions within marriage. Teach youth that we don't want them to extinguish these God-given desires and passions, but to harness them, like electricity that is channeled into an electrical outlet, providing a productive use of that power. There are blessings from bridling our passions. The scriptures teach, "bridle all your passions, that ye may be filled with love."[29]

The ability to bridle these powerful passions is an important skill not only to help them to be "filled with love" for a future spouse, but also to keep physical attraction from consuming the courtship. Physical attraction alone can deceive people into thinking they are a good match, when few or none of the other important areas are compatible at all. Dr. Brent Barlow stated that an overemphasis on sex distorts the relationship and keeps couples from exploring other, more enduring, dimensions of the relationship.[30] With physical intimacy in check, however, couples can focus on the personality, spirituality, and intelligence of a potential eternal partner, instead of being blinded by physical attraction alone.

Some fear that as the world grows more and more wicked and blatant with sin, they will not be able to resist the temptations that abound. This is untrue. Youth can be confident in their ability to overcome. They *can* control their sexuality. Their power to resist Satan's tactics is stronger than they may realize. The modern prophet Joseph Smith taught, "All beings who have bodies have power over those who have not. The devil has no power over us only as we permit him."[31] Teach youth that as they couple their strength with the Lord, they can overcome any temptation. Elder Henry B. Eyring quoted President George Albert Smith who offered this profound principle and promise:

> There is a division line well defined that separates the Lord's territory from Lucifer's. If we live on the Lord's side of the line, Lucifer cannot come there to influence us, but if we cross the line into his territory, we are in his power. By keeping the commandments of the Lord we are safe on His side of the line, but if we disobey His teachings we voluntarily cross into the zone of temptation and invite the destruction that is ever present there. Knowing this, how anxious we should always be to live on the Lord's side of the line.[32]

Teach youth to live on the Lord's side of the line. Teach them that they can avoid snares and traps by controlling their situations and circumstances. Teach them to avoid temptation by staying away from certain friends, TV, Internet sites, magazines, music, movies, and parties where temptations will be numerous.

All behavior begins as a thought. Mastery of our thoughts provides mastery of our feelings and behaviors. Help youth develop mental discipline to change thoughts when temptations creep in. Encourage them to fill their minds and their time with good things that strengthen and uplift. As they live on the Lord's side of the line, Satan cannot come there to tempt them. Teach them that prevention is better than repentance. Teach them to be wise. It is the wise and the strong who stay on the Lord's side of the line. President Hinckley has taught:

Mental control must be stronger than physical appetites or desires of the flesh. As thoughts are brought into complete harmony with revealed truth, actions will then become appropriate. The timeless proverb is as true now as when it was first spoken: "For as he thinketh in his heart, so is he" (Proverbs 23:7). Each of us, with discipline and effort, has the capacity to control his thoughts and his actions. This is part of the process of developing spiritual, physical, and emotional maturity.[33]

Self-control brings happiness. The ultimate goal is *internal* self-control, not just controlled behavior when a parent is around or a child fears getting caught. President David O. McKay stated, "The home is the best place in the world to teach the child his responsibilities, to give him *happiness in self-control*. . . . The home is the best place in which to develop obedience which [God,] nature and society will later demand."[34]

Today's youth have the strength to wait until marriage to express and receive sacred sexual expressions of love. Parents can fortify their children by meeting their emotional needs, as they teach with greater love and patience, thereby reducing vulnerability to temptation.

God's Standards

Like a road map through a dark and dangerous forest, God lovingly provides standards of moral behavior, which provide physical, emotional, and spiritual safety. Standards keep youth from falling prey to Satan's power. Moral standards keep youth from *physical* dangers, such as unwanted pregnancy, or sexually transmitted diseases; they provide *emotional* protection by maintaining self-respect, self-esteem, confidence, and peace of mind; and they provide *spiritual* safety by keeping youth from the heart-rending pain and sorrow necessary for true repentance from sexual sin.

The greatest reason for maintaining the Lord's standards is that that is how we show Him our love and our trust that He knows better than we do how to help us return home. Youth show their maturity by their ability to see the consequences of their decisions and to choose wisely. They show self-discipline by learning to control their thoughts and behavior.

Our youth are good and noble spirit children of our Heavenly Father. Teach them that their greatest tool in overcoming the wiles of the world and staying on the "strait and narrow path, which leads to eternal life,"[35] is the gift of the Holy Ghost. Teach our youth how to identify and heed the Spirit's promptings. Encourage them to develop a sweet and close relationship with their Heavenly Father whose Spirit can be with them at all times.

Precisely maintaining God's moral standards is not merely incidental or a sideline to the gospel of Jesus Christ. *It is the very key* to life and happiness. Elder Boyd K. Packer taught, "Protect and guard your gift [the sacred power of creation]. Your actual happiness is at stake. Eternal family life, now only in your anticipations and dreams, can be achieved because our Heavenly Father has bestowed this choicest gift of all upon you—this power of creation. It is *the very key* to happiness. Hold this gift as sacred and pure. Use it only as the Lord has directed."[36]

Parents and youth leaders should also stay close to their youth to encourage the development of maturity and guard them from situations that can easily get out of control. Help them to realize that there is so much good to learn and experience without sexuality enveloping every aspect of their lives.

Remember parents and leaders can and must intervene when needed. A great analogy comes from a little story of a young brother and sister who had each planted a garden. When the time came to harvest the vegetables, Cindy's were big and green and healthy. Randy was disheartened to see that his plants were small and stunted. He and his father went to check his garden plot to determine the problem. The story continues as Randy's dad pulls up a weed.

"'Here's your problem, Randy. Plants need plenty of food and sunshine to grow.'

"'But I gave them fertilizer, and I watered them every day,' Randy answered.

"'Yes, you fed them, but you didn't keep the weeds out. They stole water, nutrients, and sunshine from your plants. They stunted your radishes' growth just as breaking God's commandments would stunt your spiritual growth.'"[37]

Parents have the responsibility to keep the weeds out. Youth may not initially be appreciative of their parents' efforts, but as parents are guided by the Spirit and are tireless in lovingly giving their time and attention to the well-being of their children, their youth will ultimately come to see the great gift of love they have been given. They will also learn to trust their parents to guide them away from temptations and to equip them with the armor of God.

Elder M. Russell Ballard encouraged parents to be actively involved in helping their children make good choices, intervening when necessary:

> It is the parents' duty to intervene when they see wrong choices being made. That doesn't mean parents take from children the precious gift of agency. . . . But as parents we need to make sure they understand appropriate behavior and the conse-

quences to them if they pursue their wrongful course. Remember, there is no such thing as unlawful censorship in the home. Movies, magazines, television, videos, the Internet, and other media are there as guests and should only be welcomed when they are appropriate for family enjoyment. . . .

The same principle applies to you bishops, teachers, and other leaders in the Church as you work to assist families. You don't have to stand idly by as those over whom you have stewardship make poor moral choices. When one of our youth stands at a moral crossroad in life, almost always there is someone—a parent, a leader, a teacher—who could make a difference by intervening with love and kindness.[38]

Parents, leaders, and youth can form partnerships to restrict Satan's access to their hearts and minds. Help youth feel that you are on the same team. Teach youth to develop their talents and skills, such as being a good friend and a good conversationalist.

Our Heavenly Father knows reserving sexual relations for marriage brings the greatest happiness. This is His standard. Just as baptism is reserved until the age of eight and serving a mission is reserved until age nineteen for men and twenty-one for women, so, too, must they wait until they are legally and lawfully wedded before God authorizes engagement in sexual relations. The Lord's standards are summed up in the following statement by President Hinckley, "The way of safety and the road to happiness lie in abstinence before marriage and fidelity following marriage."[39] Elder Richard G. Scott provided a more specific standard when he said:

> Strongly tied to the sacred, private parts of the body are powerful emotions intended to be used within the covenant of marriage between a man and woman in ways that are appropriate and acceptable to them both. . . . These emotions are not to be stimulated or used for personal gratification outside of the covenant of marriage. Do not touch the private, sacred parts of another person's body to stimulate those emotions. Do not allow anyone to do that with you, with or without clothing. Do not arouse those emotions in your own body. These things are wrong. Do not do them.[40]

Sexuality is good when used within the bounds the Lord has set. Sexual passions are driving emotions given us by God, but we also have the responsibility to reverence and respect them as a sacred part of the sacrament of marriage. Sexual expression is a serious sin when it violates God's commands. Teach youth "good girls (and guys) do" . . . they just wait until marriage. Teach youth to study and follow the *For the Strength of Youth: Fulfilling Our Duty to God* booklet to stay on the Lord's side of the line. Moral standards are not to limit freedom, but to protect from sorrowful consequences.

It is critical that our youth not only understand God's standards, but also the good news of the gospel that we can repent when we make mistakes. We can be forgiven and cleansed of our sins until we remember them (with anguish) no more.

When our thoughts and actions lead us beyond the boundaries the Lord has set, one of Satan's greatest destroyers is despair. He attempts to deceive us into believing all is lost. The emotional suffering in sin can lead one to think, "Why try anymore?" Satan would love youth to believe there is no hope. But there is hope through faith and repentance. The Savior has felt each person's pains and sufferings. He knows our sorrows and how to relieve our burdens that we may be healed and made whole.[41] He loves us. "For God sent not his Son into the world to condemn the world; but that the world through him might be saved."[42]

Using an oft-used analogy, the power of the Atonement not only removes the nail from the piece of wood, nor does it simply fill the hole with wood putty, but it can restore the wood, so the hole is gone.

Using an oft-used analogy, the power of the Atonement not only removes the nail from the piece of wood, nor does it simply fill the hole with wood putty, but it can restore the wood, so the hole is gone. "Though your sins be as scarlet, they shall be as white as snow."[43] The Lord may not take away the *consequences*, but through repentance He can wash away our sins with his atoning blood. Parents and bishops can testify of hope to their youth. They can help youth open the door to the power of the Atonement to purify and cleanse their souls.

The Atonement not only cleanses us from sin, but it also has the power to heal us from sins committed upon us by others. Many carry wounds of sexual abuse, often as secret scars of shame. Our youth must understand that the scars and the wounds of sexual abuse can be washed away through the infinite power of the Atonement. The path will not be easy. Professional help is often needed. God can transform our wounds into purification of our hearts and prepare us to live again with Him, as we are purged of the painful effects of other's behaviors. It is with our Savior's wounds, bruises, and stripes that we are healed.[44] The Savior was sent by our loving Father "to heal the brokenhearted" and "to set at liberty them that are bruised."[45] "If thou believest in the redemption of Christ, thou canst be healed."[46]

Modesty. Keeping God's standards of modest dress and appearance is an important way to show our respect and appreciation for our bodies as sacred gifts from God. Appearance or dress that draws the eye away from the face to certain parts of the body is immodest. The *For the Strength of Youth* booklet gives excellent information on standards for dress and appearance. Encourage youth to wear clothing now that would also be appropriate after they have received their temple endowments. This can eliminate the need for a change of wardrobe (or attitude) after endowments are received or when attending a church-sponsored university.

Modesty is important to teach to *both* young women and young men. Be careful not to imply that *young women* must be modest, so that *young men* can control themselves. This is a dangerous message for both sexes! It incorrectly teaches young women that they are ultimately responsible for another's sexual behavior. This also incorrectly teaches young men that they are helpless to control themselves when someone *else* dresses immodestly. While modesty can help each gender avoid inappropriate arousal, it should be something they do for themselves and for God. Young men *and* young women have the ability and the responsibility to remove themselves from sexual stimuli.

Fatherly nurturing is particularly important to young women during the awkward years of sexual maturation. Some fathers, uncomfortable with their own or their daughter's developing sexuality, may avoid contact with their daughters during this delicate time. When emotional needs for love and attention are not sufficiently met in the home, young women may be tempted to dress immodestly, even provocatively, because of the male attention and approval it generates.

A negative or over-zealous approach to teaching modesty often carries over into the marital bedroom. Many women are unable to comfortably share their bodies with their husbands during lovemaking in marriage. Parents and leaders must be careful to balance their messages of modesty to avoid unnecessary marital inhibitions. This is no easy task. The objective of encouraging modest appearance and behavior during youth seems to contradict the message of being "naked and not ashamed" after marriage.[47]

One parent provided a good example of balancing the modesty message, keeping in mind that his son would one day be married. When commenting about a TV personality who was immodestly dressed, he said to his son:

> You know, son, that girl isn't very modest, is she? I don't want you to get the idea that it's okay for girls to dress that way, and I want you to set a high standard in what you encourage the girls you interact with to wear. But, you know, there is a time and a place when you're permitted to share your body and to be sexu-

ally intimate with someone. That is with your spouse after you get married. That kind of physical expression is meant to be a wonderful gift when you're married. Within the privacy of the husband and wife relationship, it's like your own little Garden of Eden where the scriptures tell us that Adam and Eve were naked and not ashamed.[48]

Dating. God has counseled youth to wait until age sixteen or later before they begin dating.[49] This allows youth to develop maturity, which is demonstrated by regularly making good choices. Many young men wisely choose to wait until after serving missions before forming serious relationships. Youth are counseled to date in groups and to avoid frequent dates with the same person.[50] Spending too much time alone with a favorite member of the opposite sex, even though intentions were innocent, has lead many good youth to the slippery slope where inappropriate intimacies are shared. This is where parents can help youth "keep the weeds out" by monitoring how much time is spent together and how much familiarity is developing.

In marriage, spending lots of time together builds emotional intimacy and closeness, which are wonderful precursors to physical intimacy. But those same precursors to physical intimacy can be dangerous outside of marriage to those unprepared for the powerful feelings of physical attraction. The best way to control appetites and passions is to avoid circumstances where youth will be tempted. Loving parents can help youth understand the purposes of emotional intimacy in marriage, which can cultivate cooperation from youth as parents help them limit their time together.

Sexual Fulfillment Takes Time and Effort after Marriage

Parents and leaders must teach beyond being chaste and marrying in the temple—beyond "happily ever after." Chastity before marriage does not ensure sexual fulfillment in marriage. Knowing what to expect of the sexual relationship is an important part of a successful transition from premarital prohibitions to mutual sexual fulfillment after marriage. Parents must instill the expectation that time, effort, study, and intimate educating between husband and wife will be needed after marriage to fine tune the symphony of sexual relations. Married couples must be willing and able to talk openly and honestly about their sexual needs and desires.

Newlywed couples who accept their sexual inexperience as a positive and healthy adventure will be better able to relax and learn without psychological pressure or feelings of failure for this greatly anticipated experience. Learning together can be one of the divinely designed ties that bind as husband and wife come to intimately "know" each other.[51]

Long ago Satan launched his campaign that "sex in any season brings
pleasure." Others have countered with the strategy "sin brings pain."
It may be time for a new, more effective and proactive campaign
with the inspiring message "righteousness brings peace."

Blessings of Righteousness

Long ago Satan launched his campaign that "sex in any season brings pleasure." Others have countered with the strategy "sin brings pain." It may be time for a new, more effective and proactive campaign with the inspiring message "righteousness brings peace." Sex education and moral training have often centered on the consequences of immorality and disobedience to God's commandments. Fear, warnings, negative consequences, and dire statistics are not the greatest motivators of righteousness. No matter how high or alarming the statistics get, teens have the attitude that says, "It won't happen to me."

Light and truth have the power to "forsake that evil one."[52] Below are ten blessings of obedience to God's commandments of moral restraint and of personal righteousness. Teach youth to understand and develop their own testimonies of the blessings of righteousness. As prompted, bear your testimony of the blessings of righteousness when discussing these blessings.

1. Companionship of the Holy Ghost. President Ezra Taft Benson counseled, "A reason for virtue—which includes personal chastity, clean thoughts and practices, and integrity—is that *we must have the Spirit and the power of God in our lives to do God's work.*"[53] Each of us has a special role to play in building God's kingdom. We need the power of the Spirit of God to fulfill our earthly missions. When we follow the Lord's standards and strive for personal righteousness, we are promised that the Holy Ghost will be our constant companion.[54] Imagine being privileged to have the power, guidance, and protection of a loving Father whose spirit can be with you constantly!

The blessings of having the Lord's spirit are many. The Spirit warns us of danger and evil, helps us know right from wrong, and helps us choose the right as we make correct decisions. The Spirit illuminates our minds so that we can understand and remember more easily. The Holy Ghost guides, teaches, inspires, and comforts.[55] There is such a serene and sweet feeling that comes from living close to the Lord. No moment of pleasure is worth losing the companionship of the Comforter. No fleeting fantasy is worth the darkness and the emptiness that result from a loss of the Spirit.

2. Peace and a Clear Conscience. The Spirit of Christ invites all to know right from wrong.[56] When the Spirit of Christ is heeded to avoid sin, or when repentance takes place after sin, peace of mind and a clear conscience are the rich rewards. Sin is a heavy burden, whereas repentance and righteousness lift the burden and bring peace. Those who are not "past feeling" will feel pricked in their heart when they are doing something wrong. Choosing righteousness protects the heart from the painful pricks of guilt, shame, and sorrow for sins committed, allowing the spirit of peace to permeate their lives. Though challenges continue and faith is tried, peace can be a constant companion amidst turmoil.

3. Happiness. Everyone wants to be happy. Happiness comes from righteousness. Satan seeks to deceive some into believing sin is more fun, but wickedness never brings long-term happiness.[57] Though sin may bring temporary pleasure, it also brings much sorrow and heartache. God created us that we might have joy.[58] Those who keep God's commandments abide in a blessed and happy state and are blessed in all things.[59]

4. Confidence in Self and in God. Righteousness creates an engaging countenance of confidence in self and in God. Confidence comes by keeping the commandments. What is there to fear when you know you are doing what pleases God? The scriptures teach that as we let virtue fill our heart and mind, then shall confidence wax strong.[60] Virtue is goodness, morality, and righteousness, which result in confidence. Confidence commands respect, and even provides an opportunity to set an example for others to follow. Sometimes all it takes is one person to stand for righteousness for others to follow. President Hinckley challenged the youth, "Prove your strength, show your independence, by saying no when enticement from peers comes your way. Your own strength will add strength to those who are weak. Your own example will give determination to others."[61]

5. Faith. Obedience to God's commandments is rewarded with faith. Faith is a sure knowledge that a loving God is in charge. Faith provides assurance and anchors the soul.[62] The shield of faith quenches the adversary's fiery darts, providing power to resist temptation.[63] According to one's faith, the Spirit guides our lives, giving knowledge and power.[64] With every act of obedience—every time unclean thoughts are expelled from the mind, every time temptations are resisted—faith increases. Increased faith makes it easier to be obedient the next time. Faith and obedience create a cycle of spiritual strength, for as we obey or *do* God's will, we come to *know* and have a testimony of God's truth.[65]

6. Self-discipline. As youth choose to keep the commandments they develop self-discipline. Choosing moral behavior keeps sexual desire in check, restraining it from accelerating out of control, which leads to bad habits, even addictions. With self-discipline, temptations can be resisted. Appetites and passions can be bridled. Self-control gives the ability to create life's circumstances, rather than being acted upon. Using agency wisely and making correct choices allow greater freedom. One who resists the temptations of premarital sexual activity is *free* from unwanted pregnancy, *free* from sexually transmitted diseases, and *free* from the attending emotional pain of sin.

7. Proper Focus in Life. Moral integrity blesses lives by building character and discipline. The development of self-discipline builds the foundations of a successful future. A proper focus keeps priorities in place, putting first things first. The fleeting nature of getting caught up in boyfriends / girlfriends, parties, movies, media, Internet attractions, and the latest fashions, cannot exceed the enduring focus of educating minds, developing talents and skills, and building spiritual strength.

8. Self-respect. To respect oneself means to appreciate, to approve, to esteem highly, to honor, admire and love. As we face the challenges of life with resolute determination to choose righteousness, we develop greater respect for ourselves. We also learn greater respect for God as we experience firsthand the blessings of obedience. When youth love and respect themselves, they can more easily love and respect others. Self-respect builds strength of character and spiritual fortitude.

9. Trust. To be trusted is an honor. Parents and others bestow trust when they see correct choices being made over a period of time. Instill a desire in youth to be trusted not only to resist temptations that may face them, but to also be trusted to stay away from *potential* temptations. Teach youth that even though they may be trustworthy, parents and leaders have greater wisdom and experience and recognize the importance of keeping youth from unnecessary temptations.

 Trust that is developed in youth carries over into marriage. Having made good choices morally in the past is a strong indicator of future marital fidelity. Fidelity brings peace and confidence to a marriage. President Kimball taught, "Abstinence before marriage and full fidelity afterward . . . is the cornerstone of trust so necessary to the precious happiness of the marriage relationship and family solidarity."[66]

10. Firm Foundation for a Strong Marriage and Family. The blessings of righteousness outlined here lay a firm foundation upon which a strong and secure marriage and family can be built. Youth can be taught to understand the connection between their choices now and their future happiness in marriage and family. Youth are counseled in the *For the Strength of Youth* booklet, "When you obey God's commandment to be sexually pure, you prepare yourself to make and keep sacred covenants in the temple. You prepare yourself to build a strong marriage and to bring children into the world as part of a loving family. You protect yourself from the emotional damage that always comes from sharing physical intimacies with someone outside of marriage."[67]

Righteousness brings many blessings; nevertheless, we must also "beware of pride," warned President Benson, for "pride is the great stumbling block."[68] If we are not careful, pride can cause *righteousness* to become *self-righteousness,* allowing Satan's influence into our hearts.

Righteousness blesses lives with the companionship of the Holy Ghost, peace, a clear conscience, happiness, confidence in self and in God, faith, self-discipline, a proper focus in life, self-respect, trust, and a firm foundation upon which to build a strong marriage and family. The First Presidency of The Church of Jesus Christ of Latter-day Saints declared, "How glorious and near to the angels is youth that is clean; this youth has a joy unspeakable here and eternal happiness hereafter. Sexual purity is youth's most precious possession; it is the foundation of all righteousness."[69]

Chapter 15—"Home" Work

- Study this chapter and the suggested resources. With this information as a guide of "what to teach," create questions and an age- and gender-appropriate outline of what you want to teach your children.

NOTES

Chapter 15 — Preparing Future Generations for
Sexual Fulfillment in Marriage: What to Teach

[1] Doctrine & Covenants 111:11.
[2] Doctrine & Covenants 10:58.
[3] John 14:6.
[4] Doctrine & Covenants 10:5.
[5] *See* Holland, "Teacher Come From God," *Ensign*, May 1998, 27.
[6] Hinckley, *Teachings of Gordon B. Hinckley*, 48.
[7] Beam, *Becoming One*, 134.
[8] Beam, *Becoming One*, 134.
[9] Holland, "Of Souls, Symbols, and Sacraments," 12.
[10] Holland, "Of Souls, Symbols, and Sacraments," 12.
[11] Holland, "Of Souls, Symbols, and Sacraments," 13. *See also* 1 Corinthians 6:16–17.
[12] Farnworth, "What's Wrong with It?" [online article].
[13] Smith, "Thoughts on Marriage Compatibility," *Ensign*, Sept. 1981, 45.
[14] "The Family: A Proclamation to the World," *Ensign*, Nov. 1995, 102.
[15] *Parent's Guide*, 20.
[16] *See* Moses 6:9; Genesis 9:6; Ether 3:16.
[17] Holland, "Of Souls, Symbols, and Sacraments," 6.
[18] Kimball, "Guidelines to Carry Forth the Work of God in Cleanliness," *Ensign*, May 1974, 7.
[19] 1 Corinthians 3:16–17.
[20] *See* Abraham 4:28.
[21] *See* Mackelprang, *Multiply and Replenish*, 49.
[22] *See* Doctrine & Covenants 29:46–47; Moroni 8:10–22.
[23] *Marriage and Family Relations Instructor's Manual*, 71.
[24] *See* Curtis and Anderson, *Living, Loving & Marrying*, 208–16.
[25] Holland, "Of Souls, Symbols, and Sacraments," 10–11.
[26] *See* 1 Nephi 3:7.
[27] Olson, "Teaching Morality to Your Children," *Ensign*, Mar. 1981, 14.
[28] *Parent's Guide*, 36.
[29] Alma 38:12.
[30] *See* Barlow, *Just for Newlyweds*, 54.
[31] Faust, "Serving the Lord and Resisting the Devil," *Ensign*, Sept. 1995, 2.
[32] Eyring, "Come Unto Christ," 42–43. *See also* George Albert Smith, *Improvement Era*, May 1935, 278.
[33] Hinckley, "Reverence and Morality," *Ensign*, May 1987, 47.
[34] McKay, *Church News*, 2003 (emphasis added).
[35] 2 Nephi 31:18.
[36] Packer, "Why Stay Morally Clean?" *Ensign*, July 1972, 113 (emphasis added).
[37] Chiles, "Garden Plots," *Friend*, May 1998, 17.
[38] Ballard, "Like a Flame Unquenchable," *Ensign*, May 1999, 87.
[39] Hinckley, "Reverence and Morality," *Ensign*, May 1987, 47.
[40] Scott, "Power of Righteousness," *Ensign*, Nov. 1998, 69.
[41] *See* Bateman, "Power to Heal from Within," *Ensign*, May 1995, 13.
[42] John 3:17.
[43] Isaiah 1:18.

[44] *See* Isaiah 53:5; Mosiah 14:3.

[45] Luke 4:18.

[46] Alma 15:8.

[47] *See* Genesis 2:25; Moses 3:25; Abraham 5:19.

[48] *See* Genesis 2:25.

[49] *For the Strength of Youth,* 24.

[50] *For the Strength of Youth,* 25.

[51] *See* Genesis 4:1; Moses 5:2.

[52] Doctrine & Covenants 93:37.

[53] Benson, *Teachings of Ezra Taft Benson,* 278 (emphasis added).

[54] *See* Doctrine & Covenants 121:45–46.

[55] *See Family Home Evening Resource Book,* 65.

[56] *See* Moroni 7:16.

[57] *See* Alma 41:10.

[58] *See* 2 Nephi 2:25.

[59] *See* Mosiah 2:41.

[60] *See* Doctrine & Covenants 121:45.

[61] Hinckley, "Reverence and Morality," *Ensign,* May 1987, 48.

[62] *See* Ether 12:4.

[63] *See* Doctrine & Covenants 27:17.

[64] *See* Alma 18:35.

[65] *See* John 7:17.

[66] Kimball, "Privileges and Responsibilities of Sisters," *Ensign,* Nov. 1978, 105.

[67] *For the Strength of Youth,* 26.

[68] Benson, "Beware of Pride," *Ensign,* May 1989, 7.

[69] *Family Home Evening Resource Book,* 260.

CHAPTER VIEW

When to Teach

1. *Before Accountability*
2. *Before Puberty*
3. *Before Dating*
4. *Before Marriage*

How to Teach

- *Fill Love Bucket First*
- *Provide Ongoing Discussions and Teaching Opportunities*
- *Prepare a Discussion Outline*
- *Make it a Special Occasion*
- *Schedule One-on-one*
- *Begin with Prayer*
- *Dialogue, Don't Lecture*
- *Teach the Correct Behavior*
- *Focus on the Blessings*
- *Teach by Example*

Our Experience

Sample Script / Dialogue for a First Sex Discussion

Chapter 16—"Home" Work

Chapter 16

PREPARING FUTURE GENERATIONS FOR SEXUAL FULFILLMENT IN MARRIAGE— WHEN AND HOW TO TEACH

When to Teach

When children are young, they are more teachable and willing to listen. The prophet Alma taught, "Learn wisdom in thy youth; yea, learn in thy youth to keep the commandments of God."[1] Teaching the topic of sexuality is no exception to the counsel to "learn in thy youth." Correct and positive teaching can provide a secure foundation upon which healthy sexuality can develop. President Hinckley shared a story illustrating why it is best to teach and train children when they are young:

> Not long after we were married, we built our first home. We had very little money. I did much of the work myself. . . . The landscaping was entirely my responsibility. The first of many trees that I planted was a thornless honey locust. . . . It was only

a wisp of a tree, perhaps three-quarters of an inch in diameter. It was so supple that I could bend it with ease in any direction. I paid little attention to it as the years passed.

Then one winter day, when the tree was barren of leaves, I chanced to look out the window at it. I noticed that it was leaning to the west, misshapen and out of balance. I could scarcely believe it. I went out and braced myself against it as if to push it upright. But the trunk was now nearly a foot in diameter. My strength was as nothing against it. . . .

When it was first planted, a piece of string would have held it in place against the forces of the wind. I could have and should have supplied that string with ever so little effort. But I did not, and it bent to the forces that came against it.

I have seen a similar thing, many times, in children whose lives I have observed. The parents who brought them into the world seem almost to have abdicated their responsibility. The results have been tragic. A few simple anchors would have given them the strength to withstand the forces that have shaped their lives.[2]

The earlier you hold age-appropriate discussions about sexuality and the body in a respectful and confident manner, the less likely children are to feel uncomfortable with such discussions. Children only learn to feel discomfort and embarrassment from those around them. To young children a discussion about sacred parts of the body is no different than a discussion about keeping their room neat and tidy.

Some parents think sexuality doesn't need to be addressed until the teen years or until an engagement. *A Parent's Guide* states, "Ideally, you should use the first eight to twelve years of a child's life to prepare him for his teenage years. If you wait until adolescence to teach your children about the changes of puberty and about intimate relationships, you may not be able to influence them as easily."[3]

Certainly preemptive teaching is best, but it's never too late. Even if your child is about to turn sixteen, or is engaged to be married, what is suggested here can still be taught and done effectively, especially with the help of the Lord. The four most critical times that teaching is needed are: (1) before the age of accountability; (2) before puberty; (3) before dating; and (4) before marriage. Each of these occasions could invite a special date between parent and child to discuss the upcoming passage of life.

Before Accountability. Before the age of accountability, children cannot sin because Satan has no power to tempt them.[4] Age eight, when a child can be baptized, is understood to be the age of accountability.[5] After age eight, your child becomes exposed to Satan's temptations. Do everything you can early on to instill the power of light and truth to fortify them against the cunning of Satan.

If children are taught at a young age about appropriate and inappropriate touch, potential abuse may be avoided. With the frequency of sexual abuse occurring to ever-younger children, they must be taught when touch is inappropriate and what to do about it. If they haven't been taught they won't know how to protect themselves.

In addition to providing protection, an appropriate attitude, and some sexual understanding *prior* to the age of accountability prepare your child to counter the world's distorted perspectives. Why allow Satan first access to the heart and mind of your child? Just as you wouldn't send your children out into the cold without coats, neither should you wait until Satan embeds his teachings to dress your children in the truth and armor of God.

It is your responsibility to determine a child's readiness for any particular sexual topic and the depth of details. Do not excuse yourself by saying your child is too young for such teachings. Be careful to distinguish a "lack of readiness" from your own inhibitions and reluctance. Do not miss out on the opportunity to be the first to build a healthy sexual foundation for your child. Otherwise you may be playing "catch up" for some time, as you strive to undo the damage done by those who distort God's plan and holy purposes for sexual relations in marriage.

Before Puberty. While "physical puberty" may begin around the age of eleven, "social puberty" often begins when a child enters school (around age 6). Before puberty children need to understand what will be happening to their bodies and know that it is a natural and wonderful part of God's plan. Proactively teaching a positive sexual attitude and approach prevents the negative, distorted, and corrupted worldly philosophies from taking hold.

During preadolescence and puberty, provide special time and attention as your children begin to experience the changes of maturation. Be there to prepare, reassure, and teach them about what they are experiencing; to calm their fears and to answer their questions. The same gender parent is best suited to explain the physiological, social, emotional, and psychological changes a child is experiencing. If the parent / child relationship is good, this open discussion will calm their fears and prevent emotional disturbances.

Mothers can provide daughters advance understanding of menstruation. They can teach that it is a normal and natural step in a young woman's life, as her body prepares for motherhood. Teach menstruation as a divine gift associated with the privilege of parenthood. Having advance understanding and a positive perspective about menstruation can make "having a period" a special part of sexual maturation instead of a frightening or traumatic experience.

Menstruation provides an excellent opportunity for mother and daughter to celebrate womanhood and discuss these new occurrences as a special occasion over a nice dinner at a restaurant or over a delicious ice cream treat. Menstruation can be celebrated as a special occasion or rite of passage for the daughter, rather than a secret shame, embarrassment, or dread.

Boys, too, need reassurance and understanding from their fathers about the normal and natural changes that will occur to their body and mind. Explaining these changes and addressing how to handle them before they occur can settle unnecessary concerns. Fathers can prepare their sons by discussing the sudden growth and possible coordination problems, frequent erections, wet dreams, voice changes, and facial and body hair.

The age of twelve might be a time of special celebration between father and son as the priesthood is received and puberty is discussed and prepared for. Both the priesthood and puberty are special and sacred milestones as a young man prepares to someday become the greatest of all things he will ever be—a father.

Before Dating. Before dating begins, parent(s) and child can welcome the upcoming birthday with a special date to practice and prepare for dating, where counsel is given and previous discussions are reviewed. Dating standards and suggestions can be shared in an air of anticipation and excitement for the approaching rite of passage. Making father / daughter and mother / son dates regular occasions ensures ongoing opportunities for parent / child bonding and heart-to-heart discussions.

Before Marriage. If parents have done their best to maintain an open relationship, and have sufficiently met emotional needs along the way, as a child prepares to marry and leave for the honeymoon parents can provide more specific lovemaking information and techniques. Where else might a daughter appropriately learn what it might mean to be "sexy"? The "good girl" who has carefully remained chaste will benefit from some very specific intimate information—if the parent / child relationship allows.

How to Teach

The following are some suggestions for how to effectively provide sex-related teachings:

Fill Love Bucket First. Investing time and effort to give extra attention and love prior to the special parent / child date can pay rich dividends. Sex discussions can be more effective if both parent and child feel love and warmth toward each other. The best way for teaching to be received and internalized by our children is to see that we are first meeting their emotional needs by creating a loving and trusting relationship. Children have basic needs to feel loved, secure, and important. Providing for your children's emotional needs prepares their heart and mind to be more receptive to your teachings and to the Spirit.

Ongoing Discussions and Teaching Opportunities. The quantity of important information alone requires that sex education be more than a one-time deal. Especially as children are young, their interest and attention span must be considered. Gone are the days of having one "big talk" about the "birds and the bees." Ongoing opportunities are needed, and parents must generally create them. Parents may think they can sit back and wait for their children to come to them with their sexual questions, but parents need to be proactive. Start planning for regular discussion opportunities before the age of accountability. After the first discussion with the same-gender parent, you can then alternate for each following discussion.

To provide sufficient ongoing opportunities to address questions and concerns that arise, a yearly discussion might even be warranted. Every other year may also be sufficient, but be sure you catch the four most important "whens"—before the age of eight, before puberty, before dating, and before marriage. Scheduling only one occasion for sex education does not provide regular opportunities for additional discussions as the child matures, or for addressing incorrect teachings that have accumulated.

If you maintain an attitude of having an ongoing discussion about sex, additional teaching opportunities may present themselves. Questions may arise from things your children hear at school, or inappropriate behavior may surface. Having regular Personal Parent Interviews or other one-on-one outings provides opportunities to address interim questions and concerns.

If worrisome behavior is noted, try to find reasons for the behavior. Talk to the child. Remain calm and resist being reactionary or judgmental. Punishment and threats will be of little long-term value. Ask them how they are doing in school. Ask about their friends and classmates. Ask if anything is bothering them. These discussions will go more smoothly if they are already a regular part of your interaction.

Prepare a Discussion Outline. You may need to do some homework to prepare yourself to teach and answer questions that may arise. Having a discussion outline allows you to think through what you want to teach and personally tailor the discussion to the age, gender, and maturity level of each child. By preparing your own discussion outline, you can re-teach yourself and you may be motivated to overcome your own negative beliefs and inhibitions.

Be truthful in your discussions and use correct terms for parts of the body to show respect for God's creations. Information and resources are provided throughout this book to help you prepare for these discussions.

Make It a Special Occasion. Sex education can become a special family tradition. If you make this an enjoyable and special tradition—perhaps at a restaurant or ice cream parlor—children will begin to eagerly anticipate their annual tradition of a special date and discussion with Mom or Dad to receive the "next installment" of their sex education. Include dinner at their favorite restaurant or an ice cream cone to make the atmosphere one of relaxed enjoyment of each other's company. If desired, the conversation can occur there in the restaurant or ice cream shop, or you may prefer to find a place with fewer distractions.

Do what works best for you and your child. Since young children have not yet learned to have anxieties about "sex talk," if you treat the experience as an enjoyable, special occasion, the child will, too—especially if you begin when they are young.

Children will begin to eagerly anticipate their annual
tradition of a special date and discussion with Mom or Dad to
receive the "next installment" of their sex education.

Schedule One-on-one. One-on-one discussions make it easier to assure the sacredness, specialness, and reverence of the occasion. A successful interaction is more likely when one parent and one child can discuss and address personal issues and questions in a casual atmosphere without the child feeling "ganged up on." This format allows questions and answers to be more freely exchanged. It also allows adjustments to be made to match the interest and maturity level of that child, including the appropriate quantity and depth of information to be provided.

Begin with Prayer. There may be no other occasion that requires more divine guidance and inspiration than that of sex-related teachings. Begin each parent / child discussion with a prayer. Before my son and I headed off to Pizza Hut for his second parent / child discussion, I asked if we could pray there in the car before we got to the restaurant. Already in the habit of praying together at the beginning of our monthly Personal Parent Interviews, he understood that we wanted to have the Spirit with us for our special discussions.

Dialogue, Don't Lecture. No one likes to sit through a lecture. Using questions and encouraging discussion can make the learning more meaningful. At times it may be better to initially answer questions with a question so that you can better understand what your child really wants and needs to know. If a child is only ready for a cupful of information, don't pour a bucketful over them. With older children, if emotions flare or disagreements arise due to expectations about dating and responsibilities, it may be useful to use the Intentional Dialogue communication tool taught in Chapter 10. The three steps of mirroring, validating, and empathizing allow both parent and child to feel heard and respected, to have their own thoughts and feelings understood. This is an extremely valuable tool for effective communication. Teach it to your children (especially teenagers) and use it regularly during one-on-one time and during parent / child dates.

Teach the Correct Behavior. Teaching is more effective when you teach what *to do* instead of what *not to do*. In my children's elementary school newsletter, the school counselor gave insightful instruction to parents and coaches on teaching the positive instead of the negative. He taught that as coaches or parents give tips, they should suggest the desired behavior rather than condemn the negative behavior. If you tell kids what they are doing wrong, they visualize themselves doing it wrong. Instead of saying "Don't pull your head away from the ball when you swing" (which is what they immediately see themselves doing) say, "Keep your eye on the ball."[6]

This counsel applies to teaching sexual purity as well. If we tell our children "don't do this," and "don't do that," they will immediately create a picture in their mind of engaging in the behavior you've just told them not to. If we instead tell them to "save sexual expression for its rightful time and place within marriage," they create a positive picture of exactly what God wants them to do. This reinforces the positive behavior instead of rehearsing the negative.

Focus on the Blessings. As you develop your own conviction of the sanctity of sexual relations, you will have more power to teach the positives and blessings of sexuality. Sprinkle awe and wonder throughout your teachings with statements such as, "Isn't your body amazing!" or, "Aren't you glad God made you this way?" or, "Isn't that a wonderful way for mommies and daddies to show their love for each other!" Likewise, in response to a daughter's question about what mommy's breasts are for, a mother can teach about breastfeeding as a special way God provided for mommies to feed their babies. The mother can emphasize what a special bonding experience it is to breastfeed her baby and how important it is to the baby's health and well-being.

Teach by Example. President Howard W. Hunter taught that the greatest thing parents can do for their children is to love their spouse.[7] In the *Marriage and Family Relations* manual published by the LDS Church, we read, "Children . . . learn true principles of moral purity by the way their parents treat each other, by the types of literature and other media that their parents allow in the home, and by the way their parents speak about the sacred power of procreation."[8] Children learn more from the *example* of their parents than from their *words*. If a child is taught "sex is sacred," but sees his mother rebuff the father's kisses, that can create confusion for the child. If parents can model a healthy acceptance and respect for their own sexuality, their children will be more likely to develop a healthy acceptance and respect for theirs.

Children need to see healthy, appropriate displays of love and affection. Let them see you model a marital relationship of kindness, love, affection, consideration, tolerance, forgiveness, and loyalty. Let them see you functioning as a team, helping and supporting each other in all things. The time and effort you put into making your marital relationship strong and secure is the greatest investment you can make for your children.

Our Experience

Personally motivated by the Sunday School Marriage and Family Relations Course we were teaching, my husband and I felt prompted to begin building a healthy sexual foundation in our oldest son. We began to pray about it and prepare for it, wanting to forestall the negative information he was already beginning to receive at school.

We determined it would be best for my husband to begin this sexual teaching with a special father and son date and I assisted by studying and preparing an outline for my husband to use. The outline / script reduced the fear of not knowing what to say and made the discussion flow more smoothly. It also gave us the opportunity to determine what specifically we wanted to cover for our son at his particular age.

After my son attended a Saturday morning basketball clinic, my husband and our son went out for lunch at McDonald's then went to a church parking lot for the discussion. We had been telling our son about this special event he would be having just with Daddy, so he was excited for it and felt honored that he was so privileged. This first talk occurred when our son was about seven and one-half years old.

About a year and a half later, when he was almost nine, it was Mommy's turn for a mother / son discussion. We decided to go to Pizza Hut for lunch one Saturday. We had the actual discussion right there in the restaurant sitting side by side in a booth. The distractions of lunch provided good little intermissions for our interaction.

My husband and I essentially used the same outline, though I may have gone into a little more depth to account for our son's increased understanding and experience. We share our script below as one example of how parents might take the information that has been given and condense it into a first sex discussion for a boy aged 7 to 10. Parents can add or remove either quantity or depth of information depending on their child's readiness.

Sample Script / Dialogue for a First Sex Discussion (7–10 Year-old Boy)

1. Introduction. Share how lucky he is to be receiving this information from his parents since many children don't. Share how we wanted to be the first ones to teach him about something very special.

2. Families.

    a. *ASK:* Why do we have families on earth? (Earthly families prepare us to be families in heaven. The most important thing you will be is a father. Being a father on earth prepares us for being a father when we get to heaven—like our Heavenly Father is.)

    b. *ASK:* Do you know you are a son of our Heavenly Father, in addition to being our earthly son? Heavenly Father is your Father in Heaven and I am your father on earth. Knowing you are a son of God helps you to know how much Heavenly Father loves you, and that we love you, too.

c. We each begin life on earth as a child away from our heavenly home, as if we were going away to school on earth to learn. But one day you will grow into a man and become a father. All that you learn and the good choices you make will help you to prepare to be a good man and a good father.

d. As you get older you will see your body grow and change. God intended this and it is wonderful.

3. Gender. Heavenly Father made you a boy on purpose. This is your gender—male. There are two genders: male and female. Gender is an essential characteristic to fulfill the specific mission God has for you on this earth. God made girls for a special purpose, too. Boys are to strive to be good daddies, and girls are to strive to be good mommies. It is more important to be a good and successful parent than anything else in the world.

a. Girls and boys are different from each other because God wants a man and a woman to make a good strong team together. They both bring different strengths to the relationship that together make them whole and strong. They are complementary to each other, like two different puzzle pieces that fit together to complete a picture. It's very important that you respect girls and understand they are different from boys and that differences are good and necessary.

b. *ASK:* Can you think of one way boys and girls are different? It's also important to know that boys' bodies and girls' bodies are different from each other for a special reason. God wanted a husband and a wife together to be able to make little babies. A daddy's body and a mommy's body work together and fit together to make babies. There is a special intimate relationship that is reserved by God for husbands and wives only after they are married. It is a sacred and special thing when a husband and wife join together to express this special love for each other, or to create children.

4. Circumcision. Even boys can look a little different from each other. *ASK:* Do you know what circumcision is? Circumcision is when part of the skin covering a boy's penis is cut off. Some boys are circumcised when they are babies and some boys are not. You should respect boys who look different than you do, and they should respect you, too.

a. *ASK:* So that I know you understand what I am saying, can you tell me something about what you've learned so far?

b. *ASK:* Do you have any questions so far?

5. *A Special Kind of Love for Husbands and Wives.* Husbands and wives show a special kind of love for each other when they hug and kiss and be together in their bedrooms. When a husband and wife join their bodies together to show love for each other it is called "physical intimacy," "making love," "having sex," "sexual relations" or "sexual intercourse." God has commanded us to save this special kind of love for our spouse after we are married.

a. *ASK:* Tell me what you understand about "sex."

b. *ASK:* Do you have any questions?

6. *Satan Tries to Mislead People about Sex.* Some people try to make the special relationship and activities between a husband and wife seem dirty or bad, when it is instead very sacred and special. Friends might try to tell you dirty jokes or be disrespectful about the relationship between a husband and wife. Don't listen to them. There should be an air of reverence and respect surrounding the intimate sexual relations between husband and wife. If anyone speaks to you or tries to portray these things without a spirit of reverence, then get away and don't listen to them. If they tell you things that upset you or cause you to have questions, please come home and ask us about it. We want to be the ones that teach you, so we can teach you correctly about God's plan and purposes for sex within marriage. We will try to tell you anything you want to know in a way that you can understand.

a. *ASK:* What should you do if someone tells dirty jokes or is disrespectful about the sexual relationship in marriage?

b. *ASK:* Has anyone told you anything about sex that wasn't correct or that caused you to have questions?

7. *Pornography.*

a. *ASK:* Do you know what pornography is? Has anyone ever tried to show you pictures of naked people? Pornography cheapens and degrades the sacred relationship between husbands and wives, fathers and mothers, and shows disrespect for our precious bodies.

b. Some people, maybe even your friends, may try to show you pictures of naked people. Don't look at these things. Get away as fast as you can. This stuff is called pornography. It is like poison for your mind. It is very difficult to get those pictures out of your mind once they are there. If you accidentally see something you shouldn't, you will need to be very careful to block those thoughts and pictures out of your mind when they enter. We can help you with this if it becomes a problem for you.

    c. (Share an experience of seeing pornography, and how it made you feel if it is relevant.)

    d. *ASK:* Why is it important to stay away from pornography?

8. Immoral Behavior. Many people who don't believe in God, or who don't keep His commandments, think it is all right for anyone to use this sacred gift even if they aren't married. This is NOT right. God has asked us to reserve sexual expression for marriage only.

    a. *ASK:* Why is it important to wait until marriage?

    b. *ASK:* What do you think are some of the consequences of having sexual relations with someone you are not married to?

9. Caring for Our Bodies. It's important that you take good care of your body. We wash regularly, get enough sleep and feed our bodies healthy foods. God has referred to our physical bodies as "temples" (like the temple we see driving down the freeway near our home). Our bodies are so special and such a precious gift from Heavenly Father that we want to take care of our bodies just as we would take care of the temple, and only put things into our bodies that are good and will strengthen us. This is why God has asked us not to smoke or drink or take harmful drugs, nor to pierce our bodies, put tattoos on them, or wear revealing clothing. All of these things will weaken our bodies and make it difficult for the Spirit to be with us anymore.

    a. *ASK:* What things can you think of that are good for the body?

    b. *ASK:* How is your body like a temple? Why do we want to make sure we take good care of our bodies and only put good things in them?

10. Protecting from Abuse. It's also important that you respect your body and protect it from misuse. Some people might try to touch you in private places that they shouldn't, such as the parts of your body that your swimming suit would cover. This is not appropriate. You should also respect others by never touching anyone in their sacred places on their body. This special kind of touching is only for husbands and wives after they are married.

    a. If anyone ever tries to make you do something, or to touch you in any way that is wrong or that makes you uncomfortable, you need to remember to do these three things: (1) strongly tell them "NO!"; (2) get away as fast as you can; (3) and tell Mom or Dad or another adult. The person who tries to hurt you might warn you not to tell anyone or tell you that they will hurt you or your family. Don't listen to them. You must tell one of us or another adult no matter what they say, so that this person won't try to hurt you or anyone else again.

b. Someone may want you to do something that might even feel sort of good, but that also makes you feel uncomfortable at the same time. You might not know for sure if something is right or wrong, but listen to what your heart tells you because that is the Holy Ghost helping you know right from wrong. When you are confused or afraid or uncomfortable, then it's probably something wrong, so come and tell us right away. You may have questions, so please know you can always ask us . . . any time. We will always have our monthly PPIs, so if it's easier for you to ask any questions then, write them down so you won't forget to ask them.

c. *ASK:* What are the three things you should do if someone tries to touch you or tries to do something that makes you uncomfortable?

11. *Respecting Our Own Bodies.* You also need to be respectful of your own body. You may be curious about your body as you grow. It is normal and natural for a boy's penis to get hard and stand up sometimes. You may feel like you need to touch or adjust it. If you can distract yourself or get up and go do something else, the erection will go away. It's very important to develop self-control and not get in a habit of touching the sacred parts of your body unnecessarily.

a. *ASK:* Do you have any questions about how your body works or what your body does?

b. We will continue to teach you additional information about your body as you grow.

12. *Future Discussions.* When you are a little older we will talk again and teach you more about these things, but please know you can ask us any questions you have at any time. You don't have to wait for a special occasion.

a. We hope you know how much we love you and want you to know about these sacred and serious things we've talked about. We want you to know God's truths about intimacy and sexuality and to know these things ahead of time, so that if you hear something about sex from others that is not correct, you will already know what is correct.

b. We want you to feel comfortable talking to us, rather than to friends or others who may not understand God's plan for us, His children. These things we have discussed are not things to talk about at school or church, but just for you to know, and for you to discuss with Mom or Dad.

13. *Give Lots of Love and Hugs.* Be sure to end with expressions of love and encouragement. Remember the power of touch to communicate love. Give lots of hugs!

God bless you parents! Good parenting is no easy task. It requires the best that is in us . . . and then some! That's where the Lord steps in to make up for what we lack. Our children deserve a healthy and positive regard for their bodies and for the pro-creative act. They also deserve to be informed and knowledgeable children, taught by loving parents who desire to shine a light into the mists of darkness that otherwise surround sexuality.

As parents teach beyond premarital issues of immorality to post-marital issues of sexual fulfillment, youth will be blessed to go into marriage with a healthy, positive sexual foundation. Husbands and wives can better utilize the honeymoon and early stage of marriage by freely and intimately learning about each other. By providing a solid foundation for marriage, mutual sexual fulfillment will occur more quickly and easily, reversing the trend of sexual "incompatibility" as a leading cause of divorce.

As parents teach beyond premarital issues of immorality to post-marital issues of sexual fulfillment, youth will be blessed to go into marriage with a healthy, positive sexual foundation.

Chapter 16—"Home" Work

- Plan and prepare to teach your children about sex before they reach age eight, before puberty, and before dating and marriage. Decide how you will teach.

- Schedule regular father / daughter and mother / son dates.

- Build the relationship by filling your child's emotional love bucket in preparation for a discussion about sex.

- Prepare your own discussion outline for the specific gender and age of your children.

- Plan a special one-on-one occasion / date for parent and child to discuss the information you've compiled in your outline.

- Begin the discussion with prayer; dialogue, don't lecture; teach correct behavior, not what shouldn't be done; focus on the positive and the blessings of the body and of sexuality.

- Model a healthy sexual attitude for your children to embrace. Set a good example of a loving, affectionate relationship with your spouse.

- Schedule regular, ongoing discussions for additional "installments" of sexual learning. Watch for other teaching opportunities.

NOTES

Chapter 16—Preparing Future Generations for Sexual
Fulfillment in Marriage: When and How to Teach

[1]Alma 37:35.
[2]*Marriage and Family Relations Instructor's Manual*, 58–59.
[3]*Parent's Guide*, 35.
[4]*See* Doctrine & Covenants 29:47.
[5]*See* Doctrine & Covenants 68:25.
[6]Grant, *Lake Hazel Elementary Newsletter*, 2.
[7]*See* Hunter, "Being a Righteous Husband and Father," *Ensign*, Nov. 1994, 49.
[8]*Marriage and Family Relations Instructor's Manual*, 72.

Appendix I

OVERCOMING PORNOGRAPHY
PROBLEMS TOGETHER

Inherent in the stewardship of marriage is the promise to work through whatever challenges couples may face. Understanding that much of the sin and neglect in marriage are rooted in emotional hurts or unmet needs can help couples have greater compassion for each other's wounds and weaknesses. President Kimball explained, "Jesus saw sin as wrong but also was able to see sin as springing from deep and unmet needs on the part of the sinner. This permitted him to condemn the sin without condemning the individual. . . . We need to be able to look deeply enough into the lives of others to see the basic causes for their failures and shortcomings."[1]

People who struggle with sexual temptations and addictions are not necessarily "evil," any more than someone with a food addiction or a gambling addiction is inherently evil. Dr. Garry A. Flint taught that addictive urges are often based on hurt of some kind.[2] Deep emotional wounds, unmet needs, and vulnerability cause some to seek unhealthy substitutes for love.

Joe Beam, a Christian pastor, shared an experience he had with a preacher who had come to him with a serious pornography problem. Through scalding tears and shame, the preacher confessed his struggles with pornography. Enlisting the help of the preacher's wife, Beam gives us an excellent example of how couples can overcome their challenges together. He recounts:

> Telling me was the toughest thing he'd ever done in his life, but he needed help and didn't know what else to do. When he finished his confession, he asked, "What do I do? How do I stop?"
>
> "Go home and tell your wife," I replied. . . .
>
> "What? Are you crazy?! If I tell her, she'll kill me!"
>
> "Well, that'll stop you," I dryly replied.
>
> For a moment, he didn't know if I was serious or not. During his confused pause, I continued, "Tell her. She won't kill you, and she won't leave you. I know

her, and I know she's gonna be hurt. She'll cry and talk about how ugly she is and how if she were prettier or sexier or younger or whatever you wouldn't do this. Of course, when she goes through all that self-recrimination, you have to reassure her that it's not her fault at all but a spiritual flaw in you. When she gets over the hurt, she'll forgive you. . . . But I'll guarantee you there's some things she will do: She'll want to know where you're going every time you go anywhere for the next year or so. She'll ask time, places, people you saw, and everything else. She'll start counting your money to see if you're spending any in unusual ways. She'll ask you directly if you're looking at that stuff again. And every time she does any of that, you'll hug her and reassure her and thank her. You will never, no matter how long it takes, show any aggravation or self-pity. Never. You understand?"

He numbly nodded his head in the affirmative, so I sent the shell-shocked sinner on his way. "Call me after you tell her so I can know how things are going. Okay?"

He nodded again and shuffled to his car. I've never seen a man walking death row to his execution, but I think his facial expression and body language must be similar to what this guy's were as he headed to his car. He was too overwhelmed and too disgusted with himself to do anything but what I told him, but he was sure I was wrong about her not leaving him.

That was five years ago, and they're doing great today. Every once in a while, she still asks him where he's been or pulls out his wallet and thumbs through his cash. He grins at her when she does.

She grins right back.

They both know she's just working on their intimacy.[3]

Pornography—Us Against It

While men primarily struggle with pornography, women too can become entangled in its web. No matter which spouse struggles with pornography, husbands and wives can work together to overcome this problem. The following are some ways couples can rid their marriage of the poison of pornography.

Pray Together. Pray together for guidance on how to overcome the temptations. Openly acknowledging your struggles before God and each other removes the shroud of secrecy and lets you begin working together on the problem. Have faith that the problem can be conquered. Developing the mental discipline to see yourself, your spouse and your relationship as you want them to be is an act of faith, which can help bring about the desired results.

Get Educated on the Problem. Both of you read and study good books and other literature to understand the poison and potential addiction of pornography. If you can, learn from others who have overcome the problem. Knowledge and understanding can increase empathy and your ability to help.

Open Discussion. Encourage open discussion regarding personal struggles and temptations, even if one of you is embarrassed. If the struggling spouse is humble and willing to accept help, and if the other spouse can be loving, patient and compassionate, you can work as a team to overcome the problem without allowing it to destroy your marriage and family. If necessary, use the Couples Dialogue taught in Chapter 10 to discuss the problem and brainstorm for solutions.

Ask for specific ways you can help. Accountability might be an effective deterrent to temptation. If your spouse is willing, ask him / her how he / she did that day with resisting temptation. Check the computer to see if pornographic sites have been visited. Suggest seeing the bishop or a counselor and volunteer to go with him. If your spouse has a true desire to overcome the problem, and if you are willing to help, your spouse can provide the best suggestions as to how you can help.

Avoid Temptations. Move computers into high-traffic areas. Avoid inappropriate chat rooms. Install filtering software. This will benefit the spouse who struggles with pornography as well as cut down the chance that other family members will accidentally run into pornographic material.

Keep TV, movies, music, or magazines that are sexually explicit, stimulating, or demeaning out of the home. Do not tolerate anything that dulls sensitivity to the Spirit or demeans the sacredness of sexuality in marriage.

Improve Your Intimate Relationship. Couples should work to create a strong and mutually fulfilling intimate relationship. They should seek to educate themselves sexually, learn from each other, and strive to better meet each other's physical intimacy needs. This can counter the draw of pornography and other sexual temptations. Address underlying unmet emotional needs, causing the vulnerability to temptation.

Seek Ecclesiastical and Professional Help. Individuals should counsel with priesthood leaders, as needed. Accountability to ecclesiastical leaders provides an outside source of support, as well as inspired counsel and guidance. Others who can share compassion or support should also be sought out. ·

Many couples will find it necessary to seek professional help to overcome problems with pornography. The underlying causes are often both spiritual and psychological.

A trained professional can not only increase the chances of success but can also help speed up the process. Couples who face these issues will need to exert significant effort and have outside help, but they can overcome this problem together.

NOTES

Appendix 1—Overcoming Pornography Problems Together

[1] Kimball, "Jesus: The Perfect Leader," *Ensign*, Aug. 1979, 5.
[2] *See* Flint, *Emotional Freedom* , 56.
[3] Beam, *Becoming One*, 201–202.

Appendix II

SEEKING PROFESSIONAL HELP

Whether you are in a marital crisis or just want to improve your marriage, professional help can be invaluable. But keep in mind couples have other avenues of marital assistance as well. According to Dr. William J. Doherty, professor of Family Social Science and Director of Marriage and Family Therapy at the University of Minnesota, the three levels of help recommended for marital problems are: (1) support people, mentors / other couples; (2) marriage educators; and (3) therapists.[1]

Support people, such as mentors or couples that have the kind of marriage you want to create, can provide perspective on your struggles as well as share their successes. If you ask a couple for their insights on creating a good marriage they will likely be happy to help.

Marriage educators could include marriage books, audio or videotapes, as well as classes to gain marital insight and relationship skills. Marriage educators may be more accessible to couples than professional therapists because books and classes generally cost less and people are more willing to read a book than to see a counselor. Since it's hard for couples to do better, if they don't *know* better, marital education is essential.

Hopefully couples will seek out support people and marriage education before their marriage is ever in crisis. Couples in crisis may initially need to bypass support people and general marriage education and get directly connected to a counselor or therapist.

Why Seek Professional Help? What Are the Benefits?

While marriage educators can provide general information and insight, therapists provide more focused and specific knowledge and guidance. Therapists can help deepen your understanding of your marriage, support, encourage and guide you in overcoming your problems, and help you develop critical relationship skills.

Marriage counseling can speed up the process of helping you find the specific knowledge and skills you need and help you integrate the knowledge and skills more quickly. With the assistance of a counselor, you will be better able to identify and address the underlying negative beliefs and issues that are causing problems in your marriage. A skilled therapist will be able to create a safe environment in which you can deal with difficult issues as well as provide structure and motivation as you make difficult but necessary changes in your life.

What to Look for in a Marriage Therapist

Finding the right therapist is vital. Shop around for a therapist who is a good match for you and your spouse. You may want to interview several on the phone to find the one that's right for you. The following are a few suggestions of what to look for and some questions to ask:

Choose a therapist who is committed to resolving your issues and strengthening your marriage. The therapist you choose should be your strongest advocate for saving your marriage. He or she should have the utmost confidence, faith, and vision regarding what your marriage can become if you will put in enough effort and endure through the challenges. Except in cases of serious abuse or danger, your therapist should operate on the assumption that most marriage problems are solvable. Divorce should be viewed as a tragic exception rather than the norm.[2]

Since marriage is not a consumer item, avoid therapists who simply help you do a cost / benefit analysis of your marriage to determine whether or not to stay married. Your therapist should be the last one to ever give up on your marriage—even when the going gets tough. Ask potential therapists what percentage of the couples they've worked with ultimately dissolved their marriages and what percentage went on to create happy marriages. Even if they can't answer the question exactly, you may learn something from their responses.

Choose a therapist skilled in marital therapy. Most counselors will say they do marriage or couple therapy but they may not necessarily be trained to do so. Marriage counseling is more involved and requires different skills than individual therapy, since more complex issues are in play when two people are involved. (Individual counseling may be helpful, however, in addressing individual issues and can be effectively combined with couple counseling.) Couple therapy requires a therapist to take an active role and to be prepared to deal with confrontation and conflict between spouses.

If you are specifically looking for help to improve physical intimacy in marriage, you might try to find a counselor who specializes in healthy sexuality within marriage. You might ask prospective counselors about their education as well as their specialties or expertise, and whether they have been trained in marital therapy. Ask them what percentage of their time is spent counseling couples versus individuals. You might also ask what percentage of their time is spent helping couples improve physical intimacy in marriage or whatever your most pressing issue is.

Choose a therapist with whom you feel comfortable and respected. Select a therapist who is warm and sensitive, and who inspires a feeling of hope and confidence. Both you and your spouse should have a good rapport with your counselor. A good therapist should never be on "her side" or "his side"—but on the side of your marriage. By calling around and asking some of the questions suggested here, or by having an initial consultation, you should be able to get a feel for whether he or she is a good match.

The counselor you choose should respect your values and feedback—particularly if you are uncomfortable with any of their recommendations. A good therapist will seek to understand and work within your value system and with respect to your religious convictions. You need to be able to distinguish the difference between a suggestion you don't feel good about and the discomfort of necessary personal growth.

Choose a therapist who will help you set goals. A good counselor will encourage you to set goals and identify your expectations regarding therapy. The therapist's expectations should also be clear. In preparation for counseling, it may be helpful to write down why you need counseling and what you want to accomplish. Having a big picture or end-result in mind can help you achieve it. Periodically you should review your goals with your counselor and determine your progress.

Learn from multiple therapists if needed. Every counselor has a different perspective and approach. The time may come when you feel you've learned all that a particular counselor has to teach you. As long as you are not running away from difficult changes they are helping you to make, trust your instincts and watch for stagnation to know when you need to move on. For example, when a counselor suggests that it may be best for you and your spouse to separate for a time, what they are really saying is that they've run out of ideas on how to help your marriage. Trust your instincts to know when the learning from one teacher is finished and a new teacher is needed.

Choose a therapist who has personally created the kind of marriage you would want. No formal schooling can replace the personal experience of having successfully waded through marital challenges. It may be difficult to assess a potential therapist's marriage, but having a good marriage is an essential credential for any marriage counselor. Popular LDS speaker, author, and marriage counselor, Lucile Johnson, used to say that the fact that she had been married for so many years was her best credential. It is a valuable credential to know that your counselor has learned and applied the principles he or she will be teaching you.

Seek divine guidance. Finding the right counselor must be a matter of prayer. The Lord knows who will best be able to teach you and He will light your way as you prayerfully seek His guidance. Trust in the Lord to guide you. Trust your instincts. There are many good counselors available if you will persist and prayerfully seek them.

Resources for Finding a Good Therapist

Get a Referral. Word-of-mouth referrals are invaluable. Get recommendations from other couples, your bishop, or other ecclesiastical leaders who will know of counselors who have been successful. For members of the LDS Church, bishops can refer you to LDS Family Services for counseling. You might also contact LDS Family Services yourself to see if they can provide local referrals to other LDS counselors. You may want to find a therapist of your same faith but it is not required if you can find one who shares similar values or one who will respect your values. The Lord can direct you to a good counselor even if there are few available.

Check out Professional and Religious Organizations. Many professional and ecclesiastical organizations provide directories that can help you find a good therapist in your area:

> ### Association of Mormon Counselors and Psychotherapists (AMCAP)
> http://www.AMCAP.net
> 2540 East 1700 South
> Salt Lake City, UT 84108
> (801) 583-6227
> Email: mail@amcap.net (Call or email to request a list of local LDS professionals.)
> *A professional organization of counselors, psychotherapists and others who adhere to the Christian principles and standards of The Church of Jesus Christ of Latter-day Saints.*

> ### American Association of Christian Counselors (AACC)
> http://www.AACC.net
> P.O. Box 739
> Forest, VA 24551

(434) 525-9470

(434) 525-9480 (Fax)

Email: memberservices@AACC.net

An association committed to assisting Christian counselors, licensed professionals, pastors, and caring church members by equipping them with Biblical truth and psycho-social insights to help hurting persons move toward personal wholeness, interpersonal competence, mental stability, and spiritual maturity.

Sexual Wholeness

http://www.SexualWholeness.com

P.O. Box 550911

Atlanta, GA 30355-3411

(404) 705-7077

(404) 705-9971 (Fax)

A non-profit Christian organization dedicated to promoting God's truths about sexuality. They have sponsored the development of the American Board of Christian Sex Therapists and are compiling a directory of Christian sex therapists.

American Board of Christian Sex Therapists (ABCST)

http://www.ABCST.org

P.O. Box 1303

Dacula, GA 30019-0023

(678) 248-4018

Email: abcst@sexualwholeness.com

The American Association of Sex Educators, Counselors, and Therapists (AASECT)

http://www.AASECT.org

P.O. Box 5488

Richmond, VA 23220-0488

(804) 644-3288

Email: aasect@aasect.org

A non-profit, interdisciplinary professional organization of members such as sex educators, sex therapists, physicians, psychologists, clergy members, lawyers, and marriage and family counselors and therapists who share an interest in promoting understanding of human sexuality and healthy sexual behavior.

Imago Relationships International

http://www.ImagoRelationships.org/Directory

335 North Knowles Avenue

Winter Park, FL 32789

(407) 644-4937

(800) 729-1121 (toll-free)

(407) 645-1315 (Fax)

A directory of certified Imago Relationship Therapists in your area who can also teach you the Couples Dialogue communication process.

American Association for Marriage and Family Therapy (AAMFT)

http://www.AAMFT.org

http://www.TherapistLocator.net

112 South Alfred Street

Alexandria, VA 22314-3061

(703) 838-9808

(703) 838-9805 (Fax)

A directory of marriage and family therapists, by area, who are also clinical members of the American Association for Marriage and Family Therapy.

Qwest Dex Online Directory

http://www.DexOnline.com

Check the phone book or this online directory for a list of marriage counselors whom you can then call and interview.

NOTES

Appendix II— Seeking Professional Help

[1] Doherty, "How Therapy Can Be Hazardous to Your Marital Health," MCFCE Conference, July 3, 1999.
[2] Doherty, "How Therapy Can Be Hazardous to Your Marital Health," MCFCE Conference, July 3, 1999.

Appendix III

RESOURCES FOR STRENGTHENING
MARRIAGES AND IMPROVING INTIMACY

Couples Dialogue Communication Tool

Emotional Freedom Technique (EFT)

Online Marriage Resources

Other Resources

Laura's Recommended Reading List

The following list includes the resources I have found to be the most enlightening and helpful in strengthening marriages and improving intimacy. This is not intended to be a comprehensive list. There are many additional resources listed at the following websites or available elsewhere. While these sites all provide helpful information and resources, their inclusion here does not imply my unlimited endorsement of all views, products, services or information contained therein.

Couples Dialogue *(See Chapter 10 in this book for the Couples Dialogue Process)*

The Couples Dialogue is an effective communication tool for couples, allowing them to be able to speak and listen in an environment where they are fully heard, validated, and understood. The Couples Dialogue Process in Chapter 10 was taken from *Getting the Love You Want: A Couples Workshop Manual*, 1997 (pp. 23-24) and *Getting the Love You Want: A Guide for Couples: Home Video Workshop Manual*, 1993 (p. 78) by Harville Hendrix, Ph.D.

To learn the Couples Dialogue and see it in action, order a copy of The Couples Dialogue video by Rick Brown, Th.M. at http://www.RickBrown.org.

Imago Relationships International

http://www.ImagoRelationships.org
335 North Knowles Avenue
Winter Park, FL 32789
(407) 644-4937
(800) 729-1121 (toll-free)
(407) 645-1315 (Fax)

To find a certified Imago Relationship Therapist in your area who can teach you the Couples Dialogue and coach you through a few sessions visit www.ImagoRelationships.org / Directory.

Emotional Freedom Technique

Emotional and neurological disturbances rooted in negative core beliefs, emotions, and energies are prevalent in couples' contemporary challenges. But God continues to provide new and effective approaches to assist us in overcoming them. One of the most valuable self-help skills for clearing or releasing inhibitions and negative beliefs is a relatively new and simple tool called the "Emotional Freedom Technique" (EFT). One counselor stated, "We can now accomplish more in five minutes of EFT than in four months of regular talk therapy."

The Emotional Freedom Technique involves a process of physically tapping on energy meridians, or points on the body, while focusing on a thought, problem, belief, emotion, or pain. The tapping addresses the body's energy system where disruptions or blockages are stored. While EFT is a simple and quick process, uncovering all the related layers of limiting core beliefs can take time and effort. The whole EFT process takes only minutes per problem (or aspect of an issue) and can be repeated until all negative emotions are cleared. The Emotional Freedom Technique (EFT) can be helpful not only to remove or reduce negative thoughts, but also to replace them with positive ones.

EFT has worked successfully for many people, including myself. It can be used effectively with a wide range of issues from negative sexual beliefs to overeating to fear of heights. For me, it was a crucial missing link that allowed me to break through and release negative sexual beliefs, emotions, and inhibitions that I had accumulated throughout my life. Without the help of EFT, I would still be struggling with sexual inhibitions and would not be writing this book.

To learn this technique, I highly recommend the book *Emotional Freedom: Techniques for Dealing with Emotional and Physical Distress*, by Garry A. Flint, Ph.D.

It is a small book with simple, easy-to-follow instructions and diagrams. There are also professional web sites where you can learn more about EFT.

EFT is particularly valuable because it can be done on your own—though you may want to consult with a therapist if you are dealing with serious issues. Professionals can assist you with other effective technologies such as Rapid Eye Therapy (RET) and Eye Movement Desensitization and Reprocessing (EMDR). RET—an energy therapy and a spiritual therapy—is an innovative form of natural healing. EMDR is the clinical counterpart to RET that is also very valuable. To learn more about EFT, RET, and EMDR, check out the resources listed below.

Emotional Freedom Techniques—Online Resources

Free EFT Self Help
http://www.123EFT.com

Emotional Freedom Techniques
http://www.EmoFree.com

Emotional Freedom (self-help book)
http://www.Emotional-Freedom.com

Rapid Eye Institute
http://www.RapidEyeTechnology.com

EMDR Institute—Eye Movement Desensitization and Reprocessing
http://www.EMDR.com

Online Marriage Resources

Strengthening Marriage.com
http://www.StrengtheningMarriage.com
Laura M. Brotherson
Email: Laura@StrengtheningMarriage.com

Excerpts from, reviews of, and other information about the book And They Were Not Ashamed—Strengthening Marriage through Sexual Fulfillment, *as well as other resources to strengthen marriages and build strong families.*

Hidden Treasures Foundation
http://www.MentalHealthLibrary.info

2550 Washington Blvd., Suite #103
P.O. Box 3074
Ogden, UT 84409-1074
(801) 621-8484
(800) 723-1760 (toll-free)
Email: hti@webpipe.net

Information on a variety of issues including marriage, sexual concerns, pornography, abuse, parenting, and depression. The information and resources are divided into the following categories: General, LDS, and Other.

The Marriage Bed.com

http://www.TheMarriageBed.com
The Marriage Bed, Inc.
5000 Tahoe Trail
Austin, TX 78745
(512) 233-2860 (Fax)
Email: paul@themarriagebed.com

A Christian source for married and engaged couples seeking information about marital intimacy. It offers information and resources on many areas of sexuality and marriage enrichment.

Family Dynamics Institute

http://www.FamilyDynamics.net
http://www.JoeBeam.com
http://www.LoveSexMarriage.net
http://www.Heartlight.org/articles/love
Joe Beam, Founder and President
305 Seaboard Lane # 319
Franklin, TN 37067
(615) 627-0751
(800) 650-9995 (toll-free)

Christian marriage and family ministry by Joe Beam, author of Becoming One: Emotionally, Spiritually, Sexually. Information and training for enriching marriages. Use the Heartlight.org articles link listed above for excellent articles on intimacy in marriage.

Smart Marriages—Coalition for Marriage, Family and Couples Education, LLC

http://www.SmartMarriages.com

Diane Sollee, Founder and Director

5310 Belt Rd NW

Washington, DC 20015-1961

Email: Diane@smartmarriages.com

(202) 362-3332

Articles, books, and audio tapes to enhance marriage, family and couple education. They organize an annual "Smart Marriages Conference."

Michael Farnworth's Web Page

http://emp.byui.edu/FARNWORTHM

Michael Farnworth, Ed.D., Faculty, Department of Child and Family Studies, BYU Idaho

Class presentations and readings on many topics such as healing the self, strengthening marriage, and parenting.

Divorce Busting.com

http://www.DivorceBusting.com

Michele Weiner Davis

P.O. Box 197

Woodstock, IL 60098

(815) 337-8000

(815) 337-8014 (Fax)

Books, tapes, articles, and phone counseling. Michele Weiner Davis is a marriage therapist and author of The Sex-Starved Marriage and Divorce Busting.

Marriage and Families

http://MarriageandFamilies.byu.edu

Email: marriage-families@byu.edu

(801) 422-4454 (email or call to subscribe to free online or print edition)

Online and hard copy peer-reviewed publication dedicated to strengthening marriages and families, published by Brigham Young University.

Utah Marriage.org

http://www.UtahMarriage.org

Resources, links, and articles on marriage.

Other Resources

Imago Relationships International

http://www.ImagoRelationships.org/shop
"Marriage as a Path to Wholeness" (2 cassettes, $17.95)
Harville Hendrix, Ph.D.

Dr. Hendrix explains the mystery of male-female relationships, why we are attracted to certain partners and how we can create a conscious marriage.

Scriptural Counsel, Inc.

130 North Spring St.
Springdale, AR 72764
(479) 751-5722
(800) 643-3477 (toll-free)
Email: scripturalcounsel@juno.com

"Sex Techniques and Sex Problems in Marriage" (1981)

Ed Wheat, M.D.
2 cassette tapes, $19.95

"Before the Wedding Night" (1982)

Ed Wheat, M.D.
2 cassette tapes, $19.95

BYU Conferences and Workshops

BYU "Family Expo" and "Families Under Fire" Conferences
136 Harman Continuing Education Building
Provo, Utah 84602-1516
(801) 422-4853
Email: cw136@byu.edu

BYU conducts two annual conferences intended to strengthen the family.

Family Expo (April)

http://ce.byu.edu/cw/cwfamily

Families Under Fire (October)

http://ce.byu.edu/cw/fuf

Yahoo Chat Groups

Yahoo Groups—LDS Marriage
http://groups.yahoo.com/group/LDS-Marriages
Email: lds-marriages-subscribe@yahoogroups.com (to subscribe)

Yahoo Groups—LDS Sexuality
http://groups.yahoo.com/group/LDS-Sexuality
Email: lds-sexuality-subscribe@yahoogroups.com (to subscribe)

Both of these are moderated email groups where members can discuss issues relating to sexuality in marriage within a gospel framework.

Laura's Recommended Reading List for Strengthening Marriage and Improving Intimacy

For help finding new or used books visit http://www.BookFinder.com.

1. *Intended for Pleasure: Sex Technique and Sexual Fulfillment in Christian Marriage* (1997) by Ed and Gaye Wheat. Ed Wheat is a medical doctor and sex therapist.

2. *Becoming One: Emotionally, Spiritually, Sexually* (1999) by Joe Beam, Christian minister and founder of Family Dynamics Institute.

3. *Passionate Marriage: Keeping Love and Intimacy Alive in Committed Relationships* (1997) by David Schnarch, Ph.D. renowned marriage and sex therapist.

4. *Sexual Happiness in Marriage: A Christian Interpretation of Sexual Adjustment in Marriage* (1987) by Herbert J. Miles, Ph.D.

5. *The Five Love Languages: How to Express Heartfelt Commitment to Your Mate* (1992) by Gary Chapman, Ph.D.

6. *The Sex-Starved Marriage* (2003) by Michele Weiner Davis, popular marriage therapist.

7. *Restoring the Pleasure: Complete Step-by-Step Programs to Help Couples Overcome the Most Common Sexual Barriers* (1993) by Clifford L. Penner, Ph.D., and Joyce J. Penner, R.N., M.N. (Christian).

8. *365 Questions for Couples* (1999) by Dr. Michael J. Beck.

9. *The Act of Marriage: The Beauty of Sexual Love* (1998) by Tim and Beverly LaHaye.

10. *Between Husband and Wife: Gospel Perspectives on Marital Intimacy* (2000) by Stephen E. Lamb, M.D. and Douglas E. Brinley, Ph.D.

11. *Getting the Love You Want: A Guide for Couples* (2001) by Harville Hendrix, Ph.D., creator of Imago Relationship Therapy and founder of the Institute for Imago Relationship Therapy.

12. *Eternal Marriage Student Manual: Religion 234 and 235* (2001) LDS Church publication. Available from http://www.LDScatalog.com.

13. *Marriage and Family Relations: Instructor's Manual* and *Marriage and Family Relations: Participant's Study Guide* (2000) LDS Church publications. Available from http://www.LDScatalog.com.

BIBLIOGRAPHY

Ballard, M. Russell. "Like a Flame Unquenchable," *Ensign*, May 1999, 85.

Ban Breathnach, Sarah. *Something More: Excavating Your Authentic Self*. New York: Warner Books, 1999.

Barlow, Brent A. "They Twain Shall Be One: Thoughts on Intimacy in Marriage," *Ensign*, Sep. 1986, 49.

——. *Just for Newlyweds*. Salt Lake City: Deseret Book, 1992.

——. *Worth Waiting For*. Salt Lake City: Deseret Book, 1995.

Bateman, Merrill J. "The Power to Heal from Within," *Ensign*, May 1995, 13.

——. *Eternal Marriage Student Manual*. Salt Lake City: The Church of Jesus Christ of Latter-day Saints, 2001, 65

Beam, Joe. *Becoming One: Emotionally, Spiritually, Sexually*. West Monroe: Howard Publishing, 1999.

Beck, Michael J., Stanis Marusak Beck and Seanna Beck. *365 Questions for Couples*. Avon Massachusetts: Adams Media Corporation, 1999.

Beckert, Charles B. "Pitfalls of Parallel Marriage" *Ensign*, Mar. 2000, 22.

Benson, Ezra Taft. "The Book of Mormon—Keystone of Our Religion," *Ensign*, Nov. 1986, 4.

——. *The Teachings of Ezra Taft Benson*. Salt Lake City: Bookcraft, 1988.

——. "The Great Commandment—Love the Lord" *Ensign*, May 1988, 4.

——. "Beware of Pride," *Ensign*, May 1989, 4.

Boyd, Susan and Associates. "Impact of Instructional Method on Retention Rate," train the trainer handout, *Ziff Institute Computer Training and Support Conference*, Oct. 24 - 27, 1993, Orlando, Florida.

Brinley, Douglas E. *Toward a Celestial Marriage: Perspectives and Practices for Building Love and Harmony in the Home*. Salt Lake City: Bookcraft, 1986.

Broderick, Carlfred. *One Flesh One Heart: Putting Celestial Love into Your Temple Marriage*. Salt Lake City: Deseret Book, 1986.

Brown, Hugh B. *You and Your Marriage*. Salt Lake City: Bookcraft, 1960.

Brown, Victor L. Jr. *Human Intimacy: Illusion & Reality*. Salt Lake City: Parliament Publishers, 1981.

Bytheway, John and Kimberly. *What We Wish We'd Known When We Were Newlyweds*. Salt Lake City: Bookcraft, 2000.

Capacchione, Lucia and Mona Brookes. *The Power of Your Other Hand: A Course in Channeling the Inner Wisdom of the Right Brain*. Franklin Lakes: New Page Books, 2001.

Chapman, Gary. *The Five Love Languages: How to Express Heartfelt Commitment to Your Mate*. Chicago: Northfield Publishing, 1992.

Chiles, Wendy. "Garden Plots," *The Friend*, May 1998, 16.

Christensen, Joe J. "Marriage and the Great Plan of Happiness," *Ensign*, May 1995, 64.

Christofferson, D. Todd. "That They May Be One in Us," *Ensign*, Nov. 2002, 71.

The Church of Jesus Christ of Latter-day Saints. *Achieving a Celestial Marriage: Student Manual*. Salt Lake City, 1976.

——. *The Holy Bible: Containing the Old and New Testaments* (authorized King James Version). Salt Lake City, 1979.

——. *Family Home Evening Resource Book*. Salt Lake City, 1983.

——. *A Parent's Guide*. Salt Lake City, 1985.

——. *Hymns of The Church of Jesus Christ of Latter-Day Saints*. Salt Lake City, 1985.

——. *The Book of Mormon: Another Testament of Jesus Christ*. Salt Lake City, 1988.

——. *The Doctrine and Covenants of The Church of Jesus Christ of Latter-day* Saints. Salt Lake City, 1988.

——. *The Pearl of Great* Price. Salt Lake City, 1988.

——. "The Family: A Proclamation to the World," *Ensign*, Nov. 1995, 102.

——. *Marriage and Family Relations: Instructor's Manual*. Salt Lake City, 2000.

——. *For the Strength of Youth: Fulfilling Our Duty to God*. Salt Lake City, 2001.

——. "News of the Church," *Ensign*, June 2003, 76.

Clarke, J. Richard. "Ministering to Needs through LDS Social Services," *Ensign*, May 1977, 85.

Cline, Victor B. "Obscenity: How It Affects Us, How We Can Deal with It," *Ensign*, Apr. 1984, 32.

Condie, Spencer J. "Finding Marital Unity through the Scriptures," *Ensign*, July 1986, 52.

Curtis, Lindsay R., and Wayne J. Anderson. *And They Shall Be One Flesh: A Sensible Sex Guide for the Bride and Groom*. Salt Lake City: Publishers Press, 1968.

——. Curtis, Lindsay R. and Wayne J. Anderson. *Living, Loving & Marrying: Thoughts for LDS Teens and Young Marrieds*. Salt Lake City: Deseret Book, 1968.

Davidson, Karen Lynn. *Our Latter-day Hymns: The Stories and the Messages*. Salt Lake City: Deseret Book, 1988.

Davis, Phyllis K. *The Power of Touch: The Basis for Survival, Health, Intimacy, and Emotional Well-Being*. Carlsbad: Hay House, 1999.

De Angelis, Barbara. *How to Make Love All the Time: The Ultimate Guide to Bringing Love into Your Life and Making it Work as Never Before*. New York: Rawson Associates, 1987.

Dew, Sheri L. "It Is Not Good for Man or Woman to Be Alone," *Ensign*, Nov. 2001, 12.

Dobson, James. *What Wives Wish Their Husbands Knew About Women*. Wheaton, Illinois: Tyndale House Publishers, 1975.

Doherty, William J. "How Therapy Can Be Hazardous to Your Marital Health," Smart Marriages Conference, July 3, 1999.

Dunn, Loren C. "How to Gain a Testimony," *Ensign*, Jan. 1973, 84.

Ellsworth, Homer. "I Have a Question," *Ensign*, Aug. 1979, 23.

Eyring, Henry B. "Come Unto Christ," *BYU Speeches / Firesides*, Oct. 29, 1989.

——. *Gifts of Love*. Salt Lake City: Deseret Book, 1995.

——. "Witnesses for God," *Ensign*, Nov. 1996, 30.

——. "That We May Be One," *Ensign*, May 1998, 66.

Farnworth, Michael. "What's Wrong With It?" [online] *Selected Readings* [cited 15 Mar., 2004]. Available from World Wide Web: <http://emp.byui.edu/FARNWORTHM/200readings/Premaritalinvolvement.htm>.

——. "Our Sexual Natures: Sections One and Two—A Doctrinal, Philosophical look at the sexual natures of men and women in marriage" [online] *Marriage Dynamics 300 lessons* [cited 15 Mar., 2004]. Available from World Wide Web: <http://emp.byui.edu/FARNWORTHM/300%20Lessons/OurSexualNatures_files/frame.htm> (slide 131 of 166).

Faust, James E. "The Refiner's Fire," *Ensign*, May 1979, 53.

——. "Heirs to the Kingdom of God," *Ensign*, May 1995, 61.

——. "The Weightier Matters of the Law: Judgment, Mercy, and Faith," *Ensign*, Nov. 1997, 53.

——. "Serving the Lord and Resisting the Devil," *Ensign*, Sep. 1995, 2.

——. "The Power of Self-Mastery," *Ensign*, May 2000, 43.

——. "Strengthening the Inner Self," *Ensign*, Feb. 2003, 5.

——. "Enriching Our Lives through Family Home Evening," *Ensign*, June 2003, 3.

——. "The Surety of a Better Testament," *Ensign*, Sep. 2003, 3.

Flinders, Neil J. "Learning to Teach as Jesus Taught: A Parent's Point of View," *Ensign*, Sep. 1974, 64.

Flint, Garry A. *Emotional Freedom: Techniques for Dealing with Emotional and Physical Distress*. Vernon: NeoSolTerric Enterprises, 2001.

Gibran, Kahlil. *The Prophet*. New York: Alfred A. Knopf Publisher, 1980.

Gochros, Harvey L. and Joel Fischer. *Treat Yourself to a Better Sex Life*. New Jersey: Prentice Hall, 1980.

Graham, Billy. "What the Bible Says About Sex," *Reader's Digest*, May 1970, 118.

Grampa Bill. Grampa Bill's G.A. [General Authority] Pages, [cited 29 Nov. 2003]. Available from World Wide Web: <http://personal.atl.bellsouth.net/w/o/wol3/hollajr1.htm>.

Grant, Andy. *Lake Hazel Elementary Newsletter*, Mar. 2003, 2.

Gray, John. *Mars and Venus in the Bedroom: A Guide to Lasting Romance and Passion*. New York: HarperCollins Publishers, 1995.

——. *Children Are From Heaven: Positive Parenting Skills for Raising Cooperative, Confident, and Compassionate Children*. New York: HarperCollins Publishers, 1999.

Grondahl, Calvin. *Freeway to Perfection: A Collection of Mormon Cartoons*. Salt Lake City: Sunstone Foundation, 1978.

Hafen, Bruce C. "Covenant Marriage," *Ensign*, Nov. 1996, 26.

Hales, Robert D. "The Aaronic Priesthood: Return with Honor," *Ensign*, May 1990, 39.

——. "Strengthening Families: Our Sacred Duty," *Ensign,* May 1999, 32.

Hendrix, Harville. *Getting The Love You Want: A Guide for Couples.* New York: HarperPerennial, 1988.

——. *Keeping the Love You Find: A Personal Guide.* New York: Pocket Books, 1992.

——. *Getting the Love You Want: A Guide for Couples Home Video Workshop Manual.* Winter Park, Florida: The Institute for Imago Relationship Therapy, 1993.

——. *Getting the Love You Want: A Couples Workshop Manual.* Winter Park, Florida: The Institute for Imago Relationship Therapy. 1997. (For more information, contact *Institute for Imago Relationship Therapy* at 1-800-729-1121.)

Hinckley, Gordon B. "Except the Lord Build the House . . . ," *Ensign*, June 1971, 71.

——. "Reverence and Morality," *Ensign*, May 1987, 45.

——. "Keeping the Temple Holy," *Ensign*, May 1990, 49.

——. "What God Hath Joined Together," *Ensign*, May 1991, 71.

——. *Teachings of Gordon B. Hinckley.* Salt Lake City: Deseret Book, 1997.

——. "Excerpts from Recent Addresses of President Gordon B. Hinckley," *Ensign*, July 1997, 72.

——. "Life's Obligations," *Ensign,* Feb. 1999, 2.

——. *Stand a Little Taller: Counsel and Inspiration for Each Day of the Year.* Salt Lake City: Deseret Book, 2001.

Holland, Jeffrey R. "Of Souls, Symbols, and Sacraments," BYU devotional address, Jan. 12, 1988.

——. "A Teacher Come from God," *Ensign*, May 1998, 25.

——. "Personal Purity," *Ensign*, Nov. 1998, 75.

——. "How Do I Love Thee?" BYU devotional address, Feb. 15, 2000, 6.

Hunter, Howard W. "Being a Righteous Husband and Father," *Ensign*, Nov. 1994, 49.

Jensen, Marlin K. "A Union of Love and Understanding" *Ensign* Oct. 1994, 47.

——. "Friendship: A Gospel Principle," *Ensign*, May 1999, 64.

Johnson, Lucile. *The Language of Love in Marriage* (talk on tape). American Fork: Covenant Communications, 1999.

Kimball, Spencer W. "Guidelines to Carry Forth the Work of God in Cleanliness," *Ensign*, May 1974, 4.

——. "John and Mary, Beginning Life Together," *The New Era*, June 1975, 4.

——. "Blessings and Responsibilities of Womanhood," *Ensign*, Mar. 1976, 70.

——. *Marriage & Divorce*, Salt Lake City: Deseret Book,1976.

——. "The Gospel Vision of the Arts," *Ensign*, July 1977, 3.

——. "Privileges and Responsibilities of Sisters," *Ensign*, Nov. 1978, 102.

——. "Jesus: The Perfect Leader," *Ensign*, Aug. 1979, 5.

——. *The Teachings of Spencer W. Kimball* , Edward L. Kimball, ed. Salt Lake City: Bookcraft, 1982.

——. *Marriage and Family Relations: Instructor's Manual.* Salt Lake City, 2000.

——. "Oneness in Marriage," *Ensign*, Oct. 2002, 40.

Klose, Kevin. "Ann Landers' Tide of Discontent." *The Washington Post*, 15 Jan., 1985. sec. C-1.

LaHaye, Tim and Beverly. *The Act of Marriage: The Beauty of Sexual Love.* Grand Rapids, Michigan: Zondervan, 1998.

Lamb, Stephen E., and Douglas E. Brinley. *Between Husband and Wife: Gospel Perspectives on Marital Intimacy.* American Fork: Covenant Communications, 2000.

Larsen, Dean L. "The Importance of the Temple for Living Members," *Ensign*, Apr. 1993, 10.

Laumann, Edward O., Anthony Paik and Raymond C. Rosen. Sexual Dysfunction in the United States: Prevalence and Predictors. *The Journal of The American Medical Association.* 281:537-44, 1999.

Lee, Harold B. "A Sure Trumpet Sound: Quotations from President Lee," *Ensign,* Feb. 1974, 77.

——. *Teachings of Presidents of the Church: Harold B. Lee.* Salt Lake City: The Church of Jesus Christ of Latter-day Saints, 2000.

Mackelprang, Romel W. "They Shall Be One Flesh": Sexuality and Contemporary Mormonism. In *Multiply and Replenish: Mormon Essays on Sex and Family,* edited by Brent Corcoran. Salt Lake City: Signature Books, 1994.

Madsen, Ann N. "Tolerance, the Beginning of Christlike Love," *Ensign,* Oct. 1983, 26.

Madsen, Truman G. *The Highest In Us.* Salt Lake City: Bookcraft, 1978.

Maxwell, Neal A. "Care for the Life of the Soul," Ensign, May 2003, 68.

Miles, Herbert J. *Sexual Happiness in Marriage: A Christian Interpretation of Sexual Adjustment in Marriage*. Grand Rapids: Pyranee / Zondervan, 1982.

McConkie, Bruce R. "Celestial Marriage," *The New Era*, June 1978, 12.

McKay, David O. *The Church News*, Apr. 26, 2003.

Nay, Annette. In "Depend Upon the Lord" [online]. [Cited 29 Nov. 2003]. Available from World Wide Web: <http://www.three-peaks.net/annette/Depend.htm>

Nelson, Russell M. "Listen to Learn," *Ensign*, May 1991, 22.

Nusbaum, Margaret R.H. and Carol D. Hamilton. The Proactive Sexual Health History. *American Family Physician* 66:1705-12, 2002.

Oaks, Dallin H. "The Great Plan of Happiness," *Ensign*, Nov. 1993, 72.

——. "The Challenge to Become," *Ensign*, Nov. 2000, 32.

O'Connor, Dagmar. "Take 6 Steps to Better Sex," *Redbook*, Feb. 1989, 90.

——. *How to Put the Love Back into Making Love*, New York: Doubleday, 1989.

Olson, Terrance D. "Teaching Morality to Your Children," *Ensign*, Mar. 1981, 14.

Packer, Boyd K. "Why Stay Morally Clean," *Ensign*, July 1972, 111.

——. *Teach Ye Diligently*. Salt Lake City: Deseret Book, 1975.

——. "Marriage," *Ensign*, May 1981, 13.

——. "A Tribute to Women," *Ensign,* July 1989, 75.

——. "Revelation in a Changing World," *Ensign*, Nov. 1989, 14.

——. "Fountain of Life." *Eternal Marriage: Student Manual, Religion 234 and 235*. Salt Lake City: The Church of Jesus Christ of Latter-day Saints, 2001.

Penner, Clifford and Joyce. *Restoring the Pleasure: Complete Step-by-Step Programs to Help Couples Overcome the Most Common Sexual Barriers*. Dallas: Word Publishing, 1993.

Perry, L. Tom. "That Spirit Which Leadeth to Do Good," *Ensign*, May 1997, 68.

——. CES Employees Meeting (quote confirmed by email, Mar. 20, 2001).

Peterson, H. Burke. "Removing the Poison of an Unforgiving Spirit," *Ensign*, Nov. 1983, 59.

Pinnock, Hugh W. "The Blessings of Being Unified," *Ensign*, May 1987, 62.

Robinson, Marie N. *The Power of Sexual Surrender*. New York: Doubleday, 1959.

Robinson, Parker Pratt. *The Writings of Parley Parker Pratt*, Salt Lake City: Deseret News Press, 1952.

Schlessinger, Laura. Letter read on air June 11, 2001.

Scoresby, A. Lynn. "Teaching Children about Physical Development," *Ensign*, June 1988, 39.

Scott, Richard G. "Finding Joy in Life" *Ensign*, May 1996, 24.

——. "The Power of Righteousness," *Ensign*, Nov. 1998, 68.

——. "First Things First," *Ensign*, May 2001, 6.

——. "Realize Your Full Potential," *Ensign*, Nov. 2003, 41.

Smith, Joseph F. "Thoughts on Marriage Compatibility," *Ensign*, Sep. 1981, 45.

Taylor, John. *Teachings of Presidents of the Church: John Taylor*. Salt Lake City: The Church of Jesus Christ of Latter-day Saints, 2001.

Tanksley, Perry. "Marriage Takes Three," Dear Cards Company: Clinton, Mississippi. www.deargreetingcards.com.

Watson, Wendy L. *Purity and Passion: Spiritual Truths About Intimacy That Will Strengthen Your Marriage*, Salt Lake City: Deseret Book, 2001.

Webster's Universal Dictionary and Thesaurus. Montreal: Tormont Publications, 1993.

Weiner Davis, Michele. *The Sex-Starved Marriage: A Couples Guide to Boosting Their Marriage Libido*. New York: Simon & Schuster, 2003.

——. *The Divorce Busting Newsletter*. 1-19-03. ©2003 Michele Weiner Davis Training Corp. Reprinted with permission of Michele Weiner-Davis. Subscribe to the FREE "Divorce Busting" newsletter at www.divorcebusting.com, the website for people who want a more loving relationship.

Wheat, Ed and Gaye. *Intended for Pleasure: Sex Technique and Sexual Fulfillment in Christian Marriage*. Grand Rapids: Fleming H. Revell, 1997.

REFERENCE GUIDE

Throughout this book I refer to many passages in the Bible and the Book of Mormon, which is regarded by Latter-day Saints as another scriptural witness of Jesus Christ. So that readers will know where to find scriptural references they are unfamiliar with, I have included a list of books within the Book of Mormon. The Book of Mormon is available online at http://Scriptures.LDS.org.

Books in *The Book of Mormon:*
Another Testament of Jesus Christ

First Book of Nephi	Book of Omni	Third Nephi
Second Book of Nephi	The Words of Mormon	Fourth Nephi
Book of Jacob	Book of Mosiah	Book of Mormon
Book of Enos	Book of Alma	Book of Ether
Book of Jarom	Book of Helaman	Book of Moroni

References to the Doctrine and Covenants (often referred to as the D&C) of The Church of Jesus Christ of Latter-day Saints and the Pearl of Great Price (which includes the book of Moses and the book of Abraham) are included in the book. These writings are accepted by Latter-day Saints as scripture and considered to be of God. The Doctrine and Covenants is a "collection of divine revelations and inspired declarations given for the establishment and regulation of the kingdom of God on the earth in the last days" (D&C Explanatory Introduction). The Doctrine and Covenants and Pearl of Great Price are also accessible online at http://Scriptures.LDS.org.

References to the *Ensign* refer to a magazine published by The Church of Jesus Christ of Latter-day Saints that contains teachings of latter-day prophets and apostles as well as other articles and information. To read the *Ensign* online, visit http://www.LDS.org.

I also frequently reference various presidents of The Church of Jesus Christ of Latter-day Saints, as well as many apostles who are recognized church leaders. Members of The Church of Jesus Christ of Latter-day Saints believe that God again speaks to man through revelation to living, modern-day prophets as He did in the days of Moses, Abraham, and Isaiah. Modern-day apostles minister in building God's kingdom on the earth as did the apostles in Jesus Christ's day. When you see a quotation by "President Hinckley" or "Elder Faust" for example, you may better understand the value of the information, knowing the source is an apostle or prophet of God.

INDEX

❧

Laura Mason Brotherson, CFLE, is a marriage and family life educator certified by the National Council on Family Relations, and has a Bachelor's degree in Family Sciences from Brigham Young University. Laura developed and taught a course on strengthening marriage that has become her groundbreaking book, *And They Were Not Ashamed—Strengthening Marriage through Sexual Fulfillment*.

As a family life educator, Laura continues to strengthen marriages and families as a frequent guest on a talk radio show about marital intimacy, and by publishing a free electronic newsletter entitled "Straight Talk about Strengthening Marriage," available on her website www.StrengtheningMarriage.com. Laura is also a regular columnist for "Meridian Magazine."

Laura plans to obtain advanced degrees in marriage and family therapy to become a marriage counselor, and a certified sex therapist where she will fill an important role in helping couples to improve emotional, spiritual and physical intimacy within a gospel framework. She also plans to write additional books on overcoming depression, on motherhood, and on gospel topics.

Laura has served as Relief Society president, Young Women president, Marriage and Family Relations instructor, and currently teaches Gospel Doctrine. She is delighted to have become an American citizen, and takes an active interest in the political affairs of this country. Her commitment to the gospel of Jesus Christ is evident in her passion to build God's kingdom by strengthening marriages and families. Laura and her husband, Kevin, are the parents of three children.

For more information, visit www.StrengtheningMarriage.com